WHERE WE ARE NOW

WHERE WE

ARE NOW

CIRCA

MITCHELL BEAZLEY

First published in Great Britain in 2008 by Mitchell Beazley,
an imprint of Octopus Publishing Group Ltd,
2–4 Heron Quays, London E14 4JP

Text, design and layout copyright © Octopus Publishing Group 2008

Commissioning Editors: Jon Asbury, Peter Taylor
Design Management: Yasia Williams-Leedham, Juliette Norsworthy
Production: Peter Hunt, Lucy Carter

Produced for Mitchell Beazley by CIRCA and Heritage Editorial
Concept by Roger East, Andrew Heritage, Duncan Youel

Project management: Heritage Editorial
Andrew Heritage, Ailsa C. Heritage

Statistical research and editorial content: CIRCA
Roger East, Catherine Jagger, Carolyn Postgate
Additional contributions by David Goldblatt,
Chris Jagger, Carina O'Reilly, Richard J. Thomas

Art direction: Duncan Youel
Designed by Duncan Youel, Nicola Plumb, Kate Stretton, Kenny Grant
Additional design and illustration by bounford.com, Advanced Illustration Ltd, Andy Crisp

Picture research: cashou.com
Louise Thomas

ISBN: 9 781845 333447

A CIP record for this book is available from the British Library

Colour reproduction by United Graphics, Singapore

Printed and bound by Toppan, Hong Kong

CONTENTS

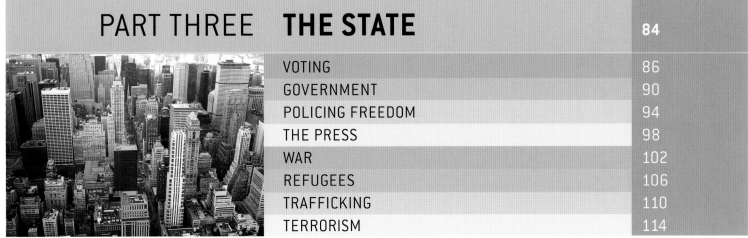

PART ONE	**THE ENVIRONMENT**	8
	CLIMATE CHANGE	10
	BIODIVERSITY	14
	DISASTERS	18
	WATER	22
	RESOURCES	26
	POPULATION	30
	MEGACITIES	34
	BUILT ENVIRONMENT	38

PART TWO	**SOCIETY**	42
	HEALTH	44
	FOOD	48
	SEX AND SOCIETY	52
	RELIGION	56
	AGEING	60
	RACE	64
	EDUCATION	68
	CRIME AND PUNISHMENT	72
	DRUGS	76
	CORRUPTION	80

PART THREE	**THE STATE**	84
	VOTING	86
	GOVERNMENT	90
	POLICING FREEDOM	94
	THE PRESS	98
	WAR	102
	REFUGEES	106
	TRAFFICKING	110
	TERRORISM	114

CONTENTS

PART FOUR — FINANCE AND COMMERCE — 118

MONEY	120
WEALTH	124
DEBT	128
GLOBALIZATION	132
WORK	136
ADVERTISING	140
FAIR TRADE	144
ARMS	148
ORGANIZED CRIME	152

PART FIVE — TECHNOLOGY — 156

ENERGY	158
COMMUNICATIONS	162
THE INTERNET	166
SURVEILLANCE	170
TRANSPORT	174
NEW TECHNOLOGIES	178

PART SIX — CULTURE — 182

LANGUAGE	184
TELEVISION	188
NEWS	192
TOURISM	196
SPORT	200
ART	204
FASHION	208
MUSIC	212
FILM	216

INDEX	220
ACKNOWLEDGEMENTS	224

INTRODUCTION

THE WORLD IS FULL of books that claim to provide you with all the facts you need. This isn't just another of those. It is full of information, certainly – but information that raises as many questions about the world as it can ever hope to answer. It is designed to provoke thought, to startle you with things you did not know, and to get you looking at familiar things in different and unexpected ways.

In short, we have done everything we can to make sure that the facts and figures in WHERE WE ARE NOW are not just dry statistics, but graphics, tables, and graphs full of juice just waiting to be squeezed out.

This book doesn't push any particular point of view – except the belief that there are issues in this world that cannot be ignored, and that solid evidence is crucial in understanding them. When it points you in directions where you want or need to know a whole lot more, it tries to provide some jumping-off points (although never a road map) to get you going.

There is a sense of urgency about it, which seems entirely appropriate for a world in rapid flux, and a consuming interest in where all this change may lead us. Yet all the topics it covers can also be looked at in terms of enduring needs, patterns of behaviour, relationships, and opportunities. Try looking at power in that way, or shelter, compromise, or threat. You may find fresh perspectives jumping out in some unexpected places as you navigate around these pages.

At the same time, the 50 topics – each presented on two double-page spreads – are grouped for ease of reference under six general headings: the Environment, Society, the State, Finance and Commerce, Technology, and Culture. Putting it all together has been hugely stimulating. If it leaves you wanting more, then it is doing exactly what it set out to do.

Roger East, CIRCA

The aftermath of Hurricane Katrina in 2005, to date the most devastating of escalating extreme weather events in North America.

WHAT HAVE BEEN IDENTIFIED AS THE MOST DANGEROUS THREATS TO THE HUMAN FUTURE? WHAT CAN, OR CAN'T, BE DONE TO AVOID OR INHIBIT THESE?

CLIMATE CHANGE
GLOBAL WARMING, GREENHOUSE GAS EMISSIONS, EXTREME WEATHER, IMPACT ON THE ENVIRONMENT

BIODIVERSITY
THE LIVING PLANET INDEX, CRITICAL BIOMES, EXTINCTIONS, PROTECTION AND SUSTAINABILITY

DISASTERS
NATURAL DISASTERS, MAN-MADE DISASTERS, COSTS AND FUTURE THREATS

THE ENVIRONMENT

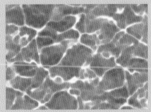

WATER
HOW MUCH WATER DO WE
NEED? HOW MUCH WATER
IS AVAILABLE? CONSERVING
WATER, SHARING WATER

RESOURCES
FOSSIL FUELS, MINERALS,
RESOURCE DEPLETION, THE
ECOLOGICAL FOOTPRINT

POPULATION
THE GENDER BALANCE, WHERE
PEOPLE LIVE, BIRTH AND
DEATH RATES, POPULATION
GROWTH

MEGACITIES
THE LARGEST CITIES, VITALITY
AND SQUALOR, QUALITY OF
LIFE, SUSTAINABLE CITIES

**BUILT
ENVIRONMENT**
CITYSCAPES, GREENING THE
CITY, LIVING IN THE CITY,
POLLUTION, WASTE AND
SANITATION, RENTAL RATES

CLIMATE CHANGE

Within 20 years, climate change has shot up the agenda to become a major focus of science and global politics. The Nobel Peace Prize in 2007 was won jointly by former US Vice-President Al Gore for raising awareness on the issue, and the UN's expert International Panel on Climate Change (IPCC) for its research and compelling analysis of the causes and consequences.

Only a few mavericks now deny that the warming of the planet is caused in large part by human activity, and that we are changing the climate in ways that are already apparent and potentially catastrophic. Even US President George W. Bush belatedly accepted this reality, if not the need to act appropriately.

The problem stems from the emission of carbon dioxide (and other "greenhouse gases" such as methane) into the atmosphere, where they hold in heat that would otherwise be reflected away from earth. CO_2 is released mainly by burning "fossil fuels" – coal, oil, and gas. Curbing carbon output can be achieved by more efficient processes, by using renewable energy, and by changing behaviour. Existing businesses, however, are reluctant to switch away from the cheapest energy, on grounds of competitiveness. As for changing behaviour, Westerners have become accustomed to high-carbon lifestyles, and people in developing countries don't easily see why they shouldn't aspire to run cars and fridges of their own.

THE KYOTO PROTOCOL

THIS IMPORTANT 1997 AGREEMENT SET GREENHOUSE GAS EMISSION CEILINGS FOR DEVELOPED COUNTRIES FOR 2008– 2012, AVERAGING OUT AS A FIVE PER CENT REDUCTION COMPARED WITH 1990. ONLY THE USA REFUSED TO TAKE PART (AUSTRALIA, A LATE CONVERT, JOINED IN DECEMBER 2007).

THE EVIDENCE

THE FOURTH REPORT OF THE IPCC IN 2007 CONFIRMED THE OVERWHELMING SCIENTIFIC CONSENSUS THAT CLIMATE CHANGE IS INDEED OCCURRING AND ATTRIBUTABLE TO HUMAN ACTIVITY.

GLOBAL AVERAGE TEMPERATURE

THE IMPACT OF CLIMATE CHANGE VARIES IN DIFFERENT AREAS AND SEASONS, BUT OVERALL IT HAS MEASURABLY RAISED THE GLOBAL AVERAGE TEMPERATURE – SO FAR QUITE GRADUALLY, THOUGH MOST RECENT YEARS HAVE BEEN AMONG THE VERY HOTTEST.

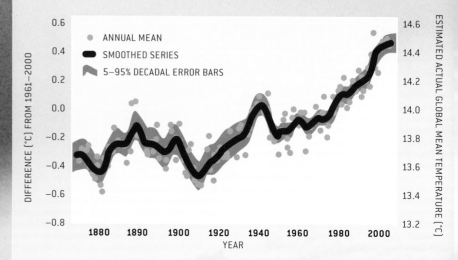

ICE COVER

STRANDED POLAR BEARS ON ICE FLOES, THE DISAPPEARANCE OF MOUNT KILIMANJARO'S YEAR-ROUND SNOWCAP, AND THE OPENING OF AN ICE-FREE NORTH-WEST PASSAGE ROUND THE AMERICAN CONTINENT, HAVE ALL SET SYMBOLIC ALARM BELLS RINGING. GLACIER SHRINKAGE FROM ALPS TO ANDES AND ALASKA TO HIMALAYAS, COMBINED WITH DRAMATIC RATES OF MELTING OF THE POLAR ICE CAPS, POSE THREE MAIN THREATS: RAISING SEA LEVELS, DISRUPTING OCEAN CURRENT CIRCULATION, AND LOSING THE WORLD'S VITAL "FOSSIL" FRESHWATER STORES.

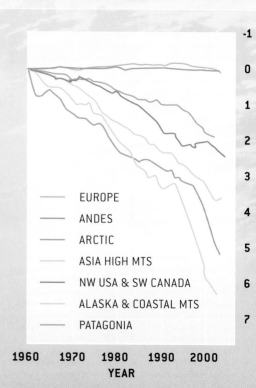

SOURCES: Intergovernmental Panel on Climate Change, www.ipcc.ch; UN Framework Convention on Climate Change, www.UNFCCC.int

CO$_2$ IN THE ATMOSPHERE

HOLDING BACK CLIMATE CHANGE ENTAILS HALTING THE RECENT RAPID RISE IN ATMOSPHERIC CO$_2$ – CAUSED MAINLY BY BURNING FOSSIL FUELS AND BY FOREST DESTRUCTION. AVOIDING CATASTROPHE COULD MEAN KEEPING IT BELOW A PEAK OF 500 PPM. SOME BELIEVE IT IS ALREADY TOO LATE.

CARBON DIOXIDE RISING OVER TIME

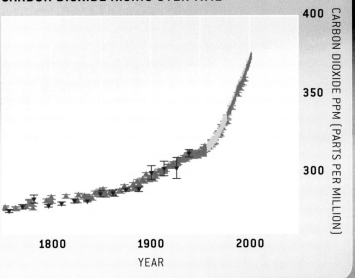

CARBON DIOXIDE PPM (PARTS PER MILLION)

YEAR

DEFORESTATION

WHILE LIVING FORESTS SOAK UP CARBON DIOXIDE, DESTROYING THEM TO EXPLOIT THE LAND NOT ONLY REMOVES THESE CRUCIAL "CARBON SINKS" – IT ALSO RELEASES THE CARBON THEY HAVE STORED UP OVER THE YEARS. BURNING FORESTS GIVE OFF MORE CO$_2$ EVERY YEAR THAN ANYTHING ELSE WE DO EXCEPT ELECTRICITY PRODUCTION.

CHANGE IN EXTENT OF FOREST 1990–2005
(1000 HECTARES)

REGION	FOREST AREA		ANNUAL RATE OF CHANGE	
	1990	2005	1990–2005	%
AFRICA	699,361	635,412	−4263	−0.61%
ASIA	574,487	571,577	−194	−0.03%
EUROPE	989,320	1,001,394	805	0.08%
NORTH AMERICA	710,790	705,849	−329	−0.05%
OCEANIA	212,514	206,254	−417	−0.20%
SOUTH AMERICA	890,818	831,540	−3952	−0.44%
WORLD	4,077,291	3,952,025	−8351	−0.20%
BRAZIL	520,027	477,698	−2822	−0.54%
CONGO DEM. REP.	140,531	133,610	−461	−0.33%
INDONESIA	116,567	88,495	−1871	−1.61%

CHANGES IN GREENHOUSE GAS EMISSIONS

THE USA IS BY FAR THE WORLD'S LARGEST EMITTER OF GREEN-HOUSE GASES – AND RISING. CHINA, ITS RAPID GROWTH POWERED LARGELY BY COAL, IS NUMBER TWO, AND COULD OVERTAKE WITHIN 20 YEARS, THOUGH PER PERSON THE CHINESE EMIT FAR LESS THAN THE AFFLUENT WEST. DESPITE ALL THE TALK OF CARBON CUTTING, FEW DEVELOPED COUNTRIES HAVE YET BROUGHT THEIR TOTALS DOWN MUCH, IF AT ALL.

CHANGES IN GHG EMISSIONS

TURKEY **72.6**
SPAIN **49.0**
PORTUGAL **41.0**
CANADA **26.6**
GREECE **26.6**
AUSTRALIA **25.1**
IRELAND **23.1**
NEW ZEALAND **21.3**
LIECHTENSTEIN **18.5**
USA **15.8**
AUSTRIA **15.7**
FINLAND **14.5**
ITALY **12.1**
NORWAY **10.3**
JAPAN **6.5**
NETHERLANDS **2.4**
BELGIUM **1.4**
SWITZERLAND **0.4**
LUXEMBOURG **0.3**

EUROPEAN COMMUNITY **−0.6**
FRANCE **−0.8**
SLOVENIA **−0.8**
DENMARK **−1.1**
MONACO **−3.1**
SWEDEN **−3.5**
ICELAND **−5.0**
CROATIA **−5.4**
UK **−14.3**
GERMANY **−17.2**
CZECH REPUBLIC **−25.0**
SLOVAKIA **−30.4**
POLAND **−31.2**
HUNGARY **−31.8**
RUSSIA **−32.0**
ROMANIA **−41.0**
BELARUS **−41.6**
BULGARIA **−49.0**
ESTONIA **−51.0**
UKRAINE **−55.3**
LATVIA **−58.5**
LITHUANIA **−60.4**

CLIMATE CHANGE

THE ECOLOGICAL IMPACT

THE EFFECT OF RISING GLOBAL AVERAGE TEMPERATURES ON WATER, ECOSYSTEMS, COASTS, AND HUMAN HEALTH

GLOBAL MEAN ANNUAL TEMPERATURE CHANGE RELATIVE TO 1980-1999 IN DEGREES CELCIUS

	0°	1°	2°	3°

"WATER STRESS" FROM SHORTAGES AND UNRELIABLE SUPPLIES SPREADS TO HUNDREDS OF MILLIONS OF PEOPLE

REDUCED WATER AVAILABILITY, MORE DROUGHTS IN MID-LATITUDE AREAS AND IN SEMI-ARID TROPICAL ZONES

MORE WATER, GENERALLY SURPLUS TO NEEDS, IN AREAS TOWARDS NORTH AND SOUTH OF GLOBE AND MOIST TROPICS

30% OF SPECIES PLACED MORE AT RISK

BLEACHING OF CORAL BECOMES NEAR-UNIVERSAL

INCREASING WILDFIRE RISKS

INCIDENCE AND SEVERITY OF FLOODS AND VIOLENT STORMS INCREASE, CAUSING WIDESPREAD DAMAGE AND LOSS

MORE PROBLEMS OF MALNUTRITION, DIARRHOEA, HEART/ RESPIRATORY CONDITIONS, INFECTIOUS DISEASES

HEAT WAVES, FLOODS, AND DROUGHTS CAUSE RISING NUMBERS OF HEALTH PROBLEMS AND ASSOCIATED DEATHS

CHANGING PATTERNS OF PRODUCTION

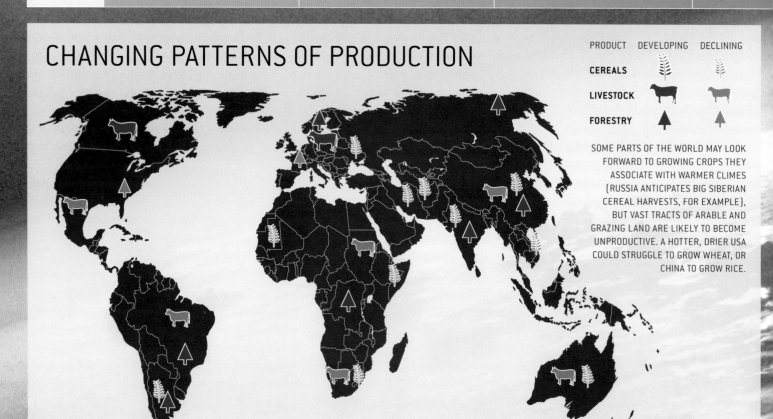

PRODUCT	DEVELOPING	DECLINING
CEREALS		
LIVESTOCK		
FORESTRY		

SOME PARTS OF THE WORLD MAY LOOK FORWARD TO GROWING CROPS THEY ASSOCIATE WITH WARMER CLIMES (RUSSIA ANTICIPATES BIG SIBERIAN CEREAL HARVESTS, FOR EXAMPLE), BUT VAST TRACTS OF ARABLE AND GRAZING LAND ARE LIKELY TO BECOME UNPRODUCTIVE. A HOTTER, DRIER USA COULD STRUGGLE TO GROW WHEAT, OR CHINA TO GROW RICE.

SOURCES: www.ipcc.ch; UN Framework Convention on Climate Change, www.UNFCCC.int; www.occ.gov.uk (Stern Review)

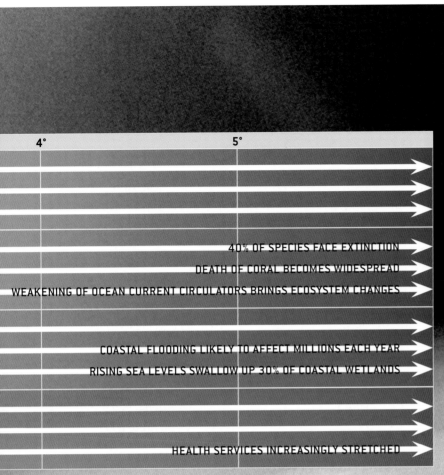

40% OF SPECIES FACE EXTINCTION

DEATH OF CORAL BECOMES WIDESPREAD

WEAKENING OF OCEAN CURRENT CIRCULATORS BRINGS ECOSYSTEM CHANGES

COASTAL FLOODING LIKELY TO AFFECT MILLIONS EACH YEAR

RISING SEA LEVELS SWALLOW UP 30% OF COASTAL WETLANDS

HEALTH SERVICES INCREASINGLY STRETCHED

4°   5°

LOWER CARBON LIVING

The steps the world has taken so far to limit greenhouse gas output have been small and faltering. The scientific consensus is that holding average temperature increases to the presumed "acceptable" threshold of 2° Celsius, will require CO_2 emission cuts at least as deep as the 20–30% proposed by the European Union by 2020, and more like 60-80% by 2050. A post-2012 successor to the Kyoto agreement will have to mandate lower country quotas accordingly, and bring the USA on board, as well as setting a framework to control rising emissions by China, India, and other fast-growing developing countries.

Great store is being set on "carbon pricing" to make businesses and whole economies more carbon-efficient. If emissions have to be kept below a certain limit, and you need a permit for every tonne of your allowed CO_2 output, then a carbon trading market can enable you to sell a permit for every tonne you save. The EU has an Emissions Trading Scheme already, though it started with such high free allowances that there was little demand (and thus a very low price) for traded permits. Properly balanced, the permit price should incentivize the carbon-cutters, and penalize the over-emitters. Market economics tells us that even businesses impervious to moral censure should change their ways to avoid such cost penalties.

Carbon quota schemes for individual households have also been proposed as the fairest way of sharing out the modest emissions permissible in a low-carbon society. Gradually ratcheting down the quota each year could gradually bring us closer to a globally equitable share – which has been dubbed "one planet living".

EXTREME WEATHER

HURRICANE KATRINA RAMMED HOME FOR ORDINARY AMERICANS THE THREAT POSED BY "EXTREME WEATHER EVENTS". CLIMATE CHANGE CANNOT BE SAID TO BE THE SPECIFIC CAUSE OF ANY ONE HURRICANE OR FLOOD, BUT HAS DISTORTED WEATHER PATTERNS TO MAKE SUCH EVENTS MORE FREQUENT AND UNPREDICTABLE.

REGION	EVENT TYPE	TEMPERATURE	COSTS AS % GDP	NOTES
GLOBAL	ALL	2°C	0.5–1.0% (0.1%)	THE INFLUENTIAL 2006 STERN REVIEW FOR THE UK TREASURY MADE A POWERFUL ECONOMIC CASE FOR TACKLING CLIMATE CHANGE. IT IS WELL WORTH INVESTING ONE PER CENT OF GDP TO DO SO, SAYS STERN, SINCE THE OVERALL DAMAGE WOULD OTHERWISE AMOUNT TO 5–20% OF ANNUAL GDP BY THE END OF THE CENTURY. THIS TABLE SHOWS STERN'S ESTIMATED COSTS, IN THE EVENT OF MODERATE CLIMATE CHANGE, FOR FIVE SPECIFIED CATEGORIES OF EXTREME WEATHER EVENTS IN DEVELOPED COUNTRIES.
USA	HURRICANE	3°C	0.13% (0.06%)	
USA	COASTAL FLOOD	1M SEA LEVEL RISE	0.01–0.03%	
UK	FLOOD	3–4°C	0.2–0.4% (0.13%)	
EUROPE	COASTAL FLOOD	1M SEA LEVEL RISE	0.01–0.02%	

ACTUAL 2005 COSTS ARE GIVEN IN BRACKETS. TEMPERATURE RISES ARE GLOBAL AVERAGES ABOVE PRE-INDUSTRIAL LEVELS. HIGHER TEMPERATURE RISES WOULD BE LIKELY TO MAKE COSTS RISE SHARPLY.

THE LIVING PLANET INDEX

The Living Planet Index, a statistical snapshot which features in the WWF's Living Planet Report, shows a rapid and continuing loss of biodiversity. Populations of vertebrate animal species, for instance, have declined by about one third since 1970. And we are using the planet's resources 25% faster than they can be renewed. Humanity's Ecological Footprint, our impact upon the planet, has more than tripled since 1961, so the consequences of our accelerating pressure on Earth's natural systems and biodiversity are both predictable and dire.

BIODIVERSITY

Biological diversity includes the number of different native species in a habitat or geographical area, the variety of different habitats in a given area, and the range of genetic variation within a species, both on land or in the sea.

There are areas of the world, particularly tropical rainforests, still rich in biodiversity, with huge numbers of species remaining to be discovered. However, mankind is changing the biodiversity of the planet at an unprecedented rate. Species and habitats are disappearing fast, and genetic diversity within species is being altered through selective breeding and genetic engineering.

In the search for the perfect crop, old varieties are dying out – whether apples, cereals, or livestock. Ownership of species developed in the lab is jealously guarded by companies, like Monsanto. The deliberate creation of sterile species is the extreme case of this, allowing worldwide control of seed sales. Monoculture, or the lack of biodiversity, contributed to several agricultural disasters in history, including the Irish potato famine, and the 19th-century collapse of the European wine industry.

	TOTAL ECOLOGICAL FOOTPRINT	TOTAL BIOCAPACITY (BILLION 2003 GHA)	LIVING PLANET INDEX
1961	4.5	9.0	
1965	5.4	9.2	
1970	6.9	9.5	1.00
1975	8.0	9.7	1.03
1980	9.3	9.9	0.99
1985	10.1	10.4	0.95
1990	11.5	10.7	0.90
1995	12.1	10.8	0.85
2000	13.2	11.1	0.71
2003	14.1	11.2	0.71

INTERNATIONAL DAY FOR BIOLOGICAL DIVERSITY 2007: THE MESSAGE

● Human activities are wiping out three animal or plant species every hour

● The world must do more to slow the worst spate of extinctions since the dinosaurs by 2010

● Extinction rates are rising by a factor of up to 1000 above natural rates

CRITICAL BIOMES: CORAL REEFS

CORAL LOSES COLOUR UNDER STRESSFUL ENVIRONMENTAL CONDITIONS. IN THE LAST DECADE, EVERY CORAL REEF IN THE WORLD HAS SUFFERED SOME SERIOUS BLEACHING – SO SEVERE IN SOME AREAS THAT THE CORAL IS DYING. A RISE IN SEA TEMPERATURE IS THE MAJOR CAUSE.

CORAL REEFS PROVIDE LIVELIHOODS FOR 100 MILLION PEOPLE, MAINLY THROUGH TOURISM AND FISHING.

ALTHOUGH THEY ONLY COVER 0.2% OF THE OCEAN FLOOR, THEY CONTAIN AN INCREDIBLE 25% OF MARINE SPECIES GLOBALLY.

 SOURCES: Convention on Biological Diversity; WWF: Living Planet Report 2006; IUCN: 2007 Red List of Threatened Species

SPECIES UNDER THREAT

THERE ARE NOW 16,306 SPECIES THREATENED WITH EXTINCTION ON THE IUCN RED LIST. THE TOTAL NUMBER OF EXTINCT SPECIES HAS REACHED 785 AND A FURTHER 65 ARE ONLY FOUND IN CAPTIVITY OR IN CULTIVATION. HOWEVER, THE PICTURE IS WORSE THAN THIS AS ONLY JUST OVER A QUARTER OF THE NUMBER OF SPECIES THAT ARE BELIEVED TO EXIST HAVE ACTUALLY BEEN ASSESSED: OF THESE, ONE IN FOUR MAMMALS, ONE IN EIGHT BIRDS, ONE IN THREE AMPHIBIANS, AND SEVEN OUT OF TEN PLANTS ARE UNDER THREAT.

	ESTIMATED NUMBER OF SPECIES	% OF SPECIES THAT ARE THREATENED	CRITICALLY ENDANGERED	ENDANGERED	VULNERABLE
MAMMALS	5416	20%	163	349	582
BIRDS	9956	12%	189	356	672
REPTILES	8240	5%	79	139	204
AMPHIBIANS	6199	29%	441	737	630
FISHES	30,000	4%	254	254	693
INSECTS	950,000	0.07%	69	129	425
MOLLUSCS	81,000	1.2%	268	224	486
OTHER INVERTEBRATES	172,375	0.3%			
PLANTS	297,326	3%	1569	2278	4600
LICHENS ETC	28,849	0.03%			
TOTAL	1,589,361	1%			

THREATENED SPECIES IN EACH COUNTRY

10 COUNTRIES WITH HIGHEST TOTAL OF ENDANGERED SPECIES	TOTAL	MAMMALS	BIRDS	REPTILES	AMPHIBIANS	FISHES	MOLLUSCS	OTHER INVERTEBRATES	PLANTS
ECUADOR	2178	33	68	10	163	15	48	3	1838
USA	1179	41	74	32	53	166	273	298	242
MALAYSIA	911	50	40	21	46	47	19	2	686
INDONESIA	850	146	116	27	33	111	3	28	386
MEXICO	840	72	59	95	198	115	5	35	261
CHINA	797	83	86	31	85	60	1	5	446
BRAZIL	725	73	122	22	25	66	21	14	382
AUSTRALIA	623	64	50	38	47	87	175	107	55
COLOMBIA	604	38	87	15	209	31	0	2	222
INDIA	560	89	75	25	63	39	2	20	247

RAINFORESTS

TROPICAL RAINFORESTS ARE THE MOST DIVERSE ECOSYSTEMS ON EARTH. A FOUR-SQUARE MILE PATCH OF RAINFOREST CONTAINS AS MANY AS 1500 SPECIES OF FLOWERING PLANTS, 750 SPECIES OF TREES, 125 SPECIES OF MAMMALS, 400 SPECIES OF BIRDS, 100 SPECIES OF REPTILES, 60 SPECIES OF AMPHIBIANS, AND 150 SPECIES OF BUTTERFLIES. MORE THAN 50% OF THE WORLD'S PLANT AND ANIMAL SPECIES INHABIT THE SEVEN PER CENT OF THE WORLD'S LAND SURFACE THAT IS COVERED IN RAINFOREST.

REASONS FOR DEFORESTATION IN THE AMAZON

CATTLE RANCHES	60-70%
SMALL-SCALE, SUBSISTENCE AGRICULTURE	30-40%
LARGE-SCALE, COMMERCIAL AGRICULTURE	1-2%
LOGGING, LEGAL AND ILLEGAL	2-4%
FIRES, MINING, URBANIZATION, ROAD CONSTRUCTION, DAMS	2-4%

BIODIVERSITY

TRYING TO SAVE THE PLANET

PROTECTING THE WORLD'S BIOMES
EXTENT OF PROTECTION OF THE WORLD'S MAJOR TERRESTRIAL BIOMES

Biome	Protected	Unprotected
TROPICAL HUMID FORESTS	23%	77% UNPROTECTED
SUBTROPICAL/TEMPERATE RAINFORESTS/WOODLANDS	17%	83% UNPROTECTED
TEMPERATE NEEDLE-LEAF FORESTS/WOODLANDS	9%	91% UNPROTECTED
TROPICAL DRY FORESTS/WOODLANDS	13%	87% UNPROTECTED
TEMPERATE BROAD-LEAF FORESTS	8%	92% UNPROTECTED
EVERGREEN FORESTS	11%	89% UNPROTECTED
WARM DESERTS/SEMI-DESERTS	10%	90% UNPROTECTED
COLD-WINTER DESERTS	8%	92% UNPROTECTED
TUNDRA COMMUNITIES	12%	88% UNPROTECTED
TROPICAL GRASSLANDS	15%	85% UNPROTECTED
TEMPERATE GRASSLANDS	5%	95% UNPROTECTED
MOUNTAIN SYSTEMS	16%	84% UNPROTECTED
ISLAND SYSTEMS	30%	70% UNPROTECTED
LAKE SYSTEMS	2%	98% UNPROTECTED

PROTECTING THE WORLD'S WETLANDS

THE ECONOMIC VALUE OF WETLANDS IS OFTEN UNDERESTIMATED. A HECTARE OF MANGROVE SWAMP CAN DELIVER "ECOSYSTEM SERVICES" WORTH AS MUCH US$900,000, NOTABLY BY PROVIDING TIMBER, FUELWOOD, HABITAT FOR ECONOMICALLY IMPORTANT SPECIES, AND SPAWNING GROUNDS FOR FISH.

RAMSAR CONVENTION ON WETLANDS:
THIS LONG-ESTABLISHED TREATY NOW PROTECTS 161 MILLION HECTARES OF WETLANDS IN 1739 SITES WORLDWIDE. THREATS RANGE FROM POLLUTION AND PRESSURE FOR DEVELOPMENT LAND, THROUGH TO RIVER DEPLETION, DIVERSION AND DAMS, AND RISING SEA LEVELS.

TEN COUNTRIES WITH LARGEST RAMSAR PROTECTED AREA (HECTARES)

Country	Hectares
CANADA	13,066,675
RUSSIA	10,323,767
CHAD	9,879,068
AUSTRALIA	7,371,873
SUDAN	6,784,600
PERU	6,780,643
BOLIVIA	6,518,073
BRAZIL	6,434,086
GUINEA	6,422,361
BOTSWANA	5,537,400

TEN LARGEST NATIONALLY DESIGNATED PROTECTED AREAS WORLDWIDE

COUNTRY	SITE NAME	SIZE (SQUARE KM)	LOCAL DESIGNATION
GREENLAND	NORTH-EAST GREENLAND	972,000	NATIONAL PARK
SAUDI ARABIA	AR-RUB'AL-KHALI	640,000	WILDLIFE MANAGEMENT AREA
KIRIBATI	PHOENIX ISLANDS PROTECTED AREA	410,500	MARINE PARK
AUSTRALIA	GREAT BARRIER REEF	344,400	MARINE PARK
USA	PAPAHANAUMOKUAKEA MARINE NATIONAL MONUMENT	341,362	CORAL REEF ECOSYSTEM RESERVE
CHINA	QIANGTANG	298,000	NATURE RESERVE
AUSTRALIA	MACQUARIE ISLAND	162,060	MARINE PARK
CHINA	SANJIANGYUAN	152,300	NATURE RESERVE
ECUADOR	GALAPAGOS	133,000	MARINE RESERVE
SAUDI ARABIA	NORTHERN WILDLIFE MANAGEMENT ZONE	100,875	WILDLIFE MANAGEMENT AREA

SOURCES: UNEP-WCMC, World Database on Protected Areas, Global Environment Outlook (GEO-4); CBD: Global Biodiversity Outlook 2 (2006)

EXAMPLES OF SUCCESSFUL REINTRODUCTIONS OF SPECIES

- **WHITE-TAILED EAGLE TO THE OUTER HEBRIDES OF SCOTLAND**
- **EUROPEAN LYNX IN SWITZERLAND**
- **GRIFFON VULTURE IN THE MASSIF CENTRAL, FRANCE**
- **LAMMERGEIER IN THE ALPS**
- **MUSK OX IN ALASKA**
- **WISENT IN POLAND, BELARUS**
- **WOLF IN WYOMING, USA**
- **ARABIAN ORYX IN OMAN**

HABITAT AND CLIMATE CHANGE

- **FLOODS AND FLOODPLAINS:** INTENSIVE AGRICULTURE AND THE LOSS OF MARSHLANDS AND FLOODPLAIN FORESTS HAVE INTERFERED WITH THE NATURAL ABILITY OF THE LAND TO DRAIN AND STORE SURFACE WATER. THE FLOW OF RIVERS IS AFFECTED BY SOIL EROSION, OFTEN CAUSED BY LARGE-SCALE AGRICULTURE, AND THE ALTERATION OF NATURAL SYSTEMS BY STRAIGHTENING MEANDERS AND BUILDING DAMS. HOUSING AND OTHER DEVELOPMENT ON FLOODPLAINS IS HAVING A SIMILAR EFFECT. CENTRAL EUROPE WAS DEVASTATED BY SEVERE FLOODS AFTER HEAVY SUMMER RAIN IN 2002 AND 2005, WHILE THE UK SUFFERED SIMILARLY IN 2007.

- **STORMS AND FORESTS:** FORESTS HELP TO MITIGATE THE EFFECT OF TROPICAL STORMS BY REDUCING FLASH FLOODWATER FLOWS AND PREVENTING SOIL EROSION. IN 2004, TROPICAL STORM JEANNE HIT THE ISLAND OF HISPANIOLA, KILLING CLOSE TO 3,000 PEOPLE IN HAITI, BUT ONLY 18 PEOPLE ACROSS THE BORDER IN THE DOMINICAN REPUBLIC. THIS DIFFERENCE IN HUMAN SUFFERING HAS BEEN LINKED TO EXTENSIVE DEFORESTATION IN HAITI, WHERE POLITICAL TURMOIL AND EXTREME POVERTY HAVE LED TO THE DESTRUCTION OF ALL BUT SOME TWO PER CENT OF THE COUNTRY'S ORIGINAL FOREST COVER.

- **TSUNAMIS AND MANGROVES:** THE PROTECTION AFFORDED BY COASTAL FORESTS WAS REVEALED AFTER THE GREAT ASIAN TSUNAMI OF DECEMBER 2004, WHEN AREAS WITH MANGROVE OR TREE COVER SUFFERED LESS DAMAGE. MANGROVES ALSO REDUCE DAMAGE FROM THE TROPICAL STORMS AND TYPHOONS WHICH REGULARLY BATTER COASTS IN THE REGION. EFFORTS TO REPLANT FORESTS HAVE BEEN HAMPERED BY DEVELOPERS. IN RECENT DECADES THE COASTAL MANGROVE FORESTS OF SOUTHEAST ASIA HAVE BEEN BEING CLEARED AT ALARMING SPEED TO MAKE WAY FOR LARGE SHRIMP FARMS AND TOURIST DEVELOPMENTS.

- **HURRICANES AND WETLANDS:** THE CATASTROPHIC FLOODING OF NEW ORLEANS IN THE UNITED STATES AS A RESULT OF HURRICANE KATRINA IN 2005 SERVES TO ILLUSTRATE THE CONSEQUENCES OF ATTEMPTING TO CONTROL GREAT RIVER SYSTEMS. THE CANALS AND LEVEES ON THE MISSISSIPI HAVE DIVERTED NATURAL SEDIMENTATION FLOWS AND ERODED COASTAL WETLANDS. PROTECTIVE BARRIER ISLANDS AND OYSTER REEFS HAVE DISAPPEARED UNDER BUILDING DEVELOPMENT, LEAVING THE LAND WIDE OPEN TO FLOODING FROM TIDAL SURGES.

HOPE FOR THE FUTURE

Conservation of natural diversity is now a global concern, but the resilience of nature is a potent weapon in the fight to halt biodiversity loss. The number of protected areas worldwide is growing slowly. Once a protection area is set up, diversity can often return.

Biodiversity can also be preserved by the creation of seed banks, and widening the range of varieties of plants and trees grown in specialist nurseries. Animal and bird species close to extinction are being bred in captivity for successful re-release into the wild.

The untapped medicinal and scientific potential still locked up in the genes of diverse species holds the best hope of enlisting powerful multinational corporations in preserving these natural resources.

PUTTING A VALUE ON NATURE:

Value of:
- Annual world fish catch – US$58 billion
- Anti-cancer agents from marine organisms – up to US$1 billion/year
- Global herbal medicine market – roughly US$43 billion in 2001
- Honeybees as pollinators for agriculture crops – US$2–8 billion/year
- Coral reefs for fisheries and tourism – US$30 billion/year

Cost of:
- Mangrove degradation in Pakistan – US$20 million in fishing losses, US$500 000 in timber losses, US$1.5 million in feed and pasture losses
- Newfoundland cod fishery collapse – US$2 billion and tens of thousands of jobs

DISASTERS

For most of human history, the great disasters have come in the form of disease, famine, and floods – rivalled only in the last century by the impact of war. Death tolls from natural disasters in recent times have tended to be highest in poor countries, where far more people live precariously on land prone to flooding or devastating drought. There is a strong argument that famine deaths should not be ascribed to natural disaster, when it is the unequal distribution of income that determines who dies.

Thanks to advances in medicine and sanitation, the scourge of disease appeared to have receded, at least since the influenza pandemic after World War I – until AIDS emerged as a huge long-term killer. On a more local scale, crowded and dirty conditions in fast-growing cities create ideal conditions for diseases like cholera and tuberculosis to run rife.

The other two major natural killers are wind storms and seismic activity. Hurricane Katrina in 2005, and Japan's Kobe earthquake a decade earlier, were by far the costliest disasters ever in terms of damage to property. The earthquake that triggered the huge tsunami caused devastation in nine countries as far afield as Somalia on the other side of the Indian Ocean.

DISASTERS SINCE 1900

TYPE OF EVENT	INCIDENCE	PEOPLE KILLED	PEOPLE AFFECTED	DAMAGE US$
DROUGHTS	533	11,707,946	1,925,620,557	83,250,245,000
EPIDEMICS	1090	9,541,759	41,456,433	7000
FLOODS	3178	6,904,596	3,043,116,780	386,061,022,000
EARTHQUAKES	1041	1,982,752	110,063,302	331,712,306,000
WIND STORMS	2883	1,210,074	772,022,434	619,055,586,000
WAVE/SURGES	61	241,505	2,534,573	10,097,277,000
TRANSPORT ACCIDENTS	4102	194,416	210,918	585,200,000
VOLCANIC ERUPTIONS	201	95,960	4,632,465	3,960,348,000
MUD/ROCK SLIDES	517	57,377	10,263,308	5,251,675,000
TECHNOLOGICAL ACCIDENTS	1085	57,110	3,280,084	4,178,519,000
INDUSTRIAL ACCIDENTS	1125	48,307	4,325,897	20,332,640,000
WILD FIRES	327	2831	5,046,000	24,463,055,000

NATURAL DISASTERS

THE DAMAGE CAUSED BY MOST NATURAL DISASTERS IS EXACERBATED BY HUMAN SHORTCOMINGS: POOR BUILDING STANDARDS IN EARTHQUAKE ZONES; UNMAINTAINED FLOOD DEFENCES; LACK OF EARLY WARNING SYSTEMS TO WARN PEOPLE TO VACATE DANGER ZONES; OR JUST A WEAK POLITICAL OR ECONOMIC SITUATION THAT IS MORE EASILY TIPPED OVER THE EDGE BY DROUGHT. MANY OF THE WORST FAMINES HAVE BEEN THE RESULT OF WAR (A FREQUENT FACTOR IN POST-COLONIAL AFRICA), OR OF EXTREME POLITICAL REGIMES (SUCH AS IN CHINA).

THE DEADLIEST DISASTERS

YEAR	EVENT	FATALITIES
1918	Worldwide influenza pandemic	45-55 million
1958-61	Famine in China	38 million
1346-52	Bubonic plague in Europe/Asia	25 million
1969	Famine in China	20 million
1769	Famine in India	10 million
1875-78	Famine in India	10 million
1876-78	Drought in China	9 million

 SOURCES: EM-DAT: OFDA/CRED International Disaster Database, Université Catholique de Louvain, Brussels; Munich Re

10 DEADLIEST NATURAL DISASTERS SINCE 1985

	EVENT	REGION	LOSSES (US$M)	FATALITIES
2004	EARTHQUAKE AND TSUNAMI	SOUTH ASIA	10,000	220,000
1991	CYCLONE, STORM SURGE	BANGLADESH	3000	139,000
2005	EARTHQUAKE	PAKISTAN, INDIA	5200	88,000
2003	HEAT WAVE	EUROPE	13,800	70,000
1990	EARTHQUAKE	IRAN	7100	40,000
1999	FLASH FLOOD, LANDSLIDES	VENEZUELA	3200	30,000
2003	EARTHQUAKE	IRAN	500	26,200
1985	VOLCANIC ERUPTION	COLOMBIA	230	25,000
1988	EARTHQUAKE	ARMENIA	14,000	25,000
1999	EARTHQUAKE	TURKEY	12,000	17,000

10 COSTLIEST NATURAL DISASTERS SINCE 1985

	EVENT	REGION	LOSSES	FATALITIES
2005	HURRICANE KATRINA	USA	US$125,000 million	1322
1995	EARTHQUAKE	KOBE, JAPAN	US$100,000 million	6430
1994	EARTHQUAKE	NORTHRIDGE, USA	US$44,000 million	61
1998	FLOODS	CHINA	US$30,700 million	4159
2004	EARTHQUAKE	NIIGATA, JAPAN	US$28,000 million	46
1992	HURRICANE ANDREW	USA	US$26,500 million	62
1996	FLOODS	CHINA	US$24,000 million	3048
2004	HURRICANE IVAN	USA/CARIBBEAN	US$23,000 million	125
1993	FLOODS	MISSISSIPPI, USA	US$21,000 million	48
2005	HURRICANE WILMA	MEXICO/USA/CARIBBEAN	US$20,000 million	42

THE KOBE EARTHQUAKE

Japan's 1995 Kobe earthquake lasted only 20 seconds, but did immense damage in this highly urbanized area, and exposed the inadequacy of the city's pre-planning. Rail lines buckled, putting the "bullet train" network out of action for months, and several elevated sections of the Hanshin expressway twisted and toppled sideways; it took over a year to reopen. Most modern buildings, constructed to withstand earthquakes, suffered little damage, but older ones collapsed and many caught fire, leaving 300,000 people homeless.

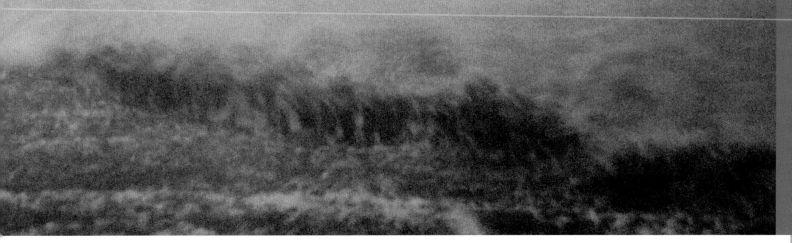

THE WORST INDUSTRIAL ACCIDENTS

INDUSTRIAL ACCIDENTS ARE VERY COMMON, PARTICULARLY WHERE SAFETY PRECAUTIONS ARE KEPT TO A MINIMUM TO HOLD DOWN COSTS. WHEN SERIOUS LARGE-SCALE ACCIDENTS OCCUR, A VEIL OF SECRECY IS SOMETIMES DRAWN OVER THEM, BY COMPANIES ANXIOUS TO PREVENT LITIGATION, OR TO PRESERVE INDUSTRIAL SECRETS, OR BY STATE AUTHORITIES KEEN "NOT TO ALARM THE PUBLIC". IT IS LIKELY THAT SEVERAL MAJOR ACCIDENTS HAVE HAPPENED IN ASIA THAT PEOPLE HAVE NEVER HEARD ABOUT.

COUNTRY	DATE	LOCATION	TYPE OF ACCIDENT	PEOPLE AFFECTED	PEOPLE KILLED
MEXICO	1984	**SAN JUAN** MEXICO CITY	GAS STORAGE TANK EXPLOSION	708,248	452
BRAZIL	2003	**MINAS GERAIS**, RIO	POISONING	550,000	0
SOVIET UNION	1957	**TCHELIABINSK** URAL	RADIATION	400,935	0
JAPAN	1999	**TOKAIMURA** NUCLEAR PLANT	RADIATION	320,600	2
INDIA	1984	**BHOPAL** PESTICIDE PLANT	GAS LEAK	300,000	2500

In December 1984 the Union Carbide plant in Bhopal, India, began leaking deadly methyl isocyanate gas – and none of the six safety systems were operational. The gas quickly spread over the city, affecting nearly half a million people. Estimates as to the initial number that died vary widely, and many more have died since or are suffering from ailments caused by the gas.

TRANSPORT DISASTERS SINCE 2000

	YEAR	COUNTRY	PLACE	FATALITIES
AIR DISASTERS				
	2003	IRAN	NEAR KERMAN	275
	2001	USA	QUEENS, NEW YORK	265
	2002	TAIWAN	PENGHU ISLAND	225
RAIL				
	2002	EGYPT	NEAR AL AYATT	377
	2004	IRAN	NEYSHABUR	300
	2002	TANZANIA	MPWAPWA	281
ROAD				
	2000	NIGERIA	OSUN STATE	150
	2000	KENYA	KAPKATUNGA	101
	2004	IRAN	NOSRAT ABAD	90
SHIPPING				
	2002	SENEGAL	NEAR GAMBIA	1200
	2006	EGYPT	RED SEA	1028
	2003	BANGLADESH	NEAR CHANDPUR	528

COAL MINE DISASTERS

Claustrophobic conditions in mines can all too easily become death traps when gas pockets explode and cause the roof to cave in. Most of the world, however, has improved safety and increased mechanization – or just reduced mining – except for China.

DEATHS IN COAL MINES IN CHINA

Several thousand miners die in China each year, despite strenuous protestations about efforts to raise safety standards. Small and old-fashioned mines are the worst. The death rate for every 100 tonnes of coal produced is 100 times that of the USA – and miners are only 2.2% as profitable in terms of output.

ANNUAL DEATHS IN CHINESE COAL MINES SINCE 2000		
	2000	5798
	2001	5670
	2002	6995
	2003	6434
	2004	6027
	2005	5986
	2006	4746

WHEN OIL TANKERS RUN INTO TROUBLE, VAST QUANTITIES OF OIL POUR INTO THE OCEAN. THE EXTENT OF DAMAGE DONE, HOWEVER, IS DEPENDENT LESS ON THE ABSOLUTE SIZE OF THE SPILLAGE THAN ON THE LOCATION; HENCE THE ENVIRONMENTAL DEVASTATION CAUSED BY THE *EXXON VALDEZ* IN A SENSITIVE ALASKAN SOUND.

MAJOR OIL SPILLS

SHIP NAME	YEAR	LOCATION	SPILL SIZE (TONNES)
ATLANTIC EMPRESS	1979	OFF TOBAGO, WEST INDIES	287,000
ABT SUMMER	1991	700 NAUTICAL MILES OFF ANGOLA	260,000
CASTILLO DE BELLVER	1983	OFF SALDANHA BAY, SOUTH AFRICA	252,000
AMOCO CADIZ	1978	OFF BRITTANY, FRANCE	223,000
HAVEN	1991	GENOA, ITALY	144,000
BRAER	1993	SHETLAND ISLANDS, UK	85,000
SEA EMPRESS	1996	MILFORD HAVEN, UK	72,000
PRESTIGE	2002	OFF THE SPANISH COAST	63,000
EXXON VALDEZ	1989	PRINCE WILLIAM SOUND, ALASKA, USA	37,000

SOURCES: EM-DAT; World Health Organization; International Tanker Owners Pollution Federation Ltd (ITOPF)

NUCLEAR DISASTERS

MANY PEOPLE REGARD CHERNOBYL AS ONE OF THE WORST MAN-MADE DISASTERS EVER, AND THE NEAR-MELTDOWN IN 1979 AT THREE MILE ISLAND IN THE USA AS PERHAPS THE WORST THAT DIDN'T QUITE HAPPEN. CHERNOBYL KILLED FEW PEOPLE IMMEDIATELY, BUT THE CREEPING EFFECTS OF RADIATION HAD A DEVASTATING EFFECT ON THE HEALTH OF THE POPULATION FOR YEARS AFTERWARDS.

DISASTERS WAITING TO HAPPEN

LONDON, UK
THE AREA OF LONDON AT RISK FROM THE FLOODING OF THE RIVER THAMES CONTAINS 26 UNDERGROUND STATIONS, 400 SCHOOLS, 16 HOSPITALS, AN AIRPORT, AND £80 BILLION WORTH OF PROPERTY. THE THAMES BARRIER WAS COMPLETED IN 1982 TO PROVIDE PROTECTION. AT THAT TIME IT WAS PREDICTED THAT THE BARRIER WOULD ONLY NEED TO CLOSE ONCE EVERY TWO OR THREE YEARS, AND WOULD HOLD BACK THE RIVER UNTIL 2030. HOWEVER, ALREADY THE BARRIER CLOSES FIVE OR SIX TIMES A YEAR, AND BY 2050 NEARLY EVERY TIDE WILL THREATEN THE CITY UNLESS A SECOND BARRIER IS BUILT.

MUMBAI (BOMBAY), INDIA
ON JULY 26 2005, NEARLY ONE METRE OF RAIN FELL IN JUST ONE DAY ON MUMBAI, ONE OF THE WORLD'S MOST DENSELY POPULATED CITIES. THE MITHI RIVER BURST ITS BANKS, SPEWING ITS BADLY POLLUTED WATER INTO THE STREETS. A THOUSAND PEOPLE DIED AS A RESULT. THE CITY WAS ONCE PROTECTED BY DRAINAGE THROUGH ITS COASTAL MANGROVE SWAMPS, CAPABLE OF ABSORBING LARGE QUANTITIES OF FLOODWATER OR OCEAN SURGES, BUT PRESSURE FOR SPACE FROM THE GROWING POPULATION HAS DESTROYED 90% OF THESE MANGROVES IN THE LAST 50 YEARS.

TUVALU, SOUTH PACIFIC
THE GRADUAL GLOBAL RISE IN SEA LEVEL WILL AFFECT LOW-LYING LAND WORLDWIDE – BUT TUVALU, IN THE SOUTH PACIFIC, HAS BEEN IDENTIFIED AS ONE OF THE FIRST COUNTRIES THAT WILL BECOME COMPLETELY SUBMERGED. THE HIGHEST POINT OF ITS CORAL ATOLLS IS CURRENTLY A MERE THREE METRES ABOVE SEA LEVEL. HIGH TIDES ALREADY FLOOD LOWER AREAS, LEAVING SALT DEPOSITS THAT DESTROY ANY CHANCE OF FARMING AND GRADUALLY ERODE THE CORAL ITSELF. THE 12,000 RESIDENTS ARE FACING A VERY REAL PROSPECT OF NEEDING TO ABANDON THEIR HOMES WITHIN THIS CENTURY.

YELLOWSTONE SUPERVOLCANO, USA
VOLCANIC ERUPTIONS CAUSE WIDESPREAD REGIONAL DAMAGE – BUT SUPERVOLCANOES CAN AFFECT THE WHOLE WORLD. ONE OF THE LARGEST SUPERVOLCANOES, LYING UNDERNEATH YELLOWSTONE PARK IN THE USA, IS OVERDUE FOR ERUPTION – ALREADY 40,000 YEARS OVER ITS NORMAL 600,000-YEAR ERUPTION CYCLE. THE GROUND HAS BEEN RISING IN THE CALDERA: 70CM HAS BEEN MEASURED OVER THE LAST FEW DECADES. WHEN IT DOES BLOW, HUGE AREAS OF THE USA WILL BE DESTROYED, THOUSANDS COULD DIE, AND ASH COULD POLLUTE THE WHOLE EARTH'S ATMOSPHERE.

DISASTERS IN THE FUTURE

Global warming and climate change are generating both more extreme weather events, and shifts in rainfall patterns that threaten major droughts.

Flooding, made worse by heavier sudden rainfall, sea-level rise, and building in flood plains, will have its biggest impact on densely populated areas, and many of the world's cities are investing heavily in flood defences. Flooding in the Yangtze river basin has brought near-annual disasters to southern China: in 1998 it caused US$24 billion in damage, killed over 3000 people, and left 14 million homeless. The vast Three Gorges Dam, the largest and most expensive in the world, was built partly to stabilize the river and prevent further floods, but there are fears of disastrous ecological impacts, as well as of faults in the structure potentially causing far greater devastation if the dam were to burst.

The recent spate of forceful hurricanes that have hit the Caribbean and east coast of the USA have been linked to small rises in the temperatures of the oceans.

As for seismic activity, the public appears far more aware of the San Andreas fault and the impact that an earthquake could have on the highly populated San Francisco area, than the much more serious volcanic threat of the Yellowstone supercaldera.

Early warning systems are increasingly successful at predicting geological events, such as earthquakes, volcanic eruptions, and tsunamis, though investment is needed to deploy the technology worldwide.

Scientists have also turned their attention to disaster threats from beyond the earth, notably including the possibility of a cataclysmic major meteor impact.

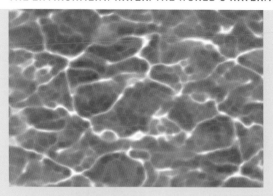

WATER

The world's annual water use increased six-fold in the 20th century – more than twice the rate of population growth. Intensive agriculture uses far more water than subsistence farming. The pressure is on to reduce the water intensity of industrial processes. And when demand exceeds supply, the environmental consequences are severe. Depletion of groundwater has wiped out over half of the world's wetlands in the last century. Some once-mighty rivers no longer reach the sea, and 20% of freshwater fish are endangered or extinct.

Freshwater scarcity has become a key political issue for the 21st century, so much so that it is often called the "new oil". Unlike oil, however, it is constantly being replenished and redistributed. Problems of scarcity are thus principally problems of uneven distribution. Where patterns of settlement and food production rely on the regularity of rain or river water, the disruption of weather patterns caused by climate change could be catastrophic.

Two centuries ago, two baths a year was considered excessive cleanliness. Today people in the affluent West commonly have daily showers, sprinklers in their gardens, and little inclination to conserve this precious resource. Yet Californian cities pay dearly for water rights, and 60% of Europe's cities are depleting their groundwater.

Poorer countries lack the infrastructure to provide clean water. Many Africans in rural areas spend several hours a day walking to their nearest well. In towns, slum-dwellers frequently only have access to supplies polluted by poor sanitation or industrial waste.

HOW MUCH WATER DO WE NEED?

FOR OUR BASIC NEEDS, EVERY INDIVIDUAL NEEDS 20–50 LITRES OF WATER FREE FROM HARMFUL CONTAMINANTS EVERY DAY. THIS EQUATES TO 7–18 CUBIC METRES A YEAR.

THE WORLD'S WATER

Around two-thirds of the earth's surface is covered by water, 97% of which is sea water: only the remaining 3% of the world's water is fresh; of this 3% over 2.5% is frozen, locked up in Antarctica, the Arctic, and glaciers, and not available to man. Thus humanity must rely on this 0.5% of the earth's water for all of its freshwater needs; Water withdrawals for irrigation have increased by over 60% since 1960; about 70% of all available freshwater is used for irrigation in agriculture. Yet because of inefficient irrigation systems, particularly in developing countries, 60% of this water is lost to evaporation or is returned to rivers and groundwater aquifers.

ACCESS TO CLEAN WATER

ALL DEVELOPED COUNTRIES RATE AT LEAST 90% AND MOST ARE 100%

RUSSIA	97%
BRAZIL	90%
SOUTH AFRICA	88%
INDIA	86%
CHINA	77%

COUNTRIES WHERE LESS THAN HALF OF THE POPULATION HAVE ACCESS TO CLEAN WATER

NIGERIA	48%
FIJI	47%
NIGER	46%
MADAGASCAR	46%
CONGO DEM. REP.	46%
MOZAMBIQUE	43%
EQUATORIAL GUINEA	43%
CHAD	42%
CAMBODIA	41%
PAPUA NEW GUINEA	39%
AFGHANISTAN	39%
SOMALIA	29%
ETHIOPIA	22%

Clean water is essential for drinking: humans require approximately two litres a day – or less than 1m³ a year. In addition, it is needed for cooking, washing, and sanitation. Around 4000 children die each day due to diseases contracted from dirty water or poor hygiene. Five out of every ten people worldwide have their own piped water supply, a further three have some public provision, but two in ten have no such access.

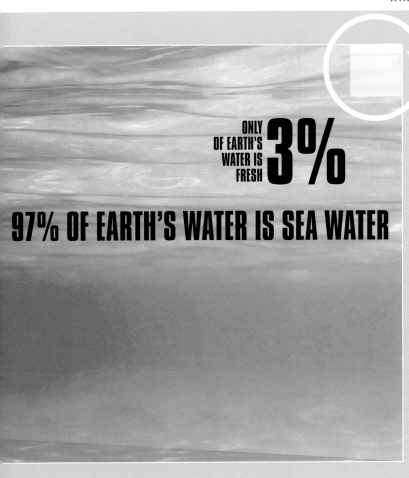

ONLY OF EARTH'S WATER IS FRESH **3%**

97% OF EARTH'S WATER IS SEA WATER

OF THIS 3% OF FRESH WATER, ONLY A SMALL PROPORTION — AROUND 0.5% OF THE EARTH'S TOTAL WATER — IS AVAILABLE TO US.

WHERE IS THIS 0.5%?

2120 KM³ IN RIVERS
5000 KM³ IN RESERVOIRS
91,000 KM³ IN NATURAL LAKES
119,000 KM³ RAINFALL FALLING ON LAND
10,000,000 KM³ IN UNDERGROUND AQUIFERS.

THE OVERWHELMING RESERVOIR OF FRESH WATER ON EARTH, 97% — OR 10,000,000 KM³ — IS STORED IN UNDERGROUND AQUIFERS. SINCE 1950 THERE HAS BEEN A RAPID EXPANSION OF GROUNDWATER EXPLOITATION, PROVIDING 50% OF ALL DRINKING WATER, 40% OF INDUSTRIAL WATER, AND 20% OF IRRIGATION WATER. THERE HAS BEEN A SEVEN-FOLD INCREASE IN GLOBAL RESERVOIR STORAGE CAPACITY SINCE 1950. THE WORLD'S RIVERS ARE OF COURSE CONSTANTLY BEING REPLENISHED BY RAINFALL AND MELTING SNOW AND ICE.

ANNUAL GLOBAL WATER USE

THE TOTAL VOLUME OF FRESH WATER USED AROUND THE WORLD IN 2007 WAS

3830 CUBIC KILOMETRES

Asia accounts for over 60% of world water use. But then it is home to 60% of people. North America's supplies allow its 8% of the world's population a lot more each. Africa's mere 5% of consumption must support 14% of the world's people. The main use by far is agriculture, notably in hotter climes. Elsewhere, in developed countries, industry uses more.

ON A GLOBAL AVERAGE, WATER USE DIVIDES AS:

10% DOMESTIC USE

20% INDUSTRIAL USE

70% AGRICULTURAL USE

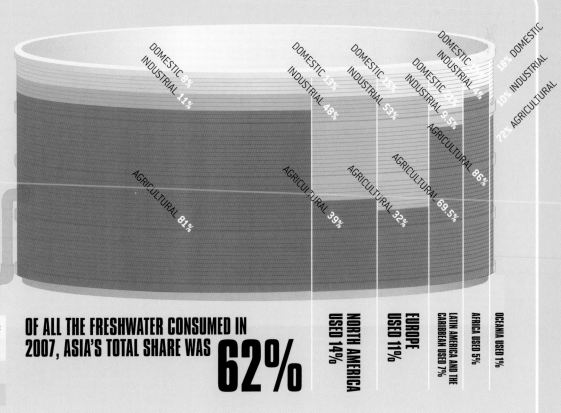

DOMESTIC 8%
INDUSTRIAL 11%
AGRICULTURAL 81%

DOMESTIC 13%
INDUSTRIAL 48%
AGRICULTURAL 39%

DOMESTIC 15%
INDUSTRIAL 53%
AGRICULTURAL 32%

DOMESTIC 9.5%
INDUSTRIAL 21%
AGRICULTURAL 69.5%

DOMESTIC 7%
INDUSTRIAL 7%
AGRICULTURAL 86%

18% DOMESTIC
10% INDUSTRIAL
72% AGRICULTURAL

OF ALL THE FRESHWATER CONSUMED IN 2007, ASIA'S TOTAL SHARE WAS **62%**

NORTH AMERICA USED 14%

EUROPE USED 11%

LATIN AMERICA AND THE CARIBBEAN USED 7%

AFRICA USED 5%

OCEANIA USED 1%

WATER

HOW MUCH WATER IT TAKES TO PRODUCE ONE KILO OF:

Paper	300 litres	Sugar Cane	1500 to 3000 litres
Potatoes	500 litres	Soya	2000 litres
Wheat	900 litres	Cotton	7 to 29,000 litres
Rice	3 to 5000 litres	Grass-fed lamb	10,000 litres
Chicken	3500 litres	Grain-fed beef	15,000 litres

DOMESTIC WATER USE

EACH AMERICAN USES OVER 360 LITRES OF WATER PER DAY: ON AVERAGE IT TAKES EIGHT LITRES TO FLUSH THE TOILET, 25 LITRES FOR A DISHWASHER CYCLE, 65 LITRES FOR A WASHING MACHINE CYCLE, AND 80 LITRES FOR A POWER SHOWER.

CUBIC METRES PER YEAR, PER CAPITA

- 132 USA
- 122 CANADA
- 115 AUSTRALIA
- 66 SPAIN
- 55 UK
- 46 GERMANY
- 24 CHINA
- 11 INDIA

2.5 million plastic bottles are thrown away every hour in the USA. For every thousand homes that consume bottled water, it is estimated that a metric ton of CO_2 is emitted each day to transport a commodity that is – in the developed world – available from the household tap.

IS BOTTLED WATER BETTER?

AVERAGE NUMBER OF LITRES CONSUMED PER PERSON PER YEAR

ITALY	183.6
MEXICO	168.5
UAE	163.5
BELGIUM	148
FRANCE	141.6
SPAIN	136.7
GERMANY	124.9
LEBANON	101.4
SWITZERLAND	99.6
CYPRUS	92
USA	90.5
SAUDI ARABIA	87.8
CZECH REPUBLIC	87.1
AUSTRIA	82.1
PORTUGAL	80.3
INDIA	79.6
GLOBAL AVERAGE	24.2

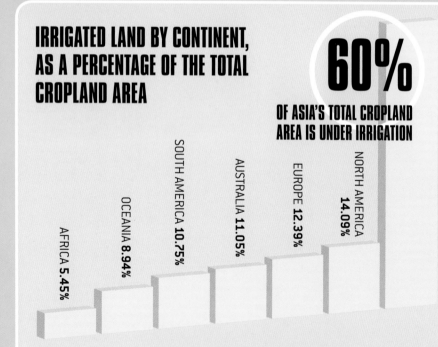

IRRIGATED LAND BY CONTINENT, AS A PERCENTAGE OF THE TOTAL CROPLAND AREA

60%

OF ASIA'S TOTAL CROPLAND AREA IS UNDER IRRIGATION

- AFRICA 5.45%
- OCEANIA 8.94%
- SOUTH AMERICA 10.75%
- AUSTRALIA 11.05%
- EUROPE 12.39%
- NORTH AMERICA 14.09%

Since 1960 water consumption for irrigation has increased by over 60%, so now around 70% of annual freshwater use is for agriculture. However, inefficient irrigation systems, particularly in developing countries, result in 60% of this water being lost to evaporation or returned to rivers and groundwater aquifers. One of the largest schemes, Libya's Great Man-Made River, draws water from an ice-age aquifer under the Sahara, but suffers from leaky pipes and evaporation.

THE COSTS OF GOING TOO FAR: THE ARAL SEA

INTENSIVE CROP IRRIGATION CAN HAVE DRAMATIC EFFECTS: CENTRAL ASIA'S ARAL SEA IS A PRIME EXAMPLE. WATER DIVERSION CAUSED THE SEA TO SHRINK BY 75%: LARGE AREAS OF VALUABLE WETLANDS WERE DESTROYED AND THE FISHING INDUSTRY COLLAPSED WITH A LOSS OF 60,000 JOBS. DRIED-OUT SOIL NOW GIVES RISE TO CLOUDS OF WIND-BLOWN DUST, CONTAINING TOXIC AGROCHEMICALS WHICH CAUSE SERIOUS LUNG DISEASE AMONG LOCAL PEOPLE. AN INTERNATIONAL PROJECT HOPES TO RESTORE PART OF THE SEA, BUT THE REGION IS INDELIBLY SCARRED.

SOURCES: International Water Management Institute; International Bottled Water Association; World Commission on Dams

THE WORLD'S DAMS

- THE WORLD COMMISSION ON DAMS ESTIMATES THAT THERE ARE AS MANY AS 48,000 DAMS OVER 15M HIGH WORLDWIDE. ABOUT HALF OF THESE ARE IN CHINA
- CHINA, TURKEY, IRAN, AND JAPAN ACCOUNTED FOR 67% OF THE TOTAL NUMBER OF DAMS UNDER CONSTRUCTION WORLDWIDE DURING 2003
- AROUND 35% OF THE 271 MILLION HECTARES OF AGRICULTURAL LAND IRRIGATED WORLDWIDE RELY ON DAMS
- 60% OF THE WORLD'S 227 LARGEST RIVERS ARE SEVERELY FRAGMENTED BY DAMS, DIVERSIONS, AND CANALS, LEADING TO THE DEGRADATION OF ECOSYSTEMS

SHARING WATER

THERE ARE MORE THAN 3800 UNILATERAL, BILATERAL, OR MULTILATERAL DECLARATIONS OR CONVENTIONS ON WATER: 286 ARE TREATIES, WITH 61 REFERRING TO OVER 200 INTERNATIONAL RIVER BASINS.

SCARCITY OF WATER FOR THE WORLD

As the world's population grows from six to nine billion, and climate change causes more extreme weather events, water stress is bound to increase. The most populous countries – India and China – both have huge rivers flowing from central Asia's great watersheds, but they suffer severely from pollution and over-exploitation, with frequent floods and droughts exacerbating the problems. India's Yamuna River rises in the Himalayas, but by the time it leaves Delhi it is laden with 950 million gallons of sewage each day. China's Yellow River is so silted up and over-abstracted that it no longer reaches the sea.

Within urban areas, the distribution and consumption of precious water is often woefully inefficient. Mexico City's old leaky pipes lose 40% of their water. London has similar problems – indeed they occur worldwide.

In developed countries, water meters are increasingly seen as the fairest routine measure to make people realize – and pay for – the amount of water they are using. In Australia, which suffered its worst drought on record in 2005–07, several state governments introduced stringent water use restrictions, advanced desalination techniques, and controversial grey-water recycling schemes (returning cleaned domestic waste water into the water supply).

Industry and agriculture also have enormous scope for savings through improved water efficiency and reuse. One Finnish paper mill, for instance, reduced its usage by over 90% over the last 20 years, by changes in the method of production and use of a recycling water facility. Evaporation losses in agriculture can be cut by drip irrigation, using perforated pipes to release water directly onto the roots of plants without flooding the entire field.

All too often, our image of Africans collecting water is one of drudgery. This South African PlayPump water system, however, harnesses the exuberance of the children to raise water from a borehole.

RESOURCES

"Resources" is a term with many meanings. Any definition of basic resources would probably start with land and water. In the international economic system, however, it refers to naturally occurring materials that have yet to be processed. Fossil fuels and minerals are the obvious examples. Supplies of these resources, however abundant or scarce, are ultimately finite as distinct from renewable – although it is customary to include non-food plantation products such as wood, cotton, and rubber within the discussion of resource availability.

Our industrialized world is dependent on stable supplies of resources. Oil dependence is particularly striking, above all for transport. Awareness that we are reaching, or have reached, "peak oil" – the point at which our total consumption to date exceeds the remaining known supplies – adds urgency to the need to find alternatives, or different ways of meeting our future needs for mobility.

At the same time, changing technology creates new resource dependence; thus uranium supplies only became relevant in the nuclear age, while tantalum was no more than a problem in tin extraction, until it became crucial in reducing the size and weight of mobile phones.

The current rate of depletion of the planet's resources is one of the two reasons, together with the acceleration of global warming, for regarding our contemporary way of life as unsustainable.

> "THE NATION BEHAVES WELL IF IT TREATS THE NATURAL RESOURCES AS ASSETS WHICH IT MUST TURN OVER TO THE NEXT GENERATION INCREASED, AND NOT IMPAIRED, IN VALUE."
> THEODORE ROOSEVELT, FORMER US PRESIDENT 1901–1909.

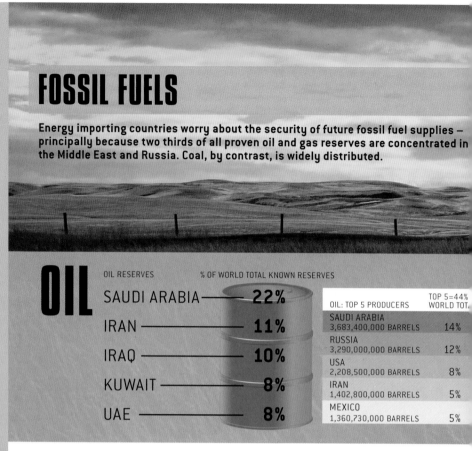

FOSSIL FUELS

Energy importing countries worry about the security of future fossil fuel supplies – principally because two thirds of all proven oil and gas reserves are concentrated in the Middle East and Russia. Coal, by contrast, is widely distributed.

OIL

OIL RESERVES — % OF WORLD TOTAL KNOWN RESERVES

SAUDI ARABIA	22%
IRAN	11%
IRAQ	10%
KUWAIT	8%
UAE	8%

OIL: TOP 5 PRODUCERS	TOP 5=44% WORLD TOT.
SAUDI ARABIA 3,683,400,000 BARRELS	14%
RUSSIA 3,290,000,000 BARRELS	12%
USA 2,208,500,000 BARRELS	8%
IRAN 1,402,800,000 BARRELS	5%
MEXICO 1,360,730,000 BARRELS	5%

COMMODITIES:
THE WORLD'S TOP PRODUCERS

Precious metals and oil have drawn prospectors, speculators, investors, and now huge multinational companies to many different parts of the world. Countries with a large share of any important resource may enjoy significant economic advantages, but over-dependence on its market price can leave them badly affected by severe fluctuations. Rare minerals can also be a curse. Conflict in the Democratic Republic of the Congo has been fuelled by the lure of its huge but largely unexploited reserves of coltan, the ore that carries the tantalum needed for making mobile phones.

URANIUM

CANADA	11627 TONNES	28%
AUSTRALIA	9516 TONNES	23%
KAZAKHSTAN	4357 TONNES	10%
RUSSIA	3431 TONNES	8%
NIGER	3093 TONNES	7%

76% OF WORLD TOTAL

DIAMONDS
TOP FIVE PRODUCERS

	CARATS	TOP 5 = 83% OF WORLD TOTAL
RUSSIA	38,000,000	22%
BOTSWANA	31,890,000	18%
AUSTRALIA	30,678,000	18%
CONGO DEM. REP.	27,000,000	16%
SOUTH AFRICA	15,775,720	9%

GOLD
TOP FIVE PRODUCERS

	KILOGRAMMES	TOP 5 = 52% WORLD TOT.
SOUTH AFRICA	294,803	12%
AUSTRALIA	263,000	11%
USA	261,098	11%
CHINA	224,050	9%
PERU	207,822	9%

GAS

GAS RESERVES	% OF WORLD TOTAL KNOWN RESERVES
RUSSIA	26%
IRAN	16%
QATAR	14%
SAUDI ARABIA	4%
UAE	3%

COAL

COAL RESERVES	% OF WORLD TOTAL KNOWN RESERVES
USA	27%
RUSSIA	17%
CHINA	13%
INDIA	10%
AUSTRALIA	9%

TANTALUM/NIOBIUM

SOUTH AFRICA 6600 TONNES	65%	90% OF WORLD TOTAL
AUSTRALIA 2500 TONNES	25%	

ROUNDWOOD

USA 471,862,342 M³	13%	
INDIA 328,677,293 M³	9%	
CHINA 286,103,128 M³	8%	44% OF WORLD TOTAL
BRAZIL 255,879,508 M³	7%	
CANADA 199,345,000 M³	6%	

RUBBER

THAILAND 3,156,958 TONNES	32%	
INDONESIA 2,350,000 TONNES	24%	
MALAYSIA 1,283,600 TONNES	13%	82% OF WORLD TOTAL
INDIA 831,000 TONNES	8%	
VIETNAM 546,100 TONNES	6%	

PHOSPHATES
TOP FIVE PRODUCERS

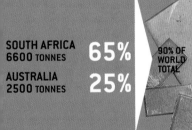

	TONNES	TOP 5 = 76% OF WORLD TOTAL
USA	38,300,000	25%
CHINA	30,450,000	20%
MOROCCO	28,788,000	19%
RUSSIA	11,286,400	7%
TUNISIA	8,203,600	5%

SILVER
TOP FIVE PRODUCERS

	KILOGRAMMES	TOP 5 = 61% OF WORLD TOTAL
PERU	3,193,146	16%
MEXICO	2,894,161	14%
CHINA	2,500,000	12%
AUSTRALIA	2,407,000	12%
CHILE	1,399,539	7%

COBALT
TOP FIVE PRODUCERS

	TONNES	TOP 5 = 78% OF WORLD TOTAL
CONGO DEM. REP.	22,000	41%
CANADA	5,533	10%
ZAMBIA	5,472	10%
RUSSIA	4,748	9%
BRAZIL	4,300	8%

RESOURCE DEPLETION

OIL, GAS, COAL
At current production levels, proven oil and gas reserves would last for only around 41 and 63 years respectively, and coal for 147 years.

VITAL MINERALS
The table below, taken from a study at the University of Augsburg, estimates how long the world's key mineral resources will last if we go on consuming them at today's rate.

INDIUM LCDS — **13**

SILVER JEWELLERY, CATALYTIC CONVERTERS — **29**

ANTIMONY DRUGS, FLAME RETARDANTS — **30**

TIN CANS, SOLDER — **40**

LEAD LEAD PIPES, BATTERIES — **42**

GOLD JEWELLERY, DENTAL — **45**

ZINC GALVANIZING — **46**

URANIUM WEAPONS, POWER STATIONS — **59**

COPPER WIRE, COINS, PLUMBING — **61**

NICKEL BATTERIES, TURBINE BLADES — **90**

TANTALUM CELLPHONES, CAMERA LENS — **116**

CHROMIUM CHROME PLATING, PAINT — **143**

PHOSPHOROUS FERTILIZER — **345**

PLATINUM JEWELLERY, CATALYSTS, FUEL CELLS FOR CARS — **360**

ALUMINIUM TRANSPORT, ELECTRICAL, CONSUMER DURABLES — **1027**

YEARS TO EXHAUSTION

FISH: MARINE RESOURCES
Many of the world's major fish populations are in crisis. Some even face extinction. The problem is persistent over-fishing – just as happened in the past with whaling. The global fishing fleet is currently two to three times larger than the oceans can support.

- Seven of the top ten marine fisheries are fully exploited or over-exploited.
- As many as 90% of all the ocean's large fish have been fished out.
- The UN FAO lists over half of the world's fisheries as fully exploited, and a quarter as either over-exploited, depleted, or recovering from depletion.
- Commercial whaling has been suspended for the last 20 years, although a few nations argue that some stocks have recovered sufficiently to allow a resumption.

WOOD USE
Almost half the world's people rely on wood as their main energy source for heating and cooking. In fact, fuel use accounts for 80% of all wood consumption in developing countries (and a remarkable 50% of the global total), and local shortages can be a major problem, notably in Bangladesh, Nepal, and Pakistan. Collecting wood for fuel is an important cause of deforestation and the expansion of deserts, particularly in Africa, although it remains less of a problem in this respect than forest clearance for farming.

Over half of all the wood harvested worldwide for building and industrial purposes – classified in official statistics as "industrial roundwood" – goes to North America, Europe, and Japan. A large proportion of this is used in making paper, consumption of which has grown sixfold since 1950. Packaging is another industry heavily reliant on wood resources. In per capita terms, each citizen of the United States uses 15 times as much "industrial roundwood" as an average citizen of a developing country.

	fuelwood 1000 m³	% world total	roundwood 1000 m³	% world total
Africa	546,059	31%	66,799	4%
Asia	774,953	44%	273,673	17%
Europe	114,968	7%	483,379	29%
North America	84,731	5%	616,975	37%
Central America	39,473	2%	3782	0%
South America	192,153	11%	160,759	10%
Oceania	8963	1%	39,776	2%
World	1,766,278	100%	1,646,667	100%

SOURCES: University of Augsburg; FAO STAT: Fisheries and Aquaculture, and Forestry; WWF: *Living Planet Index*

MATERIAL CONSUMPTION AND WASTE

- The materials consumed in the UK each year average out at 6.13 tonnes per person. The figure for Londoners comes out a little higher, at 6.65 tonnes; their average food consumption alone is equal to about ten times their body weight.
- More than 350 million tonnes of material flows through the UK construction sector each year, three quarters of it being turned into buildings and a quarter into waste; about half of that waste goes for recycling.
- As water is increasingly recognized as a valuable resource, the printing industry has reduced its once massive water consumption by 70 per cent over the last 20 years.
- Efficiency in production is only part of the equation. Over-consumption and waste both place immense strain on the world's resources. During the past three decades the amount of trash Americans have generated has risen by 87%.
- More sophisticated resource management can often be achieved by "industrial symbiosis", linking up businesses to turn the waste disposal problems of one into the raw materials or vital inputs for another. One recent example saw tomato-growers taking waste heat and carbon dioxide emissions from a chemical plant to improve growing conditions in their greenhouses.

ECOLOGICAL FOOTPRINT

This measures consumption by individuals (or communities or types of activity), and their waste, against the global availability of resources and the world's capacity to absorb waste.

Its units, global hectares (gha), reflect world-average biological productivity under prevailing technology and resource management. We are already exceeding the capacity of the planet – currently about 1.7 gha per capita – due to a combination of population increase, and rampant over-consumption in developed countries.

per capita, ecological footprint (gha)					
USA	9.6	Germany	4.5	Mexico	2.6
Canada	7.6	Russia	4.4	Brazil	2.1
France	5.6	Japan	4.4	China	1.6
UK	5.6	Italy	4.2	India	0.8

	per capita ecological footprint (gha)	the world's biocapacity (gha per capita)
1975	2.0	2.4
2000	2.2	1.8
2025	2.4	1.5
2050	2.6	1.2

- per capita ecological footprint (gha)
- the world's biocapacity (gha per capita)

RECYCLING

In the USA about 136 million people, just over half the population, recycle, but over the past three decades the amount of trash Americans have generated has risen by 87%. Americans used an estimated 84 billion plastic bags in 2006, during which time the production of plastic bags worldwide used over 12 million barrels of oil.

Countries with the highest recycling rates

Switzerland **52%** of waste recycled
Austria **49.7%** of waste recycled
Germany **48%** of waste recycled
Netherlands **46%** of waste recycled

Norway **40%** of waste recycled
Sweden **34%** of waste recycled
USA **31.5%** of waste recycled
UK **17.8%** of waste recycled

RUNNING OUT

Resource deposits rarely run out altogether, but cease to be valuable when extraction costs exceed the market price. If prices rise there may well be a commercial incentive to dig deeper, to exploit more inaccessible reserves. Oil buried many kilometres down in Brazil, or beneath the deep ocean, starts to look attractive at US$100 per barrel and rising. Oil extraction from tar sands in Canada and Venezuela, despite the enormous associated energy costs, may also become economically, if not environmentally, viable.

Effective management of living resources such as forests and fish requires respect for rules preventing damaging over-exploitation. Two joint industry-conservationist initiatives, the Forest Stewardship Council and the Marine Stewardship Council, aim to promote this by labelling sustainably-sourced produce and raising consumer awareness. It is an uphill struggle, with so much money to be made from destructive exploitation at maximum speed and minimum cost.

Rising raw material costs, however, and increasing obligations placed on industry to deal with its waste, have encouraged interest in maximum recycling and in "closed loop" manufacturing. A concept drawn from the natural world, this involves recognizing that any unwanted output – whether heat, carbon dioxide, rubble, toxic metals, or whatever – can have its own resource value as an input in another process. As the visionary engineer and architect Buckminster Fuller said: "Pollution is nothing but the resources we are not harvesting. We allow them to disperse because we've been ignorant of their value."

FIND OUT MORE: www.fao.org; www.wastewatch.org.uk; www.recycle-more.co.uk

POPULATION

There are over six billion people in today's world; by 2050 there will be nine billion. We will have added as many as the current population of China and the whole Indian subcontinent combined. Almost one in five people will then be living in the 50 least developed countries, their population having doubled – compared with almost no overall growth in the developed world. It is a fact of life that poor people have more children – and that birth rates come down when it becomes the norm for babies to survive into adulthood.

Nevertheless, many governments are pushing hard on family planning policies. The most extreme – China's one-child policy, introduced in 1979 – has cut population growth by some 400 million, but gave rise to shocking levels of female infanticide as families preferred to have a boy (thereby skewing the gender balance). Half of Chinese families (mainly in rural areas) are now allowed a second child if the first is a girl. Fertility drugs have helped others get round the policy – by making twin and triplet births abnormally common.

GENDER BALANCE

- Asia has 163 million more men than women
- China and some Indian states have 120 boy births for every 100 girls (the natural ratio is 105 to 100)
- Sex ratios among later live births are higher than first births, as pressure grows for a son
- Women are outnumbered two to one in the UAE and Qatar, where South Asian men come for work
- Women outnumber men in Russia, Ukraine, and the Baltic States, which suffer from higher male mortality rates and male emigration for work

THE USA IS THE THIRD MOST POPULOUS COUNTRY ON EARTH, WITH A POPULATION TODAY OF **303,900,000. BY 2050 THIS WILL HAVE GROWN TO 395,000,000**

BRAZIL CURRENTLY RATES FIFTH WITH **191,300,000. BY 2050 THIS WILL HAVE GROWN TO 253,100,000**

PROJECTED POPULATION GROWTH BY 2050

THE MOST POPULOUS COUNTRIES

China is home to one-fifth of the world's population. A further sixth live in India. In fact the top ten countries account for over 60% of all people. India's population is expected to overtake that of China sometime between 2030 and 2035. High growth rates in Pakistan and Nigeria will bring them up the table, while Ethiopia and the Democratic Republic of the Congo will replace Russia and Japan in the top ten. The United States is unusual among the developed world as its population is expected to continue growing, mainly due to high levels of immigration.

LARGEST POPULATIONS TODAY			LARGEST POPULATIONS IN 2050			
CHINA	1	1,331,400,000	INDIA	1	1,592,700,000	▲
INDIA	2	1,135,600,000	CHINA	2	1,392,300,000	▲
USA	3	303,900,000	USA	3	395,000,000	▲
INDONESIA	4	228,100,000	PAKISTAN	4	304,700,000	▲
BRAZIL	5	191,300,000	INDONESIA	5	284,600,000	▲
PAKISTAN	6	164,600,000	NIGERIA	6	258,100,000	▲
BANGLADESH	7	147,100,000	BRAZIL	7	253,100,000	▲
RUSSIA	8	141,900,000	BANGLADESH	8	242,900,000	▲
NIGERIA	9	137,200,000	CONGO DEM. REP.	9	177,300,000	▲
JAPAN	10	128,300,000	ETHIOPIA	10	170,200,000	▲
ETHIOPIA	14	81,200,000	JAPAN	16	112,200,000	▼
CONGO DEM. REP.	18	61,200,000	RUSSIA	17	111,800,000	▼

SOURCES: United Nations Population Fund (UNFPA); *State of the World Population*: Sex-ratio studies

PAKISTAN

CHINA IS THE MOST POPULATED COUNTRY ON EARTH, WITH **1,331,400,000 PEOPLE. PROJECTED GROWTH BY 2050 IS 1,392,300,000**

PAKISTAN'S CURRENT POPULATION IS **164,600,000. BY 2050 THIS WILL ALMOST DOUBLE TO 304,700,000**

CHINA

INDIA

BANGLADESH
TODAY: **147,100,000**
BY 2050: **242,900,000**

TOMORROW'S PARENTS

The best guide to the future size of a country's population is the number of women approaching child-bearing age. This is essentially why India's population is rising rapidly, while China's has effectively stabilized. In the least developed countries more than four in ten of the population are under 15, well above the global average of three in ten.

ETHIOPIA WILL MORE THAN DOUBLE ITS POPULATION FROM **81,200,000 TO 170,200,000 BY 2050**

INDIA IS THE SECOND MOST POPULATED NATION ON EARTH, WITH **1,135,600,000 PEOPLE. BY 2050, HOWEVER, INDIA WILL HAVE OVERTAKEN CHINA AND HAVE THE LARGEST POPULATION: 1,592,700,000**

BANGLADESH

ETHIOPIA

RUSSIA

JAPAN

INDONESIA TODAY: **228,100,000. BY 2050: 284,600,000**

CONGO DEM. REP.

NIGERIA

INDONESIA

In contrast to the developing countries, Japan and Russia's populations will be contracting, as will those of several European countries.

JAPAN NOW	**128.3 million**	
IN 2050	112.2 million	
RUSSIA NOW	**141.9 million**	
IN 2050	111.8 million	

ASTOUNDINGLY, CONGO DEM. REP.'S POPULATION WILL ALMOST TREBLE BY 2050, FROM **61,200,000 TODAY, TO 177,300,000 BY 2050**

NIGERIA WILL ALMOST DOUBLE ITS POPULATION FROM **137,200,000 TO 258,100,000 BY 2050**

WHERE THE PEOPLE LIVE

THE MOST AND LEAST CROWDED COUNTRIES ON EARTH — PEOPLE PER SQUARE KILOMETRE

MONACO IS THE MOST CROWDED COUNTRY — **16,718** PEOPLE INHABIT EACH OF ITS TWO SQUARE KILOMETRES

MONGOLIA IS THE LEAST CROWDED PLACE, WITH ONLY 1.6 PEOPLE PER SQUARE KILOMETRE

SINGAPORE 6376	INDIA 373	ITALY 199	USA 32	ICELAND 2.9
MALTA 1265	JAPAN 349	CHINA 140	BRAZIL 22	SURINAME 2.8
MALDIVES 1123	UK 249	FRANCE 110	RUSSIA 8.7	AUSTRALIA 2.6
BANGLADESH 1109	GERMANY 236		CANADA 3.5	NAMIBIA 2.4

OVER 500 PEOPLE PER SQUARE KILOMETRE — OVER 100 PEOPLE PER SQUARE KILOMETRE — OVER 10 PEOPLE PER SQUARE KILOMETRE — UNDER 10 PEOPLE PER SQUARE KILOMETRE

GOING TO TOWN

Urban areas are now home to half of the world's population. This is driven partly by migration from countryside to city, and partly by the emergence of towns in what were once rural areas. The urban population is growing fastest in Africa and Asia, whereas industrialized countries have stabilized at around 70-80%. By 2050 two-thirds of the world's population is expected to live in towns and cities.

KUWAIT 98.3 · SAN MARINO 97.5 · BELGIUM 97.2 · BAHRAIN 96.7 · MALTA 95.5 · QATAR 95.4 · VENEZUELA 93.7 · ICELAND 92.8 · URUGUAY 92.1

HIGHEST URBAN POPULATIONS

UK 89.7 · BRAZIL 84.6 · USA 81.1 · CANADA 80.2 · FRANCE 76.9 · GERMANY 75.2 · RUSSIA 72.9 · ITALY 67.7 · JAPAN 66.0 · CHINA 41.3 · INDIA 28.9

MAJOR COUNTRIES' URBAN POPULATIONS

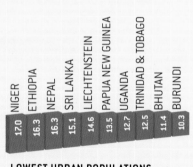

NIGER 17.0 · ETHIOPIA 16.3 · NEPAL 16.3 · SRI LANKA 15.1 · LIECHTENSTEIN 14.6 · PAPUA NEW GUINEA 13.5 · UGANDA 12.7 · TRINIDAD & TOBAGO 12.5 · BHUTAN 11.4 · BURUNDI 10.3

LOWEST URBAN POPULATIONS

BIRTH AND DEATH RATES

The world's birth rate is 20.2 live births per 1000 people, equating to almost 130 million babies born each year. There are 8.6 deaths per 1000 people – around 55 million worldwide. So the world's natural population growth is around 75 million people per year. African countries account for 37 of the top 40 birth rates, and all of the 25 highest death rates, being disproportionately afflicted by AIDS, other diseases, famine, and conflict, and lacking money to improve healthcare.

HIGHEST BIRTH RATES   **PER 1000 PEOPLE**   HIGHEST DEATH RATES

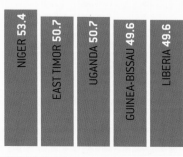

NIGER 53.4 · EAST TIMOR 50.7 · UGANDA 50.7 · GUINEA-BISSAU 49.6 · LIBERIA 49.6

BOTSWANA 27.0 · LESOTHO 25.4 · SIERRA LEONE 22.9 · ZIMBABWE 22.9 · CENTRAL AFRICAN REPUBLIC 21.9

SOURCES: World Bank: *World Development Indicators*

ANNUAL POPULATION GROWTH

ny one country's actual population growth rate is determined not just by s birth rate minus its death rate, but also by the balance of immigration and migration. Many of the former Soviet countries have high rates of emigration as eople head to Russia and Western Europe in search of better opportunities. These ceiving countries still have low or negative growth rates, however, due to their low nd falling birth rates. Asia and Africa's populations are rapidly expanding, mainly riven by the high birth rates. The majority of the world's most populous countries re trying to stem population growth as they struggle to provide for their inhabitants.

HIGHEST % GROWTH

EAST TIMOR	5.34%
BURUNDI	3.72%
UGANDA	3.61%
MARSHALL ISLANDS	3.29%
NIGER	3.24%
JORDAN	3.17%
YEMEN	3.1%
SOMALIA	3.08%
CONGO DEM. REP.	3.06%
ERITREA	3.06%

LOWEST % GROWTH (NEGATIVE GROWTH, CONTRACTION)

-0.4%	BOTSWANA
-0.43%	SWAZILAND
-0.43%	ROMANIA
-0.51%	LITHUANIA
-0.52%	RUSSIA
-0.53%	BULGARIA
-0.6%	LATVIA
-0.61%	BELARUS
-0.85%	GEORGIA
-0.87%	MOLDOVA
-1.08%	UKRAINE

CHANGING CENTRES OF POPULATION

The rate of global population growth has actually slowed appreciably since the early 1990s as fertility rates have declined (from 3.0% per annum to 2.6%), and should continue to do so (to 2.1% by 2050, the rate at which populations remain stable). But the picture is uneven: countries such as populous India, Pakistan, and Nigeria have a long way to go to stabilize their populations. Access to effective contraception, and more fundamentally the strengthening of women's rights, education, and life opportunities, are key issues in bringing down birth rates. They also pose major political challenges, not least where they encounter opposing Catholic, Islamic, or other religious authority.

Asia's gender balance will leave many young men unable to find a partner, and potentially also provoke an increase in sexual violence and trafficking of women.

In many developed countries, the ageing of the population will leave a diminishing labour force struggling to support a ballooning group of pensioners [see Ageing, pages 60-63]. Even China could soon face this dilemma due to the success of its family planning strategies. Europe will need to attract thousands more migrants from Asia and Africa to fill the gap in its labour market, as the USA is currently doing from Mexico and elsewhere. The UN estimates that there are now around 200 million migrants, one in four living in North America and one in three in Europe. Immigration is already a major political issue in the West – over problems of assimilation. Even the UK and Netherlands – known for their welcoming approach to immigration and multicultural communities – are under pressure for resources and living space due to their already high population densities.

MEGACITIES

The urban agglomeration of Tokyo is the world's largest megacity – by far. Its population is about half as big again as its nearest rivals in size – Seoul, Mexico City, and New York – and nearly three times that of London (which was the world's only megacity in 1900). In other respects Tokyo is untypical. One feature that stands out is its low incidence of violent crime. The other is its affluence. Only a handful of other megacities (New York, Los Angeles, Osaka, London, and Paris) are to be found in rich nations; the phenomenon of their recent upsurge is primarily a feature of the developing world.

Whether in developed or developing countries, megacities use a disproportionate share of resources:

● To sustain London's consumption of natural resources at the current level would need a share of the planet twice the size of that of the whole UK.

● Only one out of every three Indians lives in a city, yet cities account for 87% of India's total electricity usage.

● Los Angeles depends on the Colorado river, nearly 1000 km (620 miles) away, for much of its water. Beijing's water may soon have to come from even further afield; with the Yellow River no longer reaching the sea for most of the year, there is an ambitious project to tap China's great southern rivers to slake the capital's thirst.

LAGOS IS THE WORLD'S FASTEST-GROWING MEGACITY – AND THE DIRTIEST. In 1950 the city's population was 300,000, but by 2005 it had mushroomed to 11 million, and that number could double within as little as five years. It is a dramatic example of the problems of unplanned urban growth – congested, polluted, and dirty. Lagos has no sewage treatment facilities – and nearly all its garbage is just dumped in the city streets or into the nearby lagoon.

VITALITY AND SQUALOR

THREE-QUARTERS OF THE WORLD'S 26 BIGGEST CITIES ARE IN DEVELOPING COUNTRIES.

Some, like Karachi, Dacca, and Lagos, are still in the grip of astonishingly rapid population growth. Others, such as Seoul, Mexico City, and São Paulo, which almost trebled in size between 1970 and 2000, are now growing more slowly. Across the developing world, birth rates are actually much lower in cities than in the countryside. It is the tide of people moving from rural to urban areas that is carrying large urban centres over the ten million population threshold to become megacities. Hoping to find opportunity, new arrivals often have to contend with chronic deprivation and insecurity.

● China has launched a huge building and infrastructure programme to try to accommodate the millions moving to its cities [see overleaf]. Even so, newcomers crowd into vast sprawling settlements with a chronic shortage of amenities.

● The *favelas* (shanty towns) around Latin America's megacities are notorious for the violence and lawlessness bred of urban deprivation, yet can also bring out the cultural and economic creativity which is the positive hallmark of city life.

● Mexico City's air pollution, far worse than that of Los Angeles, results from millions of elderly cars burning gasoline at high altitude (which releases more pollutants); these emissions are locked into the city by the mountain peaks surrounding its volcanic crater.

● Some 600,000 city-dwellers across the world cannot meet their basic needs for shelter, water, or health – yet less than 10% of all international assistance funding goes to cities, the vast majority being still targeted at rural areas.

AROUND ONE MILLION PEOPLE EACH WEEK MOVE PERMANENTLY TO A CITY SOMEWHERE IN THE WORLD

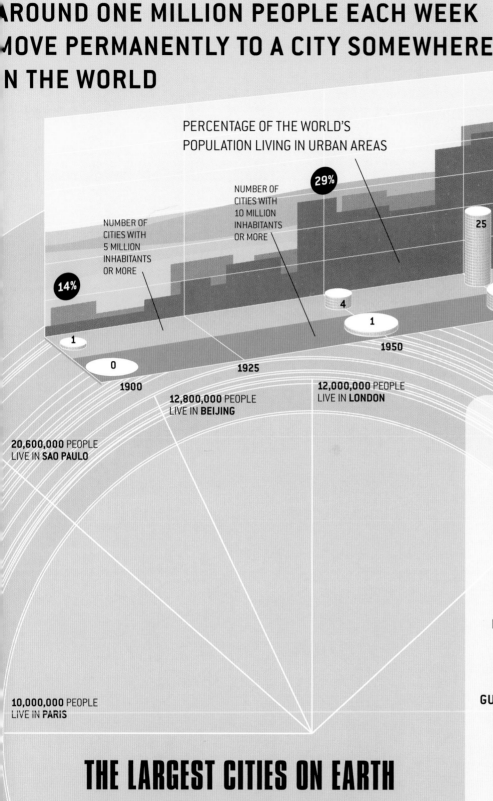

PERCENTAGE OF THE WORLD'S POPULATION LIVING IN URBAN AREAS

NUMBER OF CITIES WITH 5 MILLION INHABITANTS OR MORE

NUMBER OF CITIES WITH 10 MILLION INHABITANTS OR MORE

NUMBERS OF MEGACITIES

50%

45%

29%

14%

65

39

28

25

25

19

9

5

4

1

1

1

0

1900
1925
1950
1975
1985
1995
2000
2007

60
50
40
30
20
10
0

20,600,000 PEOPLE LIVE IN **SAO PAULO**

12,800,000 PEOPLE LIVE IN **BEIJING**

12,000,000 PEOPLE LIVE IN **LONDON**

33,600,000 PEOPLE LIVE IN **TOKYO**

10,000,000 PEOPLE LIVE IN **PARIS**

TOKYO JAPAN	**33,600,000**
SEOUL SOUTH KOREA	**23,400,000**
MEXICO CITY MEXICO	**22,400,000**
NEW YORK USA	**21,900,000**
MUMBAI (BOMBAY) INDIA	**21,600,000**
DELHI INDIA	**21,500,000**
SAO PAULO BRAZIL	**20,600,000**
LOS ANGELES USA	**18,000,000**
SHANGHAI CHINA	**17,500,000**
OSAKA JAPAN	**16,700,000**
CAIRO EGYPT	**16,100,000**
KOLKATA (CALCUTTA) INDIA	**15,700,000**
MANILA PHILIPPINES	**15,600,000**
JAKARTA INDONESIA	**15,100,000**
KARACHI PAKISTAN	**15,100,000**
GUANGZHOU (CANTON) CHINA	**14,700,000**
BUENOS AIRES ARGENTINA	**13,600,000**
MOSCOW RUSSIA	**13,500,000**
BEIJING CHINA	**12,800,000**
DACCA BANGLADESH	**12,700,000**
RIO DE JANEIRO BRAZIL	**12,600,000**
TEHRAN IRAN	**12,100,000**
LONDON UK	**12,000,000**
ISTANBUL TURKEY	**11,800,000**
LAGOS NIGERIA	**10,100,000**
PARIS FRANCE	**10,000,000**

THE LARGEST CITIES ON EARTH

AND THEIR POPULATIONS IN 2007

The United Nations coined the term megacities in the 1970s, to designate all urban agglomerations with a population of eight million or more. In the 1990s, the United Nations raised the population threshold to ten million.

MEGACITIES

FOCUS ON CHINA

This deserted and doomed cityscape (right) was unfortunate to be in the path of the massive Three Gorges Dam project. All its inhabitants were coerced into relocation by their government. Anecdotes relate that each person relocated was entitled to compensation to the value of US$25 — but that much of this compensation "disappeared" before getting to the people.

Modern Shanghai (below right) displays the energy and vision of the new China in its "space age" architecture: over the past ten years the city has been completely rebuilt and transformed into a dramatic, visionary, 21st-century metropolis.

- **BETWEEN 1990 AND 2000** THE NUMBER OF CHINESE CITIES WITH OVER ONE MILLION RESIDENTS MORE THAN DOUBLED — FROM 29 TO 61

- **TEN MILLION PEOPLE MOVE TO THE CITIES EVERY YEAR** IN SEARCH OF WORK IN THE FAST-GROWING URBAN ECONOMY

- **CHINA EXPECTS TO BUILD OVER 300 NEW CITIES** IN THE NEXT FIVE YEARS

- **IN 2010 CHINA WILL HAVE ALMOST 200 CITIES** WITH A POPULATION OF ONE MILLION RESIDENTS OR MORE, WITH A COMBINED URBAN POPULATION OF OVER 600 MILLION — ABOUT 45% OF THE TOTAL POPULATION

- **BY 2050 THE UN** ESTIMATES THAT SEVEN OUT OF TEN CHINESE WILL LIVE IN CITIES

IN ORDER TO IMPROVE THE QUALITY OF LIFE OF ITS 500 MILLION URBAN RESIDENTS, THE CHINESE GOVERNMENT NEEDS TO RESOLVE HOUSING SHORTAGES, BUILD CULTURAL, SPORTS, AND COMMERCIAL FACILITIES, AS WELL AS ROADS, PARKS, WATER RESERVOIRS, WASTE WATER TREATMENT PLANTS, AND GARBAGE DISPOSAL FACILITIES. THE GOVERNMENT ALSO NEEDS TO ADDRESS MANY REMAINING ENVIRONMENTAL ISSUES. THE CHALLENGES FACING CHINA ON PRESERVING WATER, ENERGY, AND LAND RESOURCES ALONE APPEAR OVERWHELMING.

FOR EVERY ONE PER CENT INCREASE IN ITS URBANIZATION RATE, CHINA MUST:

- **CONSUME 1800 SQUARE KILOMETRES** OF LAND

- **BUILD 400 MILLION SQUARE METRES** OF HOUSING

- **PUMP 140 MILLION CUBIC METRES** OF FRESH WATER

- **GENERATE 640 MILLION KILOWATTS** OF ENERGY

- **EXPEND 270 BILLION YUAN** OF CAPITAL

- **DISPOSE OF 1.14 BILLION CUBIC METRES** OF WASTE

— EACH YEAR

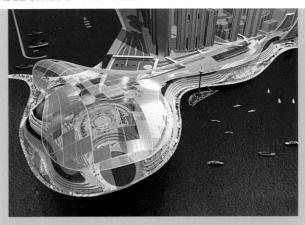

THE QUALITY OF LIFE IN MEGACITIES

Major cities have historically acted not just as the economic engines of growth, but also as the social hub and usually the political and administrative centre of their surrounding regions. Their productivity, and their cultural and intellectual creativity, make them poles of attraction in terms of opportunity, the pursuit of power, and quality of life. This remains true for today's megacities, despite the huge challenges and stresses they face.

MERCER HUMAN RESOURCE CONSULTING WORLDWIDE QUALITY OF LIVING SURVEY 2007			Base City: NEW YORK = 100	
RANK	CITY	COUNTRY	INDEX	
1	ZURICH	Switzerland	108.1	☺
2	GENEVA	Switzerland	108.0	
33	PARIS	France	102.7	☺
35	TOKYO	Japan	102.3	
39	LONDON	UK	101.2	☺
42	OSAKA	Japan	100.5	
48	NEW YORK	USA	100.0	☺
215	BAGHDAD	IRAQ	14.5	☹

The 2007 annual survey of the best cities for expatriates to live and work in, conducted by the Canadian-based human resources consultants Mercer, rates Paris in 33rd position, Tokyo 35th, London 39th, and New York 48th. The only other megacity in the top 50 is Osaka. Top positions in Mercer's survey regularly go to smaller cities such as Zurich, Geneva, Vienna, Vancouver, and Auckland. The 39 criteria for assessment emphasize factors such as personal safety, health and sanitation, transport, and public services, so safe and stable cities come out best, rather than the more dynamic places offering more spice to life. Results for each city are expressed on an index comparing it to New York, whose rating is set at 100.

SUSTAINABLE CITIES OF THE FUTURE

A project launched in 2006 at Dongtan, on a river island close to Shanghai, carries great hopes of establishing a model for sustainable urban development in China. The plan involves building a small city, to house 50,000 people in its initial phase, which will also provide local employment (rather than becoming a mere suburb of Shanghai), generate its own energy from renewable sources, manage its own waste, and carefully monitor its ecological impact on its surroundings – including a valuable wetland habitat for migratory birds. In a similar vein – but with more money and fewer constraints – Abu Dhabi announced in early 2008 a plan to build Masdar City, a "carbon neutral" and zero-waste city in the desert.

Curitiba in Brazil has the developing world's most innovative urban planning, beginning with a highly successful bus scheme and extending into pedestrianization, zoning, adult education, library and Internet access, and other areas. Other cities have tackled specific issues too. Responses to transport problems, for instance, include London's congestion charging scheme, the conversion of Delhi's buses and taxis to natural gas, a new Curitiba-inspired bus system and linked cycleway network in Bogotá, a "no driving day" scheme in Seoul, and so on. A conference of mayors of 40 major global cities in London in 2005 set up the C40 network to help share such experience more widely.

Current thinking, inspired by the successful regeneration of cities such as Barcelona, places great emphasis on preserving green spaces and distinctive features of architectural heritage, on fostering local community or "village" identities within large cities, and on designing spaces that are both safe and appealing on a human scale. The massive challenge of making megacities sustainable will depend as much on such "soft" social planning as on environmental and economic solutions.

FIND OUT MORE: www.megacitiesproject.org; www.c40cities.org; *State of the World 2007: Our Urban Future:* www.worldwatch.org

37

CITYSCAPES

THE SKYLINES AND LANDMARKS OF EVERY ONE OF THE WORLD'S CITIES REFLECT THEIR HISTORY, PHYSICAL AND HUMAN GEOGRAPHY, AND DISTINCTIVE ECONOMIC AND SOCIAL CHARACTERISTICS. SOME HAVE EVOLVED OVER A LONG PERIOD, WITH BUILDINGS OLD AND NEW JUXTAPOSED, WHILE OTHERS HAVE BEEN PLANNED FROM DAY ONE, WITH ORDERED STREETS AND PRESCRIBED PUBLIC SPACES, OR HAVE RECENTLY UNDERGONE MASSIVE REDEVELOPMENT TO CREATE GLEAMING ALL-NEW BUSINESS DISTRICTS.

BUILT ENVIRONMENT

The nature of a city's public space is crucial to its primary role as the place where people meet. But the first thing we ask of our buildings is adequate shelter. In today's fast-growing cities, even this is a big challenge. Housing solutions must also sit alongside workplaces and public buildings designed to make statements about power and wealth (whether for god, monarch or mega-corporation).

Seemingly mundane requirements like connecting up utilities and disposing of sewage – notoriously neglected in pre-19th-century London – are also key to a properly functioning modern built environment. Birmingham, "parked, paved, assized, marketed, gas & watered, and improved" from the 1870s by its pioneering mayor Joseph Chamberlain, became a model of progress. The "garden cities" movement proposed largely self-sufficient, low-density living, but demand for low-cost housing took precedence, later spawning a rash of identikit high-rise council estates. Cost and space constraints are equally evident in the US's public housing "Projects", Eastern Europe's drab tower blocks, and China's rapid urbanization.

NEW YORK

The ever-evolving Manhattan skyline gained its first skyscrapers in the late 19th century. Trinity Church, now walled in by Wall Street's tower blocks, was the tallest building until 1890. Subsequent "tallests" included the Empire State Buildings, the latter holding the world title from 1931–1972 when the ill-fated World Trade Center was completed.

PARIS

The Eiffel Tower, built for the 1889 Universal Exposition, was the world's highest man-made structure at the time. Parisians continue to take pride in up-to-the-minute "statement architecture", often to complement the city's cultural monuments.

LONDON

340,000 workers commute daily into the Square Mile of the City of London, putting immense pressure on its transportation networks, services, and buildings. The nearby Docklands area was redeveloped from the 1980s to provide additional modern office space.

GREENING THE CITY

- **TOKYO** HAS A LARGE FOREST OF 21,630 HA TO CONSERVE WATER
- **BEIJING** AIMS TO INCREASE ITS GREEN SPACE TO 40% BY THE YEAR 2010
- **NANJING** HAS PLANTED SOME 34 MILLION TREES SINCE 1994 – 23 TREES PER INHABITANT
- **MANILA** AIMS TO ACHIEVE A TREE-TO-PERSON RATIO OF ONE TO FOUR

SOURCES: FAO:*Urban Forestry in the Asia-Pacific Region – Situation and Prospects*; UN-Habitat: Global Urban Indicators Database

ST. PETERSBURG

In 1703 Peter the Great envisaged a dazzling new capital on the boggy marshlands at the mouth of the Neva river to rival the grandest European cities. Its wide boulevards, exquisite palaces, elegant bridges, and winding canals are a masterpiece of 18th-century urban planning, earning it the sobriquet of the "Venice of the North".

BEIJING

The 2008 Beijing Olympics have spurred this teeming city into a 21st-century building spree, showcasing ultra-modern designs by world-class architects. As well as the "bird's nest" National Stadium and the "water cube" National Swimming Centre, the city is also constructing a new Grand Theatre, with an oval "eggshell" exterior of titanium and glass, and an unusual interlocking "Z crisscross" to house China Central TV (CCTV) in the heart of the city's business district. CCTV's broadcasting tower, built in 1992, will remain the city's tallest building.

BERLIN

The partition of Berlin into East and West during the Cold War left swathes of land in the heart of the city undeveloped due to their proximity to the dividing Wall. Few major buildings went up here for decades, one striking exception being the Springer Building – an "in your face" icon of capitalism and press freedom overlooking Checkpoint Charlie. The East's rejoinder, the 1978 International Trade Centre, proclaimed a confidence in the communist economy which soon proved embarrassingly ill-founded. Reunification and subsequent redevelopment revitalized the city, with modern company showcases at their most conspicuous in the rebuilt Potsdamer Platz. The relocation of government from Bonn to Berlin required the construction of a new Bundeskanzleramt (Chancellor's Office), resplendent in glass to reflect the idea that Germany's modern rulers would be a model of transparency and accountability. But the most haunting public space in the old Wall zone is the Memorial to the Murdered Jews of Europe, an undulating labyrinth of 2700 concrete plinths near the Brandenburg Gate.

BUILT ENVIRONMENT

LIVING IN THE CITY

MOST URBAN DWELLERS IN THE WEST ENJOY A DOMESTIC SUPPLY OF CLEAN WATER, ELECTRICITY AND GAS, AND THE REMOVAL OF SEWAGE. THE MORE AFFLUENT THE COUNTRY, THE MORE WASTE ITS CONSUMERS GENERATE TOO. IN MUCH OF AFRICA, BY CONTRAST, MAINS WATER COUNTS AS A LUXURY, WHILE ONLY ONE INDIAN CITY-DWELLER IN FOUR (AND ONE IN TWO CHINESE AND BRAZILIANS) HAS MAINS SEWERAGE.

HOUSING TENURE

	OWNED	RENTED	SUB-TENANT	SQUATTER	HOMELESS	OTHER
AFRICA	40.8%	31.3%	4.5%	9.3%	1.0%	13.1%
ASIA-PACIFIC	61.4%	23.4%	0.3%	2.1%	1.5%	11.3%
LATIN AMERICA AND CARIBBEAN	60.6%	19.2%	0.9%	6.6%	2.9%	9.8%

URBAN WATER AND SANITATION PROVISION

	% URBAN POPULATION WITH HOUSE CONNECTIONS TO WATER SUPPLY	% URBAN POPULATION WITH HOUSE CONNECTIONS TO SEWERAGE
LIBERIA	1	12
CHAD	10	3
INDIA	47	25
PAKISTAN	49	40
CHINA	87	50
SOUTH AFRICA	87	70
BRAZIL	91	53
RUSSIA	93	85
HUNGARY	95	69
MEXICO	96	80
TURKEY	96	85
EGYPT	99	68
GERMANY	100	93
USA	100	95

AIR POLLUTION

AIR POLLUTANTS, MAINLY FROM INDUSTRIAL AND VEHICLE EMISSIONS, CAN CREATE APPALLING URBAN SMOG. THE WHO ESTIMATES THE DEATH TOLL AT 2.4 MILLION PER YEAR. THE WORST CITIES CONSTANTLY FAIL WHO MINIMUM STANDARDS.

COUNTRY	CITY	PARTICULATE MATTER (MICROGRAMS PER CUBIC METRE)
FRANCE	PARIS	11
SWEDEN	STOCKHOLM	11
CANADA	VANCOUVER	13
USA	NEW YORK	21
UK	LONDON	21
RUSSIA	MOSCOW	21
GERMANY	BERLIN	22
ITALY	ROME	29
SOUTH AFRICA	JOHANNESBURG	33
USA	LOS ANGELES	34
BRAZIL	SAO PAULO	40
JAPAN	TOKYO	40
SOUTH KOREA	SEOUL	41
MEXICO	MEXICO CITY	51
TURKEY	ISTANBUL	55
INDIA	BOMBAY (MUMBAI)	63
CHINA	SHANGHAI	73
THAILAND	BANGKOK	79
CHINA	BEIJING	89
INDONESIA	JAKARTA	104
CHINA	CHONGQING	123
CHINA	TIANJIN	125
INDIA	CALCUTTA (KOLKATA)	128
INDIA	DELHI	150
EGYPT	CAIRO	169

MUNICIPAL WASTE

	TOTAL AMOUNT OF MUNICIPAL WASTE GENERATED (1000 TONNES)	KG PER CAPITA
USA	214,253	740
AUSTRALIA	13,200	690
GERMANY	52,627	640
UK	36,841	610
FRANCE	33,467	540
ITALY	30,038	520
JAPAN	52,097	410
CANADA	12,008	380
TURKEY	25,611	360
MEXICO	33,758	320
POLAND	9925	260

SOURCES: WHO-UNICEF; OECD Factbook (2007); Cushman & Wakefield: *Main Streets Across the World* and *Office Space Across the World* (2008)

THE WORLD'S MOST EXPENSIVE OFFICES

	CITY	COUNTRY	LOCATION	TOTAL OCCUPANCY COST (US$/SQ METRE/YEAR)
1.	LONDON	UK	WEST END	3354
2.	HONG KONG	CHINA	CBD	2568
3.	TOKYO	JAPAN	CBD	2262
4.	BOMBAY	INDIA	CBD	1787
5.	MOSCOW	RUSSIA	CBD	1708
6.	PARIS	FRANCE	CBD	1524
7.	SINGAPORE	SINGAPORE	CBD	1404
8.	DUBAI	UAE	CBD	1356
9.	DUBLIN	IRELAND	2/4 DISTRICTS	1211
10.	NEW YORK	USA	MIDTOWN	1079

THE WORLD'S MOST EXPENSIVE SHOPPING STREETS

	CITY	COUNTRY	LOCATION	RENT (US$/SQ METRE/YEAR)
1.	NEW YORK	USA	FIFTH AVENUE	16,146
2.	HONG KONG	HONG KONG	CAUSEWAY BAY	13,057
3.	PARIS	FRANCE	AVENUE DES CHAMPS ELYSEES	9924
4.	LONDON	UK	NEW BOND STREET	8762
5.	TOKYO	JAPAN	GINZA	7352
6.	DUBLIN	IRELAND	GRAFTON STREET	7201
7.	ZURICH	SWITZERLAND	BAHNHOFSTRASSE	5296
8.	SYDNEY	AUSTRALIA	PITT STREET MALL	5264
9.	ATHENS	GREECE	ERMOU	4855
10.	SEOUL	SOUTH KOREA	GANGNAM STATION	4639

PAST FAILINGS, FUTURE CHALLENGES

While today's top architects build ever taller or more "expressive" buildings, our built environment has accumulated a long list of failures and shortcomings. The dynamiting of unloved tower blocks makes spectacular television footage, but urban planners also carry some of the responsibility for unsympathetically designed neighbourhoods where everyday life is dominated by the fear of violence. The spread of the "gated community", whose residents see a defended perimeter fence as their best hope of safety, is less a solution than a sign of failure. The epidemic of obesity in Western countries is also in part the product of "obesogenic environments" – built so much around the needs of the motor car that streets are unsafe for children to play or for people to walk and cycle.

The regeneration of Barcelona provides more positive inspiration. It emphasized human-scale public spaces and "liveability", and successfully used the 1992 Olympics to bring lasting improvements to the city.

The planners and architects of new towns and suburbs, as well as city centre redevelopments, have much to learn. Besides visual appearance, effective land use, housing density, transport flows, and environmental, business, and social impact, they must also address the new challenge of climate change, and deliver low or even zero carbon emissions through energy-efficient buildings and spatial planning.

Drug abuse, Afghanistan 2007/ obesity, China, 2007. Only two of the issues which are products of, and threats to, modern society.

WHILE THE CREATION OF A CIVIL SOCIETY REMAINS A CENTRAL AIM FOR MOST OF US, ENDEMIC AND LARGELY UNAVOIDABLE FACTORS PRESENT CONTINUING OBSTACLES TO THE ACHIEVEMENT OF THIS GOAL

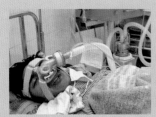

HEALTH
CAUSES OF DEATH IN THE DEVELOPED AND DEVELOPING WORLDS, LIFE EXPECTANCY, THE COSTS OF HEALTH CARE

FOOD
WHAT THE WORLD EATS, THE COST OF FOOD, OBESITY, ORGANIC FOOD, VEGETARIANS, FAST FOOD

SEX AND SOCIETY
MARRIAGE RATES, DIVORCE RATES, AGES OF CONSENT, HOMOSEXUALITY, FAMILY PLANNING, ABORTION, THE CHANGING FAMILY

RELIGION
MAJOR WORLD BELIEFS, CALENDARS, BLASPHEMY, RELIGIOUS OBSERVANCE, FUNDAMENTALISM

AGEING
LIVING LONGER, YOUNG VERSUS OLD, PENSIONS, THE COST OF CARE, THE RIGHT TO DIE

SOCIETY

RACE
MINORITIES, MELTING POTS, ETHNICITY, GENOCIDE

EDUCATION
LITERACY, STATE INVESTMENT, SCHOOL ATTENDANCE, HIGHER EDUCATION, UNIVERSITIES

CRIME AND PUNISHMENT
THE WORLD'S MOST DANGEROUS PLACES, MURDER RATES, GUN CRIME, PRISON POPULATIONS, THE DEATH PENALTY

DRUGS
ILLICIT DRUG ABUSE, SMOKING, LEGAL DRUGS, PHARMACEUTICALS, ALCOHOL

CORRUPTION
KLEPTOCRATS, BRIBERY ON THE STREET AND IN BUSINESS, TRANSPARENCY, CONTROLLING CORRUPTION

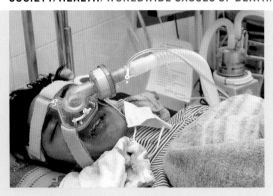

HEALTH

Despite the speed with which infectious diseases can now spread round the globe, only two of them – HIV/AIDS and tuberculosis – actually figure on the list of the top eight killers worldwide.

The striking fact is the spiralling incidence of health problems attributable to our diets (and over-consumption), stress levels, and environmental conditions. Heart disease, cancers, strokes, and lower respiratory infections loom large – the last of these ranking even above HIV/AIDS in its impact in terms of years of healthy life lost to disability and death.

New diseases are being identified at the rate of one a year. Among the major concerns are viral infections such as Ebola, Marburg haemorrhagic fever, and Nipah virus. Meanwhile, old threats such as cholera and yellow fever have re-emerged, along with the nightmare of drug-resistant strains of a range of diseases including tuberculosis, hospital-acquired infections, malaria, meningitis, and sexually transmitted infections.

WORLDWIDE CAUSES OF DEATH

	DEATHS 2002	DEATHS 2015 (PROJECTED)	DEATHS 2030 (PROJECTED)
HEART DISEASE (ISCHAEMIC)	7.2 MILLION	8.5 MILLION	9.8 MILLION
CANCERS	7.1 MILLION	9.1 MILLION	11.5 MILLION
STROKE	5.5 MILLION	6.5 MILLION	7.8 MILLION
PNEUMONIA AND OTHER RESPIRATORY INFECTIONS	4.0 MILLION	3.2 MILLION	2.6 MILLION
HIV/AIDS	2.9 MILLION	4.3 MILLION	6.5 MILLION
CHRONIC BRONCHITIS AND EMPHYSEMA	2.7 MILLION	4.0 MILLION	5.7 MILLION
TUBERCULOSIS	1.6 MILLION	1.0 MILLION	0.6 MILLION
ROAD TRAFFIC ACCIDENTS	1.2 MILLION	1.6 MILLION	2.1 MILLION

UNDER THE MICROSCOPE

- DEATHS FROM MEASLES HAVE FALLEN BY TWO-THIRDS SINCE 2000, BUT OVER 20 CHILDREN UNDER FIVE STILL DIE OF THE DISEASE EVERY HOUR
- TWO IN EVERY FIVE PEOPLE LIVE IN MALARIA-RISK AREAS. EVERY 30 SECONDS A CHILD DIES OF MALARIA
- 300 MILLION PEOPLE SUFFER FROM ASTHMA WORLDWIDE, AND 250,000 DIE OF IT EACH YEAR
- HALF OF ALL EUROPEANS WILL HAVE AN ALLERGY BY 2015
- THERE ARE 20% MORE HEART ATTACKS ON MONDAYS THAN ANY OTHER DAY IN TOKYO – DUE TO THE STRESS OF THE EARLY MORNING RISE AFTER THE WEEKEND LATE NIGHTS AND LIE-INS. JAPAN ALSO HAS ONE OF THE HIGHEST SUICIDE RATES IN THE WORLD

INFECTIOUS DISEASES

MEDIA REPORTS OF PANDEMICS TEND TO PAINT ALARMING PICTURES OF THEIR POTENTIAL THREAT. IN PRACTICE, BSE, SARS, BIRD FLU AND OTHERS HAVE SO FAR HAD LIMITED ACTUAL IMPACT ON HUMAN HEALTH – ALTHOUGH THEY CAN HAVE A MAJOR ECONOMIC IMPACT. BSE IN CATTLE IN 1990–98 COST THE UK US$39 BILLION, WHILE SARS IN 2003 COST ASIA US$30 BILLION.

BIRD FLU	OUTBREAKS IN POULTRY STOCK	HUMAN DEATHS
INDONESIA	261	107
VIETNAM	2470	52
THAILAND	1139	17
CHINA	93	20
EGYPT	1065	22
TOTAL	6241	240

TOP TEN CAUSES OF DEATH IN THE DEVELOPED AND DEVELOPING WORLDS COMPARED

DEVELOPED WORLD

DEVELOPING WORLD

Developed World	Cause	Developing World
4,666,000	HEART DISEASE (ISCHAEMIC)	2,530,000
4,047,000	STROKE	1,454,000
1,982,000	CHRONIC BRONCHITIS AND EMPHYSEMA	763,000
1,074,000	TRACHEA/BRONCHUS/LUNG CANCERS	
1,073,000	PNEUMONIA/RESPIRATORY INFECTIONS	2,806,000
742,000	STOMACH CANCER	
728,000	NEUROPSYCHIATRIC DISORDERS	
686,000	ROAD TRAFFIC ACCIDENTS	
669,000	HYPERTENSIVE HEART DISEASE	
658,000	DIABETES	
	HIV/AIDS	2,554,000
	DIARRHOEAL DISEASES	1,535,000
	MALARIA	1,246,000
	CHILDHOOD DISEASES	1,036,000
	TUBERCULOSIS	961,000
	MEASLES	546,000

WORST LIFE EXPECTANCY IN THE WORLD

GLOBAL AVERAGE IS 68

BOTSWANA	35
LESOTHO	35.2
ZIMBABWE	37.3
ZAMBIA	38.4
CENTRAL AFRICAN REPUBLIC	39.4

WHO'S DALY
(DISABILITY ADJUSTED LIFE YEAR) IS A MEASURE WHICH COMBINES THE TIME LIVED WITH DISABILITY AND THE TIME LOST DUE TO PREMATURE MORTALITY. THUS IT SHOWS THE GAP BETWEEN CURRENT HEALTH STATUS AND AN IDEAL SITUATION WHERE EVERYONE LIVES INTO OLD AGE FREE OF DISEASE AND DISABILITY. ONE DALY EQUALS ONE LOST YEAR OF "HEALTHY" LIFE.

RISK FACTORS IN DEVELOPED COUNTRIES:
INDULGENCE AND INACTIVITY ARE THE BIG KILLERS

The top five risk factors, measured as a percentage of all DALYs, add up to one-third of the total disease burden in developed countries, and are now beginning to dominate in developing countries too.

TOBACCO	12.2%
BLOOD PRESSURE	10.9%
ALCOHOL	9.2%
CHOLESTEROL	7.6%
OVERWEIGHT	7.4%
LOW FRUIT AND VEGETABLE INTAKE	3.9%
PHYSICAL INACTIVITY	3.3%
ILLICIT DRUGS	1.8%
UNSAFE SEX	0.8%
IRON DEFICIENCY	0.7%

AIDS

Despite improvements in effective treatment and prevention programmes, the number of HIV cases and deaths from AIDS continues to grow. Sub-Saharan Africa suffers the most; it is home to 63% of the global total of adults and children living with HIV. Figures are estimates.

	PEOPLE LIVING WITH HIV IN 2006	PEOPLE NEWLY INFECTED WITH HIV IN 2006	AIDS DEATHS IN 2006
SUB-SAHARAN AFRICA	24.7 MILLION	2.8 MILLION	2.1 MILLION
SOUTH AND SOUTHEAST ASIA	7.8 MILLION	860,000	590,000
EASTERN EUROPE & CENTRAL ASIA	1.7 MILLION	270,000	84,000
LATIN AMERICA	1.7 MILLION	140,000	65,000
NORTH AMERICA	1.4 MILLION	43,000	18,000
EAST ASIA	750,000	100,000	43,000
WESTERN & CENTRAL EUROPE	740,000	22,000	12,000
MIDDLE EAST & NORTH AFRICA	460,000	68,000	36,000
CARIBBEAN	250,000	27,000	19,000
OCEANIA	81,000	7100	4000
TOTAL	**39.5 MILLION**	**4.3 MILLION**	**2.9 MILLION**

HEALTH CARE

HEALTH EXPENDITURE

THE TEN COUNTRIES SPENDING THE HIGHEST
PERCENTAGES OF THEIR GDP ON HEALTH

	TOTAL	OF WHICH:	
		PRIVATE	PUBLIC
USA	15.4	8.5	6.9
MARSHALL ISLANDS	15.2	0.5	14.7
KIRIBATI	13.7	1.0	12.7
MALAWI	12.9	3.3	9.6
LEBANON	11.6	8.4	3.2
SWITZERLAND	11.5	4.8	6.7
SAO TOME & PRINCIPE	11.5	1.6	9.9
EAST TIMOR	11.2	2.4	8.8
GERMANY	10.6	2.5	8.1
FRANCE	10.5	2.3	8.2

DOCTORS AND BEDS PER 10,000 POPULATION

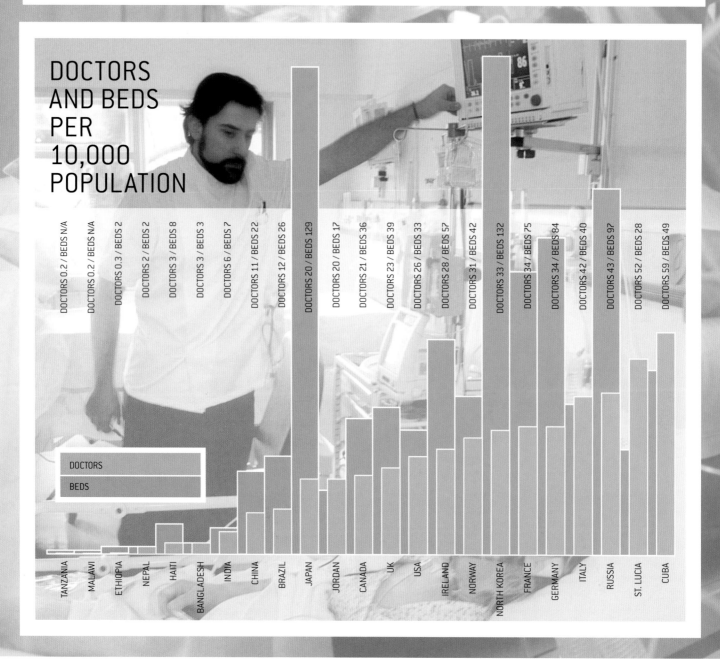

DOCTORS

BEDS

TANZANIA	DOCTORS 0.2 / BEDS N/A
MALAWI	DOCTORS 0.2 / BEDS N/A
ETHIOPIA	DOCTORS 0.3 / BEDS 2
NEPAL	DOCTORS 2 / BEDS 2
HAITI	DOCTORS 3 / BEDS 8
BANGLADESH	DOCTORS 3 / BEDS 3
INDIA	DOCTORS 6 / BEDS 7
CHINA	DOCTORS 11 / BEDS 22
BRAZIL	DOCTORS 12 / BEDS 26
JAPAN	DOCTORS 20 / BEDS 129
JORDAN	DOCTORS 20 / BEDS 17
CANADA	DOCTORS 21 / BEDS 36
UK	DOCTORS 23 / BEDS 39
USA	DOCTORS 26 / BEDS 33
IRELAND	DOCTORS 28 / BEDS 57
NORWAY	DOCTORS 31 / BEDS 42
NORTH KOREA	DOCTORS 33 / BEDS 132
FRANCE	DOCTORS 34 / BEDS 75
GERMANY	DOCTORS 34 / BEDS 84
ITALY	DOCTORS 42 / BEDS 40
RUSSIA	DOCTORS 43 / BEDS 97
ST. LUCIA	DOCTORS 52 / BEDS 28
CUBA	DOCTORS 59 / BEDS 49

SOURCES: World Health Organization: WHOSIS, *World Health Report* (2006)

CHILDHOOD IMMUNIZATION

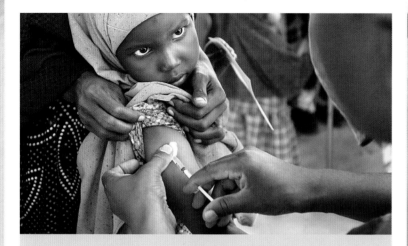

IMMUNIZATION IS A PROVEN TOOL FOR CONTROLLING DISEASE. ITS MAJOR SUCCESSES INCLUDE THE ERADICATION OF SMALLPOX, AND A 99% REDUCTION IN INFECTIONS FROM POLIOMYELITIS SINCE 1988. IT IS ALSO AMONG THE MOST COST-EFFECTIVE OF ALL HEALTH INVESTMENTS; THE UNITED NATIONS CHILDREN'S FUND (UNICEF) RECKONS THAT EVERY DOLLAR SPENT ON IMMUNIZATION CAN YIELD UP TO US$30 IN HEALTH-CARE SAVINGS. FOR US$17 A CHILD CAN BE IMMUNIZED (INCLUDING THE COST OF EQUIPMENT AND HEALTH WORKERS' SALARIES) AGAINST THE SIX DEADLIEST VACCINE-PREVENTABLE DISEASES – WHICH ARE STILL KILLING 1.4 MILLION CHILDREN UNDER FIVE EACH YEAR. DEATHS FROM MEASLES, ONCE BY FAR THE BIGGEST KILLER, WERE CUT BY TWO THIRDS BETWEEN 2000 AND 2006, TO A TOTAL OF 242,000 WORLDWIDE.

MEDICAL STAFF TRAINED ABROAD, WORKING IN OECD COUNTRIES

THE PHILIPPINES HAS BEEN TRAINING MEDICAL STAFF, ESPECIALLY NURSES, FOR EXPORT FOR MANY YEARS. 76% OF FOREIGN NURSE GRADUATES IN THE USA ARE FILIPINO. THEY ARE ENCOURAGED TO RETURN BY GRANTING PRIVILEGES SUCH AS TAX-FREE SHOPPING FOR ONE YEAR, LOANS FOR BUSINESS CAPITAL AT PREFERENTIAL RATES, AND ELIGIBILITY FOR SUBSIDIZED SCHOLARSHIPS. IN 2004 THE CENTRAL BANK OF THE PHILIPPINES REPORTED TOTAL REMITTANCES OF US$8.5 BILLION, REPRESENTING TEN PER CENT OF THE COUNTRY'S GDP.

	DOCTORS		NURSES	
	NUMBER	% OF TOTAL	NUMBER	% OF TOTAL
AUSTRALIA	11,122	21%	N/A	N/A
CANADA	13,620	23%	19,061	6%
FRANCE	11,269	6%	N/A	N/A
GERMANY	17,318	6%	26,284	3%
NEW ZEALAND	2832	34%	10,616	21%
UK	69,813	33%	65,000	10%
USA	213,331	27%	99,456	5%

PAYING FOR IT

Health-care provision varies widely from country to country. Most developed and some developing, countries have national health services, funded either by government out of tax revenue, as in the UK, or by compulsory health insurance. The US, the only wealthy developed country not to have universal free health provision, does put some public funds into basic health-care programmes for the over-65s, the disabled, and those on low incomes; private insurance is an option (taken out by all who can afford it), and contributions by employers are not compulsory.

Health services in developing countries are often extremely stretched; many African countries in particular have very low ratios of doctors to population. Their investment in training health workers can also be nullified by the "brain drain" of doctors and nurses migrating to developed countries in search of better jobs, more career opportunities, and higher salaries. Some blame medical recruitment agencies for stimulating this exodus. In a recent study of foreign nurses working in London, two thirds of the 400 in the survey had been recruited by agencies to come to the UK. South Africa's solution has been to set up a reciprocal partnership with the UK to allow the exchange of health professionals, rather than just a one-way flow, for education and practice periods. India, meanwhile, has developed sufficient expertise and facilities to encourage the rapid growth of a "health tourism" industry, where foreign patients fly in for surgery at much lower prices than they would face back home.

FOOD

Hunting, gathering, and then growing food has dominated human activity for most of our history. Without food or water, an average human being can survive for only around two weeks. Access to food and quality of nutrition remain key concerns in the modern world. What is on the menu varies widely across the world, in terms of ingredients used, cooking methods, and sheer quantity.

In the West, obtaining tasty new ingredients from around the world was a big factor behind the age of exploration and the subsequent drive for empire in the 18th and 19th centuries. Spices from the East Indies and sugar from the Caribbean added exotic flavours to European cooking, while tea, coffee, and cocoa are still among the most important internationally traded commodities – along with cereals, rice, protein-rich soybeans, meat, and fish.

Despite this globalized food trade, national cuisines vary enormously. Red meat and chicken, often in fast-food form, are the order of the day in the USA, UK, and Australia, while olive oil, pasta, and seafood reign in the Mediterranean. East Asian diets insist on large quantities of rice, white meat, and fish, while Latin Americans and Indians eat large quantities of pulses.

THE FAT OF THE LAND

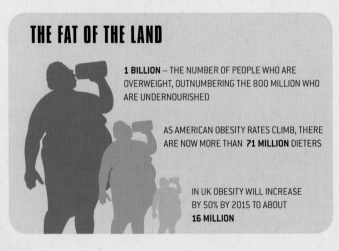

1 BILLION – THE NUMBER OF PEOPLE WHO ARE OVERWEIGHT, OUTNUMBERING THE 800 MILLION WHO ARE UNDERNOURISHED

AS AMERICAN OBESITY RATES CLIMB, THERE ARE NOW MORE THAN **71 MILLION** DIETERS

IN UK OBESITY WILL INCREASE BY 50% BY 2015 TO ABOUT **16 MILLION**

WHAT THE WORLD EATS (BILLION KCAL)

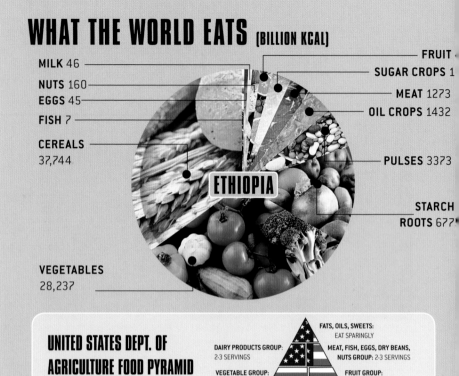

MILK 46
NUTS 160
EGGS 45
FISH 7
CEREALS 37,744
VEGETABLES 28,237

FRUIT
SUGAR CROPS 1
MEAT 1273
OIL CROPS 1432
PULSES 3373
STARCH ROOTS 677

ETHIOPIA

UNITED STATES DEPT. OF AGRICULTURE FOOD PYRAMID FOR IDEAL FOOD CONSUMPTION

FATS, OILS, SWEETS: EAT SPARINGLY
DAIRY PRODUCTS GROUP: 2-3 SERVINGS
MEAT, FISH, EGGS, DRY BEANS, NUTS GROUP: 2-3 SERVINGS
VEGETABLE GROUP: 3-5 SERVINGS
FRUIT GROUP: 3-4 SERVINGS
BREAD, CEREAL, RICE, PASTA GROUP: 6-11 SERVINGS

WHO SPENDS WHAT ON FOOD

PROPORTION OF THE HOUSEHOLD BUDGET SPENT ON EACH FOOD TYPE (%)

COUNTRY	BEVERAGES & TOBACCO AS % OF TOTAL FOOD EXPENDITURE	BREADS & CEREALS AS % OF TOTAL FOOD EXPENDITURE	DAIRY AS % OF TOTAL FOOD EXPENDITURE
AZERBAIJAN	2.894	39.017	5.644
TANZANIA	4.745	39.548	3.558
NIGERIA	2.731	34.08	5.613
ARMENIA	5.204	18.856	6.229
ALBANIA	5.125	20.635	17.365
RUSSIA	15.459	14.26	13.265
BRAZIL	12.315	16.798	14.036
ITALY	16.184	11.317	13.901
UK	47.53	8.306	6.884
FRANCE	21.358	10.887	11.799
JAPAN	23.148	22.279	4.793
GERMANY	28.246	14.872	7.109
CANADA	29.481	11.429	11.185
USA	28.71	11.387	8.587

SOURCES: Food and Agriculture Organization: FAOSTAT; US Department of Agriculture, Economic Research Service

DIETARY ENERGY CONSUMPTION

TOP 10
KCAL/PERSON/DAY

USA – 3770	ZAMBIA – 1930
PORTUGAL – 3750	SIERRA LEONE – 1930
AUSTRIA – 3740	ETHIOPIA – 1860
LUXEMBOURG – 3710	TAJIKISTAN – 1840
IRELAND – 3690	SOMALIA – 1760
GREECE – 3680	COMOROS – 1750
ISRAEL – 3680	ETHIOPIA – 1640
ITALY – 3670	BURUNDI – 1640
BELGIUM – 3640	CONGO DEM. REP. – 1610
FRANCE – 3640	ERITREA – 1520

BOTTOM 10
KCAL/PERSON/DAY

NUTS 1631
FISH 3495
PULSES 4810
EGGS 5713
VEGETABLES 8348
STARCHY ROOTS 13,405
FRUIT 13,827

CEREALS 169,786

SUGAR CROPS 31,770

OIL CROPS 40,853

MILK 46,139

MEAT 56,346

USA

					COUNTRY	
16	1.071	13.038	14.4	13.72	AZERBAIJAN	73.507
02	6.377	24.223	9.598	8.649	TANZANIA	73.239
46	15.222	15.437	12.883	8.888	NIGERIA	72.974
8	1.57	34.36	8.179	16.022	ARMENIA	69.657
14	0.307	22.637	18.994	5.392	ALBANIA	69.264
52	4.13	16.237	22.921	9.465	RUSSIA	34.346
22	2.309	14.833	24.54	11.546	BRAZIL	22.715
56	5.401	19.142	23.584	6.614	ITALY	16.593
71	2.254	12.018	12.573	9.164	UK	16.374
51	4.75	12.389	24.921	11.045	FRANCE	15.345
61	17.024	12.787	7.818	11.49	JAPAN	14.878
72	1.871	8.279	20.299	17.052	GERMANY	13.093
08	2.651	18.119	16.456	8.57	CANADA	11.68
71	1.194	14.662	19.583	14.106	USA	9.726
OILS AS % OF TOTAL FOOD ...ITURE	FISH AS % OF TOTAL FOOD EXPENDITURE	FRUITS & VEGETABLES AS % OF TOTAL FOOD EXPENDITURE	MEAT AS % OF TOTAL FOOD EXPENDITURE	OTHER FOODS AS % OF TOTAL FOOD EXPENDITURE	COUNTRY	TOTAL FOOD EXPENDITURE AS % OF TOTAL HOUSEHOLD EXPENDITURE

FOOD

OBESITY

OVEREATING IS A MAJOR PROBLEM IN THE WEST. ABUNDANCE OF FOOD AND LACK OF EXERCISE ARE THE MAIN REASONS WHY AROUND A QUARTER OF WESTERNERS ARE OBESE. IN THE CAR-LOVING USA, THE WORLD'S FATTEST NATION, TWO IN THREE PEOPLE QUALIFY AS OVERWEIGHT AND HALF OF THEM ARE DEFINED AS OBESE. THE COST OF PROVIDING HEALTH CARE FOR OBESITY-RELATED ILLNESSES IS BALLOONING.

MALES AGE 15+	2002	2005	2010
AUSTRALIA	21.2	23.8	28.4
CANADA	23.1	23.7	25.5
FINLAND	18.0	18.9	20.9
MEXICO	20.3	24.0	30.1
NEW ZEALAND	19.7	23.0	28.9
SPAIN	15.6	15.6	17.3
UK	18.7	21.6	23.7
USA	32.0	36.5	44.2

FEMALES AGE 15+	2002	2005	2010
AUSTRALIA	22.5	24.9	29.1
CANADA	22.2	23.2	25.7
FINLAND	17.5	17.8	19.4
MEXICO	31.6	34.3	41.0
NEW ZEALAND	26.7	31.5	39.9
SPAIN	14.5	15.8	17.3
UK	21.3	24.2	26.3
USA	37.8	41.8	48.3

ORGANIC FOOD

A GROWING PERCENTAGE OF OUR FOOD IS MARKETED AS "ORGANIC", MEANING THAT IT COMES FROM PRODUCERS WHO HAVE RECEIVED CERTIFICATION FOR THEIR FARMING METHODS. THEIR CROPS MUST BE GROWN WITHOUT USE OF CONVENTIONAL PESTICIDES, ARTIFICIAL FERTILIZERS, HUMAN WASTE, OR SEWAGE SLUDGE, AND PROCESSED (IF AT ALL) WITH NO IONIZING RADIATION OR FOOD ADDITIVES. ORGANIC LIVESTOCK REARING AVOIDS ROUTINE USE OF ANTIBIOTICS OR GROWTH HORMONES. THE ORGANIC MARKET WAS WORTH US$40 BILLION IN 2006, AND IS EXPECTED TO ALMOST DOUBLE BY 2012.
ORGANIC FARMING HAS GONE GLOBAL; THERE ARE PRODUCERS IN 120 COUNTRIES. EUROPEAN FARMERS HAVE TAKEN TO IT MOST, SO FAR, IN TERMS OF THE PERCENTAGE OF LAND CONVERTED.

LIECHTENSTEIN **26.4%**
AUSTRIA **12.9%**
SWITZERLAND **10.27%**
FINLAND **7.22%**
ITALY **6.86%**
SWEDEN **6.8%**
GREECE **6.24%**
DENMARK **6.2%**
CZECH REP. **5.97%**
SLOVENIA **4.6%**

COUNTRIES WITH MOST HECTARES UNDER ORGANIC MANAGEMENT 2006

31 MILLION HECTARES WORLDWIDE ARE FARMED ORGANICALLY, AND TWICE THAT AREA IS CERTIFIED FOR WILD FOOD HARVESTING. THE THREE PLACES WITH MOST ORGANIC LAND ARE ALL HUGE FARMING COUNTRIES. AUSTRALIA HAS GREAT TRACTS OF GRAZING FOR ORGANIC LIVESTOCK. CHINA'S RECENT RUSH TO ORGANIC HORTICULTURE AIMS TO RECTIFY ITS REPUTATION FOR DANGEROUSLY HIGH PESTICIDE USE. BETWEEN 2005 AND 2006 IT LEAPT FROM 11TH TO SECOND IN THE WORLD LEAGUE, AND AS MUCH AS 30% OF ITS FARMLAND COULD CONVERT BY 2010.

AUSTRALIA **11,300,000**
CHINA **3,400,000**
ARGENTINA **2,800,000**
ITALY **1,052,002**
USA **930,810**
BRAZIL **803,180**
URUGUAY **760,000**
GERMANY **734,027**
SPAIN **725,254**
UK **695,619**

SAYING NO TO MEAT

INDIA HAS THE MOST VEGETARIANS (AND VEGANS) IN THE WORLD. ABOUT A QUARTER OF ITS BILLION INHABITANTS AVOID EATING MEAT, AS RECOMMENDED BY THE HINDU, JAIN, AND BUDDHIST FAITHS. MOST ARE LACTO-VEGETARIANS (THEY DRINK MILK BUT AVOID EGGS).

THE INTERNATIONAL VEGETARIAN UNION (IVU) PROVIDES THE FOLLOWING STATISTICS FOR EUROPE:

SWEDEN 60,000 TOTAL: **8M** POPULATION: **0.75%**

POLAND 75,000 TOTAL: **38M** POPULATION: **0.2%**

FRANCE 500,000 TOTAL: **56M** POPULATION: **0.9%**

NETHERLANDS 700,000 TOTAL: **16M** POPULATION: **4.4%**

GERMANY 700,000 TOTAL: **56M** POPULATION: **1.25%**

UK 3,500,000 TOTAL: **57M** POPULATION: **6.1%**

WHAT, NO McDONALD'S!

IT IS NOT EASY TO GET A BIG MAC IN AFRICA — IT IS ONLY AVAILABLE IN EGYPT, MAURITIUS, MOROCCO, NIGERIA, AND SOUTH AFRICA.

ELSEWHERE, YOU CAN FIND A McDONALD'S IN EVERY COUNTRY EXCEPT:

- **CENTRAL AMERICA/CARIBBEAN:** ANTIGUA & BARBUDA, BARBADOS, BELIZE, CUBA, DOMINICA, GRENADA, HAITI, JAMAICA, ST KITTS & NEVIS, ST LUCIA, ST VINCENT & THE GRENADINES, TRINIDAD & TOBAGO

- **SOUTH AMERICA:** BOLIVIA, GUYANA

- **EUROPE:** ALBANIA, ARMENIA, BOSNIA & HERZEGOVINA, VATICAN CITY

- **ASIA:** AFGHANISTAN, BANGLADESH, BHUTAN, BURMA (MYANMAR), CAMBODIA, EAST TIMOR, IRAN, IRAQ, KYRGYZSTAN, LAOS, MALDIVES, MONGOLIA, NEPAL, NORTH KOREA, SYRIA, TAJIKISTAN, TURKMENISTAN, UZBEKISTAN, VIETNAM, YEMEN

- **OCEANIA:** KIRIBATI, MARSHALL ISLANDS, MICRONESIA, NAURU, PALAU, PAPUA NEW GUINEA, SOLOMON ISLANDS, TONGA, TUVALU, VANUATU

UK TAKEAWAY RESTAURANTS

FISH & CHIP SHOPS

1910 – ABOUT **25,000**   1927 – ABOUT **35,000**   2003 – ABOUT **8600**

KEBAB SHOPS NOW – ABOUT **20,000**

TECHNO-FIXING FUTURE FAMINE?

Where people live longest, as in Japan and Georgia, they often ascribe it to the high nutritional value of their diet. While obesity plagues the West, the developing countries suffer most from malnutrition because people cannot afford a well-balanced menu, or simply cannot get enough to eat. Many charities and NGOs now use proactive campaigns to invest in local farming as a major element in combating the threat of famine.

Scientific approaches to producing food have produced great advances down the ages, but new technologies have also thrown up great controversies. The "Green Revolution" of the 1970s and 1980s promised to end world hunger by promoting newly-bred high-yielding crop varieties, backed by huge irrigation schemes. The adverse effects, however, included drawing subsistence farmers into dependence on the seed and pesticide merchants. Traditional crop varieties were also lost in the process.

Similar hopes and fears surround the current debate on genetic modification (GM), with the added nightmare vision of modified varieties cross-breeding with unpredictable effects. The agri-food giant Monsanto leads both the pro-GM lobby, and the commercial production of crop varieties engineered to be immune to its systemic pesticides. Around 90% of US-grown soybeans are GM, whereas the European Union has maintained a moratorium on growing most GM varieties pending further research.

Animals too can be modified. In 2003 US farmers got the go-ahead to use cloned animals for the food market. A report by scientists in 2007 predicted that such cloned meat would be a part of the American diet by 2009.

SEX AND SOCIETY

Human reproduction, like that of most mammal species, involves sexual intercourse. Humans are unusual, however, in also having sex for sensual pleasure and to express inter-personal connections. This makes sexuality, and the human relationships associated with it, of central importance to society. Marriage gives legal, social, and often religious backing to the partnership of two adults, and is widely seen as the best framework for bringing up children. Laws on marriage, however, have generally become less rigid as society places greater emphasis on individual freedom, making it easier for couples to end their union by divorce. Appalling abuse within relationships still continues: in Russia a woman is killed by her partner, spouse, or boyfriend every 35 minutes.

Sexual attraction is not easily confined within socio-legally sanctioned partnerships, and can be subversive of them. Homosexuality has been practised openly in some societies throughout history, but stigmatized, condemned, and driven "underground" in others, notably under the influence of Judaic, Christian, or Islamic religious doctrine. More liberal attitudes have prevailed only recently and partially in many Western countries.

RELATIONSHIPS

- THE WORLD'S ONE BILLION MARRIED COUPLES ACCOUNT FOR NEARLY HALF OF ALL ADULTS
- COHABITATION WITHOUT MARRIAGE IS CHOSEN BY THREE IN TEN COUPLES IN SWEDEN, MORE THAN ONE IN FIVE IN AUSTRALIA, MORE THAN ONE IN SIX IN MEXICO, AND AROUND ONE IN 12 IN THE USA
- OVER HALF OF NEW MARRIAGES IN THE USA ARE LIKELY TO END IN DIVORCE
- DIVORCE IS ILLEGAL IN MALTA AND THE PHILIPPINES
- IN US SURVEYS, 50% OF MEN CLAIM TO HAVING EIGHT OR MORE SEXUAL PARTNERS IN THEIR LIFETIME, WHILE 50% OF WOMEN CLAIM THREE OR FEWER
- AROUND FOUR PER CENT OF MEN AND TWO PER CENT OF WOMEN ARE AVOWEDLY HOMOSEXUAL

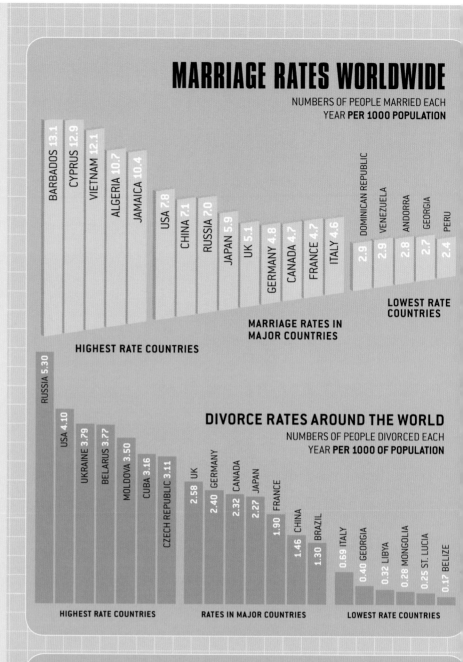

MARRIAGE RATES WORLDWIDE

NUMBERS OF PEOPLE MARRIED EACH YEAR **PER 1000 POPULATION**

HIGHEST RATE COUNTRIES
- BARBADOS 13.1
- CYPRUS 12.9
- VIETNAM 12.1
- ALGERIA 10.7
- JAMAICA 10.4

MARRIAGE RATES IN MAJOR COUNTRIES
- USA 7.8
- CHINA 7.1
- RUSSIA 7.0
- JAPAN 5.9
- UK 5.1
- GERMANY 4.8
- CANADA 4.7
- FRANCE 4.7
- ITALY 4.6

LOWEST RATE COUNTRIES
- DOMINICAN REPUBLIC 2.9
- VENEZUELA 2.9
- ANDORRA 2.8
- GEORGIA 2.7
- PERU 2.4

DIVORCE RATES AROUND THE WORLD

NUMBERS OF PEOPLE DIVORCED EACH YEAR **PER 1000 OF POPULATION**

HIGHEST RATE COUNTRIES
- RUSSIA 5.30
- USA 4.10
- UKRAINE 3.79
- BELARUS 3.77
- MOLDOVA 3.50
- CUBA 3.16
- CZECH REPUBLIC 3.11

RATES IN MAJOR COUNTRIES
- UK 2.58
- GERMANY 2.40
- CANADA 2.32
- JAPAN 2.27
- FRANCE 1.90
- CHINA 1.46
- BRAZIL 1.30

LOWEST RATE COUNTRIES
- ITALY 0.69
- GEORGIA 0.40
- LIBYA 0.32
- MONGOLIA 0.28
- ST. LUCIA 0.25
- BELIZE 0.17

HOMOSEXUALITY

Homosexuality (of either gender) is illegal in: Afghanistan, Algeria, Angola, Bahrain, Bangladesh, Barbados, Benin, Bhutan, Botswana, Brunei, Burma, Burundi, Cameroon, Congo Dem. Rep., Eritrea, Ethiopia, Gambia, Grenada, Guinea, Guyana, India, Iran, Jamaica, Kenya, Kuwait, Lebanon, Liberia, Malaysia, Mauritius, Morocco, Mozambique, Namibia, Nigeria, Oman, Pakistan, Papua New Guinea, Qatar, Samoa, Saudi Arabia, Senegal, Singapore, Somalia, Sri Lanka, Sudan, Swaziland, Syria, Tajikistan, Tanzania, Togo, Tonga, Trinidad & Tobago, Tunisia, Turkmenistan, Tuvalu, Uganda, UAE, Uzbekistan, Yemen, Zambia, and Zimbabwe.

Where homosexuality is legal, most countries have the same minimum age for consensual homosexual or heterosexual sex, except for: Canada (heterosexual: 12 or 14 years; male homosexual: 18 years), Chile (hetero: 14; homo:18), Vanuatu (hetero: 15; homo: 18), Bahamas, Rwanda, and Suriname (hetero: 16; homo: 18), Indonesia (hetero: 16 for women and 19 for men, homo: 18), and South Africa (hetero: 14; homo: 19).

SAME-SEX UNIONS

Europe is leading the way in recognizing same-sex unions. The Netherlands was the first country to grant full legal equality to gay marriage in 2001, and Belgium, Spain, Canada, and South Africa have so far followed suit. Canada granted the world's first same-sex divorce in 2004. Objection to the idea of gay marriage remains largely entrenched in traditional opinions and religious edict. The evangelical Christian Right in the USA vigorously opposes the legitimization of gay relationships as equivalent to the marriage of a man and a woman.

● **THE US SUPREME COURT** RECENTLY STRUCK DOWN LAWS THAT OUTLAWED CONSENSUAL, SAME-SEX ADULT SEXUAL ACTIVITY

● **SAME-SEX INTERCOURSE** IS ILLEGAL IN THE US MILITARY

● **SAME-SEX "MARRIAGE"** IS LEGAL IN MASSACHUSETTS

● **43 US STATES LEGALLY DEFINE "MARRIAGE"** AS BETWEEN A MAN AND WOMAN. SOME OF THESE STATES HAVE LEGALIZED SAME-SEX "UNIONS"

● **SAME-SEX "UNION" IS LEGAL,** WITH ALL THE RIGHTS AND RESPONSIBILITIES OF MARRIAGE, IN CONNECTICUT, VERMONT, NEW JERSEY, CALIFORNIA, AND NEW HAMPSHIRE

● **SAME-SEX "UNION" IS LEGAL,** WITH A SUBSET OF THE RIGHTS AND RESPONSIBILITIES OF HETEROSEXUAL MARRIAGE, IN MAINE, HAWAII, WASHINGTON D.C., AND OREGON

● **26 US STATES HAVE** CONSTITUTIONALLY BARRED SAME-SEX "MARRIAGES", AND DEFINED CIVIL MARRIAGE AS THE LEGAL UNION OF A MAN AND WOMAN. SOME OF THESE STATES ALSO BAN ANY LEGAL RECOGNITION OF SAME-SEX UNIONS THAT WOULD BE EQUIVALENT TO CIVIL MARRIAGE

MINIMUM LEGAL AGES FOR SEX AND MARRIAGE

FOR HETEROSEXUAL RELATIONSHIPS

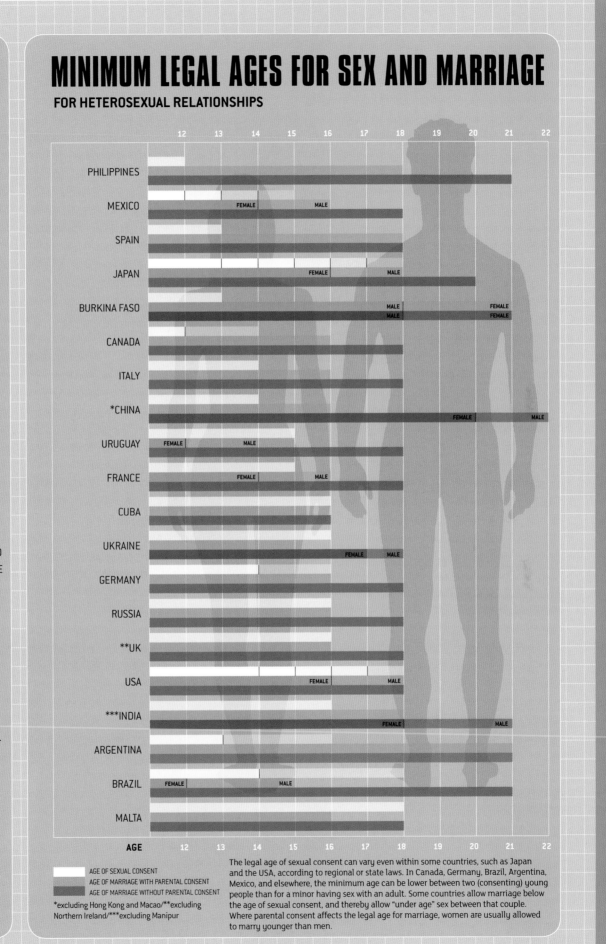

Legend:
- AGE OF SEXUAL CONSENT
- AGE OF MARRIAGE WITH PARENTAL CONSENT
- AGE OF MARRIAGE WITHOUT PARENTAL CONSENT

*excluding Hong Kong and Macao/**excluding Northern Ireland/***excluding Manipur

The legal age of sexual consent can vary even within some countries, such as Japan and the USA, according to regional or state laws. In Canada, Germany, Brazil, Argentina, Mexico, and elsewhere, the minimum age can be lower between two (consenting) young people than for a minor having sex with an adult. Some countries allow marriage below the age of sexual consent, and thereby allow "under age" sex between that couple. Where parental consent affects the legal age for marriage, women are usually allowed to marry younger than men.

GIVING BIRTH

AVERAGE AGE OF FIRST-TIME MOTHERS

SPAIN	30 YEARS OLD
USA	25 YEARS OLD
INDONESIA	21 YEARS OLD
NIGERIA	20 YEARS OLD

FAMILY SIZES

COUNTRY	NUMBER OF CHILDREN
NIGER	8
CONGO DEM. REP.	7
YEMEN	6
NIGERIA/ETHIOPIA	5
PAKISTAN/SUDAN	4
INDIA/SOUTH AFRICA/ISRAEL	3
BRAZIL/MEXICO/USA/INDONESIA	2
RUSSIA/ITALY/JAPAN/GERMANY/SPAIN	1

WHO DO CHILDREN LIVE WITH IN THE UK?

MARRIED COUPLE*	66%
COHABITING COUPLE*	11%
LONE MOTHER	22%
LONE FATHER	2%

*NOT NECESSARILY THEIR TWO PARENTS

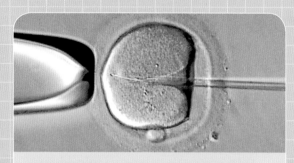

THE NUMBER OF BABIES PRODUCED WORLDWIDE USING IVF AND DONOR INSEMINATION IS AROUND 200,000 A YEAR

FAMILY PLANNING AND CONTRACEPTION

PERCENTAGE OF MARRIED WOMEN USING CONTRACEPTIVES

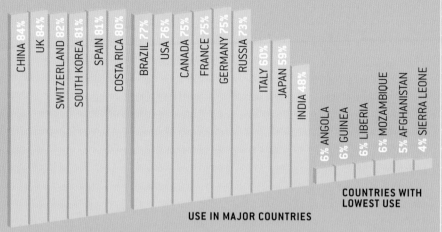

COUNTRIES WITH HIGHEST USE

USE IN MAJOR COUNTRIES

COUNTRIES WITH LOWEST USE

CHINA 84% · UK 84% · SWITZERLAND 82% · SOUTH KOREA 81% · SPAIN 81% · COSTA RICA 80% · BRAZIL 77% · USA 76% · CANADA 75% · FRANCE 75% · GERMANY 75% · RUSSIA 73% · ITALY 60% · JAPAN 59% · INDIA 48% · ANGOLA 6% · GUINEA 6% · LIBERIA 6% · MOZAMBIQUE 6% · AFGHANISTAN 5% · SIERRA LEONE 4%

Although one in every four births worldwide is the result of an unplanned pregnancy, two-thirds of the world's married couples have used modern family planning (birth control) methods. Female sterilization is the most common method (23% of all married couples), ahead of intrauterine devices (18%) and the pill (9%). Male contraception, three times more popular in developed countries than in the developing world, is the choice of only 11% of married couples worldwide, and depends more often on condom use than on male sterilization (vasectomy). Ten billion condoms are currently used annually; four billion of them for family planning, and over six billion to protect against sexually-transmitted infections. This still leaves more than nine in every ten risky sexual acts unprotected by condoms, despite HIV awareness initiatives by governments in most countries. Half of the new HIV infections in China in 2005 occurred through unprotected sex.

TEENAGE BIRTHS

Percentage of women aged 15-19 who give birth, per year

By the age of 16, most girls in Niger are married, often in polygamous relationships, and many have given birth. In their lifetime they will have on average 7.6 children – the highest rate in the world. In developed countries, most "teenage mums" are unmarried.

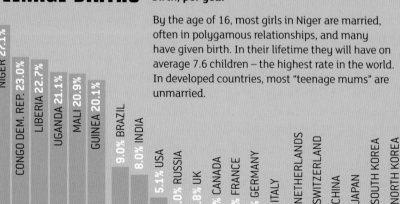

NIGER 27.1% · CONGO DEM. REP. 23.0% · LIBERIA 22.7% · UGANDA 21.1% · MALI 20.9% · GUINEA 20.1% · BRAZIL 9.0% · INDIA 8.0% · USA 5.1% · RUSSIA 3.0% · UK 2.8% · CANADA 1.5% · FRANCE 1.4% · GERMANY 1.1% · ITALY 0.7% · NETHERLANDS 0.5% · SWITZERLAND 0.5% · CHINA 0.5% · JAPAN 0.4% · SOUTH KOREA 0.3% · NORTH KOREA 0.2%

HIGHEST COUNTRIES · MAJOR COUNTRIES · LOWEST COUNTRIES

ABORTION NUMBERS

ESTIMATES OF INDUCED ABORTIONS IN
MILLIONS, BY REGION

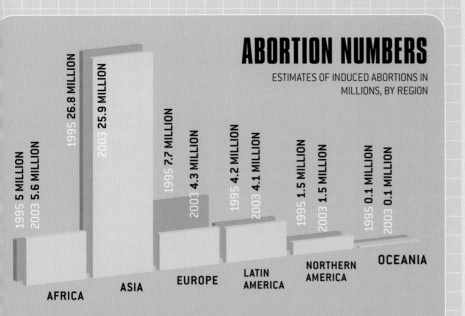

AFRICA
- 1995 5 MILLION
- 2003 5.6 MILLION

ASIA
- 1995 26.8 MILLION
- 2003 25.9 MILLION

EUROPE
- 1995 7.7 MILLION
- 2003 4.3 MILLION

LATIN AMERICA
- 1995 4.2 MILLION
- 2003 4.1 MILLION

NORTHERN AMERICA
- 1995 1.5 MILLION
- 2003 1.5 MILLION

OCEANIA
- 1995 0.1 MILLION
- 2003 0.1 MILLION

The number of induced abortions worldwide has declined from over 45 million a year to under 42 million between 1995 and 2003. This includes an estimated 20 million unsafe abortions, which can kill or cause serious injury, infertility, and increased health care costs.

- The world's lowest abortion rate is in Western Europe (12 per 1000 women aged 15-44), where contraceptive services and use are widespread. Safe medical abortion is usually accessible here, and legal on often quite broad grounds. Northern Europe's abortion rate is somewhat higher (17 per 1000 women), and it is 21 per 1000 in Canada and the USA.
- Across the developed countries as a whole, the average unsafe abortion rate is two per 1000 women aged 15–44. By contrast there are up to 39 unsafe abortions per 1000 women in Eastern Africa and 33 per 1000 in South America.
- Africa, Asia, and South America have the highest overall rates of abortion, despite the legal restrictions in force in most countries in these regions.
- China accounts for a third of the 26 million abortions in Asia.
- Eastern Europe has seen the most marked reductions in abortion rates since 1995.

THE LEGALITY OF ABORTION

CHILE, EL SALVADOR, MALTA, NICARAGUA, AND THE VATICAN CITY BAN ANY WOMAN FROM HAVING AN ABORTION WITH NO EXCEPTIONS. IN GERMANY IT REMAINS ILLEGAL, BUT THIS IS NOT ENFORCED. THE USA AND AUSTRALIA HAVE VARYING LEGISLATION BY STATE. OTHER COUNTRIES HAVE A VARIETY OF LEGAL THRESHOLDS, WHICH ARE USUALLY MOST RESTRICTIVE IN CATHOLIC AND MUSLIM SOCIETIES.

ILLEGAL	**5 COUNTRIES** (CHILE, EL SALVADOR, MALTA, NICARAGUA, AND THE VATICAN CITY)
ONLY LEGAL FOR PROTECTION OF MATERNAL HEALTH	**101 COUNTRIES** (INCLUDING IRELAND)
ALSO LEGAL IN CASES OF RAPE	**6 COUNTRIES** (INCLUDING HONG KONG, AND THAILAND)
ALSO LEGAL FOR FOETAL DEFECTS	**16 COUNTRIES** (INCLUDING ISRAEL, NEW ZEALAND, AND SPAIN)
ALSO LEGAL FOR SOCIOECONOMIC REASONS	**12 COUNTRIES** (INCLUDING ICELAND, INDIA, AND UK)
LEGAL ON REQUEST	**56 COUNTRIES** (INCLUDING ARMENIA, AZERBAIJAN, BAHRAIN, CANADA, CHINA, AND SWITZERLAND)

FAMILIES OF THE FUTURE

The support network (and constraining ties) of the extended family, with several generations and cousins living under the same roof, have become a rarity in the West. Even in Asia, young couples (and individuals) increasingly move away to set up home, either because they can afford to, or because they must do so in search of work.

The more modern norm of the "nuclear family" unit (one man, one woman, plus children) is now under challenge in its turn. Western couples increasingly cohabit either before or instead of marriage, and separation and divorce rates continue to rise, leaving many single parents (usually the mother) to bring up children alone. Many commentators blame juvenile delinquency and even adult criminality on a broken family history. Single women not in long-term relationships are also making the choice to have children, often late in life after building a career. As family units get smaller this puts increased pressure on housing resources and on the need for nursery facilities. Single parents can find themselves trapped in a system where childcare costs make it uneconomic to go out to work, pushing them towards dependence on social security benefits.

Meanwhile, the need for a male-female coupling to conceive children is being challenged by artificial reproductive techniques. Taboos on human cloning could prove fragile in the face of ambitious laboratories and changing social behaviour. Some feminists see men as becoming biologically redundant, while women remain essential to carry fertilized eggs through to the point of childbirth – potentially heralding the dawn of an all-female race.

RELIGION

Religion can be institutional, personal, or habitual; it means different things to different people. It is often a matter of cultural identity and a shared sense of community values. Wars have frequently been fought in the name of contending religious beliefs. On the other hand, faith and spirituality can provide ways of transcending everyday concerns, answering questions about the purpose of existence, and explaining how human life fits into what believers see as God's creation.

For more than 80% of the world's population, religion is a part of life, whether through rituals, traditional practices, daily prayers, or simply self-definition. Many people consider themselves culturally or ethnically part of a religion, while seldom if ever practising its rites. Conversely, some practise traditional rituals without accepting that they are religious – notably the 87% or so Japanese people who deny they are followers of Shinto yet many of whom visit local temples as a matter of course. Not all religions involve attendance at a church, mosque, or temple.

A sixth of the world's population profess no religion. Atheists are convinced there is no god (and may find sufficient explanations in science), while agnostics just consider that such things cannot be proven one way or the other. At various points in history both non-belief and unorthodox (heretical) belief have attracted persecution by devotees of a dominant religion.

WHERE THE MAJORITIES ARE...

- **CHRISTIANITY:** 108 COUNTRIES
- **ISLAM:** 39 COUNTRIES
- **HINDUISM:** 10 COUNTRIES
- **BUDDHISM:** 3 COUNTRIES
- **SHINTO:** 1 COUNTRY
- **JUDAISM:** 1 COUNTRY

MAJOR WORLD BELIEFS

Of the five billion or so people who profess a religion, most are Christians, Muslims (followers of Islam), or Hindus. The major faiths can be classified as either Abrahamic (Christianity, Islam, and also Judaism) or Dharmic (Hinduism, and also Buddhism and Sikhism): this represents similarities of origin and some shared beliefs.

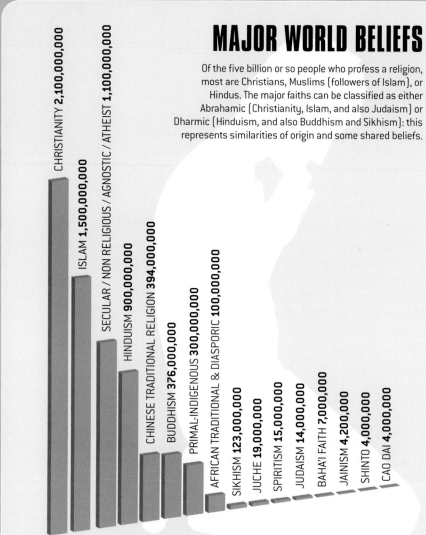

CHRISTIANITY 2,100,000,000
ISLAM 1,500,000,000
SECULAR / NON RELIGIOUS / AGNOSTIC / ATHEIST 1,100,000,000
HINDUISM 900,000,000
CHINESE TRADITIONAL RELIGION 394,000,000
BUDDHISM 376,000,000
PRIMAL-INDIGENOUS 300,000,000
AFRICAN TRADITIONAL & DIASPORIC 100,000,000
SIKHISM 123,000,000
JUCHE 19,000,000
SPIRITISM 15,000,000
JUDAISM 14,000,000
BAHA'I FAITH 7,000,000
JAINISM 4,200,000
SHINTO 4,000,000
CAO DAI 4,000,000

CHRISTIANS AND MUSLIMS

COMPARATIVE PERCENTAGES OF MUSLIMS AND CHRISTIANS OVER TIME:

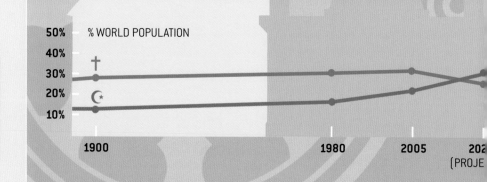

% WORLD POPULATION

50%
40%
30%
20%
10%

1900   1980   2005   202
(PROJE

SOURCES: www.adherents.com; Canadian Society of Muslims (muslim-canada.org)

THE TOP SEVEN RELIGIONS

While Christianity has the most adherents worldwide, it also has the most internal fractures. Roman Catholicism has the greatest share of followers (around one billion), making it the single largest creed in the world. The two other main branches are Eastern Orthodoxy and the many different Protestant faiths. Islam has fewer divisions, but most notably fractures along Sunni and Shi'a lines, the former being the larger group. Hinduism and Buddhism are also divided, though their denominations reflect different paths to the same goal.

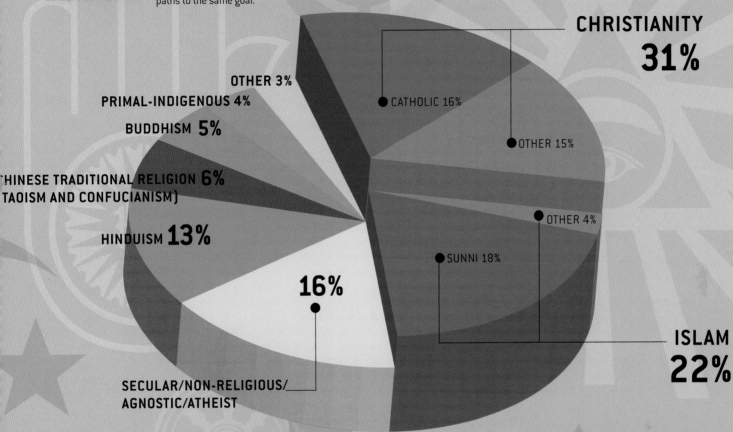

CHRISTIANITY 31%
CATHOLIC 16%
OTHER 15%

OTHER 3%
PRIMAL-INDIGENOUS 4%
BUDDHISM 5%
CHINESE TRADITIONAL RELIGION 6% (TAOISM AND CONFUCIANISM)
HINDUISM 13%
16%
SECULAR/NON-RELIGIOUS/ AGNOSTIC/ATHEIST

OTHER 4%
SUNNI 18%
ISLAM 22%

DEFINITIONS OF RELIGION

✝	CHRISTIAN	MONOTHEISTIC RELIGION, BASED ON THE TEACHINGS OF THE SON OF GOD, JESUS CHRIST, AND HIS APOSTLES, AND ON THE BIBLE
☪	ISLAM	MONOTHEISTIC RELIGION, BASED ON THE TEACHINGS OF MUHAMMAD, THE FINAL PROPHET OF GOD
	HINDUISM	BELIEF IN DESTINY (KHARMA) AND CYCLES OF REINCARNATION, WITH A MORAL LAW (DHARMA) AND A CLASS SYSTEM OF SOCIAL ORGANIZATION
ॐ	BUDDHISM	PHILOSOPHIES AND BELIEFS BASED ON THE TEACHING OF GAUTAMA BUDDHA
☬	SIKHISM	MONOTHEISTIC RELIGION, BASED ON THE TEACHINGS OF THE TEN GURUS, WITH CYCLES OF REINCARNATION LEADING TO ULTIMATE SALVATION
✡	JUDAISM	MONOTHEISTIC RELIGION, IN WHICH GOD REVEALED HIMSELF TO ABRAHAM, MOSES, AND THE OTHER HEBREW PROPHETS, AND BASED ON THE TANAKH, THE TALMUD, AND TRADITIONS
✺	BAHA'I FAITH	MONOTHEISTIC RELIGION, BASED ON THE TEACHINGS OF BAHA'U'LLAH, AND THE EVENTUAL SPIRITUAL UNITY OF MANKIND
✋	JAINISM	PHILOSOPHIES AND BELIEFS BASED ON THE TEACHINGS OF THE 24 TIRTHANKARS, STRIVING FOR PERFECTION OF MAN AND LIBERATION OF THE SOUL
⛩	SHINTO	ANIMISTIC BELIEF, WORSHIPPING SPIRITS THAT MANIFEST THEMSELVES IN NATURAL OBJECTS AND PROCESSES
👁	CAO DAI	MONOTHEISTIC RELIGION, OF A UNIVERSAL GOD, COMBINING THE TEACHINGS OF BUDDHA, JESUS CHRIST, MUHAMMAD, CONFUCIUS, LAO TSE (TAOISM), AND MANY OTHER HISTORICAL FIGURES

CALENDARS

RELIGIONS ARE THE ORIGIN OF MANY OF THE WORLD'S DIFFERENT CALENDAR SYSTEMS. THE CHRISTIAN CALENDAR IN ITS GREGORIAN VERSION IS THE BASIS OF THE COMMON ERA CONVENTION. COMMON ERA 2008 BEGINNING JANUARY 1 CORRESPONDS TO:

MUSLIM	1428 A.H.	NEW YEAR BEGINS ON JANUARY 10 2008 CE
JULIAN	2007 AD	NEW YEAR BEGINS ON JANUARY 14 2008 CE
CHINESE	4644 AC OR 4704 AC OR CYCLE 78 OR 77, YEAR 24 (DING-HAI)	NEW YEAR BEGINS ON FEBRUARY 7 2008 CE
BAHA'I	164 OR JAVÁB (12) VAHID 9 KULL-I-SHAY 1	NEW YEAR BEGINS ON MARCH 21 2008 CE
HINDU (SAKA, AS STANDARDIZED BY INDIAN GOVT)	1929	NEW YEAR BEGINS ON MARCH 21 2008 CE
IRANIAN	1386	NEW YEAR BEGINS ON MARCH 21 2008 CE
ETHIOPIAN	2000	NEW YEAR BEGINS ON SEPTEMBER 11 2008 CE
COPTIC	COPTIC	NEW YEAR BEGINS ON SEPTEMBER 9 2008 CE
JEWISH	1724	NEW YEAR BEGINS AT SUNSET ON SEPTEMBER 29 2008 CE
JAPANESE	2668 OR HEISEI 20	NEW YEAR BEGINS ON JANUARY 1 2009 CE
BUDDHIST	2552	NEW YEAR BEGINS ON JANUARY 1 2009 CE

BLASPHEMY LAWS

Many countries have blasphemy laws, setting a legal definition of where freedom of speech gives unacceptable offence. There is an argument that such laws should protect all faiths equally, or none. In practice they usually defend the dominant religion, and can be misused as a political weapon against minorities. Dan Brown's best-selling book *The Da Vinci Code* was banned in many countries for blaspheming against Christianity, while Mel Gibson's 2004 film *The Passion of the Christ* earned the dubious distinction of a ban under various Christian and Muslim jurisdictions and in Israel too. "Blasphemers" driven into hiding or exile by an Islamic fundamentalist *fatwa* demanding their murder have included British author Salman Rushdie, over his 1988 novel *The Satanic Verses*, and Bangladeshi author Taslima Nasreen in 1993.

SOURCES: Harris Interactive Inc: The Harris Poll® #78 (October 20 2005) and #80 (October 31 2006)

RELIGION IN THE USA

THESE THREE POLLS, CONDUCTED IN THE USA BY HARRIS INTERACTIVE® , QUESTIONED ADULTS ABOUT THEIR ATTITUDES TO RELIGION AND THE RIGHT TO LIFE.

CERTAINTY OF BELIEF

		CATHOLIC	PROTESTANT	JEWISH	BORN-AGAIN CHRISTIAN
✓	CERTAIN THERE IS A GOD	84%	90%	64%	97%
?	NOT SURE WHETHER OR NOT THERE IS A GOD	11%	7%	24%	LESS THAN 0.5 %
✗	CERTAIN THERE IS NO GOD	5%	3%	12%	3%

BASE: A SAMPLE OF 2242 US ADULTS

RELIGIOUS ATTENDANCE 2006

ATTENDANCE AT CHRISTIAN CHURCHES IN EUROPE HAS BEEN DECLINING STEADILY OVER THE LAST CENTURY, BUT AMERICANS ARE MUCH MORE ARDENT CHURCHGOERS – PARTICULARLY AMONG THE NEW EVANGELICAL FAITHS. SUPPORTERS REGARD THIS AS REFLECTING GREATER RELIGIOUS AWARENESS, AS WELL AS THE MORE "ACCESSIBLE" FORMAT OF MANY SERVICES.

BASE: A SAMPLE OF 2242 US ADULTS

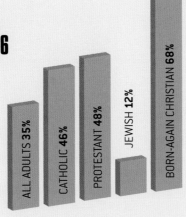

- ALL ADULTS 35%
- CATHOLIC 46%
- PROTESTANT 48%
- JEWISH 12%
- BORN-AGAIN CHRISTIAN 68%

SANCTITY OF LIFE

PERCENT SAYING STRONGLY OR SOMEWHAT FAVOUR ABORTION RIGHTS

TOTAL	CATHOLIC	EPISCOPALIAN / ANGLICAN	LUTHERAN	METHODIST	NON-DENOMINATIONAL	PRESBYTERIAN	BAPTIST	OTHER CHRISTIAN	JEWISH	AGNOSTIC / ATHEIST	BORN-AGAIN CHRISTIAN	VERY RELIGIOUS	EVANGELICAL BORN-AGAIN CHRISTIAN
63%	56%	83%	67%	75%	50%	72%	53%	49%	83%	90%	30%	39%	28%

BASE: A SAMPLE OF 2242 US ADULTS

TAKING FAITH TOO FAR?

A correlation between strong faith and economic hardship, observable in many parts of the world, is often explained in terms of religious belief providing solace against stress. aliving are relatively high in the USA (and the more affluent Arab countries) requires a different explanation – perhaps that poverty is not the sole source of stress.

In the USA, televangelism brings preachers into people's homes. Over two billion people have listened to some of Billy Graham's broadcasts on TV and radio. Benny Hinn and his "Miracle Crusades" attract massive audiences at stadiums worldwide.

Although most religions include respect for human life and for neighbouring peoples, militant fundamentalists not only follow their religious doctrines as strictly as possible, but also consider any other way of life inherently wrong. Taking this to its extreme can lead to the view that conflict with other religions is a holy duty. The medieval crusaders used militant Christianity as their justification, while today there are some Islamic fundamentalists who interpret the idea of holy struggle (jihad) to mean violence against non-Muslims.

Fundamentalism is a growing phenomenon in modern society. It is also a growing source of tension, between countries and within them. The embrace of terrorism by extremist fringe fundamentalist elements is one factor that has made these issues impossible to ignore, however distant they may once have felt from the centres of global power. Understanding the interplay of religion, stress, core values, and identity is as crucial to any response as strengthening the defence of "homeland security".

AGEING

Every one of us is ageing and, across the globe, more and more people are surviving into "old age." There are 650 million people over 60 now – and this is predicted to rise by 2050 to two billion, with two-thirds of them in developing countries.

Over the 20th century, medical advances and healthier living conditions have enabled far more people to live active and productive retirements. As we live longer, even our perception of how old is "old" is shifting. The UK alone has 2.7 million people over 80. Even centenarians, once a great rarity, are more numerous. Indeed they are almost commonplace in such places as the Russian Caucasus; in one district of Adygeya one in every 2000 people is 100 or over. These pockets of unusual longevity, however, are usually explained less in terms of modern medicine and living conditions, more by low-stress traditional lifestyles, clean air and water, and diets with natural rather than processed food.

EACH MONTH THE WORLD'S ELDERLY POPULATION
INCREASES BY 795,000

INCREASE IN POPULATION OVER TIME

YEAR	POPULATION AGED 90-99 (MILLIONS)	POPULATION AGED 100+ (MILLIONS)	% OF WORLD POPULATION OVER 90
1950	1.3	0.02	0.05
1975	2.5	0.03	0.06
2000	8.0	0.18	0.13
2025	26.8	1.15	0.34
2050	70.0	3.77	0.81

LIVING LONGER

BY 2050 THE NUMBER OF OLD PEOPLE WILL HAVE TRIPLED

The proportion of people aged over 65 years is growing faster than any other age group, as a result of both longer life expectancy and declining fertility rates. Only in sub-Saharan Africa has there been little increase in life expectancy over the last 50 years, mainly due to conflicts and the impact of the AIDS epidemic. As female life expectancy is higher than male, women tend to outnumber men by two to one in the oldest age groups.

WOMEN CAN EXPECT TO LIVE AN AVERAGE OF 4.5 YEARS LONGER THAN MEN

HOW MANY PEOPLE ARE OVER 65?
% OF POPULATION OVER 65, BY REGION

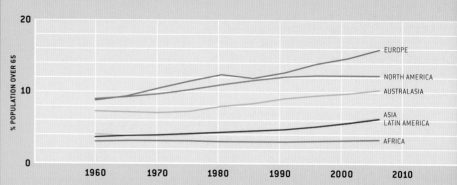

HOW LONG DO WE LIVE?
AVERAGE LIFE EXPECTANCY FROM BIRTH IS INCREASING WORLDWIDE, EVEN IN AFRICA. ASIA HAS SHOWN THE BIGGEST CHANGE, AN INCREASE OF OVER 20 YEARS IN HALF A CENTURY.

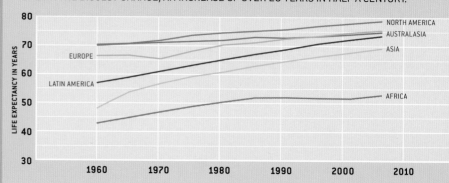

LIFE EXPECTANCY, BY INCOME
PEOPLE LIVING IN RICH COUNTRIES HAVE ALWAYS HAD A MUCH HIGHER LIFE EXPECTANCY THAN THOSE IN POOR COUNTRIES. THE GAP HAS NARROWED SLIGHTLY, BUT THE POOREST NATIONS ARE STILL BELOW THE RICH NATIONS' LEVEL OF 50 YEARS AGO.

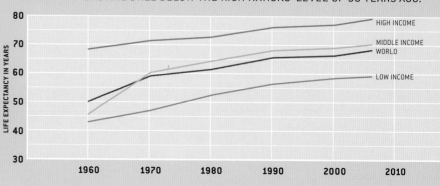

SOURCES: UN Population Division: *World Population Prospects* (2006); World Bank: *World Development Indicators*

YOUNG VERSUS OLD

RATIO OF POPULATION OVER 65 TO THOSE OF WORKING AGE

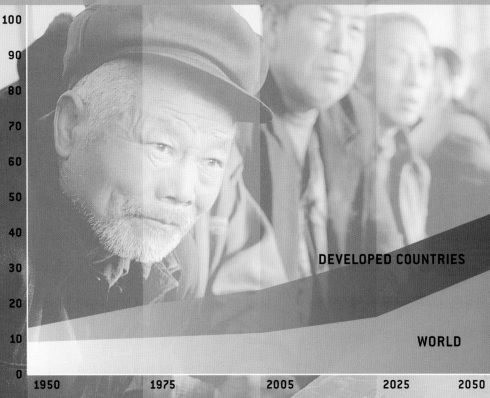

100
90
80
70
60
50
40
30
20
10
0

DEVELOPED COUNTRIES

WORLD

1950   1975   2005   2025   2050

OLD-AGE DEPENDENCY RATIO

THE OLD-AGE DEPENDENCY RATIO IS THE NUMBER OF THE POPULATION AGED 65 YEARS OR OVER TO EVERY 100 PEOPLE AGED 15-64 (WORKING AGE)

POPULATIONS OVER 65

THE PROPORTION OF THE POPULATION THAT IS OVER 65 IS HIGHEST IN DEVELOPED COUNTRIES

TOP TEN COUNTRIES

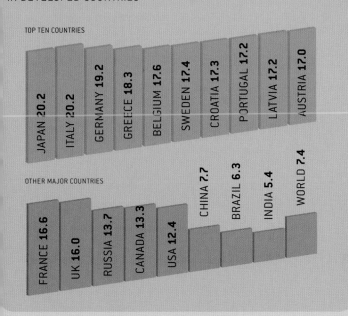

JAPAN 20.2
ITALY 20.2
GERMANY 19.2
GREECE 18.3
BELGIUM 17.6
SWEDEN 17.4
CROATIA 17.3
PORTUGAL 17.2
LATVIA 17.2
AUSTRIA 17.0

OTHER MAJOR COUNTRIES

FRANCE 16.6
UK 16.0
RUSSIA 13.7
CANADA 13.3
USA 12.4
CHINA 7.7
BRAZIL 6.3
INDIA 5.4
WORLD 7.4

LIFE EXPECTANCY BY COUNTRY

MEDICAL ADVANCES IN THE 20TH CENTURY HAVE HAD A HUGE EFFECT ON LIFE EXPECTANCY. NOW A NEWBORN BABY IN JAPAN CAN EXPECT TO LIVE TO OVER 82 YEARS OF AGE.

JAPAN	82.1	SWITZERLAND	81.2
ICELAND	81.1	AUSTRALIA	80.6
SPAIN	80.6	SWEDEN	80.6
ITALY	80.3	FRANCE	80.2
CANADA	80.2	UK	79.0
GERMANY	78.9	USA	77.7
CHINA	71.8	BRAZIL	71.2
RUSSIA	65.5	INDIA	63.5

PENSIONS

INCREASING LIFE EXPECTANCY MEANS THAT STATES HAVE TO SUPPORT PENSIONERS FOR LONGER. MANY COUNTRIES ARE LOOKING TO RAISE THE PENSIONABLE AGE IN ORDER TO KEEP THE TOTAL BILL DOWN.

RETIREMENT AGE AND EXPECTED NUMBER OF YEARS IN RETIREMENT

COUNTRY	PENSIONABLE AGE*	YEARS IN RETIREMENT**	COUNTRY	PENSIONABLE AGE	YEARS IN RETIREMENT
PORTUGAL	55	27	UNITED KINGDOM	65/60	16/24
ITALY	57	27	AUSTRIA	65/60	17/25
LUXEMBOURG	60	22	GERMANY	65/61	16/24
BELGIUM	60	23	SWITZERLAND	65/63	18/25
GREECE	60	23	AUSTRALIA	65/63	18/23
CANADA	60	24	DENMARK	65	17
FINLAND	60	24	IRELAND	65	17
FRANCE	60	24	NETHERLANDS	65	18
SPAIN	60	24	NEW ZEALAND	65	19
JAPAN	60	26	NORWAY	67	16
SWEDEN	61	23	ICELAND	67	17
UNITED STATES	62	22			

* WHERE TWO FIGURES ARE SHOWN MALE FIGURES COME FIRST
** IF RETIRING AT PENSIONABLE AGE (BASED ON LIFE EXP AT 65)

MEAN PENSIONABLE AGE IN OECD COUNTRIES

The average age at which you could draw your pension in the developed world fell steadily over the second half of the 20th century from 65 for men and 63 for women to 62 for men and 61 for women, but now it has started rising again and is expected to be at least a year higher for men and two years higher for women in 2035.

UNIVERSAL PENSIONS

The UN has proposed that every country in the world should provide its elderly with a basic pension of at least US$1 a day, to avoid them living in complete poverty. It estimates that this will cost on average less than one per cent of GDP – but it could consume as much as ten per cent of tax revenue in countries like India.

BURDENING CHINA'S CHILDREN

China's one-child policy has reduced the country's young-to-old dependency ratio – so today's "only child" will be solely responsible for supporting two parents and four grandparents. If the child is unable or unwilling to shoulder this burden – or if the elderly outlive their progeny – they could find themselves destitute. It is not just a family-based problem. The shrinking labour force must become more productive and pay more taxes if the economy is going to cope with supporting the elderly. Increasingly schools are closing and converting to care homes for the elderly population: China will have 400 million elderly by 2050.

THE RIGHT TO DIE
EUTHANASIA AND ASSISTED SUICIDE

The controversial subject of the right to die has provoked passionate debate around the globe. Supporters argue that terminally ill people, or those with incurable physical or mental illnesses, should be able to opt for euthanasia, in either its active form (where medical staff take deliberate action to end a patient's life) or passively (where medical staff withdraw medical treatment with the deliberate aim of ending life). An alternative that has been legal in Switzerland since 1942 is assisted suicide, where the means, eg medicine, is provided to allow a patient to end their own life. This has created the phenomenon of suicide tourism: people travelling to countries where euthanasia or assisted suicide are legal in order to end their lives.

COUNTRIES IN WHICH EUTHANASIA IS PERMITTED BY LAW UNDER CERTAIN CIRCUMSTANCES
SWITZERLAND (1942 – assisted suicide)
ALBANIA (1999 – euthanasia)
BELGIUM (2002 – euthanasia)
THE NETHERLANDS (2002 – euthanasia)
LUXEMBOURG (2008 – euthanasia)
JAPAN (no national laws against euthanasia)

SOURCES: AARP Public Policy Institute; American Association of Homes and Services for the Aging (AAHSA); OECD; United Nations

THE COST OF CARE

● Typical care-home costs in the UK average around US$3000 per person per month. NHS funding only subsidizes those with less than US$40,000 of capital.
● Italian "guests" at homes run by Roman Catholic nuns pay US$1770 a month for their care.
● A private room in a US retirement home averages US$6500 a month, though in big cities it can cost US$10,000 a month
● 87-year-old Bea Muller has been a permanent resident on Cunard's *Queen Elizabeth II* since January 5 2000. "Frequent traveller" discounts mean her overall costs amount to about US$5000 a month. One previous Cunard guest, Clair Macbeth, lived on board for 14 years.

LOOKING AFTER THE ELDERLY IN THE USA

MORE THAN TWO-THIRDS OF THE US ADULTS NOW AT RETIREMENT AGE WILL NEED SOME FORM OF LONG-TERM CARE LATER IN THEIR LIFE, EITHER AT HOME OR IN A RESIDENTIAL CARE FACILITY. TODAY THE PICTURE IS:
● OVER 1.4 MILLION NURSING HOME RESIDENTS
● AVERAGE AGE ON ENTRY: 79
● AVERAGE LIFETIME STAY PER INDIVIDUAL: 1 YEAR
● WOMEN ARE ALMOST THREE TIMES AS LIKELY TO LIVE IN NURSING HOMES THAN MEN
● OVER 745,000 OLDER ADULTS IN CONTINUING CARE RETIREMENT COMMUNITIES
● NEARLY 1.4 MILLION INDIVIDUALS RECEIVE HOME HEALTH SERVICES, GETTING ON AVERAGE 200 VISITS IN A LIFETIME
● ABOUT THREE TIMES AS MANY PEOPLE RECEIVE CARE AT HOME SOLELY FROM INFORMAL CAREGIVERS
● AN ESTIMATED 34 MILLION AMERICANS PROVIDE SOME CARE FOR A FAMILY MEMBER AGE 50 OR OLDER
● THE AVERAGE LONG-TERM CARE INSURANCE PREMIUM PAID BY INDIVIDUALS OVER 65 IS US$2862 PER YEAR

"GOLDEN OLDIES" BECOME "SILVER SHOPPERS"

FOR THE FIRST TIME EVER BRITAIN'S OVER-60S OUTNUMBER THE UNDER-16S AND THEIR SPENDING IS FORECAST TO REACH £46BN BY 2008. UK CONSUMERS AGED 65-74 WILL INCREASE THEIR RETAIL EXPENDITURE BY OVER 75% ACROSS THE NEXT TEN YEARS. THIS WILL MAKE THEM THE FASTEST-GROWING AGE SEGMENT BY SOME DISTANCE, ALTHOUGH THE OVER 75S WILL ALSO SEE ABOVE AVERAGE TOTAL SPENDING GROWTH.

SILVER SURFERS
Internet use has overtaken traditional pastimes of DIY and gardening, according to an AXA survey of over-65s in 11 countries. Of those who go online:
● 84% use email for keeping in touch with friends and relatives
● the next most popular online activity was "looking for information", selected by 83%
● 40% are regular e-shoppers: travel tickets are the most popular purchase
● 35% go online for banking activities

One in 12 of all US adults who have Internet access are over 65. In a recent survey, over half of US pensioners questioned said they had watched videos online, with one in eight using YouTube. In the UK almost two out of every three of those coming up to retirement are using the web, compared with just a third in 2001.

THE CHALLENGE OF AGEING

Increasing longevity is a result of successful public health policies and economic development – but is also a major 21st-century challenge for the nations that have achieved this. Health care itself will need investment to meet the needs of the elderly: training for health professionals on old-age care; preventing and managing age-associated chronic diseases; designing sustainable policies on long-term care; and developing age-friendly services and settings.

The cost of residential aged care in Australia has more than doubled in ten years to over A$5 billion. The cost of caring for old people in the UK is expected to increase from its 1995 level of £11 billion to more than £45 billion in 2051. Governments need to start adapting their policies to prepare for this level of funding, which will include increasing taxation on the dwindling labour force, and raising the pensionable age to lengthen working lives.

Money also needs to be spent on adapting society and the environment for an ageing population. Buildings and transportation networks must be modified to be age-friendly, or created with the needs of the elderly in mind. Adaptations permeate the whole of society, such as larger-type font on letters, induction loops for hearing aids in theatres, and fashion lines to please older tastes.

But this is not a one-way process. Pensioners themselves are able to provide services to the community, through volunteer work, the passing on of experience and knowledge, childcare help for their families, and prolonged participation in the paid labour force after pensionable age. The longer older people can remain healthy and active, the more they can contribute and the better quality of life they can enjoy.

RACE

Classifying humans by race has been a pretext for such appalling horrors and injustices as slavery, the Holocaust, and apartheid. Racism wrongly attributes stereotyped personality traits and even abilities to racial origins. Modern genetics exposes most notions of "racial purity" as untrue, but does support the concept of five broad racial groups with specific physiological characteristics (Caucasian, Black African, Indigenous American, East Asian, and Pacific Islander), with sub-divisions within each. More specific ethnic identities are often based on acquired social characteristics like language and religion.

MINORITY RIGHTS: PEOPLES LIVING UNDER THREAT

RANK	COUNTRY	PEOPLE FROM MINORITIES UNDER THREAT 2008
1	SOMALIA	22.8 MILLION
2	IRAQ	22.6 MILLION
3	SUDAN	21.6 MILLION
4	AFGHANISTAN	20.9 MILLION
5	BURMA (MYANMAR)	20.1 MILLION
6	CONGO DEM. REP.	19.9 MILLION
7	PAKISTAN	19.2 MILLION
8	NIGERIA	18.9 MILLION
9	ETHIOPIA	17.8 MILLION
10	CHAD	17.6 MILLION

CANADA

Most Canadians are descended from immigrants from Britain, France, Ireland, and other European countries. Many now identify themselves simply as Canadian. The 2001 census allowed multiple ethnic-origin answers: 6.7 million people chose only "Canadian" and five million more included it among their choices.

GUYANA & TRINIDAD

Guyana and Trinidad have large communities of south Asians (usually called East Indians), whose ancestors were brought over as labourers in the 19th century. Politics in both countries is split between African and Indian-dominated parties.

BOLIVIA

Amerindians make up two-thirds of Bolivia's population, but the country only got its first Amerindian president in 2006.

BRAZ

Brazil has been heralded as a "racial democracy": 54% white, 38% mixed race, 6% black, and 2% other including 220,000 Amerindians. However, the blacks in particular suffer higher infant mortality and poverty and more racial and job discrimination than other groups.

 SOURCES: Minority Rights Group International: *State of the World's Minorities 2008*

MELTING POTS

Israel has had huge influxes of Jewish immigrants since the creation of the state in 1948, from Europe, North Africa, and the former Soviet Union. Arabs are now just 17.5% of the population. Hopes for a "land-for-peace" deal with Palestinians in Israeli-occupied territory are mired in conflict.

ISRAEL

Few countries are as racially homogeneous as the Koreas, a consequence of the peninsula's geographical remoteness and historical isolation.

KOREAS

In the small Gulf states of Qatar and the United Arab Emirates, the vast numbers of Iranians and south Asians that come there for work actually outnumber the Arabs. There are also large expatriate Western communities. Only one in five inhabitants of Qatar are native-born.

QATAR & UAE

SUDAN

The Sahara Desert divides Sudan's Arab north and Black African south. The country's population remains highly polarized by geography, ethnicity, and religion. The Arab-led government in Khartoum waged a long and brutal war against southern rebels in the late 20th century. Ethnic cleansing by Arab militia against blacks in Darfur in the west has now caused a humanitarian crisis.

FIJI

SOUTH AFRICA

The pre-1994 apartheid era classified and segregated South Africans as White, Coloured, Indian or Black. Whites had a monopoly (and still have an unproportional share) of wealth and political power, while making up only 14% of the population. The majority black population suffered the worst discrimination and deprivation.

Fiji's population is split between indigenous Melanesians and Indians, descended from workers brought over under British colonial rule. Fear of being outnumbered and outvoted sparked off Fijian nationalist military coups to preserve their political ascendancy.

RACE

USA ETHNIC SPLIT

Americans identify themselves by both race and ancestry. White non-Hispanics have had a political near-monopoly (until the 2008 presidential contest) but may no longer be the overall majority population by 2050; the proportion of Hispanics is rising rapidly. The mid-20th century Civil Rights Movement fought to end racial discrimination, but African Americans still fare badly on indicators such as average earnings, access to health care, and disproportionately high prison numbers.

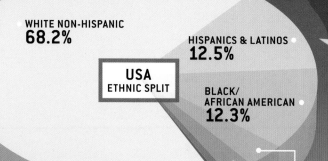

USA ETHNIC SPLIT

- WHITE NON-HISPANIC **68.2%**
- HISPANICS & LATINOS **12.5%**
- BLACK/ AFRICAN AMERICAN **12.3%**
- ASIAN **3.6%**
- MULTIRACIAL AMERICANS **2.4%**
- NATIVE AMERICANS **0.9%**
- NATIVE HAWAIIANS/ PACIFIC ISLANDERS **0.1%**

USA TOP 15 ANCESTRIES

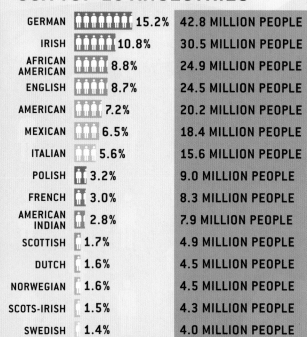

Ancestry	%	People
GERMAN	15.2%	42.8 MILLION PEOPLE
IRISH	10.8%	30.5 MILLION PEOPLE
AFRICAN AMERICAN	8.8%	24.9 MILLION PEOPLE
ENGLISH	8.7%	24.5 MILLION PEOPLE
AMERICAN	7.2%	20.2 MILLION PEOPLE
MEXICAN	6.5%	18.4 MILLION PEOPLE
ITALIAN	5.6%	15.6 MILLION PEOPLE
POLISH	3.2%	9.0 MILLION PEOPLE
FRENCH	3.0%	8.3 MILLION PEOPLE
AMERICAN INDIAN	2.8%	7.9 MILLION PEOPLE
SCOTTISH	1.7%	4.9 MILLION PEOPLE
DUTCH	1.6%	4.5 MILLION PEOPLE
NORWEGIAN	1.6%	4.5 MILLION PEOPLE
SCOTS-IRISH	1.5%	4.3 MILLION PEOPLE
SWEDISH	1.4%	4.0 MILLION PEOPLE

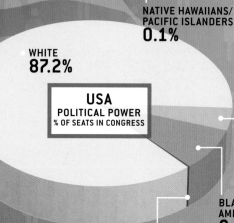

USA POLITICAL POWER
% OF SEATS IN CONGRESS

- WHITE **87.2%**
- LATINO **4.3%**
- BLACK/AFRICAN AMERICAN **8.4%**
- NATIVE AMERICAN **0.1%**

RUSSIA

RUSSIAN ETHNIC MINORITIES

Russia has recognized 21 homelands of specific ethnic minorities, granting them the administrative status of "republic." Most are in the Caucasus, in the Volga basin, and along the Chinese border. Each has its own government and can make its language co-official with Russian. However, a history of migration means that the "titular nationality" accounts for less than half of the population in half of the republics.

RUSSIA ETHNIC MINORITIES

- TURKIC **8.4%**
  OF WHICH: TATARS 3.8%
  BASHKIRS 1.2%
  CHUVASHS 1.1%
- CAUCASIAN **3.3%**
  OF WHICH: CHECHENS 0.9%
- INDO-EUROPEAN **84.1%**
  OF WHICH: RUSSIANS 79.8%
  UKRAINIANS 2%
  ARMENIANS 0.8%
- FINNO-UGRIC **1.9%**
- OTHER **2.3%**

CHINESE ETHNIC MINORITIES
CHINA OFFICIALLY RECOGNIZES 56 MINORITIES – TOP TEN ETHNICITIES ARE:

CHINESE PEOPLES	% OF POPULATION	POPULATION
HAN	92.70%	1,136,703,824
HUANG	1.27%	15,555,800
MANCHU	0.72%	8,846,800
HUI	0.70%	8,612,000
MIAO	0.60%	7,383,600
UYGUR	0.59%	7,207,000
YI	0.54%	6,578,500
TUJIA	0.47%	5,725,000
MONGOLIAN	0.39%	4,802,400
TIBETAN	0.37%	4,593,100

GENOCIDE

Genocide means killing (or trying to kill) an entire racial group. Nazi Germany's systematic programme of sending Jews to death camps created a Holocaust without parallel in human history. Other uses of the term "genocide" are often contentious or imprecise, referring to any large-scale killing of people of a particular ethnic group – and sometimes including famine victims in the death toll.

1915–17	Armenians	500,000–1 million	"Genocide" by Ottoman Turks
1939–45	Holocaust	5.9 million	Jews killed by Germans
1971	Bangladesh	1–3 million	Bengalis die in conflict with Pakistan
1972	Burundi	50,000–100,000	Hutus killed by Tutsis
1975–79	Cambodia	1.7 million	Cambodians killed by Khmer Rouge
1974–99	East Timor	102,800	East Timorese killed by Indonesians
1982	Sabra-Shatila	700–3500	Palestinians killed in Lebanon by Maronite Christian/Phalange
1993	Burundi	400,000	Tutsis killed by Hutus
1994	Rwanda	937,000	Tutsis and moderate Hutus killed by Hutu
1995	Srebrenica	8000	Worst Serb ethnic cleansing of Bosniaks in Bosnian War
2002	Darfur	2 million	African Sudanese victims of Janjaweed militia killings and famine

CHANGING THE FACE OF RACE

The terrible consequences of racial division, from genocide to discrimination to personal prejudice, mean that any use of race as a descriptive classification is fraught with danger. Few would dispute, however, that it is useful in some fields, for instance in medical research and diagnosis, where susceptibility to conditions like sickle cell anaemia is strongly correlated with racial origins.

More contentious, but nevertheless now widely accepted in many modern societies, is the idea that race should be one consideration in positive discrimination. This involves recognizing the legacy of disadvantage suffered by minority groups, and taking steps to even it out by giving preference to minority candidates, for example in university admissions or job recruitment.

The idea of redressing past wrongs is a recurring theme in international politics too. At the global level, the greatest divide is perhaps that between the former imperial powers – essentially the Europeans and more recently the USA – and the countries they colonized. At the height of the imperial age, the notion took hold that the imperialists belonged to a white race (reinforced by a doctrine that leadership was its destiny), and the rest of the world consisted of black and Asian subject races. In a post-colonial age, attitudes are still coloured by this relatively recent past, even if official doctrines of racial superiority have become taboo.

On the other hand, as societies increasingly intermingle and interact economically, culturally, and sexually, it is conceivable that distinctions between races will become increasingly meaningless – and genetically unfounded. Futurologists have suggested that in the future the human race may be just that: a single race.

EDUCATION

Modern societies consider that every child has a right to education, for personal development, to realize their potential, and to enable them to participate in society. All but a few countries make education compulsory – both to protect that right, and to create the kind of educated workforce that a competitive economy needs.

The concept of democracy relies on the electorate being sufficiently educated to have a grasp of the issues on which they vote. Schools are also expected to turn out citizens who share a set of common values – whether or not "citizenship" is a formal part of the teaching curriculum. Traditionally these values were often explicitly religious ones. Now there may be more emphasis on the nation's history and cultural achievements. Many societies do still give religious organizations a major teaching role, but others are determinedly secular; in France, for instance, pupils at state schools may not wear religious symbols in class.

DURATION OF PRIMARY SCHOOL EDUCATION

8 YEARS	1 COUNTRY (IRELAND)
7 YEARS	22 COUNTRIES
6 YEARS	113 COUNTRIES
5 YEARS	24 COUNTRIES
4 YEARS	28 COUNTRIES
3 YEARS	3 COUNTRIES (ARMENIA, RUSSIA, TURKMENISTAN)

EDUCATION IS NOT COMPULSORY IN OMAN, SIERRA LEONE, THE GAMBIA, UGANDA, VANUATU, PAKISTAN, AND PAPUA NEW GUINEA

THE MEANING OF LITERACY

UNESCO DEFINES LITERACY AS "THE ABILITY TO READ AND WRITE, WITH UNDERSTANDING, A SHORT SIMPLE SENTENCE ABOUT ONE'S EVERYDAY LIFE." IN DEVELOPED COUNTRIES THIS EXCLUDES ONLY ONE TO TWO PER CENT OF ADUL BUT IN LOW-INCOME COUNTRIES 40% CANNOT READ OR WRITE AT ALL.

ADULT LITERACY, AVERAGE PERCENTAGE BY REGION

	MALE	FEMALE
	87%	77%
WORLD AVERAGE	98.8	96.2
EUROPE & CENTRAL ASIA	94.6	86.8
EAST ASIA & PACIFIC	90.6	89.1
LATIN AMERICA & CARIBBEAN	82.6	63.1
MIDDLE EAST & NORTH AFRICA	68.8	50.4
SUB-SAHARAN AFRICA		

WHAT THE STATE SPENDS ON EDUCATION (AS PERCENTAGE OF GNP)

LOWEST SPENDERS	
	0.84
BURMA (MYANMAR)	0.85
NIGERIA	0.86
INDONESIA	0.87
SUDAN	0.95
CONGO DEM. REP.	

HIGHEST SPENDERS	
	8.04
SWEDEN	8.09
CUBA	8.09
DENMARK	8.09
MARSHALL ISLANDS	9.37
UZBEKISTAN	

SOURCES: World Bank: *World Development Indicators*; UNESCO; OECD: Programme for International Student Assessment (PISA) 2006

STAYING ON FOR SECONDARY SCHOOL (ENROLMENT AS A PERCENTAGE OF THE APPROPRIATE AGE GROUP)

KAZAKHSTAN 99.9
ITALY 99.7
BARBADOS 99.5
FRANCE 98.9
CUBA 98.5
NETHERLANDS 98.1
SRI LANKA 97.0
BOTSWANA 95.1
MEXICO 93.7
TURKEY 91.6
SUDAN 89.5
INDIA 85.1
BRAZIL 80.5
ISRAEL 73.4
BURUNDI 32.8

ADULT LITERACY, AVERAGE PERCENTAGE BY INCOME

	MALE	FEMALE
HIGH INCOME	98.9	98.4
UPPER MIDDLE INCOME	94.2	92.0
MIDDLE INCOME	93.5	86.7
LOWER MIDDLE INCOME	93.2	84.6
LOW & MIDDLE INCOME	84.8	72.6
LOW INCOME	71.5	49.9

COUNTRIES WITH THE LOWEST LITERACY RATES

	MALE	FEMALE
GUINEA	42.6	18.1
NIGER	42.9	15.1
AFGHANISTAN	43.1	12.6
CHAD	40.8	12.8
MALI	32.7	15.9
BURKINA FASO	31.4	16.6

RATIO OF GIRLS TO BOYS IN PRIMARY AND SECONDARY EDUCATION, PER 100 BOYS

COUNTRIES WITH MOST GIRLS IN SCHOOL

KIRIBATI	HONDURAS	LIBYA	MONGOLIA	SURINAME
106	107	108	108	113

COUNTRIES WITH FEWEST GIRLS IN SCHOOL

AFGHANISTAN	CHAD	GUINEA-BISSAU	YEMEN	COTE D'IVOIRE
55	60	65	66	68

ENROLMENT IN HIGHER EDUCATION (PERCENTAGE OF APPROPRIATE AGE GROUP)

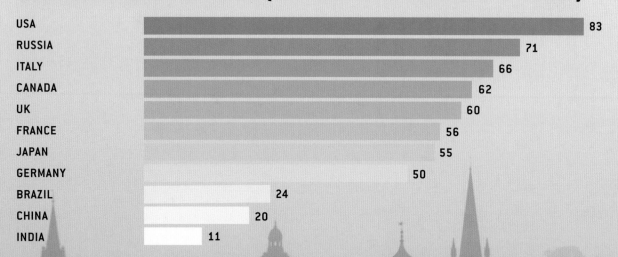

USA	83
RUSSIA	71
ITALY	66
CANADA	62
UK	60
FRANCE	56
JAPAN	55
GERMANY	50
BRAZIL	24
CHINA	20
INDIA	11

THE TOP FIVE UNIVERSITIES 2007

1	HARVARD UNIVERSITY, USA
2=	UNIVERSITY OF CAMBRIDGE, UK
2=	UNIVERSITY OF OXFORD, UK
2=	YALE UNIVERSITY, USA
5	IMPERIAL COLLEGE LONDON, UK

SOURCES: Times Higher Ed Supplement – Quacquerelli Symonds (THES–QS) World University Rankings; US Dept of Education

HOOLED IN THE USA: WHO GETS QUALIFIED?

(RCENTAGE OF TOTAL DEGREES AWARDED AT EACH LEVEL)

		BA		MA		PhD
HITE, NON-HISPANIC		70.0		60.3		56.2
ACK, NON-HISPANIC		8.7		7.8		5.1
SPANIC	BA	6.3	MA	4.4	PhD	3.2
REIGN STUDENTS *		3.2		14.0		25.3
HER/UNSPECIFIED		11.8		13.5		10.2

S POSTGRADUATE QUALIFICATIONS ARE A MAGNET FOR STUDENTS FROM AROUND THE RLD. INDIA, CHINA, AND SOUTH KOREA ACCOUNT FOR OVER HALF THE INTERNATIONAL AKE. A QUARTER OF ALL DOCTORATES NOW GO TO FOREIGN STUDENTS.

E GLOBAL DEGREE MARKET

DEMIC INSTITUTIONS, INCREASINGLY KEEN TO ATTRACT FEE-PAYING FOREIGN DENTS, COMPETE FIERCELY IN THIS RAPIDLY GROWING MARKET. THE THES–QS KINGS LOOK AT RESEARCH QUALITY, GRADUATE EMPLOYABILITY, INTERNATIONAL LOOK, AND TEACHING QUALITY. UNIVERSITIES IN THE USA AND UK ENJOY THE HUGE ANTAGE THAT ENGLISH IS THE DOMINANT LANGUAGE OF GLOBALIZED EDUCATION. E HAVE SET UP CAMPUSES IN ASIA TO CATER FOR LOCAL DEMAND.

MBER OF UNIVERSITIES PER COUNTRY IN THE TOP 200 LIST

A	55	INDIA	3
K	29	ISRAEL	3
STRALIA	13	SOUTH KOREA	3
PAN	11	MALAYSIA	2
ETHERLANDS	11	NEW ZEALAND	2
RMANY	10	RUSSIA	2
NADA	7	SINGAPORE	2
ANCE	7	IRELAND	1
ITZERLAND	7	ITALY	1
ELGIUM	6	MEXICO	1
HINA	6	NORWAY	1
ONG KONG	4	SPAIN	1
VEDEN	4	TAIWAN	1
STRIA	3	THAILAND	1
ENMARK	3		

TOMORROW'S LITERACY

Knowledge and information have become an integral part of the global economy. While the developing world, with its abundance of cheap labour, is serving as a workhouse for data-crunching, developed countries rely more and more on information-based industries and services. To compete in this international "knowledge economy," skilled workers, advanced research capabilities, and the creation of intellectual property are key factors.

The correlation between literacy and earning potential remains strong, but educational requirements go well beyond the "three Rs" of reading, writing, and arithmetic. Alongside the emphasis on scientific knowledge, communications and information technology skills rank highly. There is a strong argument that the understanding of literacy today should include such skills. Where once the ability to sign your own name was considered the test for literacy, the test of the future may have more to do with handling IT equipment, engaging successfully in virtual networks like Myspace or Facebook, and setting up a blog.

MBA STUDENTS

THE MASTER'S DEGREE IN BUSINESS ADMINISTRATION (MBA) HAS COME TO BE SEEN AS THE PASSPORT TO WELL-PAID WORK IN THE CORPORATE WORLD. THE USA, WHERE IT FIRST CAUGHT ON, TURNS OUT 250,000 MBA GRADUATES A YEAR – FIVE TIMES THE OUTPUT OF EUROPE'S 500 BUSINESS SCHOOLS, THOUGH DEMAND IS DRIVING RAPID GROWTH HERE TOO.

CRIME AND PUNISHMENT

The media gives such prominence to reporting violent crime that most people overestimate the threat they face. In some places, however, statistics confirm a fearsome reputation. In South Africa, for instance, although murder and robbery rates have fallen slightly, the incidence of rape remains horrifyingly high; security cameras and high fences protect offices and homes, and carjacking is such a problem that some people paint the licence number on their car roof so police helicopters can follow them if they are stolen.

Mass shootings, a particularly high-profile phenomenon, seem to take place disproportionately in the United States, although other countries with notorious incidents include the UK and even Switzerland. The massacre on the campus at Virginia Tech in April 2007 was the deadliest in US history, killing 32 students and teachers.

Serial killers attract popular notoriety, avid media attention, and lurid sobriquets – the Angel of Death, the Cyber Sex Killer, the Yorkshire Ripper – as the gruesome details of their crimes unfold. Between 1975 and 1998 British doctor Harold Shipman murdered at least 215 elderly patients.

GLOBAL GUN CRIME

- **OVER 1,000,000 PEOPLE ARE INJURED BY GUNS EVERY YEAR**
- **OVER 200,000 PEOPLE ARE GUN HOMICIDE VICTIMS EVERY YEAR**
- **AROUND 50,000 ARE GUN SUICIDE VICTIMS EVERY YEAR**

Gun laws vary widely around the world, but lots of these lethal weapons are legal. A study of 65 multiple-victim shootings in the United States, spanning 40 years, found that only one third were committed with illegally-acquired firearms. On an average day in the United States eight children are killed by guns.

HIGH-PROFILE KILLERS · Recent mass shootings by individuals

DATE	PLACE	TOTAL DEAD (Victims+killer/s)
Nov 7 2007	**Jokela High School** Tuusula, Finland	8 + 1
Apr 16 2007	**Virginia Tech campus** Blacksburg, USA	32 + 1
Apr 26 2002	**Johann Gutenberg Gymnasium** Erfurt, Germany	16 + 1
Sep 27 2001	**Regional Parliament building** Zug, Switzerland	14 + 1
Jul 29 1999	**Brokerage firms** Atlanta, USA	12 + 1
Apr 20 1999	**Columbine High School** Littleton, USA	13 + 2
Apr 28 1996	**Port Arthur** Australia	35
Mar 13 1996	**Primary School** Dunblane, Scotland	17 + 1

MURDER VICTIMS BY AGE AND GENDER

ESTIMATED MURDER VICTIMS PER 100,000 POPULATION

AGE GROUP	MALES	FEMALES
0 TO 4	5.8	4.8
5 TO 14	2.1	2.0
15 TO 29	19.4	4.4
30 TO 44	18.7	4.3
45 TO 59	14.8	4.5
60+	13.0	4.5
TOTALS	**73.8**	**24.5**

KIDNAPPINGS

IN 2000, KIDNAPPING FOR RANSOM WAS A LUCRATIVE BUSINESS IN COLOMBIA. SINCE THEN THE UNWELCOME TITLE OF "KIDNAP CAPITAL OF THE WORLD" HAS MOVED TO MEXICO AND THEN TO IRAQ – WHERE SEIZING AND HOLDING FOREIGNERS FOR POLITICAL ENDS IS PART OF THE PICTURE, BUT THOUSANDS OF ORDINARY IRAQIS ALSO GET TAKEN HOSTAGE FOR RANSOM.

IRAQ	2006	19,548
MEXICO	2004	3,000
COLOMBIA	2000	3,572

MURDER RATES IN MAJOR COUNTRIES

COUNTRY	LATEST AVAILABLE
USA	5.6
SCOTLAND	2.6
CANADA	2.0
FRANCE	1.6
ENGLAND&WALES	1.3
AUSTRALIA	1.3
ITALY	1.2
GERMANY	1.0

Russia has the highest homicide rate in Europe, and Switzerland, surprisingly, the highest in western Europe – but the chances of being a murder victim there are only half as bad as in the United States. Such figures are not only a reflection of how violent society is; also part of the equation are such factors as the efficiency of paramedics and hospital treatment.

THE WORLD'S MOST DANGEROUS PLACES

COUNTRIES WITH THE HIGHEST MURDER RATES (PER 100,000 PEOPLE)

Crime rates across countries are difficult to measure, as police forces often record their statistics differently and may even differ in what is considered a crime. Even the reliability of homicide statistics can be questioned, with varying standards of police behaviour and differing legal definitions of murder, homicide, manslaughter etc.

COUNTRY	LATEST AVAILABLE
VENEZUELA	42
SOUTH AFRICA	41
COLOMBIA	39
JAMAICA	34
EL SALVADOR	32
BRAZIL	27
GUATEMALA	26
RUSSIA	20
ECUADOR	18
KAZAKHSTAN	16

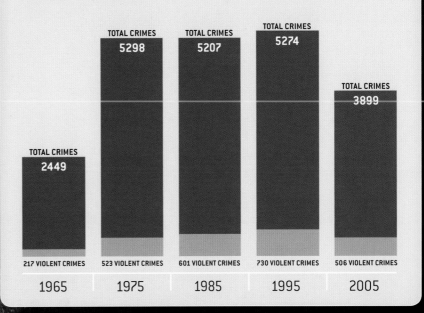

TWO NATIONAL RAP SHEETS

SOUTH AFRICAN CRIME RATES

PER 100,000 POPULATION

	2001/2	2002/3	2003/4	2004/5	2005/6	2006/7
MURDER	47.8	47.4	42.7	40.3	39.5	40.5
RAPE	121.1	115.3	113.7	118.3	117.1	111.0
CARJACKING	35.4	32.3	29.7	26.7	27.3	28.7
TOTAL CRIME	5823	5976	5687	5293	4769	4611

UK CRIME RATES

ENGLAND AND WALES, PER 100,000 POPULATION

	2001/2	2002/3	2003/4	2004/5	2005/6	2006/7
MURDER	1.5	1.8	1.5	1.5	1.3	1.3
RAPE	15.1	19.3	20.9	20.0	20.0	18.6
TOTAL CRIME	9286	10,059	10,141	9491	9305	9077

CRIME RATES IN THE USA
PER 100,000 POPULATION

Crime in general rose sharply during the 1960s and 1970s but has declined since 1995. There are clear differences in crime rates between states. Baltimore in Maryland, cursed by high unemployment and a serious drugs problem, has a homicide rate of 43.5 per 100,000 inhabitants, giving it the nickname of "Murder City".

Year	TOTAL CRIMES	VIOLENT CRIMES
1965	2449	217
1975	5298	523
1985	5207	601
1995	5274	730
2005	3899	506

RWANDA 67,000 (7.28 per 1000 population)

USA 2,186,230 (7.26 per 1000 population)

RUSSIA 858,900 (6.03 per 1000 population)

CUBA 55,000 (4.87 per 1000 population)

UK 77,962 (1.30 per 1000 population)

CANADA 34,096 (1.05 per 1000 population)

ITALY 59,960 (1.03 per 1000 population)

GERMANY 78,581 (0.95 per 1000 population)

FRANCE 52,908 (0.87 per 1000 population)

JAPAN 79,055 (0.62 per 1000 population)

IN THE CLINK — HIGHEST PRISON POPULATIONS WORLDWIDE

The worldwide figure of 9.25 million people in prison is probably an underestimate, as so many countries do not accurately report prison statistics. The United States accounts for more than a quarter of that total figure, partly because custodial sentences are mandatory for drugs crimes – for which 57% of federal prisoners have been convicted. So many black men get sent to jail that the federal government predicts one in four of them will be imprisoned at some point in their lives.

DEATH PENALTY

A large majority of countries have abolished the death penalty in law or practice. According to Amnesty International:

- 91 countries and territories have abolished the death penalty for all crimes;
- 11 countries have abolished the death penalty for all but exceptional crimes such as wartime crimes;
- 33 countries can be considered abolitionist in practice: they retain the death penalty in law but have not carried out any executions for the past ten years or more and are believed to have a policy or established practice of not carrying out executions;
- 62 other countries and territories retain and use the death penalty, but far fewer actually execute prisoners in any one year.

Over 50 countries have abolished the death penalty for all crimes since 1990. Only four have reintroduced it, and two of those – Nepal and the Philippines – have since abolished it again, while neither of the other two (Gambia and Papua New Guinea) have actually used it.

SOURCES: R. Walmsley: *World Prison Population List*; **Amnesty International**

EXECUTIONS, 2006

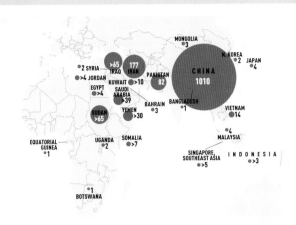

Singapore has one of the lowest murder rates in the world – and the highest rate of executions per capita, averaging 30 a year among a population of just four million. It was one of 25 countries to implement the death penalty that year, when **there were at least 1591 people executed worldwide, the great majority of them (91%) in China, Iran, Pakistan, Iraq, Sudan, and the USA. The total number was certainly significantly higher than this.** In the United States, 37 of the 50 states have the death penalty on their statute books, under legislation passed since a Supreme Court ruling in 1976 which ended its four-year suspension nationwide. In those 30 years there have been some 1100 executions, two-thirds of them in just five states (Texas, Virginia, Oklahoma, Florida, and Missouri); Texas alone has executed over 400 people, by lethal injection. Two-thirds of US death sentences eventually get overturned or commuted; California, the state with most people on death row (660), has only actually executed 13 in 30 years.

METHODS OF EXECUTION

EXECUTIONS HAVE BEEN CARRIED OUT BY THE FOLLOWING METHODS SINCE 2000: BEHEADING in Saudi Arabia; ELECTROCUTION in the USA; HANGING in Egypt, Iran, Iraq, Japan, Jordan, Pakistan, Singapore, and other countries; LETHAL INJECTION in China, Guatemala, Thailand, and the USA; SHOOTING in Belarus, China, Somalia, Taiwan, Uzbekistan, Vietnam, and other countries; STONING in Afghanistan and Iran.

Many Muslim countries use Sharia principles based on the Koran and other Islamic teachings as their legal framework, extending to areas of social life, such as proper dress and appearance, that are not generally subject to the law in Western countries. A strict interpretation of Sharia can include the application of severe punishments such as stoning to death for adultery/fornication, amputation for theft, and lashing for drinking alcohol. In 2002 a young Nigerian woman was stoned to death for bearing a child out of wedlock.

SHARIA LAW

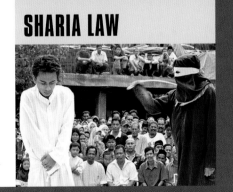

IS PRISON NECESSARY?

Prisons in England and Wales currently hold 148 people per 100,000 of the population, the highest rate in Western Europe, but well below Russia (615) or the USA (737 per 100,000). The physical limit comes when jails are bursting. Private companies in the US have made business out of building and running more prisons, whereas England and Wales – despite creating 17,000 prison places in the last 30 years – cannot keep pace with "demand". Measures like pressing prison ships into service are only stopgaps; the future requires more radical changes in sentencing policy and in how we keep tabs on offenders.

Restorative justice is an approach designed to encourage offenders to take responsibility for the consequences of their crime, and can provide for "punishments" negotiated with the victims. It has been found to work for violent crime as well as "petty" crime.

Community service orders are a non-custodial option for less serious crimes. Electronic "tagging", to track offenders' movements, is another, with far-reaching potential. It costs a tenth of the £24,000 annual cost of a prison place. Only a handful of UK offenders have so far been tagged instead of getting prison sentences, but around 27,000 have been released early to serve out the remainder of their term "on the tag". Neither of these options appear to reduce rates of reoffending, despite concerns that prisons are "schools for crime" rife with drugs and violence – or, in an opposing view, so comfortable that old lags deliberately get themselves back "inside".

CIGARETTES

FORTUNE 500 – TOP FOUR CIGARETTE MANUFACTURERS, 2007

RANK	COMPANY	GLOBAL 500 RANK	REVENUES ($ MILLIONS)	PROFITS ($ MILLIONS)	PROFITS AS % OF REVENUE
1	**ALTRIA GROUP** (FORMERLY PHILIP MORRIS)	71	70,324	12,022	17
2	**BRITISH AMERICAN TOBACCO**	404	17,961	3,488	19
3	**JAPAN TOBACCO**	415	17,536	1,802	10
4	**ALTADIS** (FRENCH/SPANISH GROUP)	482	15,687	568	4

DRUGS

A lot of people take drugs. Even leaving aside alcohol, tobacco, and the misuse of prescription drugs, 159 million people worldwide used cannabis/marijuana in 2005/6, according to the UN's World Drug Report. Narcotics like cocaine and heroin have fewer users, but attract more concern over their effects on individuals and society.

Coca leaves have long been chewed in South America for their stimulant effects (as has khat in East Africa and Arabia). Coca farmers, however, face mounting pressure as eradication schemes funded by Western governments target the source of illegal cocaine. Typically ingested nasally in powder form, cocaine is also smoked in extremely pure (freebase) form or, increasingly, as the easier-to-manufacture crack cocaine. Cheap crack quickly spread through the urban housing estates or "projects" of the United States from the 1980s, causing severe social problems and disproportionately affecting the black community; between 1984 and 1994 the murder rate for black teenagers more than doubled.

Heroin, refined from opium and typically injected, has a powerful but short-lived "high", followed by withdrawal symptoms – nausea, diarrhoea, cramps, and insomnia – that increase the craving for the relief of another "fix".

- **THE GLOBAL ILLICIT DRUGS TRADE** IS ESTIMATED TO BE WORTH BETWEEN $300-400 BILLION
- **THE US GOVERNMENT** COLLECTS AROUND $15 BILLION IN TAX REVENUE ON TOBACCO AND ALCOHOL SALES EACH YEAR
- **A 10% INCREASE IN THE PRICE OF CIGARETTES** REDUCES CONSUMPTION BY ABOUT 4% IN HIGH-INCOME COUNTRIES AND 8% IN LOW AND MIDDLE-INCOME COUNTRIES

TOBACCO KILLS FIVE MILLION PEOPLE A YEAR — ONE IN TEN OF ALL ADULT DEATHS

BY 2020 THIS IS EXPECTED TO RISE TO TEN MILLION DEATHS A YEAR

MORE THAN TEN MILLION CIGARETTES ARE SMOKED EVERY MINUTE

EACH CIGARETTE SMOKED TAKES SEVEN MINUTES OFF THE SMOKER'S LIFE

CIGARETTE CONSUMPTION

5763 BILLION IN 2006

5500 BILLION IN 2000

5419 BILLION IN 1990

4388 BILLION IN 1980

3112 BILLION IN 1970

2150 BILLION IN 1960

1686 BILLION IN 1950

OF WHICH:

35% **CHINA**
7% **USA**
6% **RUSSIA**
5% **JAPAN**
3% **INDONE**

COUNTRIES WITH HIGHEST REPORTED SMOKING RATES AMONG MEN

YEMEN **77%**

DJIBOUTI **75%**

CAMBODIA/CHINA **67%**

KAZAKHSTAN/SOUTH KOREA **65%**

ARMENIA **62%**

ALBANIA/RUSSIA/SAMOA **60%**

GUINEA **59%**

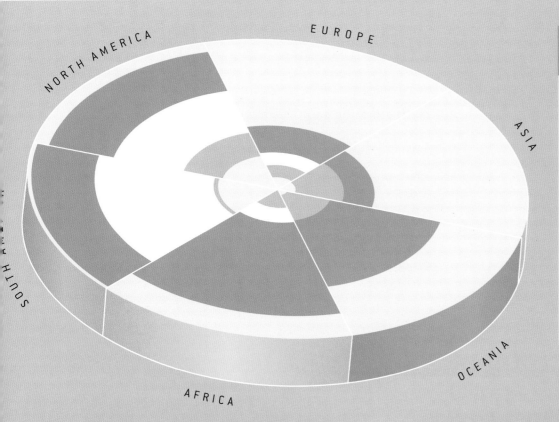

GLOBAL DRUG ABUSE

	OPIATES
	CANNABIS
	COCAINE-TYPE
	AMPHETAMINE-TYPE
	OTHERS

Opiates dominate the "hard drugs scene" in Asia and generally also in Europe. Cocaine-type drugs, on the other hand, are more widely used in the Americas. The proportion of people in the Americas who undergo treatment for drug abuse problems is significantly higher than elsewhere, but this is less a reflection of the scale of the drugs problem than of the availability of such treatment and the money to pay for it.

HOW MANY PEOPLE USE DRUGS, AND PROBLEM USE WORLDWIDE, 15–64 YEAR-OLDS

TYPE OF HABIT	NUMBER OF PEOPLE	PERCENTAGE
TOBACCO USE	**1200 MILLION**	28%
DRUGS: ONCE A YEAR	**200 MILLION**	4.8%
DRUGS: ONCE A MONTH	**110 MILLION**	2.6%
PROBLEM DRUG USE	**25 MILLION**	0.6%

THE TEEN DRUG SCENE

On an average day in the USA, nearly 1.2 million teenagers smoke cigarettes. Over half that number (631,000) drink alcohol, and almost as many (586,000) use marijuana. Nearly 50,000 use inhalants "recreationally", while 27,000 use hallucinogens, 13,000 use cocaine, and 3800 use heroin.

TREATMENT DEMAND – HOW MANY PEOPLE ARE TREATED FOR DRUGS PROBLEMS?

NUMBER OF DRUG TREATMENTS
PER MILLION INHABITANTS

EUROPE **847**

ASIA **117**

AMERICAS **3674**

AFRICA **29**

OCEANIA **2288**

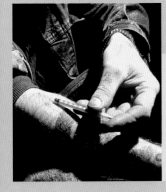

HEROIN AND COCAINE PRICES IN USA AND EUROPE

STREET PRICE OF HEROIN: (US$ PER GRAM)			STREET PRICE OF COCAINE: (US$ PER GRAM)		
	1990	NOW		1990	NOW
USA	433	201	USA	284	107
EUROPE	267	71	EUROPE	180	85

FIND OUT MORE: *Tobacco Atlas* www.who.int; *World Drug Report* www.unodc.org; www.oas.samhsa.gov/nsduhLatest.htm; teens.drugabuse.gov

77

LEGAL DRUGS

- **THREE-QUARTERS OF ALL DRUGS SALES** ARE IN NORTH AMERICA, EUROPE, AND JAPAN. AFRICA ACCOUNTS FOR JUST OVER 1%.
- **IN 2007, THE TOP TEN PHARMACEUTICAL** COMPANIES ENJOYED $349 BILLION IN SALES, OF WHICH $75 BILLION WAS PROFIT.
- **ALSO IN 2007, THE TOP FOUR PHARMACEUTICAL** COMPANIES ENJOYED $185 BILLION IN SALES, OF WHICH $47 BILLION WAS PROFIT — A VERY HIGH PROFIT MARGIN OF OVER 25%.
- **HALF OF THE CURRENT R&D EXPENDITURE** WORLDWIDE, ESTIMATED AT $70-$90 BILLION, IS FUNDED PUBLICLY.

PRESCRIPTION DRUGS

Depression afflicts one in ten Americans, and the WHO predicts that by 2020 depression will be second only to heart disease as the leading cause of disability worldwide. **Prescriptions of powerful antidepressants such as Prozac, Zoloft, and Paxil have more than doubled** in the United States in the last ten years, creating a $11-billion-a-year industry for these drugs, and one in twenty Americans are now taking them. But as with all previous "wonder drugs", side effects have emerged, including in rare cases an increase in suicidal tendencies. In the UK, more than three million adults and young people are now dependent on antidepressants. **Worldwide, 54 million people have taken Prozac.** Even more alarming is the resort to pharmaceuticals to cope with Attention Deficit Hyperactivity Disorder (ADHD) in children. **More than 20 million children in the United States have been prescribed** drugs such as Ritalin, Adderall, or Modafinil. Three million prescriptions are written each month for Ritalin alone. However, these drugs are highly addictive, and if ingested nasally in powder form they give a "high" that has earned them the nickname of "kiddie coke". **One Ritalin tablet can fetch $5 in the schoolyard** as children on prescriptions sell on to others. Tablets can also be obtained illegally over the Internet. In a survey at a US college, one in six respondents admitted to taking prescription drugs illicitly.

FORTUNE 500 — PHARMACEUTICAL COMPANIES REVENUES, 2007

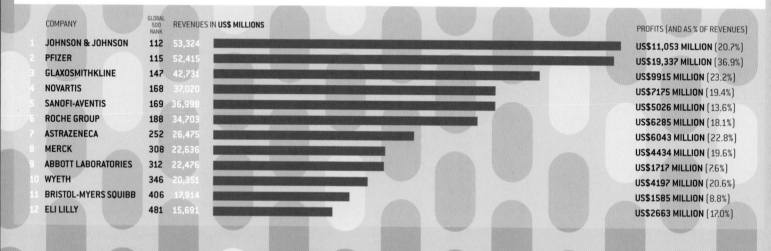

	COMPANY	GLOBAL 500 RANK	REVENUES IN US$ MILLIONS	PROFITS (AND AS % OF REVENUES)
1	JOHNSON & JOHNSON	112	53,324	US$11,053 MILLION (20.7%)
2	PFIZER	115	52,415	US$19,337 MILLION (36.9%)
3	GLAXOSMITHKLINE	147	42,731	US$9915 MILLION (23.2%)
4	NOVARTIS	168	37,020	US$7175 MILLION (19.4%)
5	SANOFI-AVENTIS	169	36,998	US$5026 MILLION (13.6%)
6	ROCHE GROUP	188	34,703	US$6285 MILLION (18.1%)
7	ASTRAZENECA	252	26,475	US$6043 MILLION (22.8%)
8	MERCK	308	22,636	US$4434 MILLION (19.6%)
9	ABBOTT LABORATORIES	312	22,476	US$1717 MILLION (7.6%)
10	WYETH	346	20,351	US$4197 MILLION (20.6%)
11	BRISTOL-MYERS SQUIBB	406	17,914	US$1585 MILLION (8.8%)
12	ELI LILLY	481	15,691	US$2663 MILLION (17.0%)

PHARMACEUTICALS — GENERIC V PATENT DRUGS

Pharmaceutical companies jealously guard their intellectual property by patenting drugs around the world to ensure a return on their (often expensive) research and development. Patents typically give their holders a monopoly on a drug's production and sale for at least 20 years, preventing competitors from undercutting them on price. Painkillers containing aspirin are a classic example; with aspirin now out of patent its generic form costs a mere fraction of the brand name products.

However, in developing countries patented drugs are frequently unaffordable for poorer patients - spurring campaigns to allow the use of generic versions even before patents expire. The problem became especially acute in the wake of the AIDS pandemic, and centred on the ethics of restricting access to antiretroviral (ARV) drug treatment.

A triple-combination of ARVs costs $10,000-$15,000 per patient per year in the United States and Europe. Generic drug producers, however, have offered to sell the equivalent medicines for as low as $300 per patient per year. In Brazil the production and sale of generic ARVs caused prices to fall by 82%. India, "the pharmacy of the developing world" due to its less strict patent-protection regime, supplied 84% of the ARVs prescribed by Médecins sans Frontières worldwide.

The World Health Organization set a target to provide three million of the world's poorest HIV sufferers with antiretroviral drugs by the end of 2005; however, by that year only some 1.3 million were receiving them. The World Trade Organization has now amended its rules on this area of intellectual property rights to free up access to generics, within limits acceptable to the global pharmaceutical giants.

ALCOHOL CONSUMPTION

AVERAGE ANNUAL CONSUMPTION, PER ADULT, OF ALCOHOL IN LITRES OF PURE
ETHANOL (WHERE BEER HAS AROUND 4% VOLUME, WINE 12%, AND SPIRITS 35%)

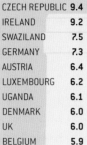

BEER

CZECH REPUBLIC	9.4
IRELAND	9.2
SWAZILAND	7.5
GERMANY	7.3
AUSTRIA	6.4
LUXEMBOURG	6.2
UGANDA	6.1
DENMARK	6.0
UK	6.0
BELGIUM	5.9

WINE

LUXEMBOURG	9.4
FRANCE	8.4
PORTUGAL	7.2
ITALY	7.0
CROATIA	6.4
SWITZERLAND	6.2
ARGENTINA	5.6
SPAIN	5.1
GREECE	4.8
DENMARK	4.6

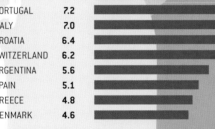

SPIRITS

MOLDOVA	10.9
RUSSIA	7.6
ST. LUCIA	7.3
DOMINICA	7.2
THAILAND	7.1
BAHAMAS	7.1
LATVIA	6.6
HAITI	6.5
BELARUS	6.3
LAOS	6.1

THE PRICE OF DRINK

JORDAN HAS A 200% SALES TAX ACROSS THE BOARD ON BEER, WINE, AND SPIRITS.
ICELAND IS NEXT HIGHEST WITH TAXES OF 64%, 58%, AND 80% RESPECTIVELY.
IN MANY MUSLIM COUNTRIES, IT IS PROHIBITION RATHER THAN TAXATION THAT TARGETS
DRINKERS. THE MOST COMPLETE BANS ON THE PRODUCTION, IMPORTATION, OR
CONSUMPTION OF ALCOHOL EXIST IN SAUDI ARABIA, KUWAIT, LIBYA, AND SUDAN, WITH
SEVERE PENALTIES FOR VIOLATION.

TO BAN OR NOT TO BAN

Attitudes vary between countries about the dangers of
various drugs. This is one explanation for differing legal
controls – along with social acceptability, practicality,
and the importance of tax revenues. The Dutch approach
of treating drug use as a public health rather than a
criminal issue now allows the open sale of cannabis
for personal use in so-called coffee shops. This has
been challenged, however, because of increases in
the strength of the drug, and distaste for the growing
"drug tourism" phenomenon of visitors travelling to the
Netherlands to buy and use it there.

Despite alcohol's health risks – cirrhosis of the liver,
malnutrition, cancer, diabetes – its capacity to reduce
inhibition has made it a socially and legally acceptable
drug in most of the world. Indeed, where water quality is
poor, fermented beverages can be much safer.

Some Muslim countries forbid alcohol, and most
governments regulate its sale and consumption to some
extent, but in Western societies the idea of prohibition
(famously and unsuccessfully tried in the USA between
1920 and 1933) appears ever more remote. On the
contrary, in the UK, for example, drinking hours in pubs
have been greatly extended, although drink-driving
incurs stricter penalties and there is growing concern
about under-age drinking and binge drinking.

The world's other principal legal addictive drug,
nicotine, has lately become less socially acceptable
in the United States and Western Europe. Prompted
by evidence that tobacco smoke can damage others
near enough to breathe it – so-called "passive smokers"
– around 50 countries worldwide have introduced bans
since 2002 on smoking cigarettes or pipes in public
places. Taxes on tobacco have often been cranked up
too, so government revenues should not suffer from any
success in cutting overall consumption.

THE WORLD HEALTH ORGANIZATION (WHO) CALCULATES
HOW MANY YEARS OF HEALTHY LIFE ARE LOST TO
DISEASES ATTRIBUTED TO DRUGS WORLDWIDE:

% OF YEARS LOST, CAUSED BY	MALE	FEMALE
SMOKING	6.3%	1.6%
ALCOHOL	6.5%	1.3%
ILLICIT DRUGS	1.1%	0.4%

IND OUT MORE: www.accessmed-msf.org; www.avert.org/generic.htm; www2.potsdam.edu/hansondj; www.who.int; www.smokefreeworld.com

79

JUST HOW MUCH DID THESE FI

ESTIMATES OF FUNDS ALLEGEDLY EMBEZZLED

SUHARTO: US$ 15-35 BILLION
MOHAMED SUHARTO, PRESIDENT OF INDONESIA, 1967-98

MARCOS: US$ 5-10 BILL
FERDINAND MARCOS, PRESIDENT OF PHILIPPINES, 1

CORRUPTION

Corruption can cause global crises, as in the notorious case of fraudulent accounting by the giant Enron corporation. The tentacles of scandals may spread far and wide: Indian Foreign Minister Natwar Singh (above) resigned in late 2005 over kickbacks in the UN–Iraq oil-for-food affair. When payments are made routinely for personal favours, or to obtain services from public officials that should be provided as of right, poor people end up paying a disproportionate amount of their income in bribes. A survey by anti-corruption NGO Transparency International (TI) found that in Cameroon, Paraguay, Cambodia, and Mexico up to half of all households had paid a bribe in the previous year, compared with fewer than five per cent in wealthy Western countries.

Corruption can take the form of patronage, where contracts, jobs, or promotions are awarded to the friends, family, and business associates of influential office-holders and politicians. Rewarding loyalty ahead of competence is obviously improper when public money pays the wages. Political party funding rules vary widely between counties; France, for instance, bans corporate donations and places strict ceilings on campaign spending. One argument for the public funding of political parties is to stop them feeling bound to deliver on promises made to their financial backers rather than their voters.

WHAT IS CORRUPTION?

TRANSPARENCY INTERNATIONAL DEFINES CORRUPTION AS THE MISUSE OF ENTRUSTED POWER FOR PRIVATE GAIN.

BRIBE: A PAYMENT OR GIFT GIVEN TO INFLUENCE THE BEHAVIOUR OR JUDGMENT OF A PERSON IN AUTHORITY.

GRAFT: THE IMPROPER USE OF A POSITION OF AUTHORITY FOR PRIVATE FINANCIAL ADVANTAGE.

KICKBACK: A KIND OF BRIBE WHEREBY A FIRM GETS A GOVERNMENT CONTRACT BY LETTING THE ALLOCATING OFFICIAL POCKET PART OF ITS FEE.

FRAUD: DECEPTION FOR UNLAWFUL GAIN OR UNJUST ADVANTAGE.

TRANSPARENCY: OPENNESS ABOUT THE MECHANISMS AND PROCESSES BEHIND ADMINISTRATIVE DECISIONS, BUSINESS TRANSACTIONS, OR CHARITABLE WORK.

GREASING POLICE PALMS

Percentage of "people who had had contact with th police in the past year" who have paid a bribe

NORTH AMERICA: Canada and USA **2%**

1%

EU AND OTHER WESTERN EUROPEAN COUNTRIES: Austria, Czech Republic, Denmark, Finland, France, Germany, Greece, Iceland, Italy, Luxembourg, Netherlands, Norway, Poland, Portugal, Spain, Sweden, Switzerland, and UK

20% **NEWLY INDEPENDENT STAT** Moldova, Russia, and Ukrain

16% **SOUTHEAST EUROPE:** Albania, Bulgari Croatia, Kosovo, Macedonia, Romania Serbia, and Turkey

LATIN AMERICA: Argentina, Bolivia, Chile, Colombia, Dominican Republic, Mexico, Panama, Paraguay, Peru, and Venezuela **32%**

19% **ASIA-PACIFIC:** Fiji, Hong Kong, India, Indonesia, Japan, South Korea, Malaysia, Pakistan, Philippines, Singapore, Taiwan, and Thailand

55% **AFRICA:** Cameroon, Congo, Gabon, Kenya, Morocco, Nigeria, Senegal, and South Africa

MORE BRIBERY   8% AVERAGE   **LESS BRIBERY**

SOURCES: Transparency International: *Global Corruption Report* (2007) and *Bribe Payers Index* (2006)

LEPTOCRATS STEAL FROM THEIR COUNTRIES?

MOBUTU: US$ 5 BILLION
MOBUTU SESE SEKO, PRESIDENT OF ZAIRE, 1965-97

ABACHA: US$ 2-5 BILLION
SANI ABACHA, PRESIDENT OF NIGERIA, 1993-98

MILOSEVIC: US$ 1 BILLION
SLOBODAN MILOSEVIC, PRESIDENT OF SERBIA/YUGOSLAVIA, 1993-98

BUSINESS AND BRIBERY

HOW MUCH IS BUSINESS AFFECTED BY BRIBERY? Taken from Transparency International's **Global Corruption Report 2007**, a survey of 50 international companies. The graph below shows the percentage of companies believing they lost business in 2006 through competitors paying bribes

HONG KONG **66%**

NETHERLANDS **26%**

USA **20%**

BRAZIL **42%**

GERMANY **28%**

FRANCE **32%**

UK **22%**

SQUEAKY CLEAN AT HOME BUT WHAT ABOUT ABROAD?

THE LIKELIHOOD OF COMPANIES PAYING BRIBES ABROAD. Transparency International's **Bribe Payers Index 2006** studied 30 countries to investigate the likelihood of companies paying bribes outside of their own borders.

Rank	Country or territory	Average scores out of 10 10 is NO bribes and 0 is ALL bribes
1	SWITZERLAND	7.81
2	SWEDEN	7.62
5	CANADA	7.46
6	UK	7.39
7	GERMANY	7.34
9	USA	7.22
11	JAPAN	7.10
15	FRANCE	6.50
20	ITALY	5.94
28	RUSSIA	5.16
29	CHINA	4.94
30	INDIA	4.62

CORRUPTION

TRANSPARENCY INTERNATIONAL PUBLISHES AN ANNUAL CORRUPTION PERCEPTIONS INDEX (CPI), WHICH ATTEMPTS TO MEASURE "THE DEGREE TO WHICH CORRUPTION IS PERCEIVED TO EXIST AMONG PUBLIC OFFICIALS AND POLITICIANS". THIS WAS MEASURED IN 2007 THROUGH 14 DIFFERENT SOURCES, INCLUDING SURVEYS FROM 12 DIFFERENT INDEPENDENT INSTITUTIONS. IN THE 2007 CPI, **DENMARK, FINLAND, AND NEW ZEALAND WERE PERCEIVED TO BE LEAST CORRUPT,** WHILE **IRAQ, BURMA (MYANMAR), AND SOMALIA WERE PERCEIVED TO BE THE MOST CORRUPT.**

WORLDCOM

THE TELECOMMUNICATIONS GIANT WORLDCOM FILED THE LARGEST CORPORATE BANKRUPTCY IN HISTORY ON JULY 21 2002. REVELATIONS OF FALSE ACCOUNTING, INFLATING THE COMPANY'S ASSETS BY $11 BILLION, SAVAGED INVESTOR CONFIDENCE, AND CUT BILLIONS OF DOLLARS IN VALUE FROM US AND GLOBAL MARKETS.

CASH-FOR-HONOURS

IN 2006 TONY BLAIR BECAME THE FIRST BRITISH PRIME MINISTER TO BE QUESTIONED BY POLICE, AFTER NOMINATING SEVERAL PEOPLE FOR PEERAGES WHO HAD LOANED MONEY TO THE LABOUR PARTY. NO EVIDENCE WAS FOUND TO PROVE THAT THE PEERAGES HAD BEEN PROMISED AT THE TIME OF THE LOANS.

OIL-FOR-FOOD

THE UN'S OIL-FOR-FOOD PROGRAMME IN IRAQ WAS SYSTEMATICALLY ABUSED BETWEEN 1995 AND 2003. CONCESSIONS WERE OFFERED ON OIL CONTRACTS, OIL COUPONS OFFERED AS BRIBES, AND KICKBACKS PAID TO SUPPLIERS OF HUMANITARIAN GOODS. EVEN UN SECRETARY-GENERAL KOFI ANNAN WAS IMPLICATED.

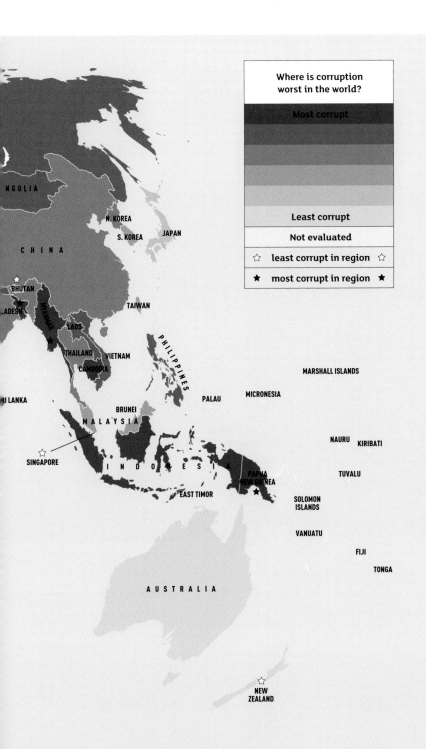

Where is corruption worst in the world?

Most corrupt

Least corrupt

Not evaluated

☆ least corrupt in region ☆

★ most corrupt in region ★

CONTROLLING CORRUPTION

In an age of global electronic finance, massive fraud can be curiously depersonalized. The biggest known case ever was uncovered by the major French bank Société Générale in early 2008, when secret deals by "rogue trader" Jerome Kerviel cost it 4.9 billion euros – three times what unauthorized trading by Nick Leeson (above) had cost Barings Bank in 1995. Kerviel and Leeson depended on nobody's active complicity, but only on their knowledge of how to "work the system". The same is true of most trading in wrongly valued shares, commodities, junk bonds, and other "financial derivatives". In cases of insider trading, it is the privileged information of company insiders that can be turned to corrupt profit.

The battle against corruption may be waged through legislation, such as on political party funding. To combat the problems of differing standards and definitions around the world, there is a trend towards bringing a company's overseas activities under the jurisdiction of the country where it is headquartered. Ultimately, however, deterring corruption depends on increasing the risk of exposure. International efforts revolve increasingly around ways of improving transparency and increasing the flow of information about how governments, businesses, and political parties receive and spend money.

Foreign aid is one area where corruption frequently prevents the benefits reaching their intended recipients. The Anti-Corruption Resource Centre (U4), backed by the overseas development departments of several Western countries, provides extensive online resources to donors on themes such as corruption in the health and education sectors, public financial management, and co-ordination between donor agencies to prevent corruption, as well as case studies on how corruption problems have been managed in developing countries in the past.

MONTESINOS AND FUJIMORI

PERUVIAN SPY CHIEF VLADIMIRO MONTESINOS WAS CAUGHT ON CAMERA IN 2000 OFFERING MONEY TO OPPOSITION SENATORS TO SECURE SUPPORT FOR PRESIDENT ALBERTO FUJIMORI. BOTH MEN FLED INTO EXILE. MONTESINOS WAS ALSO ACCUSED OF TORTURING SHINING PATH REBELS AND OTHER POLITICAL OPPONENTS.

BOFORS ARMS DEAL

THE BOFORS SCANDAL OF THE 1980s STILL HAUNTS INDIAN POLITICS, ALTHOUGH THE THEN PRIME MINISTER RAJIV GANDHI WAS POSTHUMOUSLY CLEARED IN 2004 OF TAKING KICKBACKS FROM THE SWEDISH ARMS FIRM IN RETURN FOR A CONTRACT TO SUPPLY HOWITZER FIELD GUNS TO THE INDIAN ARMY.

Tibetan Buddhist monk, 2008/ illegal immigrant, 2007.
The state uses a variety of methods to protect itself from
threats.

THE SPREAD OF LIBERAL DEMOCRACY PROCEEDS APACE, OFTEN BY FORCE OR COERCION, BUT NOT WITHOUT ENCOUNTERING SOME SERIOUS PROBLEMS. AND WHAT DO WE MEAN BY DEMOCRACY ANYWAY?

VOTING
SUFFRAGE, THE PRICE OF
THE US PRESIDENCY, WHO
VOTES FOR WHAT? VOTES FOR
WOMEN, ELECTORAL SYSTEMS

GOVERNMENT
THE COLLAPSE OF
COMMUNISM? DEMOCRACY
ON THE RISE, WORLD
GOVERNMENTS, THE COST OF
GOVERNMENT

POLICING
FREEDOM
ABUSING PRIVACY,
SURVEILLANCE SOCIETIES,
CROSSING BORDERS,
DETENTION OF SUSPECTS,
SECURITY FIRMS

THE STATE

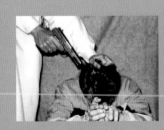

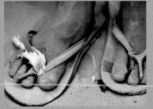

THE PRESS
PRIVACY AND THE PRESS, FREEDOM OF SPEECH, JOURNALIST CASUALTIES, ENEMIES OF THE INTERNET

WAR
DEATHS IN CURRENT ARMED CONFLICTS, FLASHPOINTS, PEACEKEEPING, SMART WEAPONS

REFUGEES
HOST COUNTRIES, EXODUS COUNTRIES, REFUGEES AND INTERNALLY DISPLACED PERSONS

TRAFFICKING
TRADE IN HUMANS, PACKAGE PRICES, DRUG SMUGGLING AND SEIZURES

TERRORISM
TACTICS AND INCIDENTS, CIVILIAN DEATHS, GROUPS, MOTIVES AND IDEOLOGY, EXTRAORDINARY RENDITION

VOTING

In most Western societies we are used to voting. For some matters we may seek everyone's agreement, but choices and decisions are commonly regarded as fair if they have majority support. Voting is seen as conferring legitimacy – to the extent that it is now used across the world even by regimes which are not genuinely democratic, and do not offer real choices at the polls. International organizations often send "monitors" to report on whether polls are free and fair.

The secrecy of the ballot is an important safeguard against voter intimidation. When the Democratic Republic of the Congo recently experimented with a system of counting voters lined up according to their chosen candidate, this was widely condemned – although, on a smaller scale, most meetings customarily take decisions by a show of hands.

OLD ENOUGH TO VOTE?

In most countries the minimum voting age is 18 years. Czechoslovakia was the first country to lower their voting age to 18, in 1946, although there are now four countries in the world where citizens as young as 16 have the right to vote.

Austria, Brazil, Cuba, and Nicaragua	16
East Timor, Indonesia, North Korea, Seychelles, and Sudan	17
Rest of world	18
South Korea	19
Bahrain, Cameroon, Japan, Nauru, Taiwan, and Tunisia	20
CAR, Fiji, Gabon, Kuwait, Lebanon, Malaysia, Maldives, Oman, Samoa, Saudi Arabia, Singapore, Solomon Islands, and Tonga	21

THE PRICE OF THE
US PRESIDENCY

WHAT THE CANDIDATES SPENT IN 2004:

GEORGE W. BUSH (REPUBLICAN)
$345.3m

JOHN KERRY (DEMOCRAT)
$309.7m

OTHER PARTIES
$6.7m

An additional $56.2 million from private funding was spent, during the primary selection rounds, by candidates competing for their party nominations.

US election budgets used to focus on press coverage and whistlestop travel. Today, the bandwagon continues, but in addition television broadcasts, websites and straightforward advertising on billboards and commercial breaks have added to the burden, not to mention gladhanding rallies staged like pop festivals.

200
200
199
199
198
198
198
1976

Feeling manipulated? Voters sometimes express anger against mainstream politicians by voting for fringe candidates. There are always several of these in US presidential elections, though they rarely get much support. In the 2002 French presidential election, however, the left-of-centre vote was so fragmented that even the main socialist candidate was eliminated in the first round, allowing the extreme right-winger Le Pen through to the run-off against the right-of-centre incumbent Jacques Chirac.

2004

$717.9m

REPUBLICAN VICTORY

Presidential candidates have to raise enormous sums of money for their campaigns. In 2004 Bush and Kerry each received $75 million in state funding, as the nominees of the main two parties, but also raised a total of half a billion dollars in private contributions.
Even before the first primary in the 2008 election race, Democrat candidates Hillary Clinton and Barack Obama had each built up impressive war chests of over $100 million, with Republican candidates not far behind. Predictions of the total final spend surpass $1 billion.

2000

$343.1m

REPUBLICAN VICTORY

1996

$239.9m

DEMOCRAT VICTORY

1992

$192.2m

DEMOCRAT VICTORY

1988

$210.7m

REPUBLICAN VICTORY

1984

$103.6m

REPUBLICAN VICTORY

1980

$92.3m

REPUBLICAN VICTORY

$66.9m

DEMOCRAT VICTORY 1976

FIND OUT MORE: www.opensecrets.org; www.youthrights.org; www.aceproject.org

VOTING

WHO BOTHERS TO VOTE TODAY?
PERCENTAGE TURNOUT IN KEY RECENT ELECTIONS

98% SOUTH AFRICA
95% AUSTRALIA
84% ITALY, FRANCE
83% BRAZIL
78% GERMANY
68% JAPAN
65% CANADA
64% GLOBAL AVERAGE
64% RUSSIA, USA
61% UK
58% INDIA

Voting in South Africa is not compulsory. In Australia, however, voting is compulsory, and sanctions may be taken against those who refuse. It is compulsory in Italy too, but not enforced. Countries which hold direct presidential elections usually record higher turnouts in those polls than in parliamentary elections. Well over 80% of French voters turned out in the presidential election of 2007.

WHAT DO WE VOTE FOR?

WHO CAN'T VOTE?

Certified insanity is a common reason for ineligibility to vote. A curiosity of the UK system is that peers of the realm are also debarred from voting in elections to the main parliamentary chamber, the House of Commons. Black South Africans were denied meaningful voting rights under the racist apartheid regime until as recently as 1994. In traditional Islamic societies, women's rights are limited, although some Arab states have now allowed them to vote – although voting of any kind is a rarity.

IN THE USA:
70m RECORD AMERICAN IDOL VOTE
126m LAST US ELECTION VOTE

IN THE UK:
7.5m RECORD BIG BROTHER VOTE
5.7m 18-34 YEAR-OLDS IN LAST UK ELECTION

SOURCES: International Parliamentary Union (IPU); International Institute for Democracy and Electoral Assistance (International IDEA)

VOTES FOR WOMEN

Extending voting rights to women was a controversial issue in the USA, the UK, and some other developed countries in the latter part of the 19th century. Despite high-profile "suffragette" campaigns, it was not completed until 1920 in the USA and 1928 in the UK. Meanwhile, New Zealand had become the first country to give full voting rights to women in 1893. It was not until 1990 that all European adult women were entitled to vote, with the lifting of restrictions by Switzerland's last canton. A few Arab states have yet to follow suit.

ELECTORAL SYSTEMS

CONSTITUENCY-BASED MAJORITY SYSTEMS:

√ Voters elect candidates rather than parties

X A party could get lots of votes, but if its candidates don't win it gets no seats

X One party could win a large proportion of seats relative to its total vote

First Past the Post: The candidate with most votes (a simple plurality) in each constituency wins.

Two-Round System: A candidate needs to win 50% of the constituency vote (an absolute majority). If no-one does, the top two go into a second round run-off.

Alternative Vote: Voters rank all the candidates in their constituency. The one with fewest first preference votes is eliminated, and their votes are re-allocated to the second choice. This continues until one candidate has an absolute majority.

PROPORTIONAL REPRESENTATION SYSTEMS:

√ Results reflect the national vote distribution

√ Most parties get representation

X Voters cannot reject unpopular candidates if their parties choose them

X Parties rarely win a parliamentary majority, so coalitions are necessary

Basic List PR: Each party lists its candidates. Voters choose between party lists. Parties receive seats in proportion to their overall vote, and allocate them to candidates highest on their lists.

Parallel System: Some seats are elected from constituencies, the rest chosen from party lists. Voters mark their choice of candidate in their constituency and from a party list.

Mixed Member Proportional: Some seats are elected from constituencies, the rest allocated by party to make each party's total proportional to the number of votes won by its candidates.

Single Transferable Vote: If a candidate scores less than a set quota of first-preference votes, they are ejected from the race and their votes are transferred to the next choices.

TOMORROW'S VOTE

Denmark was the first country to introduce voting by mail, in 1915, mainly for the benefit of sailors. Postal voting is now quite widespread, though generally used by relatively few people. When Estonia offered Internet voting in its national elections in March 2007, the experiment was keenly watched to see if this kind of innovation could help raise the turnout. Over 30,000 votes were cast online, 5.5% of the total. Although the vast majority of voters still preferred to use polling stations, "electronic democracy" had been shown to be a trend to watch for the future.

Making it easy to vote won't tackle the problem of a so-called "democratic deficit", where voters at local or even national level are so apathetic or cynical about the outcome of elections that they do not bother to participate. In the USA, for example, some presidential elections have seen a turnout of barely 50%. Younger democracies have also suffered a rapid disenchantment. The tiny Balkan country of Montenegro, long under Tito's Yugoslav dictatorship, won its independence from Serbia in 2006 on a referendum turnout of only just over 55%.

The invention of the telegraph enabled American democracy to be spread across the continent, but today new technologies seem to cause little but trouble. The "damaged chads" scandal, indicating faulty voting punchcards, in the US 2000 elections caused havoc, and new digital display voting machines have proved unreliable and confusing.

GOVERNMENT

It is staggering how much government has grown in one lifetime. One simple measure is the number of sovereign states, which has approximately trebled in the last 60 years to reach the current (mid-2007) figure of 194. This is partly due to the break-up of the colonial empires centred on London, Paris, and other European capitals, which had ruled whole swathes of Asia, Africa, Australasia, and the Caribbean. Decolonization doubled the number of independent states by the mid-1960s, and brought the total to 168 by 1990. The following decade saw the break-up of the Soviet Union and the former Yugoslavia. In the 21st century, East Timor and Montenegro have become independent. There are perhaps 20 or so remaining candidates for separate nationhood.

The great majority of these new states are republics, and most would count themselves as democracies, although a fair number passed through periods of single-party or military rule. Democracy can conflict, however, with other cherished principles of the state. In Turkey, for example, the military has deposed four elected governments within the last 60 years in defence of the secular principles laid down by the country's founder, Kemal Atatürk.

BOLIVIA HAS HAD MORE COUPS THAN ANY OTHER COUNTRY – 192 SINCE INDEPENDENCE IN 1825

COMOROS HAS HAD 20 COUPS IN THE LAST 30 YEARS

ITALY HAS HAD 61 GOVERNMENTS IN THE LAST 61 YEARS

PAKISTAN HAS BEEN UNDER MILITARY RULE FOR HALF OF ITS EXISTENCE AS AN INDEPENDENT STATE

VIETNAM: 52,742,000	HUNGARY: 10,680,000
ETHIOPIA: 41,930,000	CUBA: 9,724,000
POLAND: 36,745,000	BULGARIA: 8,906,000
ROMANIA: 22,553,000	ANGOLA: 7,700,000
YUGOSLAVIA: 22,425,000	CAMBODIA: 5,756,000
NORTH KOREA: 18,490,000	LAOS: 3,800,000
EAST GERMANY: 16,737,000	ALBANIA: 2,672,000
CZECHOSLOVAKIA: 15,437,000	SOUTH YEMEN: 2,040,000
AFGHANISTAN: 14,367,000	MONGOLIA: 1,962,000
MOZAMBIQUE: 13,413,000	

USSR: 271,200,000

CHINA: 1,008,175,000

1988
21 COUNTRIES
1,587,454,000
30.5% OF THE WORLD'S POPULATION OF 5.2 BILLION LIVING UNDER COMMUNIST RULE IN 1988

VIETNAM: 81,400,000
NORTH KOREA: 22,700,000
CUBA: 11,300,000
LAOS: 5,700,000

CHINA: 1,300,000,000

2008
5 COUNTRIES
1,421,000,000
22% OF THE WORLD'S POPULATION OF 6.4 BILLION LIVING UNDER COMMUNIST RULE IN 2008

THE COLLAPSE OF COMMUNISM?

Amid great excitement, pro-democracy movements swept away a succession of one-party Communist regimes in eastern Europe in 1989. Communism's heartland, the Soviet Union, fell two years later. Now, in multi-party systems there as elsewhere, communists are just one (rarely very successful) competitor for electoral support. China's 1.3 billion people, however, and North Korea, Vietnam, Laos, and Cuba, remain in the grip of single-party communist rule.

DEMOCRACY IN NAME ONLY

The word "democratic" is included in eight countries' official names, but it is rarely a good sign. North Korea, which styles itself the Democratic People's Republic of Korea, is probably the world's most totalitarian regime. Even countries with periodic multi-party elections may fail the "democracy test", as Zimbabwe (left) and perhaps 40 others do, because of the restriction and intimidation of opponents, gags on the media, and widespread ballot-rigging.

SOURCES: UN; US Census Bureau; European Union

DEMOCRACY ON THE RISE

ALMOST TWO-THIRDS OF ALL COUNTRIES NOW HOLD REGULAR DEMOCRATIC ELECTIONS – AND THE LARGEST DEMOCRACY, INDIA, HAS SOME 700 MILLION REGISTERED VOTERS. Military coups have become relative rarities, and their instigators usually promise a return to civilian rule once they have imposed order on the political process – though such "interventions" can seriously impede the development of democratic institutions, as in Pakistan. Fear of retribution, or reluctance to give up their power of patronage, does sometimes encourage even elected leaders to cling to office; the incumbent president in Kenya was accused of this, and of stealing the elections of early 2008 by falsifying the results.

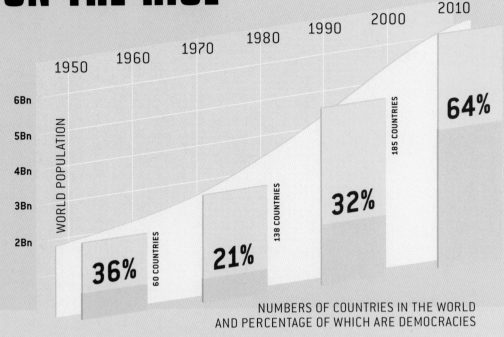

1950 1960 1970 1980 1990 2000 2010

WORLD POPULATION

6Bn
5Bn
4Bn
3Bn
2Bn

36% 60 COUNTRIES

21% 138 COUNTRIES

32% 185 COUNTRIES

64% 194 COUNTRIES

NUMBERS OF COUNTRIES IN THE WORLD AND PERCENTAGE OF WHICH ARE DEMOCRACIES

NATION OR SUPERSTATE?
THE GROWING EUROPEAN UNION

The US federal structure, balancing the powers of central government with the 50 states' rights, has inspired scores of federal systems across the world. At the supra-national level the expanding European Union, which outstrips the USA in population and economic size, has extended its remit from economic to financial, social, and even foreign policy – provoking anti-EU sentiment in some member countries over the erosion of national sovereignty.

NORWAY
SWEDEN (1995)
FINLAND (1995)
ESTONIA (2004)
LATVIA (2004)
RUSSIA
LITHUANIA (2004)
DENMARK (1973)
UNITED KINGDOM (1973)
IRELAND (1973)
NETHERLANDS (1952)
GERMAN UNIFICATION (1990)
POLAND (2004)
BELARUS
BELGIUM (1952)
GERMANY (1952)
CZECH REP. (2004)
LUX (1952)
SLOVAKIA (2004)
UKRAINE
AUSTRIA (1995)
HUNGARY (2004)
FRANCE (1952)
SWITZ.
SLOVENIA (2004)
ROMANIA (2007)
ITALY (1952)
BULGARIA (2007)
PORTUGAL (1986)
SPAIN (1986)
GREECE (1981)
TURKEY
MALTA (2004)
CYPRUS (2004)

	Population of EU	Number of countries	Population of USA
1958	169m	6	173m
1973	257m	9	210m
1981	273m	10	228m
1986	323m	12	239m
1990	345m	12	248m
1995	372m	15	265m
2004	459m	25	292m
2007	492m	27	301m

GOVERNMENT

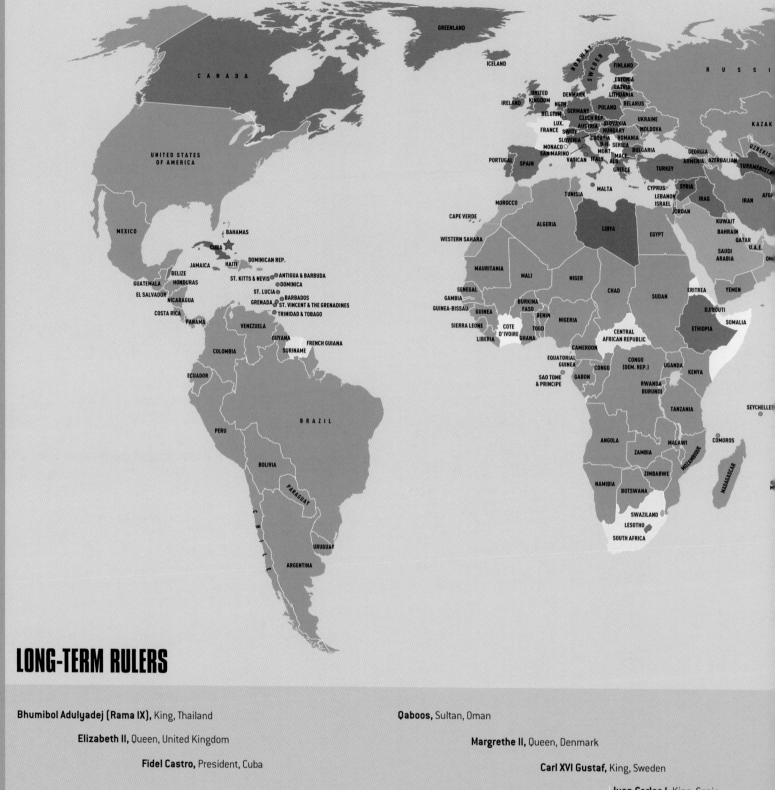

LONG-TERM RULERS

Bhumibol Adulyadej (Rama IX), King, Thailand

Qaboos, Sultan, Oman

Elizabeth II, Queen, United Kingdom

Margrethe II, Queen, Denmark

Fidel Castro, President, Cuba

Carl XVI Gustaf, King, Sweden

Juan Carlos I, King, Spain

Hassanal Bolkiah, Sultan, Brunei / **Omar Bongo,** President, Gabon

Col. MUAMMAR QADDAFI, "Leader of the Revolution", Libya

1946	**1952**	**1959**	**1967**	**1969**	**1970**	**1972**	**1973**	**1975**
First electronic digital computer	First hydrogen bomb detonated	Dalai Lama flees Tibet	Beatles release Sgt. Pepper's Lonely Hearts Club Band	First moon landings	Concorde makes its first supersonic flight	State of Bangladesh created	World Trade Center opened	Vietnam War ends with fall of Saigon to North Vietnamese troops

SOURCES: CIRCA: *People in Power*; World Bank: *World Development Indicators*

WORLD GOVERNMENT

Types of Government	Totals
Monarchies	10
Non-party systems	4
One-party states	8
Presidential systems	81
Parliamentary systems	69
Mixed presidential-parliamentary systems	8
Mixed monarchical-parliamentary systems	4
Transitional regimes	3
Others	6
★ Communist regimes today ★	5

MONGOLIA

N. KOREA
S. KOREA
JAPAN
CHINA
NEPAL
BHUTAN
BANGLADESH
IA
TAIWAN
BURMA (MYANMAR)
LAOS
THAILAND
VIETNAM
CAMBODIA
PHILIPPINES
SRI LANKA
MARSHALL ISLANDS
PALAU
MICRONESIA
BRUNEI
MALAYSIA
SINGAPORE
NAURU
KIRIBATI
INDONESIA
PAPUA NEW GUINEA
TUVALU
EAST TIMOR
SOLOMON ISLANDS
VANUATU
FIJI
TONGA
AUSTRALIA
NEW ZEALAND

GOVERNMENT EXPENDITURE AS A PERCENTAGE OF GDP

USA	RUSSIA	JAPAN	GERMANY	CANADA	ITALY	UK	FRANCE	EAST TIMOR
15.8	16.5	18	18.6	19.5	20.3	21.8	23.7	51.2

TOO MUCH GOVERNMENT?

We expect government to protect us from crime and foreign aggression, and to help define (and enforce) functional rules such as traffic regulations. The modern state, however, goes much further than that. It not only regulates but promotes and participates in economic activity, keeps an ever closer watch on society [*see* Policing Freedom, pages 90-93], and taxes its citizens to pay for everything from wars to welfare, and from schools to bureaucrats. Libertarians, and free market economists, see this as suffocating freedom and enterprise.

In developed countries, governments now typically spend a four times larger share of their nations' income than they did a century ago – even in the USA, where reducing the burden of "big government" has been something of a Republican crusade.

Liberal democracies generally make a point of not interfering with freedom of belief, but their legal systems may still enshrine some religious values, for instance over abortion, or trading on holy days. Some Islamic states go further, applying sharia law which is based explicitly on religious doctrine. Out-and-out theocracy (rule by religious leaders, as in Iran) is rare in modern times, but religious radicals pose a potent threat to several governments, claiming as they do that they owe a higher allegiance to faith than state.

The biggest challenge of all, however, comes from the twin phenomena of technology and globalization, stretching the capacity of any government to control the movement of work, money, and information around the world.

PARIAH STATES

Governments regarded internationally as unacceptable may be shunned as pariah states, such as the former apartheid regime in South Africa. The UN can in theory intervene if they are a threat to peace; however, unless they invade a neighbour, UN members rarely agree. Major powers occasionally take it upon themselves to step in. The Islamic fundamentalist Taliban regime in Afghanistan was invaded by a US-led coalition in late 2001 after being blamed for supporting al-Qaeda terrorists, and Saddam Hussein's dictatorship in Iraq was also overthrown by US-led military force in 2003, in a bid (among other things) to "establish democracy" there.

POLICING FREEDOM

Liberal societies have always struggled to strike the "right" balance between individual freedoms, the rights of others, curbing antisocial behaviour, and providing security from external threats. Too much policing can limit the very liberties purportedly being defended.

The rapid development of technology in this area has profound effects. It provides ever more sophisticated techniques for governments and security forces (and commercial organizations too) to identify individuals, monitor their communications, and track their movements. The right to personal privacy is difficult to square with the intrusiveness of such techniques, the sheer quantity of data that is now gathered on people – whether in police DNA databases or on supermarket shopping patterns – and the possibilities for linking up and analysing these different data sets. Meanwhile, the spectre of terrorism is used to justify ever-closer scrutiny of our behaviour.

Limits to the infringement of privacy can be set by law, or even enshrined in constitutions. A huge amount of policing can now be done, however, without its subjects even knowing they are being watched – thereby tempting the security forces to stretch the interpretation of what is permissible in the name of protecting freedom.

> "THOSE WHO DESIRE TO GIVE UP FREEDOM IN ORDER TO GAIN SECURITY WILL NOT HAVE, NOR DO THEY DESERVE, EITHER ONE."
> BENJAMIN FRANKLIN
>
> 46% OF ADULTS THINK THAT PRESIDENT BUSH'S PROGRAMMES DO NOT STRIKE THE RIGHT BALANCE BETWEEN INVESTIGATIONS OF POTENTIAL TERRORISM AND THE PROTECTION OF CIVIL LIBERTIES.

ABUSING PRIVACY

UK-BASED HUMAN RIGHTS GROUP PRIVACY INTERNATIONAL HAS DEVELOPED A RANKING SYSTEM COVERING 47 MAJOR COUNTRIES, WEIGHING UP THEIR LEVELS OF PUBLIC SURVEILLANCE AND STATE CONTROL, AND THE EFFECTIVENESS OF LEGAL SAFEGUARDS IN THESE AREAS. THE USA, AND ENGLAND AND WALES, CAME OUT ALMOST AS BADLY AS CHINA AND RUSSIA IN THE 2007 RANKINGS – AND NO COUNTRY SCORED HIGH ENOUGH TO BE FLAGGED AS ACHIEVING "SIGNIFICANT PROTECTIONS AND SAFEGUARDS," LET ALONE THE TOP RANK OF "CONSISTENTLY UPHOLDING HUMAN RIGHTS STANDARDS."

LOWER SCORES ARE WORSE

1 ENDEMIC SURVEILLANCE SOCIETIES

RUSSIA	1.3	CHINA	1.3
MALAYSIA	1.3	ENGLAND & WALES	1.3
SINGAPORE	1.4	USA	1.5
THAILAND	1.5	TAIWAN	1.5

2 EXTENSIVE SURVEILLANCE SOCIETIES

PHILIPPINES	1.8	FRANCE	1.9
INDIA	1.9	DENMARK	2.0
BULGARIA	2.0	LITHUANIA	2.0

KEY TO RANKINGS

1.1–1.5	INDICATES AN ENDEMIC SURVEILLANCE SOCIETY
1.6–2.0	INDICATES AN EXTENSIVE SURVEILLANCE SOCIETY
2.1–2.5	INDICATES A SOCIETY WITH A SYSTEMIC FAILURE TO UPHOLD SAFEGUARDS
2.6–3.0	INDICATES A SOCIETY WITH SOME SAFEGUARDS BUT WEAKENED PROTECTIONS
3.1–3.5	INDICATES A SOCIETY WITH ADEQUATE SAFEGUARDS AGAINST ABUSE
3.6–4.0	INDICATES A SOCIETY WITH SIGNIFICANT PROTECTIONS AND SAFEGUARDS
4.1–5.0	INDICATES A SOCIETY THAT CONSISTENTLY UPHOLDS HUMAN RIGHTS STANDARDS

SOURCES: Harris Interactive Inc: The Harris Poll® #132 (28 December, 2007); Privacy International: 2007 International Privacy Ranking

COUNTRIES WITH THE WORST RECORDS

● **CONSTITUTIONAL PROTECTION**
AUSTRALIA, MALAYSIA, SINGAPORE, UK

● **STATUTORY PROTECTION**
INDIA, JAPAN, SINGAPORE, SOUTH AFRICA, USA

● **PRIVACY ENFORCEMENT**
BRAZIL, CHINA, INDIA, JAPAN, MALAYSIA, PHILIPPINES, RUSSIA, SINGAPORE, SOUTH AFRICA, TAIWAN, USA

● **IDENTITY CARDS AND BIOMETRICS**
BELGIUM, BULGARIA, LITHUANIA, MALAYSIA, NETHERLANDS, POLAND, PHILIPPINES, SLOVAKIA, SINGAPORE, SPAIN, TAIWAN, THAILAND, UK, USA

● **DATA-SHARING**
AUSTRIA, BELGIUM, CHINA, CZECH REPUBLIC, DENMARK, FINLAND, FRANCE, MALAYSIA, NETHERLANDS, NORWAY, RUSSIA, UK

● **VISUAL SURVEILLANCE**
CHINA, HUNGARY, LITHUANIA, MALAYSIA, SINGAPORE, SWITZERLAND, UK, USA

● **COMMUNICATION INTERCEPTION**
BULGARIA, CHINA, CYPRUS, CZECH REPUBLIC, GREECE, HUNGARY, INDIA, ITALY, LITHUANIA, MALAYSIA, NETHERLANDS, NEW ZEALAND, PHILIPPINES, POLAND, RUSSIA, SINGAPORE, SPAIN, TAIWAN, THAILAND, UK, USA

● **WORKPLACE MONITORING**
LITHUANIA, SINGAPORE, SWEDEN, USA

● **GOVERNMENT ACCESS TO DATA**
CHINA, DENMARK, FRANCE, INDIA, ISRAEL, MALAYSIA, PHILIPPINES, RUSSIA, SINGAPORE, SLOVAKIA, SWEDEN, THAILAND

● **COMMUNICATIONS DATA RETENTION**
CHINA, DENMARK, FRANCE, GERMANY, IRELAND, ITALY, NETHERLANDS, POLAND, RUSSIA, SLOVAKIA, SLOVENIA, SOUTH AFRICA, SWEDEN, UK

● **SURVEILLANCE OF MEDICAL, FINANCIAL, AND MOVEMENT**
AUSTRALIA, BRAZIL, DENMARK, ISRAEL, MALAYSIA, NORWAY, RUSSIA, SPAIN, SWEDEN, TAIWAN, THAILAND, UK, USA

● **BORDER AND TRANS-BORDER ISSUES**
AUSTRALIA, DENMARK, FRANCE, ICELAND, ISRAEL, JAPAN, MALAYSIA, NORWAY, RUSSIA, SWITZERLAND, TAIWAN, UK, USA

● **LEADERSHIP**
AUSTRIA, BELGIUM, CHINA, FRANCE, GERMANY, HUNGARY, IRELAND, JAPAN, LUXEMBOURG, NETHERLANDS, RUSSIA, SINGAPORE, SPAIN, SWEDEN, TAIWAN, UK, USA

● **DEMOCRATIC SAFEGUARDS**
CHINA, MALAYSIA, RUSSIA, SINGAPORE, THAILAND

3 SYSTEMIC FAILURE TO UPHOLD SAFEGUARDS

NETHERLANDS	2.1	SLOVAKIA	2.1
SWEDEN	2.1	BRAZIL	2.1
NORWAY	2.1	LATVIA	2.2
JAPAN	2.2	AUSTRALIA	2.2
ISRAEL	2.2	POLAND	2.3
SPAIN	2.3	AUSTRIA	2.3
CYPRUS	2.3	NEW ZEALAND	2.3
SOUTH AFRICA	2.3	MALTA	2.4
SWITZERLAND	2.4	CZECH REP.	2.5
FINLAND	2.5	IRELAND	2.5
SCOTLAND	2.5		

4 SOME SAFEGUARDS BUT WEAKENED PROTECTIONS

BELGIUM	2.7	ICELAND	2.7
SLOVENIA	2.8	PORTUGAL	2.8
LUXEMBOURG	2.8	GERMANY	2.8
ITALY	2.8	ESTONIA	2.8
ARGENTINA	2.8	ROMANIA	2.9
HUNGARY	2.9	CANADA	2.9

5 ADEQUATE SAFEGUARDS AGAINST ABUSE

GREECE	3.1

CROSSING BORDERS

WITHIN EUROPE, THE WIDENING SCHENGEN ZONE ALLOWS MEMBER COUNTRY NATIONALS TO TRAVEL WITHOUT VISAS OR PASSPORTS. IT SOUNDS LIKE A GREAT INCREASE IN THEIR FREEDOM – BUT THE FLIP SIDE IS THAT PARTICIPATING COUNTRIES POOL EVER MORE DATA ON THEM, IN THE SCHENGEN INFORMATION SYSTEM DATABASE. THE UK AND IRELAND HAVE OPTED OUT OF THE ZONE – OUT OF RELUCTANCE TO RELINQUISH NATIONAL BORDER CONTROLS, RATHER THAN AVERSION TO CENTRALIZING DATA.

SCHENGEN MEMBERS: 22 EU COUNTRIES (WITH CYPRUS EXPECTED TO JOIN IN 2009, AND BULGARIA AND ROMANIA POSSIBLY IN 2011) PLUS ICELAND AND NORWAY (AND SWITZERLAND FROM LATE 2008).

IN THE USA, ENTRY RESTRICTIONS ARE GETTING TIGHTER, PARTICULARLY SINCE THE 9/11 TERRORIST ATTACKS. THE VISA WAIVER PROGRAM, UNDER WHICH CITIZENS OF SELECTED COUNTRIES MAY ENTER THE US WITHOUT NEEDING A VISA, IS OPEN TO JUST 27 COUNTRIES. THE POTENTIAL EXPANSION OF THE VWP IS OPENLY USED AS A TOOL TO INFLUENCE POLICY, ESPECIALLY ON SECURITY ISSUES, IN COUNTRIES THAT WOULD LIKE TO BE INCLUDED.

BIOMETRIC PASSPORTS

BIOMETRIC PASSPORTS CONTAIN TINY CHIPS HOLDING IMAGES OF THE OWNER: A FACIAL IMAGE, INCREASINGLY FINGERPRINT IMAGES, AND OCCASIONALLY IRIS SCAN IMAGES. OVER 40 COUNTRIES NOW ISSUE THEM, THOUGH NON-BIOMETRIC ONES REMAIN VALID UNTIL EXPIRY. FROM 2009 ALL EU PASSPORTS WILL FEATURE A DIGITAL FINGERPRINT AND PHOTOGRAPH, BUT RUMOURS THAT THE NEW PASSPORTS WOULD REQUIRE DNA INFORMATION HAVE BEEN DENIED. BOTH THE EU AND USA PLAN TO REQUIRE ALL VISITORS TO HOLD BIOMETRIC PASSPORTS.

2004	Belgium, Pakistan, USA
2005	Australia, Germany, New Zealand, Thailand
2006	Austria, Czech Republic, Denmark, Finland, France, Greece, Hungary, Iceland, Ireland, Italy, Lithuania, Netherlands, Poland, Portugal, Singapore, Slovenia, Somalia, Spain, Switzerland, UK
2007	Brunei, Canada, Estonia, Iran, Latvia, Macedonia, Ukraine, Venezuela
2008	Moldova, Serbia, Slovakia, Taiwan

FINGERPRINTING AND DNA

FINGERPRINTS, USED BY POLICE FOR OVER 100 YEARS, ARE NOW SCANNED AND DATABASED FOR WIDER COMPARISONS, BUT THE NEW BIG THING IS DNA PROFILING. DNA EVIDENCE FIRST SECURED A MURDER CONVICTION IN 1987, AND HAS REVOLUTIONIZED PATERNITY TESTING AND TRANSPLANT TISSUE MATCHING. SOME FAVOUR COLLECTING SAMPLES FROM EVERYBODY; THE UK DATABASE ALREADY HOLDS 4.5 MILLION.

ID CARDS

ID CARDS ARE COMPULSORY IN: BELGIUM, BRAZIL, CHINA, GERMANY, RUSSIA
ID CARDS EXIST IN: AUSTRALIA, CANADA, FRANCE, ITALY, SWEDEN
NO ID CARDS IN: INDIA, JAPAN, NEW ZEALAND, UK, USA

IN THE UK PASSPORTS AND DRIVER'S LICENCES ARE WIDELY USED TO VERIFY IDENTITY, BUT THERE IS ONGOING DEBATE ABOUT INTRODUCING ID CARDS. IN THE USA, WHERE ONLY 20% OF CITIZENS OWN PASSPORTS, THE DRIVER'S LICENCE HAS BECOME THE DE FACTO ID CARD.

DETENTION OF SUSPECTS

THE THREAT OF TERRORISM HAS PROMPTED WESTERN GOVERNMENTS TO REVIEW THE LEGAL SITUATION FOR DETAINING SUSPECTS WITHOUT TRIAL OR WITHOUT CHARGE, DESPITE THE FUNDAMENTAL LOSS OF HUMAN RIGHTS THAT THIS ENTAILS. THE UK GOVERNMENT IN 2005 PROPOSED A LENGTHY 90-DAY PERIOD, BUT PARLIAMENT REFUSED TO GO FURTHER THAN DOUBLING THE EXISTING 14-DAY PERIOD. THE US GOVERNMENT HOLDS "ENEMY COMBATANTS" IN ITS OFFSHORE GUANTÁNAMO BAY FACILITY INDEFINITELY – DECLARING THEM BEYOND US JURISDICTION.

XXXXXXXXXXXXXXXXXXXXXXXXXXXX UK: 28 DAYS
XXXXXXXXXXXX AUSTRALIA: 12 DAYS
XXXXXXX TURKEY: 7.5 DAYS
XXXXXXX IRELAND: 7 DAYS
XXXXXX FRANCE: 6 DAYS
XXXXX RUSSIA, SPAIN: 5 DAYS
XXXX ITALY: 4 DAYS
XXX DENMARK, NORWAY: 3 DAYS
XX GERMANY, NEW ZEALAND, SOUTH AFRICA, USA: 2 DAYS
X CANADA: 1 DAY

SOURCES: Liberty: *Terrorism Pre-Charge Detention Comparative Law Study*; European Union; Privacy International: Big Brother Awards

THE GREAT FIREWALL OF CHINA

An army of Chinese public security officials does daily battle with the Internet and its libertarian ethos. The "Golden Shield" project, derided worldwide as the Great Firewall of China, monitors who is online, blocks sensitive postings in chat rooms and discussion forums, and prevents connections to websites with unwelcome content – including Wikipedia, the BBC until recently, and anything linked with dissidents or the Dalai Lama. Web searches for terms like "Falun Gong" return empty pages. Hackers both inside and outside China constantly develop ways round the Firewall, in a race against the authorities' efforts to find and close the loopholes. China has an estimated 20 million bloggers, and the Internet-savvy do get their messages out, but mass public use suffers from these government controls – aided by the controversial collaboration of global Internet giants Google and Yahoo, who argue that to do business in China you must obey its rules.

BIG BROTHER AWARDS

PRIVACY INTERNATIONAL held its first International Big Brother Awards in 2007. Winners were given a golden statue of a boot stamping upon a human head, in reference to George Orwell's prescient novel *1984*.

● Most invasive company: **Choicepoint** (for their vast databases of personal data, sold to nearly anyone who wishes to pay)

● Worst Public Official: **Stewart Baker** (for role in US surveillance policies, most recently the EU-US agreement on Passenger Name Records transfers)

● Most Heinous Government: **UK** (for being the greatest surveillance society among democratic nations)

● Most Appalling Project or Technology: **International Civil Aviation Organization** (for implementing a variety of invasive policies behind closed doors, including the biometric passport and passenger data transfer deals)

LOSING THE PLOT

Global insecurity over terrorism has led governments to pay much closer attention to the people who cross their borders. Yet possible terrorists represent a minuscule fraction of cross-border traffic – a mere handful, for instance, of the 300 million people who cross Europe's 1792 designated frontier checkpoints each year.

Willingly or reluctantly, ordinary citizens surrender aspects of their freedom and convenience with every tightening of security in the name of "policing freedom" – just as strict airport security checks are imposed on the mass of innocent travellers, and even such minor "anti-terrorist" measures as the removal of litter bins or left luggage lockers affect the wider public.

The rising volume of computerized data on individuals, whether collected from surveillance, official records, personal computing, or the "data mining" of commercial transactions, has led to fears over the misuse of that data – and the possibility of massive fraud, exploitation, or "identity theft" if it falls into the wrong hands. Notoriously, in November 2007, the UK Customs and Revenue department lost financial data on 25 million households – stored on just two CDs.

SECURITY FIRMS IN IRAQ

● 170 PRIVATE SECURITY FIRMS OPERATE THERE
● THIRD-LARGEST INTERNATIONAL CONTRIBUTOR OF FORCES TO THE WAR EFFORT IN IRAQ – AFTER US AND BRITISH TROOPS
● PRIVATE CONTRACTORS OFTEN EARN IN EXCESS OF US$100,000 A YEAR
● JOBS INCLUDE THE PROTECTION OF PERSONNEL WORKING FOR PRIVATE COMPANIES AND NON-GOVERNMENT ORGANIZATIONS
● THE US MILITARY OUTSOURCED MORE THAN US$1.5 BILLION IN SECURITY OPERATIONS IN 2007, USING 20,000–30,000 CONTRACTORS TO OFFSET CHRONIC TROOP SHORTAGES

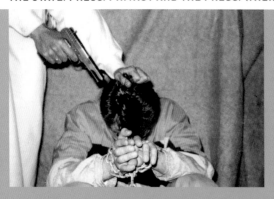

PRESS

The idea that the press should be free of state control is an extension of the idea that free speech should be a right. Most Western countries hold freedom of the press to be necessary for a healthy democracy, with the press seeing itself as representing a notional "fourth estate" and a safeguard against arbitrary government.

Freedom of the press can also be curtailed by self-censorship on the part of journalists afraid to offend powerful figures. Another risk is the concentration of media ownership within ruling elites, giving them powerful vehicles for influencing the public, and marginalizing unwelcome reporting and independent opposition viewpoints.

There is also the danger that lack of public interest could make an active and politically engaged mainstream media sector unviable, leaving the press to focus largely on entertainment, even when there are few or no legal constraints on its freedom.

The fate of journalist Daniel Pearl (above), executed by al-Qaeda in Pakistan, reminds us of the cost of maintaining a free press.

PRIVACY AND THE PRESS

Most free societies do accept some controls on the press as desirable. One increasingly controversial area is the infringement of privacy – and not just of celebrities railing against paparazzi journalists. Codes of conduct often set standards in such sensitive areas as respecting the grief of accident, crime, or disaster victims and their relatives, or reporting about the children of public figures. Privacy laws vary widely between countries, as do legal restrictions on libel, obscenity, and incitement to violence. Suing for libel is so much easier in England than in the USA (and can secure such punitive damages) that so-called "libel tourism" now occurs, where plaintiffs get judgments against what are basically US publications via their (much smaller) UK editions or Internet presence.

WHAT ALLOWS A COUNTRY TO RANK HIGH?

- LAWS PROTECTING FREEDOM OF SPEECH
- LOW STATE OWNERSHIP OF MEDIA OUTLETS
- A BALANCED OWNERSHIP OF THE PRESS ACROSS THE POLITICAL SPECTRUM
- MULTICULTURAL AND LANGUAGE BROADCASTING
- PROTECTION OF SOURCES OF STORIES
- PROBING INVESTIGATIVE JOURNALISM PERMITTED
- ACTIVE JOURNALIST UNIONS DEFENDING THE WORKFORCE'S INTERESTS
- EFFECTIVE INVESTIGATION BY AUTHORITIES INTO VIOLATIONS AGAINST JOURNALISTS

WHEN FREEDOM OF SPEECH OFFENDS...

Cartoons of the Prophet Muhammad published in September 2005 by the Danish *Jyllands-Posten* deeply offended Muslims worldwide. Did the paper have a right to publish them under freedom of expression? Should they have been self-censored out of sensitivity to readers' views? Should there be national, or even global, rules? Should Islam be treated differently to other religions? In the ensuing confrontation, several papers worldwide republished the cartoons in solidarity; demonstrations and violence resulted in over 100 deaths, and an anti-Danish consumer boycott was launched.

WHAT MAKES A COUNTRY RANK LOW?

- ACTIVE CENSORSHIP OF REPORTS
- ARRESTS OF POLITICAL ACTIVISTS AND JOURNALISTS
- IMPRISONMENTS WITHOUT TRIAL
- LAWS CRIMINALIZING PRESS OFFENCES
- INTIMIDATION OF AND VIOLENCE AGAINST JOURNALISTS
- INTERNET RESTRICTIONS ON FREEDOM OF INFORMATION
- CONSTRAINTS ON MOVEMENT OF FOREIGN JOURNALISTS WITHIN THE COUNTRY
- RESTRICTIONS OR TAXES ON PRODUCTION MATERIALS

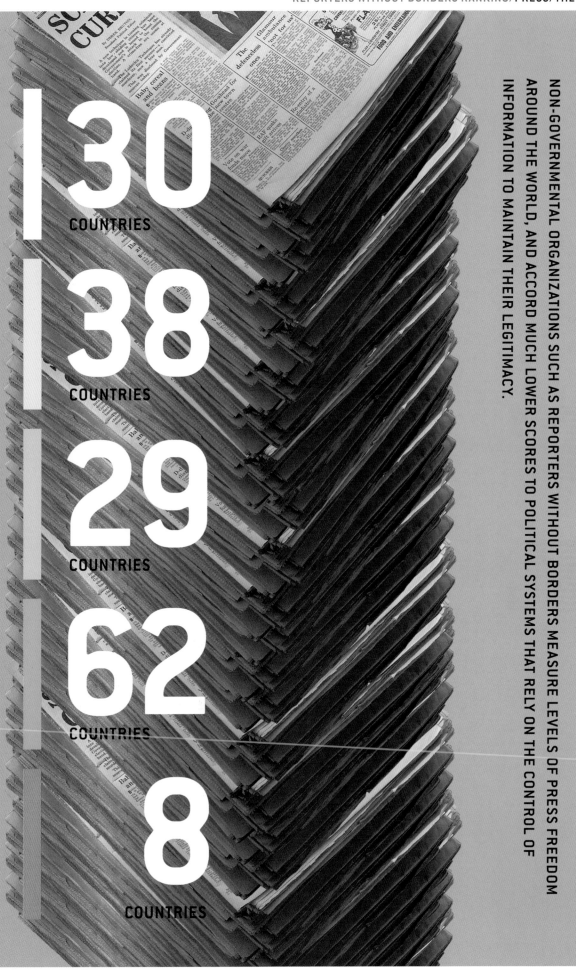

SAMPLE COUNTRIES
WITH RANKINGS

GOOD

1/ FINLAND, ICELAND,
IRELAND, NETHERLANDS
8/ SLOVAKIA, SWITZERLAND
14/ HUNGARY, LATVIA,
PORTUGAL, SLOVENIA
23/ BENIN, GERMANY,
JAMAICA
27/ UK, LITHUANIA

SATISFACTORY

35/ AUSTRALIA,
BULGARIA, FRANCE, MALI
50/ ISRAEL
53/ BOTSWANA, CROATIA,
TONGA, USA
66/ MADAGASCAR
68/ ECUADOR

NOTICEABLE
PROBLEMS

75/ BRAZIL
76/ ARGENTINA
92/ MALAYSIA
93/ COMOROS

DIFFICULT
SITUATION

105/ INDIA, UKRAINE
133/ EGYPT
142/ CONGO DEM. REP.,
PHILIPPINES
146/ SINGAPORE
147/ RUSSIA

VERY SERIOUS
SITUATION

161-168/ SAUDI ARABIA,
IRAN, CHINA,
BURMA, CUBA,
ERITREA,
TURKMENISTAN,
NORTH KOREA

30
COUNTRIES

38
COUNTRIES

29
COUNTRIES

62
COUNTRIES

8
COUNTRIES

NON-GOVERNMENTAL ORGANIZATIONS SUCH AS REPORTERS WITHOUT BORDERS MEASURE LEVELS OF PRESS FREEDOM AROUND THE WORLD, AND ACCORD MUCH LOWER SCORES TO POLITICAL SYSTEMS THAT RELY ON THE CONTROL OF INFORMATION TO MAINTAIN THEIR LEGITIMACY.

JOURNALIST CASUALTIES IN 2007

- 86 JOURNALISTS AND 20 MEDIA ASSISTANTS WERE KILLED
- AT LEAST 887 ARRESTED
- 1,511 PHYSICALLY ATTACKED OR THREATENED
- 67 KIDNAPPED
- 528 MEDIA OUTLETS CENSORED

ALL THE NEWS THAT'S FIT TO DIE FOR

Journalism is a hazardous business in Iraq, where 153 journalists have been killed since the 2003 invasion, along with a further 54 media assistants (fixers, drivers, translators, technicians, security staff). But journalists can be in physical danger outside war zones too. More than 200 have been murdered in Russia since 1993, including the high-profile killing in 2006 of investigative journalist Anna Politkovskaya, known for her critical appraisals of the Putin government.

28   23   38   32   31   25   4

1997   1998   1999   2000   2001   2002   20

NUMBERS OF JOURNALISTS KILLED WORLDWIDE

SOURCES: Reporters without Borders: *Press Freedom Barometer*, *The War in Iraq*, and *Internet Enemies*

64

85   86

62

2004   2005   2006   2007

THE JOURNALISTS' MEMORIAL, PARIS, FRANCE

PRESS FREEDOM IN THE FUTURE

Restrictions on the press range from blatant censorship, to intimidation, kidnap, and murder. However, such hazards are not always the fault of governments. In 2007, a newspaper editor was killed in California by a bakery worker incensed over coverage of his company's financial state.

In Turkey the same year, Hrant Dink, editor of the bilingual Turkish-Armenian newspaper *Agos*, was murdered by a teenaged extreme nationalist. The killer objected to Dink's continued assertion of Turkey's responsibility for the genocide of Armenians in the early 20th century. To some extent, the state can be blamed for the political environment that produced this murder; "denigrating Turkishness" with reference to the Armenians was a charge on which Dink had been prosecuted three times and convicted once, ironically for an article in which he asked diaspora Armenians to abandon their rage against Turks.

The public thirst for instant news and dramatic film footage around the clock has made journalism ever more demanding and potentially risky, involving broadcasts by satellite from extreme circumstances as stories break, the "embedding" of journalists in armies for front-line coverage, and assignments into restrictive regimes for exposés. Essential equipment in such circumstances is no longer just the journalist's trusty notepad and pencil, but a videophone and bulletproof jacket.

ENEMIES OF THE INTERNET

THESE COUNTRIES IMPOSE CONTROL ON CYBERSPACE: **BELARUS, BURMA, CHINA, CUBA, EGYPT, IRAN, NORTH KOREA, SAUDI ARABIA, SYRIA, TUNISIA, TURKMENISTAN, UZBEKISTAN, AND VIETNAM**
CYBER DISSIDENTS: NUMBERS OF PEOPLE JAILED
**CHINA 60, VIETNAM 4, SYRIA 3
TUNISIA 1, LIBYA 1, IRAN 1**

WAR

Once seen as "the continuation of diplomacy by other means", war in the modern era has become hugely destructive. It is generally only considered when all else fails – though wars have been fought with distressing frequency even throughout the last 40 years. Majority opinion – and international law – still considers war to be legitimate in certain circumstances, although usually only when it involves resisting aggression.

In the first half of the 20th century, warfare shifted from being an essentially local affair to the global scale. And for most of the second half of that century the Cold War between the rival US and Soviet superpowers overshadowed the globe with the threat of nuclear Armageddon, while turning the state-level actors in local and regional conflicts into proxy Cold War warriors.

In the 21st century, the idea of a "global war on terror" is something different again, articulated principally by the US administration of George W. Bush. In this view, the biggest security consideration is the need to root out, wherever they may be in the world, the amorphous groups that foster instability in poorer countries and promote terrorism against the West. The most notorious such group, the militant Islamist al-Qaeda, for its part preaches a global jihad or "holy war", using terror tactics to strike into the heartland of its enemies with the ostensible aim of restoring the rule of a Muslim Caliphate.

TURNING AWAY FROM WAR

Some regions formerly riven by warfare – such as Western Europe – have seen countries turn instead to the integration of their economies and their militaries, a move that is likely to prevent open conflict for the foreseeable future. The NATO military alliance now fights wars a long way from its borders, attempting to isolate local threats to security before the instability can spread.

DEATHS IN CURRENT ARMED CONFLICTS

4,00

NUMBER OF WARS SINCE 1950

Data points: 13 (1950), 15 (1955), 12 (1960), 28 (1965), 31 (1970), 36 (1975), 37 (1980), 41 (1985), 50 (1990), 34 (1995), 35 (2000), 28 (20...)

DEATHS IN MAJOR CONFLICTS

AMERICAN CIVIL WAR 1861-65	620,000
BOER WAR 1899-1902	118,000
MEXICAN REVOLUTION 1910-20	200,000
CHINA 1917-28	178,000
CHINA 1928-37	406,000
WORLD WAR I 1914-18	15,000,000
WORLD WAR II 1939-45	72,000,000

SOURCES: AKUF & Institute of Political Science, University of Hamburg; Project Ploughshares 2007; Icasualties.org

0,000

DEAD IN THE DEMOCRATIC REPUBLIC OF THE CONGO SINCE 1990

2,000,000

DEAD IN SUDAN SINCE 1983

1,500,000

DEAD IN AFGHANISTAN SINCE 1978

500,000
DEAD IN UGANDA SINCE 1987

DEATHS IN POST-WWII CONFLICTS

400,000
DEAD IN SOMALIA SINCE 1988

KOREAN WAR 1950-53	2,800,000	
RWANDA/BURUNDI 1959-95	1,350,000	
ETHIOPIA 1962-92	1,400,000	
VIETNAM WAR 1965-73	1,415,000	
NIGERIA 1966-70	1,000,000	
BANGLADESH 1971	1,250,000	
CAMBODIA, KHMER ROUGE 1975-78	1,650,000	
MOZAMBIQUE 1975-92	1,000,000	
IRAN-IRAQ WAR 1980-88	1,000,000	
GULF WAR 1991	30,000	

400,000
DEAD IN SUDAN/DARFUR SINCE 2003

300,000
DEAD IN BURUNDI SINCE 1993

200,000 DEAD IN ALGERIA SINCE 1992

200,000 DEAD IN COLOMBIA SINCE 1964

150,000 DEAD IN PHILIPPINES/ MINDANAO SINCE 1971

120,000 DEAD IN ISRAEL/ PALESTINE SINCE 1948

100,000 DEAD IN SRI LANKA SINCE 1948

92,000 DEAD IN IRAQ SINCE 2003

IRAQ WAR FROM 2003

50,000 DEAD IN NIGERIA SINCE 1990

US/UK MILITARY DEATH TOLL	4105	
ESTIMATED IRAQI CIVILIAN DEATH TOLL	88,048	

40,000 DEAD IN PHILIPPINES SINCE 1969

30,000 DEAD IN CHECHNYA SINCE 1999

FIND OUT MORE: www.crisisgroup.org; www.flashpoints.info; www.icasualties.org; www.ploughshares.ca; www.iraqbodycount.org

103

WAR

WARS, FLASHPOINTS, AND PEACEKEEPERS

RUSSIA

GEORGIA
UNOMIG **142**

Chechnya
1999

Kosovo

AZERBAIJAN

UNMIK **2087**

ARMENIA

MIDDLE EAST

TURKEY   Kurdistan

UNTSO

CYPRUS
UNFICYP **917**

IRAQ
2003

AFGHA

LEBANON

IRAN

ISRAEL
Palestine
1948

Golan Heights

WESTERN
SAHARA

ALGERIA
1992

UNIFIL **13,225**

UNDOF **1046**

MINUSTAH **8810**

MINURSO **232**

SUDAN
1983

ERITREA

HAITI

CHAD   Darfur
2003

YEMEN

NIGERIA
1990

UNMIS **10,022**

UNMEE **1681**

SIERRA LEONE

LIBERIA

COTE D'IVOIRE

CENTRAL
AFRICAN REP

ETHIOPIA

SOMALIA
1988

COLOMBIA
1964

UNMIL **15,296**

CONGO
(DEM. REP.)
1990

UGANDA 1987

UNOCI **9205**

BURUNDI 1993

MONUC **18,357**

COMOROS

ZIMBABWE

NEW NUCLEAR THREATS

THE NIGHTMARE OF SUPERPOWER CONFLICT HAS RECEDED
QUITE MARKEDLY SINCE THE END OF THE COLD WAR IN THE
1990s. THE THREAT OF NUCLEAR WAR REMAINS, HOWEVER
– NOW USUALLY ENVISAGED AS ARISING FROM AGGRESSIVE
AND ERRATIC BEHAVIOUR OF LEADERS IN POWER-HUNGRY
EMERGING NUCLEAR WEAPONS STATES, OR TERRORIST USE
OF EASILY ASSEMBLED "DIRTY BOMBS".

SMART WEAPONS

ADVANCES IN WEAPON SOPHISTICATION NOW ALLOW GUIDED
MISSILES TO BE TARGETED WITH INCREASING ACCURACY, DOWN
TO THE LEVEL OF SPECIFIC BUILDINGS OR EVEN SMALLER
TARGETS. ENTHUSIASTS FOR SUCH "SMART WEAPONS" SEE THEM
AS POTENTIALLY AVOIDING THE MASSIVE LOSS OF CIVILIAN LIFE
EXPERIENCED IN WORLD WAR II – BUT THE MUDDLE OF BATTLE
REMAINS SO PREVALENT THAT SUCH NOTIONS HAVE TO BE SEEN
IN A REALISTIC PERSPECTIVE, WHERE PEOPLE EVEN GET KILLED
ACCIDENTALLY BY THE "FRIENDLY FIRE" OF THEIR OWN SIDE.

CURRENT ARMED CONFLICTS

1978	start date of conflict	1978
	over 2 million deaths	
	1-2 million deaths	
	500,000-1 million deaths	
	200,000-500,000 deaths	
	50,000-200,000 deaths	
	up to 50,000 deaths	
	flashpoints	
UN	UN peacekeeping forces and strengths deployed 2007	UN

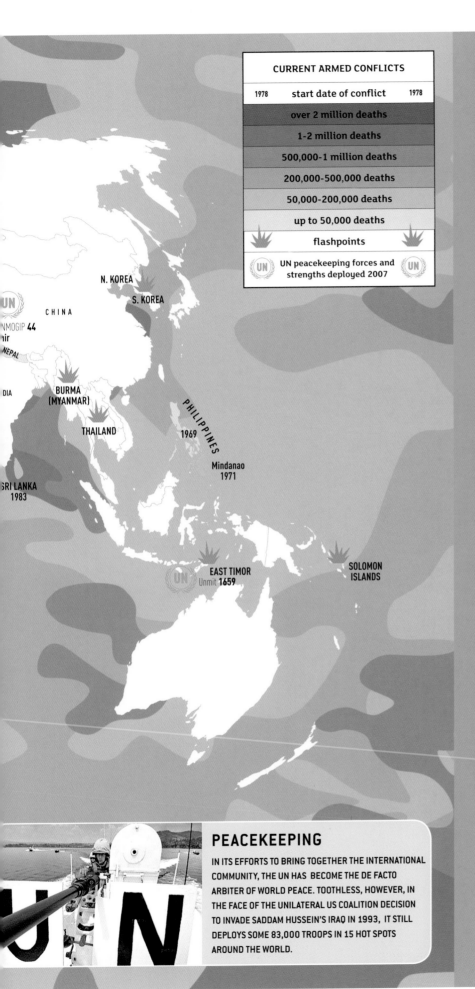

WAR IN THE FUTURE

Future wars will not be confined to conflicts based on terrorist threats (from a Western point of view) and neo-imperialism (from the perspective of some Muslims), though these terms may be exploited. Rather, the sources of many of the world's conflicts will remain local, and will be about territory, resources, and ethnicity.

The increasing availability of more basic arms and technology to any faction continues to fuel brutal civil conflicts and insurgencies, where civilians are still by far the biggest victims. The West has responded to this threat in a multitude of ways, including financial and other assistance to poorer countries and supporting UN peacemaking interventions, although its responsibility as the ultimate source of much of the weaponry should not be forgotten.

At the global level, old divisions have not completely broken down. And NATO, for all its recent expansion, cannot impose its peace on every country that may pose a future threat. A proposed US missile shield above Europe may be aimed at countering the threat of attack from Iran or North Korea, but one consequence of it has been to anger Russia severely. On an even wider scale, the threat of armed confrontation in space – for some time a largely commercial environment – raised its head again when China in early 2007 launched a ballistic missile to destroy a satellite.

PEACEKEEPING

IN ITS EFFORTS TO BRING TOGETHER THE INTERNATIONAL COMMUNITY, THE UN HAS BECOME THE DE FACTO ARBITER OF WORLD PEACE. TOOTHLESS, HOWEVER, IN THE FACE OF THE UNILATERAL US COALITION DECISION TO INVADE SADDAM HUSSEIN'S IRAQ IN 1993, IT STILL DEPLOYS SOME 83,000 TROOPS IN 15 HOT SPOTS AROUND THE WORLD.

A WORLD WITHOUT WAR

THE LEAGUE OF NATIONS (FORMED 1920), AND ITS SUCCESSOR, THE UNITED NATIONS (FORMED 1947), WERE BOTH ESTABLISHED IN THE WAKE OF GLOBAL CONFLICTS, WITH THE AIM OF AVOIDING THE REPETITION OF SUCH CATACLYSMS. IT HAS BECOME CLEAR, HOWEVER, THAT LOCALIZED ISSUES CAN RARELY BE SOLVED BY THE INTERVENTION OF GLOBAL ARBITRATORS OR PEACEKEEPERS. UNFORTUNATELY WAR SEEMS TO BE NOT JUST A "CULTURAL ACTIVITY", AS SOME HISTORIANS WOULD HAVE IT, BUT AN ENDEMIC ASPECT OF THE HUMAN CONDITION.

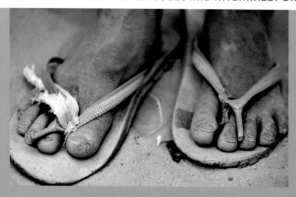

REFUGEES

Today's world has (officially) almost 9.9 million refugees. Millions of Palestinians have lived in refugee camps for decades; over two million Afghans live in huge camps, mostly in Pakistan – where they face further upheaval as the authorities move to close the camps and repatriate them. This pattern of exodus, privation, encampment, and – hopefully – eventual resettlement or return has been repeated across the centuries. That is why the post of UN High Commissioner for Refugees (UNHCR) was set up in 1950, in the wake of the bloody partition of India and the huge postwar European movements of refugees.

Encouragingly, decreasing numbers of new refugees are fleeing their countries. The total in 2006 of 117,000 was the lowest in nearly 30 years. But official refugees are only part of the story – because the UNHCR only places people in this category if they have fled persecution by crossing an international border. The most hideous "refugee" crisis of the 21st century, in Darfur, is mainly happening within Sudan – so its victims are not officially classed as refugees but as Internally Displaced Persons (IDPs). The Internal Displacement Monitoring Centre estimates there are 5.8 million IDPs in Sudan – and 24.5 million worldwide. The international community is under no legal obligation to help such people, but the UNHCR now provides care for 12.8 million of them.

- AT THE END OF 2006 THE NUMBER OF GLOBAL REFUGEES INCREASED TO 9.9 MILLION – THE FIRST RISE IN NUMBERS SINCE 2000.

- AT THE END OF 2006 THERE WERE 24.5 MILLION INTERNALLY DISPLACED PERSONS IN 44 COUNTRIES – LITTLE CHANGE SINCE 2001.

REFUGEES AND INTERNALLY DISPLACED PERSONS (IDP

1997-2006 END OF YEAR TOTALS			BY REGION 2006		
YEAR	REFUGEES	IDPs	REGION	REFUGEES	IDPs
1997	12,015,400	17,400,000	AFRICA	2,607,559	11,800,
1998	11,480,900	19,300,000	ASIA	4,416,502	5,800,
1999	11,687,200	21,300,000	EUROPE	1,733,705	2,800,
2000	12,129,600	21,200,000	CENTRAL AND SOUTH AMERICA	40,577	4,100,
2001	12,116,800	25,000,000	NORTH AMERICA	995,325	
2002	10,594,100	25,000,000	OCEANIA	84,039	
2003	9,680,300	24,600,000			
2004	9,559,100	25,300,000			
2005	8,394,400	23,700,000			
2006	9,877,707	24,400,000			

P TEN REFUGEE
OSTING COUNTRIES

TOP TEN REFUGEE
EXODUS COUNTRIES

06		2006	
KISTAN	1,044,462	AFGHANISTAN	2,107,519
AN	968,370	IRAQ	1,450,905
A	843,498	SUDAN	686,311
RIA	702,209	SOMALIA	464,253
RMANY	605,406	CONGO DEM. REP.	401,914
RDAN	500,229	BURUNDI	396,541
NZANIA	485,295	VIETNAM	374,279
	301,556	OCCUPIED PALESTINIAN TERRITORY	334,142
INA	301,027	TURKEY	227,232
AD	286,743	ANGOLA	206,501

REFUGEES

A WORLD DISPLACED: REFUGEES BY REGION

A snapshot of refugee populations around the world risks missing the point that the refugee picture is – almost by definition – an ever-moving one. In 2006 alone, over 700,000 former refugees returned home. Over 400,000 of these were in Asia, and most of the rest in Africa. Stateless people, however, cannot go home – they have none. The UNHCR counts 5.8 million of them, but other estimates run as high as 11 million worldwide. The 250,000 Biharis stranded in Bangladesh are a case in point. Rejected by the new state after its war of independence in 1971, because they had sided with Pakistan, they were equally unwanted, for ethnic, cultural, and economic reasons, in post-1971 Pakistan. Statelessness is not confined to poor countries. Estonia's citizenship laws require stringent language tests, leaving 160,000 ethnic Russians stateless there.

The nations neighbouring Sudan's southern borders are bearing the brunt of Sudan's ethnic conflicts. Kakuma in Kenya is the world's largest refugee camp, a temporary city in the desert for some 95,000. Within Sudan, Darfur Gereida (above) is the world's largest IDP camp, with a population of 120,000.

North America
Total: 716,806
190,295 / 526,511

Western Europe
Total: 1,818,850
232,727 / 21 / 30,625 / 1,555,477

Eastern Eur
Total: 2,900,
1,051,143 / 410

North Africa
Total: 239,123
29,500 / 13,472 / 196,151

Central and South America
Total: 713,070
37,749 / 10,843 / 53 / 200,000 / 464,425

West Africa
Total: 1,031,030
269,778 / 377,167 / 278,861 / 27,316 / 77,908

Central Africa
Total: 1,359,175
119,019 / 35,003 / 11,500 / 1,193,653

Southern Africa
Total: 434,427
53,824 / 151,966 / 228,637

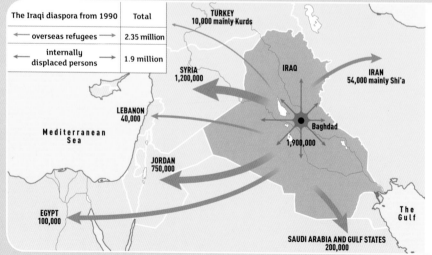

The Iraqi diaspora from 1990	Total
⟵ overseas refugees	2.35 million
⟷ internally displaced persons	1.9 million

TURKEY
10,000 mainly Kurds

SYRIA
1,200,000

IRAQ

IRAN
54,000 mainly Shi'a

LEBANON
40,000

Baghdad
1,900,000

Mediterranean Sea

JORDAN
750,000

EGYPT
100,000

The Gulf

SAUDI ARABIA AND GULF STATES
200,000

THE IRAQI DIASPORA

First the Jews, then the Palestinians, then the Kurds, now Iraqis; the pattern of Middle Eastern peoples forced to leave their homes and homelands shifts as new power bases emerge.

SOURCES: UNHCR Statistical Online Population Database (Data extracted May 2 2007 and January 23 2008)

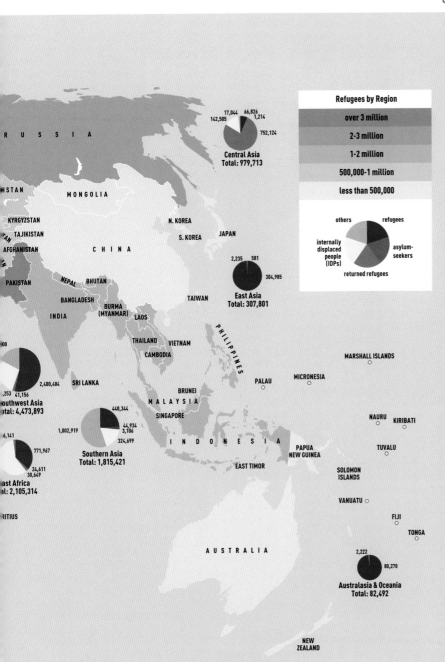

Refugees by Region

| over 3 million |
| 2-3 million |
| 1-2 million |
| 500,000-1 million |
| less than 500,000 |

others   refugees
internally
displaced
people
(IDPs)   asylum-
seekers
returned refugees

Central Asia
Total: 979,713
17,044 66,826
142,505 1,214
752,124

East Asia
Total: 307,801
2,235 581
304,985

Southwest Asia
Total: 4,473,893
2,400,484
...,253 41,156

Southern Asia
Total: 1,815,421
440,344
1,002,919
44,934
3,106
324,699
6,141

...ast Africa
...l: 2,105,314
771,967
24,611
30,649

Australasia & Oceania
Total: 82,492
2,222
80,270

CLIMATE REFUGEES

It is a perennial problem for prosperous countries to distinguish "genuine" refugees, with a right to asylum, from so-called "economic migrants", who have no such rights although their plight may be as desperate. Already the USA and most of Europe's prosperous countries are struggling to tighten their borders against a feared (and sometimes actual) influx of the latter, while regularizing the status of those who have already "got in".

The consequences of climate change threaten to make this problem unimaginably more acute. According to one estimate, by the middle of the century, 200 million people may become permanently displaced due to rising sea levels, heavier floods, and more intense droughts. Even the world's most prosperous countries will not be immune to these issues – but, by every projection, climate stress will hit hardest of all in the developing world. The most authoritative assessment of its impact to date, in social and economic rather than just meteorological terms, is the review commissioned by the UK government from Sir Nicholas Stern in 2006. According to the Stern Review, with global warming of 3 or 4°C, rising sea levels will result in tens or even hundreds of millions more people flooded each year. Coastal Asia (especially Bangladesh and Vietnam) faces particularly acute problems, along with small islands in the Caribbean and the Pacific, and large coastal cities, such as Tokyo, New York, Cairo, and London. Accelerated desertification and volatility of seasonal monsoons risk creating famine on an unprecedented scale, driving already poor populations to seek some means of livelihood elsewhere, and swelling the number of "climate refugees" desperately heading for the global North.

COLOMBIA'S DISPLACED

With almost four million people fleeing gang-controlled rural areas for the (relative) safety of Colombia's cities, a demographic shift of massive proportions is occurring unannounced. With a national population of some 46 million, one in every 12 Colombians is an IDP.

THE TRADE IN PEOPLE

TRAFFICKING

The biggest illegal trafficking businesses today are in people and narcotics. For the operators, high risks and complex logistics are offset by the huge amounts of money at stake – attracting the involvement of the world's most powerful organized crime groups. The trade in cocaine trafficking into Europe, for example, is now largely controlled by the Calabria-based 'Ndrangheta through its close ties with Colombian drug cartels.

Human trafficking preys both on would-be immigrants (who pay extortionate sums to be taken illegally across national borders), and on targets who are duped, doped, or conned by offers of work, taken abroad, and then enslaved, by the sex trade, but sometimes for domestic purposes. Women and girls are the main targets of trafficking for domestic slave labour, prostitution, or with very young children, adoption. The people smugglers' "clients" are also highly vulnerable to exploitation due to their lack of legal travel documents.

THE TRADE IN PEOPLE

- 800,000 PEOPLE A YEAR ARE TAKEN ILLEGALLY ACROSS NATIONAL BORDERS BY THE HUMAN TRAFFICKING INDUSTRY, AND MILLIONS MORE ARE TRAFFICKED WITHIN THEIR OWN COUNTRIES.
- 80% OF TRANSNATIONAL TRAFFICKING VICTIMS ARE FEMALE AND UP TO 50% ARE MINORS.
- 87% OF CASES INVOLVE THE VICTIMS ENDING UP BEING SUBJECTED TO SEXUAL EXPLOITATION.
- 28% OF CASES INVOLVE THE VICTIMS ENDING UP BEING SUBJECTED TO FORCED LABOUR.
- ANNUAL PROFITS REACH UP TO US$32 BILLION.

PACKAGE PRICES FOR HUMAN SMUGGLING

MOROCCO TO MELILLA & CEUTA	LAND	US$600
SENEGAL TO CANARY ISLANDS	SEA	US$1000
MOROCCO TO SPAIN	SEA	US$1200
MOROCCO TO CANARY ISLANDS	SEA	US$1900
LIBYA TO ITALY	SEA	US$2500
PAKISTAN TO AFRICA TO EUROPE	AIR/LAND/SEA	US$15,000

SOURCES: US Dept of State: *Trafficking in Persons Report* (2007); UNODC: *Trafficking in Persons: Global Patterns*

INCIDENCE OF PEOPLE TRAFFICKING – BY COUNTRIES OF ORIGIN, TRANSIT, AND DESTINATION

	ORIGIN	TRANSIT	DESTINATION		ORIGIN	TRANSIT	DESTINATION
THAILAND	VERY HIGH	VERY HIGH	VERY HIGH	MEXICO	HIGH		
ALBANIA	VERY HIGH	VERY HIGH		MOROCCO	HIGH		
BULGARIA	VERY HIGH	VERY HIGH		NEPAL	HIGH		
ROMANIA	VERY HIGH	HIGH		PHILIPPINES	HIGH		
UKRAINE	VERY HIGH	HIGH		UZBEKISTAN	HIGH		
CHINA	VERY HIGH		HIGH	VIETNAM	HIGH		
BELARUS	VERY HIGH			ITALY		VERY HIGH	VERY HIGH
LITHUANIA	VERY HIGH			BELGIUM		HIGH	VERY HIGH
MOLDOVA	VERY HIGH			GERMANY		HIGH	VERY HIGH
NIGERIA	VERY HIGH			GREECE		HIGH	VERY HIGH
RUSSIA	VERY HIGH			TURKEY		HIGH	VERY HIGH
POLAND	HIGH	VERY HIGH	HIGH	BOSNIA & HERZEGOVINA		HIGH	HIGH
HUNGARY	HIGH	VERY HIGH		FRANCE		HIGH	HIGH
CZECH REPUBLIC	HIGH	HIGH	HIGH	SERBIA		HIGH	HIGH
BURMA (MYANMAR)	HIGH	HIGH		MACEDONIA		HIGH	
SLOVAKIA	HIGH	HIGH		MONTENEGRO		HIGH	
CAMBODIA	HIGH		HIGH	ISRAEL			VERY HIGH
INDIA	HIGH		HIGH	JAPAN			VERY HIGH
PAKISTAN	HIGH		HIGH	NETHERLANDS			VERY HIGH
ARMENIA	HIGH			USA			VERY HIGH
BANGLADESH	HIGH			AUSTRALIA			HIGH
BENIN	HIGH			AUSTRIA			HIGH
BRAZIL	HIGH			CANADA			HIGH
COLOMBIA	HIGH			CYPRUS			HIGH
DOMINICAN REPUBLIC	HIGH			DENMARK			HIGH
ESTONIA	HIGH			HONG KONG			HIGH
GEORGIA	HIGH			SAUDI ARABIA			HIGH
GHANA	HIGH			SPAIN			HIGH
GUATEMALA	HIGH			SWITZERLAND			HIGH
KAZAKHSTAN	HIGH			TAIWAN			HIGH
LAOS	HIGH			UAE			HIGH
LATVIA	HIGH			UK			HIGH

PROSECUTING TRAFFICKERS, NOT VICTIMS

THE BIGGEST CHALLENGE IN BRINGING HUMAN TRAFFICKERS TO JUSTICE IS GETTING VICTIMS TO COME FORWARD AND GIVE EVIDENCE. INTERNATIONAL GUIDELINES HAVE BEEN LAID DOWN FOR THEIR PROTECTION, CARE, AND SHELTER, AS FOR ANY VICTIM OF A SERIOUS CRIME – BUT IT IS COMPLICATED BY THEIR FEAR OF PUNISHMENT FOR CONSEQUENTIAL CRIMES, SUCH AS LACK OF OFFICIAL DOCUMENTATION, OR PROSTITUTION.

PROSECUTIONS BY REGION	2003		2006	
AFRICA	50	1%	170	3%
EAST ASIA AND PACIFIC	1727	22%	1321	23%
EUROPE	2231	28%	2950	51%
NEAR EAST	1004	13%	295	5%
SOUTH AND CENTRAL ASIA	2805	35%	629	11%
WESTERN HEMISPHERE	175	2%	443	8%
TOTAL	7992		5808	

GLOBAL DRUG PRODUCTION 2005/6

PRODUCTION, METRIC TONS

OPIUM (2006)		6610
AFGHANISTAN	92%	
MYANMAR	5%	
OTHER	3%	
COCAINE (2006)		984
COLOMBIA	62%	
PERU	28%	
BOLIVIA	10%	
CANNABIS (2005)		42,000
AFRICA	26%	
NORTH AMERICA	23%	
SOUTH + CENTRAL AMERICA	23%	
ASIA	22%	
EUROPE	5%	
OCEANIA	1%	

GLOBAL DRUG SEIZURES 2005

LAW ENFORCEMENT AUTHORITIES CLAIM THAT THEY ARE SEIZING A GROWIN PROPORTION OF GLOBAL DRUG PRODUCTION. THE ACTUAL AMOUNT OF COCAINE SEIZED HAS DOUBLED IN THE LAST DECADE. THE RISE IN HEROIN SEIZURES HAS BEEN LESS DRAMATIC, BUT IS STILL OFFICIALLY BELIEVED TO HAVE MORE THAN KEPT PACE WITH THE INCREASE IN PRODUCTION, SO EIGH PER CENT LESS HEROIN IS REACHING THE STREET.

METRIC TONS (OR EQUIVALENT)

COCA LEAF	3209	
COCAINE	752	(ESTIMATED 42% INTERCEPTION RATE OF TOTAL TRAFFICKED*)
OPIUM	342	
KHAT	98	
HEROIN	58	(ESTIMATED 26% INTERCEPTION RATE OF TOTAL TRAFFICKED*)
MORPHINE	32	

42% OF GLOBAL COCAINE PRODUCTION AND 26% OF GLOBAL HEROIN PRODUCTION WERE SEIZED IN 200 CONSEQUENTLY NEVER MAKING IT TO END USERS.

[*THE GLOBAL INTERCEPTION RATE WAS CALCULATED (BY UNODC) ON THE BASIS OF A GLOBAL COCAINE PRODUCTION OF 980 MT IN 2005 AND GLOBAL SEIZURES OF 756 MT AT STREET PURITY, WHICH, GIVEN A GLO AVERAGE COCAINE PURITY OF 55 PER CENT IN 2005 (AS REPORTED BY MEMBER STATES TO UNODC IN THE A REPORTS QUESTIONNAIRES), WOULD BE EQUIVALENT TO PURE COCAINE SEIZURES OF SOME 416 MT.]

DRUGS PRODUCTION AND SEIZURES

COCAINE SEIZURES ARE HAPPENING CLOSER TO THE SOURCE OF PRODUCTION, WHICH IS ALMOST ENTIRELY IN SOUTH AMERICA. SEIZURES OF OPIUM AND OPIATE PRODUCTS – HEROIN AND MORPHINE – ARE MOSTLY HAPPENING ALONG TRANSIT ROUTES BETWEEN ASIA AND EUROPE, RATHER THAN NEAR THE MAIN CULTIVATION AREAS IN AFGHANISTAN AND BURMA (MYANMAR).

OPIUM SEIZURES BY COUNTRY 2005 (TOP TWO) METRIC TONS (OR EQUIVALENT)

IRAN	231	68% OF GLOBAL TOTAL SEIZURES (342 M TONS)
AFGHANISTAN	91	27% OF GLOBAL TOTAL SEIZURES

HEROIN SEIZURES BY COUNTRY 2005 (TOP FIVE) METRIC TONS (OR EQUIVALENT)

CHINA	8.9	15% OF GLOBAL TOTAL SEIZURES (58.4 M TONS)
TURKEY	8.2	14% OF GLOBAL TOTAL SEIZURES
AFGHANISTAN	7.1	12% OF GLOBAL TOTAL SEIZURES
IRAN	5.6	10% OF GLOBAL TOTAL SEIZURES
RUSSIA	4.7	8% OF GLOBAL TOTAL SEIZURES

MORPHINE SEIZURES BY COUNTRY 2005 (TOP TWO) METRIC TONS (OR EQUIVALENT)

PAKISTAN	22.2	69% OF GLOBAL TOTAL SEIZURES (32 M TONS)
IRAN	6.9	22% OF GLOBAL TOTAL SEIZURES

SOURCES: UN Office on Drugs and Crime (UNODC): *World Drug Report 2007*

COCA LEAF SEIZURES BY COUNTRY 2005 (TOP THREE)

METRIC TONS (OR EQUIVALENT)

PERU	1588	49% OF GLOBAL TOTAL SEIZURES (3209 M TONS)
BOLIVIA	902	28% OF GLOBAL TOTAL SEIZURES
COLOMBIA	665	21% OF GLOBAL TOTAL SEIZURES

COCAINE SEIZURES BY COUNTRY 2005 (TOP FIVE)

METRIC TONS (OR EQUIVALENT)

COLOMBIA	217	29% OF GLOBAL TOTAL SEIZURES (752 M TONS)
USA	175	23% OF GLOBAL TOTAL SEIZURES
VENEZUELA	59	8% OF GLOBAL TOTAL SEIZURES
SPAIN	48	6.5% OF GLOBAL TOTAL SEIZURES
ECUADOR	43	6% OF GLOBAL TOTAL SEIZURES

PREVENTION THAT CANNOT CURE

Border security makes good news copy – both its successes and its failures. Images like the Sangatte "reception centre" near the mouth of the tunnel from France to Britain speak both of its intensity and its human tragedy. No feasible barriers, however, can entirely hold back the powerful forces that drive the trafficking industry; demand for its "products", whether human or narcotic, and demand for its "services", in the case of would-be economic migrants seeking a better life. Demand for sex and drugs won't go away, so – unless it is met in other ways – improvements in policing and awareness can only hope to limit the trafficking. Interestingly, cannabis is now increasingly produced in Western countries rather than illegally imported, using hydroponics in hidden indoor growing rooms.

As for desperate would-be migrants, their global numbers seem likely to increase, especially with growing population pressures worldwide and the impact of climate change set to make the persistent rich/poor divide even more acute. There is a real danger that tighter immigration controls – and border enforcement – will therefore have the perverse effect of turning more people towards the "professional" services of the smuggling gangs.

TERRORISM

It is notoriously hard to define "terrorism". It has a political goal, though this may be as unspecific as striking back at a perceived oppressor. It is typically the weapon of the weak against the strong, and there is a truism that one man's terrorist is another's freedom fighter. Where "struggle" becomes terrorism is when it targets not just state personnel but civilians, to spread fear and intimidate. Methods include assassination, mutilation, targeted or apparently random bombings, blowing up planes, hostage taking, hijacking and, recently, "suicide bombings" – brought together with devastating effect in the 9/11 attacks in 2001. Many ideas have had to be re-examined since that day. It wrought unprecedented death and destruction in two nerve centres of Western power – the World Trade Center and the Pentagon. The US-led "war on terror", launched in response, saw the supposed power of the modern state unable to achieve swift and decisive results; critics also condemned the resort to methods at odds with the values of liberal democracy.

AIR HIJACKINGS

- AIRCRAFT HIJACKING GAINED A HIGH PROFILE IN THE 1960s WHEN PLANES WERE FORCED TO FLY TO CASTRO'S CUBA ("OFF LIMITS" FOR AMERICANS). NEARLY HALF OF ALL HIJACKINGS HAVE BEEN FOR REFUGEE ESCAPES RATHER THAN TERRORIST ATTACKS.

- FROM THE LATE 1960s, PALESTINIANS MADE HIJACKING A POLITICAL WEAPON, OFTEN USING THE PASSENGERS AS HOSTAGES TO DEMAND THE RELEASE OF JAILED FELLOW MILITANTS.

- HIJACKERS RARELY ACHIEVED THEIR OBJECTIVES AND OFTEN DIED AS ARMED FORCES STORMED GROUNDED PLANES. BOMBS IN LUGGAGE ON PLANES BECAME MORE FEARED AS A TERRORIST TACTIC – BUT 9/11 CHANGED THAT.

SEPTEMBER 11 2001

- **FOUR PLANES** SEIZED BY 19 HIJACKERS
- **US$4-500,000 SPENT** BY TERRORISTS IN PLANNING THE ATTACKS
- **1966 PEOPLE** TRAPPED AT OR ABOVE IMPACT ZONES IN TWIN TOWERS, ONLY 18 OF WHOM ESCAPED FROM SOUTH TOWER
- **2993 DEATHS** AND 24 MISSING PRESUMED DEAD
- **99 DAYS** BEFORE RUBBLE FINALLY STOPPED SMOULDERING
- **US$1.2 TRILLION** LOST IN VALUE FROM US STOCKS IN THE WEEK
- **30% OF OFFICE SPACE** IN LOWER MANHATTAN DAMAGED OR DESTROYED
- **US$23 BILLION** TO CLEAN UP SITE AND REPAIR DAMAGE

 SOURCES: Memorial Institute for the Prevention of Terrorism (MIPT): Terrorism Knowledge Base, www.tkb.org

TERRORISM

CIVILIAN DEATHS FROM TERRORIST ATTACKS
1990–2007

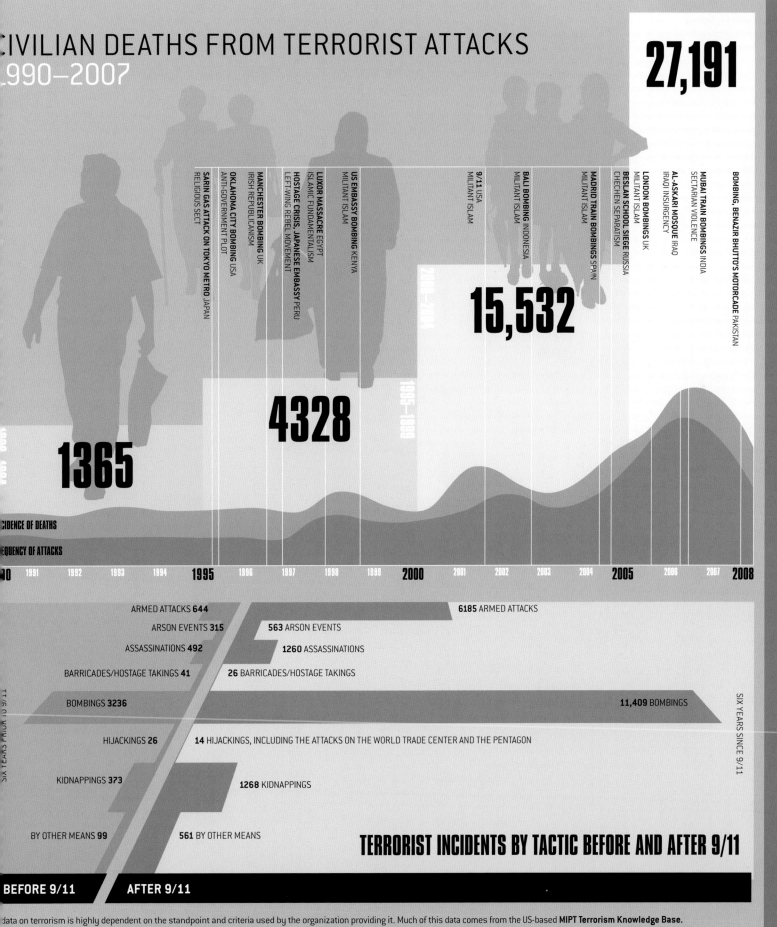

27,191

SARIN GAS ATTACK ON TOKYO METRO JAPAN
RELIGIOUS SECT

OKLAHOMA CITY BOMBING USA
ANTI-GOVERNMENT PLOT

MANCHESTER BOMBING UK
IRISH REPUBLICANISM

HOSTAGE CRISIS, JAPANESE EMBASSY PERU
LEFT-WING REBEL MOVEMENT

LUXOR MASSACRE EGYPT
ISLAMIC FUNDAMENTALISM

US EMBASSY BOMBING KENYA
MILITANT ISLAM

9/11 USA
MILITANT ISLAM

BALI BOMBING INDONESIA
MILITANT ISLAM

MADRID TRAIN BOMBINGS SPAIN
MILITANT ISLAM

BESLAN SCHOOL SIEGE RUSSIA
CHECHEN SEPARATISM

LONDON BOMBINGS UK
MILITANT ISLAM

AL-ASKARI MOSQUE IRAQ
IRAQI INSURGENCY

MUBAI TRAIN BOMBINGS INDIA
SECTARIAN VIOLENCE

BOMBING, BENAZIR BHUTTO'S MOTORCADE PAKISTAN

15,532

2000–2007

1995–1999

4328

1990–1994

1365

INCIDENCE OF DEATHS

FREQUENCY OF ATTACKS

1990 1991 1992 1993 1994 **1995** 1996 1997 1998 1999 **2000** 2001 2002 2003 2004 **2005** 2006 2007 **2008**

SIX YEARS BEFORE 9/11

ARMED ATTACKS **644** | **6185** ARMED ATTACKS

ARSON EVENTS **315** | **563** ARSON EVENTS

ASSASSINATIONS **492** | **1260** ASSASSINATIONS

BARRICADES/HOSTAGE TAKINGS **41** | **26** BARRICADES/HOSTAGE TAKINGS

BOMBINGS **3236** | **11,409** BOMBINGS

HIJACKINGS **26** | **14** HIJACKINGS, INCLUDING THE ATTACKS ON THE WORLD TRADE CENTER AND THE PENTAGON

KIDNAPPINGS **373** | **1268** KIDNAPPINGS

BY OTHER MEANS **99** | **561** BY OTHER MEANS

SIX YEARS SINCE 9/11

TERRORIST INCIDENTS BY TACTIC BEFORE AND AFTER 9/11

BEFORE 9/11 | **AFTER 9/11**

data on terrorism is highly dependent on the standpoint and criteria used by the organization providing it. Much of this data comes from the US-based **MIPT Terrorism Knowledge Base**.

TERRORISM

GROUPS, MOTIVES, AND IDEOLOGY

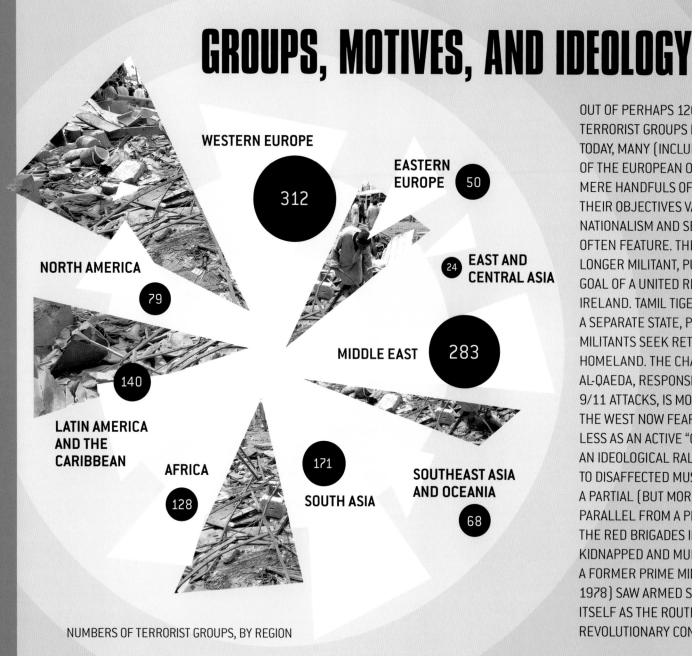

WESTERN EUROPE
312

EASTERN EUROPE 50

EAST AND CENTRAL ASIA 24

NORTH AMERICA 79

MIDDLE EAST 283

LATIN AMERICA AND THE CARIBBEAN 140

AFRICA 128

SOUTH ASIA 171

SOUTHEAST ASIA AND OCEANIA 68

NUMBERS OF TERRORIST GROUPS, BY REGION

OUT OF PERHAPS 1200-1300 TERRORIST GROUPS IN THE WORLD TODAY, MANY (INCLUDING MOST OF THE EUROPEAN ONES) HAVE MERE HANDFULS OF MEMBERS. THEIR OBJECTIVES VARY WIDELY. NATIONALISM AND SEPARATISM OFTEN FEATURE. THE IRA, NOW NO LONGER MILITANT, PURSUED THE GOAL OF A UNITED REPUBLICAN IRELAND. TAMIL TIGERS DEMAND A SEPARATE STATE, PALESTINIAN MILITANTS SEEK RETURN OF THEIR HOMELAND. THE CHALLENGE OF AL-QAEDA, RESPONSIBLE FOR THE 9/11 ATTACKS, IS MORE GENERAL. THE WEST NOW FEARS ITS IMPACT LESS AS AN ACTIVE "CELL" THAN AS AN IDEOLOGICAL RALLYING-CALL TO DISAFFECTED MUSLIM YOUTH. A PARTIAL (BUT MORE LOCALIZED) PARALLEL FROM A PREVIOUS AGE, THE RED BRIGADES IN ITALY (WHO KIDNAPPED AND MURDERED A FORMER PRIME MINISTER IN 1978) SAW ARMED STRUGGLE ITSELF AS THE ROUTE TO CREATING REVOLUTIONARY CONSCIOUSNESS.

EXTRAORDINARY RENDITION

This is a bizarre jargon term for a shadowy CIA practice, used mainly since 9/11, whereby terrorist suspects are held in (or taken to) jails outside the USA to extract evidence from them. The aim is to get round US safeguards on the use of torture, which carry little weight with interrogators in places like Egypt, Syria, or Jordan. For fear of international condemnation, most countries are anxious to avoid being implicated in any way.

SOURCES: Memorial Institute for the Prevention of Terrorism (MIPT): Terrorism Knowledge Base, www.tkb.org

CAMP DELTA, GUANTANAMO BAY

APPROXIMATELY 750 SUSPECTS HAVE BEEN HELD AT GUANTANAMO BAY. APPROXIMATELY 250 HAVE BEEN RELEASED, OR TRANSFERRED TO THE CUSTODY OF THEIR NATIVE COUNTRIES. SOME OF THESE WERE THEN QUICKLY RELEASED, SINCE THERE WAS NO EVIDENCE OF INVOLVEMENT IN ANY CRIMES. THE BUSH ADMINISTRATION CONTINUES TO CLASSIFY MANY OF THESE RELEASED DETAINEES AS "ILLEGAL COMBATANTS".

NUMBERS AND NATIONALITIES OF MEN HELD AT GUANTANAMO BAY DETAINMENT CAMP	
SAUDI ARABIAN	104
YEMENI	87
AFGHANI	77
PAKISTANI	63
MOROCCAN	18
CHINESE	15
KUWAITI	15
RUSSIAN	9
TURKISH	9
ALGERIAN	8
BRITISH	8
FRENCH	7
JORDANIAN	7
TUNISIAN	7
NATIONALITY UNCLEAR	27
OTHER	50
CURRENT TOTAL	**511**

THE CHANGING FACE OF TERROR

The psychological impact of 9/11 was heightened by the way it turned the industrialized world's own technology and systems against itself. Its immediate weapons were American airliners and collapsing prestige office blocks. Television caught the shocking images and imprinted them on the global consciousness. And al-Qaeda followed through with masterly exploitation of the media, keeping its cause in the headlines with filmed messages, kidnappings, and video clips.

9/11 also underlined the difficulty of stopping terrorists with no fear of death. Readiness to die had already become a cult in some militant circles. Tamil Tiger separatists in Sri Lanka in the 1980s and 1990s trained young recruits to strap explosives to their bodies, walk up to their targets, and press the detonator. Radical Islam gave suicidal action a religious underpinning, promising the rewards of martyrdom in the afterlife to those who undertook it. Suicide bombings by Palestinian militants have become chillingly familiar in Israel. 9/11 brought the phenomenon to the USA, and London later felt its impact in the bus and tube bomb attacks of July 2005.

In both 9/11 and the ensuing US-led "war on terror", divisions between states appear less significant than the rift between global "haves" and "have-nots" – the beneficiaries of the existing system, and the dispossessed with nothing to lose. At the same time, the US State Department still maintains its list of (and sanctions against) countries deemed to be "state sponsors of terrorism". For many years it had seven countries on it: Cuba, Iran, Iraq, Libya, North Korea, Sudan, and Syria. Iraq came off the list when the US-led invasion overthrew the Saddam Hussein regime, while a more co-operative Libya was officially taken off in 2006.

MONEY, THEY SAY, MAKES THE WORLD GO AROUND. IT ALSO
MAKES BILLIONAIRES AND BANKRUPTS AND ILLUSTRATES THE
YAWNING GAP BETWEEN THE HAVES AND HAVE-NOTS

FINANCE

The Tokyo Stock exchange/Container port, Hong Kong. Greasing the wheels of commerce.

MONEY
MAKING MONEY, INFLATION,
EXCHANGE RATES, GOLD
RESERVES, HOW WE PAY

WEALTH
THE RICHEST/THE POOREST,
LIVING BELOW THE POVERTY
LINE, RICH LIST DONORS,
INCOME TAX

DEBT
NATIONAL DEBT, LIVING
BEYOND OUR MEANS, STUDENT
DEBT, THE CREDIT CRUNCH

GLOBALIZATION
TRADING AROUND THE CLOCK,
GLOBAL BUSINESS, THE WTO,
TRADE BLOCS, UNFAIR TRADE

AND COMMERCE

WORK
WHO WORKS WHERE?
WORKING WOMEN, WHO
WORKS HARDEST? STRIKES,
SWEATSHOPS

ADVERTISING
ADVERTISING SPEND, THE TOP
AGENCIES, POPULAR MEDIA: TV
AND THE INTERNET

FAIR TRADE
LABELLING, PREMIUMS AND
GUARANTEES, COCOA, TEA,
COFFEE, BANANAS, MARKET
SHARES

ARMS
THE BIG SPENDERS,
MILITARY PERSONNEL, ARMS
MANUFACTURERS, GOING
NUCLEAR, WMD

ORGANIZED CRIME
TYPES OF ORGANIZED CRIME,
MONEY LAUNDERING,
TRAFFICKING, ID THEFT,
SYNDICATES

MONEY

The value of money rests entirely on what it can be exchanged for – whether goods or services, or the future promise of either. Different currencies, coexisting in international trade, once had their values fixed in relation to gold. The pound sterling had its own spell as the standard, then the US dollar. Now a system of floating exchange rates creates a constantly changing balance between the values of the main global currencies. Prices for globally traded commodities are generally quoted in dollars, however; several other currencies are tied to it, and it is accepted and even preferred in many developing countries. Its fastest-rising challenger is the euro, set up in 1999 in the world's largest-ever currency union (and coming into use as currency from 2002). Intended as the European Union's common currency, it was adopted by most member states, but not the UK, Denmark, or Sweden.

Some communities have developed alternative kinds of money for local use. The LETS – Local Exchange Trading Scheme – idea originated in Vancouver in 1983, to establish rates of exchange between goods and services offered by its participants. Despite a wide range of similar initiatives, LETS schemes remain confined to the fringe of today's highly money-oriented Western society.

THE SEVEN-CENT NICKEL

DUE TO RISING METAL PRICES, THE METAL IN A US NICKEL (75% COPPER, 25% NICKEL) IS NOW WORTH SEVEN CENTS – MORE THAN THE FACE VALUE OF THE COIN! A SIMILAR PROBLEM LED TO THE WITHDRAWAL FROM CIRCULATION OF THE OLD US CENT IN 1982, AND ITS SUBSTITUTION FOR A COIN OF A DIFFERENT METAL COMPOSITION. THE OLD CENT WOULD NOW COST OVER TWO CENTS TO PRODUCE. IN THE UK, "COPPER" COINS SUDDENLY BECAME MAGNETIC IN 1992, DUE TO THE SWITCH TO STEEL RATHER THAN BRONZE UNDER THE COPPER COATING.

MAKING MONEY

THE AMOUNT OF ACTUAL CURRENCY IN CIRCULATION CAN BE A REFLECTION OF A COUNTRY'S WEALTH, BUT IT IS ALSO STRONGLY AFFECTED BY THE AVAILABILITY OF CREDIT. NEW NOTES AND COINS MUST BE PRODUCED REPLACE WORN-OUT CURRENCY. IN THE USA, EACH $5 BILL HAS A LIFESPAN OF AROUND 15 MONTHS, WHIL THE LESS-USED $100 BILL AVERAGES OVER EIGHT YEARS, AND COINS CIRCULATE FOR 25 YEARS.

A FISTFUL OF DOLLARS

COUNTRY	VALUE OF BANKNOTES AND COINAGE IN CIRCULATION PER INHABITANT (US$)
JAPAN	5569
SWITZERLAND	4479
HONG KONG	2948
USA	2677
SINGAPORE	2205
EURO AREA	2192
SWEDEN	1546
CANADA	1346
UK	1213

EUROZONE USED SINCE:

1999	AUSTRIA, BELGIUM, FINLAND, FRANCE, GERMANY, IRELAND, ITALY, LUXEMBOURG, NETHERLANDS, PORTUGAL, SPAIN
2001	GREECE
2007	SLOVENIA
2008	CYPRUS, MALTA

PROSPECTIVE MEMBERS (AND POSSIBLE TARGET DATES FOR ADOPTION)

2009	SLOVAKIA
2010	ESTONIA, LITHUANIA
2011	CZECH REPUBLIC
2012	BULGARIA, POLAND
2013	LATVIA
2014	HUNGARY, ROMANIA

ELIGIBLE COUNTRIES THAT HAVE NOT OPTED FOR MEMBERSHIP: DENMARK, SWEDEN, UK

OTHER COUNTRIES USING THE EURO: MONACO, SAN MARINO, VATICAN CITY

OTHER COUNTRIES USING THE EURO WITHOUT FORMAL AGREEMENT: ANDORRA, KOSOVO, MONTENEG

CFA FRANC USED SINCE:

1945	BURKINA FASO, BENIN, CAMEROON, CENTRAL AFRICAN REPUBLIC, CHAD, CONGO, COTE D'IVOIRE, GABON, NIGER, SENEGAL, TOGO
1984	MALI
1985	EQUATORIAL GUINEA
1997	GUINEA-BISSAU

EASTERN CARIBBEAN DOLLAR USED SINCE 1965: ANTIGUA & BARBUDA, DOMINICA, GRENADA, ST. KITTS & NEVIS, ST. LUCIA, AND ST. VINCENT & THE GRENADINES

OTHER COUNTRIES USING US DOLLAR: EAST TIMOR, ECUADOR, MARSHALL ISLANDS, MICRONESIA, PAL

OTHER COUNTRIES USING EQUIVALENT CURRENCY WORTH ONE US DOLLAR: BAHAMAS, CUBA, PANAM

 SOURCES: Bank for International Settlements; World Bank: *World Development Indicators*

WORTHLESS MONEY

HYPERINFLATION IS A SPIRAL CREATED BY SHORTAGES OF GOODS ON THE ONE SIDE, AND AN OVERSUPPLY OF MONEY ON THE OTHER – OFTEN BECAUSE THE STATE PRINTS VAST QUANTITIES TO PAY ITS EMPLOYEES AND OTHER OBLIGATIONS. EVERYDAY NECESSITIES BECOME UNAFFORDABLE, AND PRICES RISE SO RAPIDLY THAT MONEY QUICKLY LOSES ITS VALUE – SO NOBODY WANTS TO HOLD IT, AND ITS INTERNATIONAL EXCHANGE RATE PLUMMETS, WHILE HARD-EARNED DOMESTIC SAVINGS ARE WIPED OUT TOO.

A DECADE OF HYPERINFLATION: 1993–2002   OVER 100%   OVER 1000%

		1993	1994	1995	1996	1997	1998	1999	2000	2001	2002
AFRICA	ZIMBABWE	27.59	22.26	22.59	21.43	18.74	31.82	58.52	56.00	132.00	139.00
	CONGO DEM. REP.	1986.90	23,773.13	541.91	492.44	198.52	29.15	284.89	550.01	313.72	38.09
	ANGOLA	1379.41	948.81	2671.79	4145.11	219.18	107.28	248.20	325.00	169.73	95.60
	SUDAN	101.38	115.40	68.38	132.82	46.65	17.11	15.99	5.69	5.85	8.30
	ZAMBIA	183.31	54.60	34.93	43.07	24.42	24.46	26.79	26.03	21.39	22.23
ASIA	MONGOLIA	268.15	87.58	47.00	36.59	9.36	7.49	11.62	6.24	0.93	5.18
	LAOS	6.27	6.78	19.59	13.02	27.51	90.98	128.42	25.08	7.81	10.63
FORMER SOVIET STATES	RUSSIA	874.62	307.63	197.47	47.74	14.77	27.67	85.74	20.78	21.46	15.79
	UKRAINE	4734.91	891.19	376.75	80.33	15.94	10.58	22.68	28.20	11.96	0.76
	BELARUS	1190.23	2221.02	709.35	52.71	63.94	72.87	293.68	168.62	61.13	42.54
	AZERBAIJAN	1129.04	1664.53	411.74	19.90	3.67	-0.80	-8.52	1.86	1.48	2.83
	ARMENIA	..	5244.2	175.95	18.68	13.96	8.67	0.65	-0.79	3.15	1.06
	GEORGIA	..	..	162.72	39.36	7.09	3.57	19.19	4.06	4.65	5.56
	KAZAKHSTAN	..	1877.37	176.16	39.18	17.41	7.15	8.30	13.18	8.35	5.84
	LATVIA	108.77	35.93	24.98	17.61	8.44	4.66	2.36	2.65	2.49	1.94
	LITHUANIA	410.24	72.15	39.66	24.62	8.88	5.07	0.75	1.01	1.30	0.30
EUROPE AND AMERICAS	TURKEY	66.10	106.26	88.11	80.35	85.73	84.64	64.87	54.92	54.4	44.96
	ROMANIA	255.17	136.76	32.24	38.83	154.76	59.10	45.80	45.67	34.47	22.54
	MACEDONIA	..	126.58	16.37	2.30	2.60	-0.10	-0.70	5.80	5.50	1.80
	BULGARIA	72.88	96.06	62.05	121.61	1058.37	18.67	2.57	10.32	7.36	5.81
	CROATIA	1500.00	107.33	3.95	4.30	4.17	6.40	3.46	5.27	4.77	1.70
	SURINAME	143.51	368.48	235.56	-0.70	7.15	18.98	98.93	59.4	38.64	15.49
	BRAZIL	1927.98	2075.89	66.01	15.76	6.93	3.20	4.86	7.04	6.84	8.45

SINCE 2003 THE PROBLEM HAS ONLY AFFLICTED ZIMBABWE. ITS OFFICIAL INFLATION RATES SINCE INFLATION EXCEEDED 100%:

2001	2003	2005	2007
132%	385%	586%	66,212%
2002	**2004**	**2006**	**2008**
139%	624%	1281%	100,580%

HYPERINFLATION TODAY

PERIODS OF WAR OR ECONOMIES IN TRANSITION (SUCH AS THE EX-COMMUNIST STATES IN THE 1990S) ARE COMMONLY ASSOCIATED WITH HYPERINFLATION. A MORE RECENT EXAMPLE IS ZIMBABWE, WHOSE EARLY 2008 INFLATION RATE OF OVER 100,000% CORRESPONDS TO A DOUBLING OF PRICES IN LITTLE MORE THAN A MONTH.

WORLD EXCHANGE RATES

INTERPLAY BETWEEN CURRENCIES HAS A HUGE IMPACT ON GLOBAL FINANCIAL VALUES. THESE FIGURES LOOK AT THE VALUES OF THE US DOLLAR, POUND STERLING, AND JAPANESE YEN IN RELATION TO THE EURO SINCE ITS INTRODUCTION IN 1999. INITIALLY ALL THREE ROSE AGAINST A WEAK EURO, BUT THIS TREND WAS SOON REVERSED. IN 2002–2004 THE DOLLAR FELL SHARPLY; ITS RECOVERY LASTED ONLY TWO YEARS, WHILE THE YEN FELL, AND BY 2008 THE POUND WAS LOSING GROUND TOO.

	US$1	£1	100 YEN
1999	0.848248	1.406272	0.747775
2000	0.99108	1.601025	0.973236
2001	1.061233	1.583531	0.923702
2002	1.106439	1.596934	0.83661
2003	0.957304	1.533742	0.803859
2004	0.794155	1.417535	0.74228
2005	0.740357	1.413927	0.720254
2006	0.845594	1.456664	0.716538
2007	0.75358	1.484781	0.633874
2008	0.680828	1.348982	0.610389

GOLD RESERVES

GOLD AND SILVER WERE USED FOR CENTURIES AS CURRENCY. GOLD IN PARTICULAR IS STILL AN IMPORTANT MONETARY ASSET, FREE OF ANY POLITICAL AFFILIATION AND REGARDED AS A LONG-TERM SAFE INVESTMENT AGAINST INFLATION. WORLDWIDE, CENTRAL BANKS TODAY HOLD ABOUT ONE-EIGHTH OF THEIR TOTAL RESERVES AS GOLD BULLION. MOST OF THE REST IS HELD IN FOREIGN CURRENCIES, WITH A GROWING NUMBER OF BANKS SWITCHING RECENTLY FROM DOLLARS TO EUROS AS THE SAFER INVESTMENT.

MANY PEOPLE IN DEVELOPING COUNTRIES STILL INVEST IN GOLD (OFTEN IN THE FORM OF JEWELLERY) TO STORE THEIR WEALTH. PRIVATELY-HELD GOLD IN INDIA IS WORTH US$920 BILLION – FOUR TIMES THE AMOUNT HELD IN FORT KNOX AND ABOUT ONE-FIFTH OF ALL GOLD EVER MINED.

COUNTRIES WITH HIGHEST GOLD RESERVES	GOLD (US$MILLIONS)	GOLD % OF TOTAL RESERVES
USA	173,047.0	76.1
GERMANY	72,817.0	64.1
FRANCE	57,208.9	57.1
ITALY	52,165.1	66.3
SWITZERLAND	27,447.8	42.5
JAPAN	16,280.6	1.8
NETHERLANDS	13,636.7	57.2
CHINA	12,191.3	1.1
TAIWAN	8999.7	3.3
SPAIN	8019.7	43.5
RUSSIA	8516.1	2.6
PORTUGAL	8139.5	79.9
INDIA	7611.4	3.9
VENEZUELA	7590.3	24.5
UK	6601.0	13.4
AUSTRIA	6143.0	45.5
LEBANON	6102.7	32.2

SOURCES: De Nederlandsche Bank; World Gold Council; American Bankers Association/Dove Consulting

OW WE PAY

US IN-STORE SPENDING:

CASH	33%
DEBIT CARDS	33%
CREDIT CARDS	19%
PAPER CHEQUES	11%
GIFT/PREPAID CARD	4%

US ONLINE SPENDING:

CREDIT CARDS	55%
DEBIT CARDS	25%
P2P SERVICE	9%
INTERNET CHEQUES	3%
PAPER CHEQUES	3%
MONEY ORDER	3%
PREPAID CARD/ACCOUNT	1%
OTHER	1%

US BILL PAYMENTS:

PAPER CHEQUES	49%
ONLINE BILL PAYMENT	24%
AUTOMATIC PAYMENT	21%
CASH	3%
MONEY ORDER	3%

VIRTUAL MONEY

Advances in technology and the availability of "plastic money" has cut to one third the proportion of transactions in US stores that involve actual cash. Americans generally prefer debit cards to credit cards, although the latter can be financially more efficient, either because of an "old-fashioned" dislike of the idea of debt, or simply out of fear for their self-control.

The Internet now offers efficient and immediate control over personal finance, with free and easy payments and transfers, and access to an expanding range of savings and investment products.

South Korea is a world leader in the use of mobile phones to pay for everyday goods. Two-thirds of owners do this already, and a quarter of all VISA cards are supplied as phones – customers "wave" their phone at the checkout. Up to 50 million people worldwide are expected to adopt "wave-and-pay" mobiles within a decade, with other flexible options including PIN-secured larger transactions and links to bank accounts. In the UK, an early example of payment by mobile phone was implemented by NCP car parks where, curiously, machines do not accept the otherwise ubiquitous debit or credit cards.

Novel payment systems will expand as people get used to the technology, assuming that electronic security improves. Electronic money is much cheaper for the state than printing and minting cash. One advantage of Singapore's pioneering SELT (Singapore Electronic Legal Tender) is the potential to eliminate banknote forgery. Australia is tackling the same issue with what is literally "plastic money" – banknotes made of polymers.

WEALTH

In global terms, the gulf in wealth between richest and poorest is immense. The top one per cent of the world's adult population owns 40% of the wealth, while the bottom 50% owns only one per cent.

Half the world's population struggles to live below the UN-defined poverty line (the equivalent of less than US$2 a day). Development aid directed at the even more desperate state of "absolute poverty", people with income equivalent to under US$1 a day, has had some success, and the UN's Millennium Development Goals promise to halve absolute poverty by 2015, but that would still leave 15% of the world's population trapped in this misery.

International comparisons of monetary wealth can seem confusing because of the wide variations in what things cost. These figures are therefore expressed in terms of "purchasing power parity" (PPP), a concept developed by economists to equate money to the amount of goods and services it will pay for locally.

Within societies, wealth and poverty are relative; one community's rich person is another's relative pauper.

GNH – GROSS NATIONAL HAPPINESS

The pursuit of happiness, including cultural, environmental, and spiritual well-being as well as material wealth, is official policy in the remote Himalayan kingdom of Bhutan. Measuring so-called Gross National Happiness (GNH) is a direct challenge to the almost universal practice of rating a country's economic success by growth in Gross National Product (GNP). GNP focuses on goods and services produced and consumed in terms of their material value alone, takes little or no account of the environmental damage it might cause, and simply misses out much of what makes us happy or unhappy. The need for a better measure, once confined to fringe "alternative" economics, is now being taken seriously by mainstream thinkers and politicians. Bhutan may not be alone for long in pursuing GNH.

THE VERY RICHEST

COUNTRIES WITH THE MOST BILLIONAIRES BY COUNTRY OF CITIZENSHIP

	NUMBER	TOTAL NET WORTH IN US$ BILLIONS
USA	415	1359
GERMANY	54	239
RUSSIA	53	282
INDIA	36	191
UK	29	80
TURKEY	25	36
JAPAN	24	64
CANADA	23	84
HONG KONG	21	111
BRAZIL	20	46

THERE ARE 33 BILLIONAIRES UNDER 40 YEARS OLD

THE WORLD'S YOUNGEST BILLIONAIRE IS ALBERT VON THURN UND TAXIS OF GERMANY

THE RICHEST COUNTRIES

BY AVERAGE INCOME PER ANNUM

LIECHTENSTEIN HAS THE HIGHEST AVERAGE NATIONAL INCOME:

US$85,444

1	LIECHTENSTEIN **US$85,444**	2	LUXEMBOURG **US$76,040**
3	NORWAY **US$66,530**	4	SWITZERLAND **US$57,230**
5	QATAR **US$53,762**	6	DENMARK **US$51,700**
7	ICELAND **US$50,580**	8	IRELAND **US$45,580**
9	USA **US$44,970**	10	SAN MARINO **US$44,607**
11	SWEDEN **US$43,580**	12	NETHERLANDS **US$42,670**
13	FINLAND **US$40,650**	14	UK **US$40,180**
15	AUSTRIA **US$39,590**	16	BELGIUM **US$38,600**
17	JAPAN **US$38,410**	18	GERMANY **US$36,620**
19	FRANCE **US$36,550**	20	CANADA **US$36,170**

SOURCES: World Bank: *World Development Indicators*; UN's World Institute for Development Economic Research (WIDER)

THE POOREST COUNTRIES

BY AVERAGE INCOME PER ANNUM

BURUNDI HAS THE LOWEST
AVERAGE NATIONAL
INCOME:

US$100

THE LOWEST AVERAGE INCOME PER ANNUM IN EACH CONTINENT		
EUROPE:	**MOLDOVA**	US$1100
LATIN AMERICA:	**BOLIVIA**	US$1100
OCEANIA:	**SOLOMON ISLANDS**	US$680
NORTH & CENTRAL AMERICA:	**HAITI**	US$480
ASIA:	**NEPAL**	US$290
AFRICA:	**BURUNDI**	US$100

WORLD AVERAGE US$7439

RUSSIA	US$5780
BRAZIL	US$4730
CHINA	US$2010
INDIA	US$820

HOW SOCIETIES SPLIT

Extremes of wealth and poverty within countries are most dramatic in some of the smallest economies.
Namibia's richest tenth of the population own 64% of the wealth and the poorest tenth own 0.5%. In Haiti the richest tenth own 48% while the poorest own 0.7%. In the world's major economies, the split looks like this:

COUNTRY	WEALTH OWNED BY RICHEST 10% OF POPULATION	WEALTH OWNED BY POOREST 10% OF POPULATION
BRAZIL	45%	0.9%
CHINA	35%	1.6%
INDIA	31%	3.6%
RUSSIA	31%	2.4%
UK	30%	2.0%
USA	30%	1.9%
ITALY	27%	2.3%
CANADA	25%	2.6%
FRANCE	25%	3.0%
GERMANY	22%	3.2%
JAPAN	22%	4.8%

LIVING BELOW THE POVERTY LINE

US$2

In most African countries a large proportion of the population lives below the UN-defined poverty line of an income of US$2 a day. More than 92% of Nigerians struggle to survive on less than this amount. The situation is almost as bad in South Asia: almost 90% of Cambodians earn less than US$2 a day. None of the major industrialized countries admit to having citizens that poor.

PERCENTAGES OF POPULATIONS LIVING ON LESS THAN US$2 PER DAY (PPP)

INDIA	80.36%
INDONESIA	52.42%
CHINA	34.89%
SOUTH AFRICA	34.07%
BRAZIL	21.15%
RUSSIA	12.14%
MEXICO	11.6%

WEALTH

THE RICH LIST 2008

In 2008 Microsoft founder Bill Gates was overtaken as the world's richest person by investment market specialist Warren Buffett. Gates ranked third, behind Mexico's communications guru Carlos Slim Helu. Of the 1125 billionaires on the list, 48 were aged under 40, the youngest being 23-year-old Facebook founder Mark Zuckerberg. Over 40% lived in the USA and 8% in Russia, the second largest contingent. Germany, India, and China were all well represented too, while new entrants to the list in 2008 included the first two black Africans, from South Africa and Nigeria.

RANK	NAME	CITIZENSHIP	AGE	NET WORTH	RESIDENCE
1	WARREN BUFFETT	USA	77	US$62BN	USA
2	CARLOS SLIM HELU	MEXICO	68	US$60BN	MEXICO
3	WILLIAM GATES III	USA	52	US$58BN	USA
4	LAKSHMI MITTAL	INDIA	57	US$45BN	UK
5	MUKESH AMBANI	INDIA	50	US$43BN	INDIA
6	ANIL AMBANI	INDIA	48	US$42BN	INDIA
7	INGVAR KAMPRAD	SWEDEN	81	US$31BN	SWITZERLAND
8	KP SINGH	INDIA	76	US$30BN	INDIA
9	OLEG DERIPASKA	RUSSIA	40	US$28BN	RUSSIA
10	KARL ALBRECHT	GERMANY	88	US$27BN	GERMANY

GIVING IT AWAY

BILLION-DOLLAR CHARITABLE DONATIONS AND PLEDGES IN THE USA:
Following in the footsteps of entrepreneurs-turned-philanthropists like Carnegie (1835-1919) and Gulbenkian (1896-1972), Warren Buffett has emerged as by far the biggest donor, ahead of Bill Gates.

YEAR	DONOR	AMOUNT PLEDGED	AMOUNT PAID	SOURCE OF WEALTH	RECIPIENTS
2007	LEONA HELMSLEY	US$4BN	—	HOTELS AND REAL ESTATE	Leona M & Harry B Helmsley Foundation
2007	BARRON HILTON	US$1.2BN	—	HOTELS	Conrad N Hilton Foundation
2006	WARREN BUFFETT	US$43.5BN	US$1.9BN	INVESTMENTS	Gates Foundation/Buffett Foundations/NoVo Foundation
2006	HERBERT & MARION SANDLER	US$1.3BN	US$1.3BN	FINANCE AND INVESTMENTS	Sandler Family Supporting Foundation
2004	BILL & MELINDA GATES	US$3.4BN	US$627MN	TECHNOLOGY	Bill & Melinda Gates Foundation
2004	SUSAN BUFFETT	US$2.6BN	US$2.6BN	INVESTMENTS	Buffett Foundations/Spirit Foundation
2003	JOAN CROC	US$1.9BN	US$1.9BN	FAMILY WEALTH	National Public Radio/Salvation Army and others
2002	WALTER ANNENBERG	US$1.4BN	US$1.4BN	PUBLISHING	Annenberg Foundation and others
2001	GORDON & BETTY MOORE	US$6.1BN	US$5.8BN	TECHNOLOGY	California Institute of Technology and others
2001	BILL & MELINDA GATES	US$2BN	US$2BN	TECHNOLOGY	Bill & Melinda Gates Foundation
2001	JAMES & VIRGINIA STOWERS	US$1.1BN	US$1.1BN	FINANCE	Stowers Institute for Medical Research and others
2000	BILL & MELINDA GATES	US$5BN	US$5BN	TECHNOLOGY	Bill & Melinda Gates Foundation
1999	BILL & MELINDA GATES	US$2.4BN	US$2.4BN	TECHNOLOGY	MIT, United Negro College Fund and others
1997	TED TURNER	US$1BN	US$1BN	MEDIA AND ENTERTAINMENT	United Nations Foundation and others

INCOME TAX

Most countries have progressive tax rates – so high earners pay higher rates of personal tax than those on a lower income. In a few countries, including Russia, Saudi Arabia, and Jamaica, everyone pays at the same rate. In some oil-rich Middle Eastern countries there is no income tax at all. Taxing the wealthy too hard is now widely seen as likely to "discourage enterprise" or just drive them abroad, so only three countries have rates of 50% or more on the highest incomes. The picture is complicated, however, by regional/municipal taxes in many countries, compulsory contributions for health care or social security (as in Australia or the UK), and special levies such as Zimbabwe's for tackling AIDS or Germany's for west-east solidarity.

THE TOP RATES OF PERSONAL INCOME TAX

NETHERLANDS	52%
AUSTRIA	50%
BELGIUM	50%
CHINA	45%
GERMANY	45%
FRANCE	40%
UK	40%
ITALY	39%
JAPAN	37%
USA	35%
TURKEY	35%
INDIA	30%
CANADA	29%
BRAZIL	27.5%
HONG KONG	20%
RUSSIA	13%

 SOURCES: Forbes.com: The World's Billionaires 2008; Indiana University, Center on Philanthropy: The Slate 60

HE WORLD'S MOST EXPENSIVE...

OUSE – US$122 MILLION
PDOWN COURT IN WINDLESHAM, SURREY, UK, WITH 103 ROOMS (ABOVE RIGHT)

CULPTURE – US$57.2 MILLION
000-YEAR-OLD LIMESTONE LION FIGURINE FROM MESOPOTAMIA, AUCTIONED IN 2007

IRTHDAY PARTY – US$27.2 MILLION
OTH BIRTHDAY PARTY HELD BY THE SULTAN OF BRUNEI IN 1996 (TOP)

AR – US$10 MILLION
930 BUGATTI TYPE 41 ROYALE KELLNER COACH, AUCTIONED IN 1987

VHEEL RIMS – US$1 MILLION
OUR WHEEL RIMS SET WITH 110,000 CARATS OF GEMSTONES, FREE BENTLEY ATTACHED

OMPUTER MOUSE – US$24,180
OLD SET WITH DIAMONDS, MADE BY SWISS MANUFACTURER *PAT SAYS NOW* (ABOVE LEFT)

OOK – US$30.8 MILLION
EONARDO DA VINCI'S *CODEX LEICESTER*, SOLD TO BILL GATES IN 1994

VINE – US$160,000
1787 CHATEAU LAFITE, SOLD IN 1985

TAMP – US$2.3 MILLION
WEDEN THREE SKILLING BANCO, YELLOW COLOUR ERROR, 1855

HONE NUMBER – US$3 MILLION
HE NUMBER **666 6666**, AUCTIONED IN 2006 IN QATAR

VEDDING CAKE – US$20 MILLION
HE DIAMOND CAKE, CREATED BY MIMI SO JEWELLERS AND NAHID LA PATISSERIE ARTISTIQUE

THE RICH AND THE POOR

Super-rich elites within countries are not a new phenomenon, but the concentration of wealth in their hands is increasing. Few countries buck this trend – and certainly not such emerging economic giants as India, or recovering giant Russia. In once-egalitarian China the super-rich have come to be regarded as exemplary models of "wealth creation", and high-profile billionaires campaign for cuts in their income tax.

The lifestyles of the wealthy are traditionally associated with huge mansions, luxury yachts, private planes, the finest goods, and access to the most desirable services. The less envied image is of the stressed, results-driven executive or entrepreneur whose waking hours are solely focussed on generating wealth.

Besides this negative personal impact, critics of an obsession with wealth also point to the exploitation of cheap human labour which it often entails, and to its environmental impacts too. Few people now believe that technology can unlock the door to infinite wealth creation without human labour. Fewer still believe that the earth's resources are inexhaustible or that we can just expect the planet to soak up industrial pollution without imposing rapidly rising costs.

Speculative writers have pondered the possibility of broadening the field of resources that can be plundered. Some rest their hopes on harvesting what lies on the deep ocean floor, or beneath the melting polar ice. Others look to the Moon, asteroids, and other planets. Either way, the wealth amassed on earth must ultimately be recycled through the economy, to create purchasing power in the markets on which wealth creation depends.

DEBT

In 2000, Times Square's 13-digit national debt clock had to be stopped at US$5.6 trillion as government debt actually began decreasing and it couldn't run backwards. But defici soon resumed and the clock is facing a new dilemma – it won't have enough digits if the debt total reaches US$10 trillion.

DEFINING DEBT

GOVERNMENT (OR NATIONAL) DEBT: THE AMOUNT THE GOVERNMENT OWES TO INDIVIDUALS, BUSINESSES, AND FOREIGN GOVERNMENTS

GOVERNMENT DEFICIT: THE TOTAL ANNUAL LOSS A GOVERNMENT MAKES BETWEEN ITS EXPENDITURE AND ITS INCOME (LARGELY FROM TAXES), PLUS INTEREST ON LOANS

EXTERNAL DEBT: THE AMOUNT OWED TO FOREIGN GOVERNMENTS, INTERNATIONAL INSTITUTIONS, AND INVESTORS

TOTAL DEBT: THE GOVERNMENT DEBT PLUS THE AMOUNT OWED BY BUSINESSES AND INDIVIDUALS AT HOME AND ABROAD

The US government owes over US$9 trillion – over half of it to "the public", that is to say to individuals and businesses (both US and foreign) and foreign governments; the rest is held by US government trust funds and the Federal Financing Bank. Interest payments on this huge national debt form the third-largest spending sector in the federal budget, behind defence and welfare payments, but well ahead of education and health. Moreover, federal government spending so greatly exceeds its tax take and other income that a hefty budget deficit adds to the debt each year, to the tune of US$163 billion in 2007.

Huge as it is, the government debt (or national debt) is just a fraction of the staggering US$44 trillion total debt owed by the USA as a whole This puts the USA way up at the top of the world's debt league – in which most leading industrialized countries also feature prominently. The USA also has the biggest external debt – over $10 trillion owed overseas.

Third World country foreign debts, although smaller in absolute terms, frequently amount to such large proportions of their GNP that a major part of national income is drained off to service the repayments and interest.

EMPIRE OVERDRAWN

THE US FEDERAL BUDGET DEFICIT IN 2004, AT US$413 BILLION, WAS THE LARGEST IN THE HISTORY OF THE WORLD. THE GOVERNMENT HAS CHIPPED AWAY AT THE ANNUAL DEFICIT IN SUBSEQUENT YEARS, BUT NOT BY ENOUGH TO BALANCE THE BUDGET, SO ITS DEBT GROWS EVER LARGER.

The USA is not the only nation to effectively run its budget on a credit basis. This is the model for most countries who operate on a free market economy. The problem – or art – is controlling various aspects of the national economy so that nobody notices, and nobody gets hurt. The key to this is controlling the balance of external and internal payments, and keeping a lid on inflation. Within a complex economy largely operating outside governmental control this is difficult enough, but with the growth of globalized corporations whose interests are subject to local market dynamics, the power of a state even as large as that of the USA is limited.

US$930
US$389BN
US$290BN
US$257BN
US$43BN
1940   1950   1960   1970

IN DEBT TO THE WORLD – THE TOP TEN EXTERNAL DEBTORS

IRELAND OWES US$1,392,000,000,000

JAPAN OWES US$1,547,000,000,000

SPAIN OWES US$1,591,000,000,000

NETHERLANDS OWES US$1,899,000,000,000

ITALY OWES US$1,957,000,000,000

FRANCE OWES US$3,461,000,000,000

GERMANY OWES US$3,904,000,000,000

UK OWES US$8,280,000,000,000

USA OWES US$10,040,000,000,000

TOTAL FOR ALL DEBTOR COUNTRIES

US$44,610,000,000,000

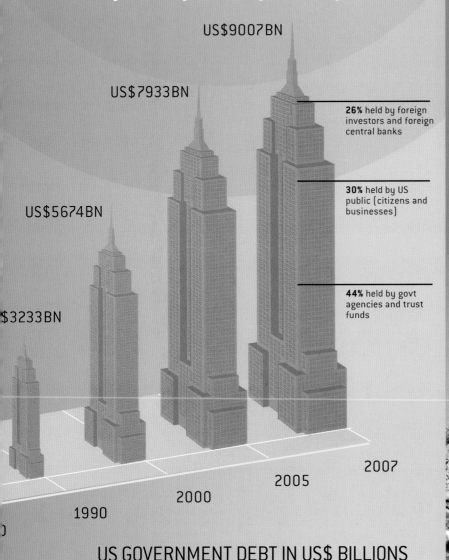

US$9007BN

US$7933BN

US$5674BN

$3233BN

26% held by foreign investors and foreign central banks

30% held by US public (citizens and businesses)

44% held by govt agencies and trust funds

1990 2000 2005 2007

US GOVERNMENT DEBT IN US$ BILLIONS

FOR EUROPEAN RECOVERY
SUPPLIED BY THE
UNITED STATES OF AMERICA

$4.5BN PAID

Britain finally paid off its post-World War II Marshall Plan reconstruction aid debt of US$4.5 billion to the USA in 2006.

PAYING OFF OLD DEBTS?

Taxpayers in the Philippines will be paying off the foreign debt run up by former President Ferdinand Marcos (below) until 2025.

$27BN OWED

OVER 24 MILLION TRANSACTIONS, WORTH £1.3BN, ARE MADE USING PLASTIC CARDS EACH DAY IN THE UK

LIVING BEYOND OUR MEANS: BRITAIN IS THE DEBT CAPITAL OF EUROPE

THE BRITISH ARE AMONG THE BIGGEST BORROWERS IN THE WORLD, WITH PERSONAL DEBT TWICE AS HIGH AS OTHER EUROPEANS. Spiralling house prices, low interest rates, and a stable economy have fuelled borrowing, together with easy access to credit, a cultural shift that has made debt socially acceptable, and relaxed insolvency laws.

The average UK household owes over £50,000, increasing at over £10 per day. The majority is home mortgage debt, but the remaining £9000 is largely unsecured, a third of it owed on credit cards. More than half the credit cards in Europe are in the UK, although as many as two-thirds of these do have their bills paid off regularly. Student loans mean graduates now leave university saddled with substantial debts. Far from rushing into the job market, many then delay seeking jobs while racking up further debt.

Debt appears to be part of the luggage of the human condition moving into the future. Easy credit helps sustain a boom in consumer spending. Reining it in could, conversely, provoke an economic downturn. A worrying increase in personal insolvencies, shows how easily this rising debt can become unsustainable, especially when an individual's work or personal situation changes.

BORROWING AGAINST A FUTURE
AVERAGE STUDENT DEBT AT GRADUATION

SWEDEN	US$24,050
USA	US$19,300
CANADA	US$14,750
UK	US$14,300
NEW ZEALAND	US$10,620
AUSTRALIA	US$10,615
NETHERLANDS	US$9,050
GERMANY	US$5,825

OWING MORE THAN YOU EARN

HOUSEHOLD DEBT, THE AMOUNT OF DEBT IN RELATION TO INCOME, HAS INCREASED DRAMATICALLY IN THE WORLD'S MORE SUCCESSFUL ECONOMIES IN RECENT YEARS

AVERAGE HOUSEHOLD DEBT IN THE UNITED STATES IS RUNNING AT 42% MORE THAN INCOME

GERMANY 102%

JAPAN 121%

UK 138%

USA 142%

SOURCES: UN: Millennium Development Goals; World Bank: World Development Indicators

AFRICA IN DEBT

[T]HE LIVE 8 CONCERTS IN JULY 2005, WATCHED BY AN ESTIMATED [A] BILLION PEOPLE, CAMPAIGNED FOR THE MAJOR DEVELOPED [C]OUNTRIES (THE G8) TO CANCEL DEBT AND IMPROVE AID, EDUCATION, [A]ND WELFARE TO THE WORLD'S POOR. THE G8 SUMMIT LATER THAT [M]ONTH AGREED A TOTAL DEBT CANCELLATION OF US$40 BILLION [F]OR AT LEAST 19 OF THE WORLD'S POOREST COUNTRIES, INCLUDING [1]3 IN AFRICA. THIS LEFT SIX VERY VULNERABLE COUNTRIES ON THE [C]ONTINENT IN A SERIOUS SITUATION.

BUYING THE FUTURE ON CREDIT

Much of the Third World's foreign debt was accumulated decades ago. This was partly because newly independent countries needed funds for infrastructure, education, and health projects. However, money also went on white elephant projects, on arms purchases, and into the pockets of corrupt ruling elites - saddling later generations with crippling debts from loans which never gave them any benefits.

Some campaigners want these "odious debts" to be written off, and partly blame the lenders for having made loans irresponsibly in the first place. Less radically, the UN's agreed Millennium Development Goals focus on making the debt of developing countries sustainable. For the poorest, this may well mean writing it off, but for others it can mean relating debt service costs to revenues earned from exports.

The US crisis in 2007 over excessive "sub-prime lending" (to people without good credit ratings) rebounded on the loan industry when these borrowers could not afford the repayments – and also highlighted how quickly and widely the repercussions can spread, in an age of interlinked financial markets. The dependence of lenders on global investment markets – like UK mortgage lender Northern Rock, whose crash provoked public panic and government intervention – indicates that the lenders are no more reliable than the borrowers.

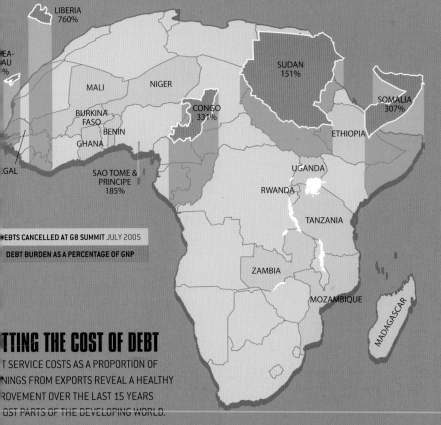

LIBERIA 760%

[GUIN]EA-[BISS]AU [...]%

MALI

NIGER

SUDAN 151%

SOMALIA 307%

BURKINA FASO

BENIN

GHANA

CONGO 331%

ETHIOPIA

[SENE]GAL

SAO TOME & PRINCIPE 185%

UGANDA

RWANDA

TANZANIA

ZAMBIA

MOZAMBIQUE

MADAGASCAR

[D]EBTS CANCELLED AT G8 SUMMIT JULY 2005

DEBT BURDEN AS A PERCENTAGE OF GNP

[CU]TTING THE COST OF DEBT

[DEB]T SERVICE COSTS AS A PROPORTION OF [EAR]NINGS FROM EXPORTS REVEAL A HEALTHY [IMP]ROVEMENT OVER THE LAST 15 YEARS [IN M]OST PARTS OF THE DEVELOPING WORLD.

[RATI]O OF DEBT SERVICING TO EXPORTS	1990	2004
[DEV]ELOPING REGIONS	16.4%	7.0%
[NOR]THERN AFRICA	39.8%	10.9%
[SUB]-SAHARAN AFRICA	11.5%	5.8%
[LATI]N AMERICA AND CARIBBEAN	20.5%	14.6%
[WES]TERN ASIA	4.7%	0.9%
[SOU]THERN ASIA	17.7%	14.7%
[SOU]THEASTERN ASIA	16.7%	9.2%
[OCE]ANIA	14.0%	1.2%
[COM]MONWEALTH OF [INDE]PENDENT STATES [TRAN]SITION COUNTRIES	3.9%	5.5%
[SOU]THEASTERN EUROPE	9.4%	8.9%

TO FIND OUT MORE: www.creditaction.org.uk; www.educational policy.org; www.makepovertyhistory.org; www.jubileedebtcampaign.org.uk

131

GLOBALIZATION

It's a 24/7, joined-up world. The global market place conforms to both the economic logic of capitalism, and the rules established by intergovernmental pacts to regulate it. The underlying principles are the free movement of capital, labour, and materials. The public at large distrust it, but buy into it, in much the same way that they use their large supermarket but prefer their corner shop. The Internet and communications revolution help take trade and knowledge transfers further beyond the scope of national restriction. Countries dare not lag behind in dismantling protective barriers, for fear of losing competitive advantage to their neighbours.

Over the years much manufacturing industry, once concentrated in the developed economies of the West, has moved to the growing Tiger economies of Southeast Asia and Latin America, and now to China with its vast resources of cheap labour. Fierce global competition leaves the West little option but to cut costs, by employing migrants on low wages or outsourcing work to cheaper locations. Advances in technology have made it possible for many jobs to be done anywhere in the world. Most recently India has become a huge outsourcing market, not only for call centres, but also for many highly-skilled professions, as its well-educated population can be paid prices a tenth of those in the West.

MADE IN CHINA

80% OF ALL TOYS
50% OF ALL SHOES AND TEXTILES
40% OF ALL LAPTOP COMPUTERS
38% OF ALL MOBILE PHONES
32% OF ALL FURNITURE

New York

Paris

Moscow

Beijing

Sydney

TRADING ROUND THE CLOCK: THE WORLD'S MAJOR STOCK MARKETS

IT IS SAID THAT THE WORLD'S FINANCIAL MARKETS NEVER SLEEP, AND CERTAINLY WITH LONGER STOCK EXCHANGE TRADING HOURS, AND 24/7 TRADING ON FOREIGN CURRENCY MARKETS, THERE ARE ALWAYS TRADERS AWAKE AND BUSY SOMEWHERE AROUND THE GLOBE.

STOCK EXCHANGE	TRADING HOURS (GMT)	COMPANIES (% FOREIGN)	MARKET VALUE	TOTAL SHARE TURNOVER
AUSTRALIAN SECURITIES EXCHANGE	00:00–6:00 HRS	2002 (4%)	US$1450BN	US$1000BN
TOKYO STOCK EXCHANGE	00:00–02:00 and 03:30–06:00 HRS	2415 (1%)	US$4630BN	US$5450BN
SHANGHAI STOCK EXCHANGE	01:30–03:30 and 05:00–07:00 HRS	860 (0%)	US$3020BN	US$3560BN
HONG KONG STOCK EXCHANGE	03:00–08:00 HRS	1240 (1%)	US$2970BN	US$1700BN
MILAN STOCK EXCHANGE	07:00–16:30 HRS	306 (2%)	US$1130BN	US$1980BN
LONDON STOCK EXCHANGE	08:00–16:30 HRS	3300 (22%)	US$4210BN	US$9140BN
MADRID STOCK EXCHANGE	08:00–16:35 HRS	3547 (1%)	US$1830BN	US$2490BN
FRANKFURT STOCK EXCHANGE	08:00–19:00 HRS	868 (12%)	US$2120BN	US$3640BN
NASDAQ	14:30–21:00 HRS	3064 (11%)	US$4390BN	US$12,400BN
NYSE	14:30–21:00 HRS	2296 (18%)	US$2070BN	US$28,700BN

Many companies involved in international business the world over also expect their employees to work outside their own countries' normal 9-5 hours: some work on Eastern Daylight Time if the USA is their main focus, but many multinationals work on GMT as the "middle zone" between Asia and America.

GLOBAL BUSINESS

NEITHER OF THE ICONIC GIANTS OF GLOBALIZATION, MCDONALD'S AND MICROSOFT, ACTUALLY MAKE IT INTO THE LIST OF THE WORLD'S TEN LARGEST CORPORATIONS. IT IS DOMINATED BY THE OIL AND AUTOMOBILE INDUSTRIES, BUT HEADED BY WAL-MART WHOSE STAGGERING US$351 BILLION REVENUE IS ALMOST SEVEN TIMES THAT OF MICROSOFT, AND MORE THAN THE COMBINED GNP OF THE WORLD'S 82 POOREST COUNTRIES.

COMPANY	SECTOR	US$ BILLION REVENUE	EMPLOYEES	COUNTRIES OF OPERATION
WAL-MART STORES USA	RETAIL	351	1,900,000	6900 STORES IN 14 COUNTRIES
EXXON MOBIL USA	OIL & GAS	347	106,400	35,000 SERVICE STATIONS IN 100 COUNTRIES
ROYAL DUTCH SHELL NETHERLANDS/UK	OIL & GAS	319	108,000	46,000 SERVICE STATIONS IN 90 COUNTRIES
BP UK	OIL & GAS	274	97,000	24,600 SERVICE STATIONS IN 100 COUNTRIES
GENERAL MOTORS USA	MOTOR VEHICLES	207	280,000	FACTORIES IN 33 COUNTRIES; VEHICLES MARKETED WORLDWIDE
TOYOTA MOTOR JAPAN	MOTOR VEHICLES	205	299,394	FACTORIES IN 23 COUNTRIES; VEHICLES MARKETED IN 170 COUNTRIES
CHEVRON USA	OIL & GAS	201	62,500	25,800 SERVICE STATIONS IN 74 COUNTRIES
CONOCOPHILLIPS USA	OIL & GAS	172	38,400	20,000 SERVICE STATIONS IN 40 COUNTRIES
TOTAL FRANCE	OIL & GAS	168	95,070	17,000 SERVICE STATIONS IN 130 COUNTRIES
GENERAL ELECTRIC USA	TECHNOLOGY, MEDIA, FINANCIAL SERVICES	168	319,000	OPERATES IN MORE THAN 100 COUNTRIES

GLOBALIZATION INDEX

WARWICK UNIVERSITY'S CENTRE FOR THE STUDY OF GLOBALIZATION AND REGIONALIZATION (CSGR) RANKS 103 COUNTRIES BASED ON ECONOMIC, SOCIAL, AND POLITICAL FACTORS. ECONOMIC VARIABLES LOOK AT TRADE, INVESTMENT, AND INCOME; SOCIAL VARIABLES INCLUDE IMMIGRATION, OVERSEAS REMITTANCES, TOURIST ARRIVALS, LEVELS OF COMMUNICATION, AND CULTURE; POLITICAL VARIABLES INCLUDE LEVELS OF DIPLOMATIC REPRESENTATION AND MEMBERSHIP OF INTERNATIONAL ORGANIZATIONS.

	OVERALL GLOBALIZATION INDEX	ECONOMIC GLOBALIZATION INDEX	SOCIAL GLOBALIZATION INDEX	POLITICAL GLOBALIZATION INDEX
SINGAPORE	1	3	2	93
BELGIUM	2	7	14	7
CANADA	3	36	7	6
UK	4	34	11	5
USA	5	74	18	2
AUSTRIA	6	28	6	12
SWEDEN	7	43	9	11
SWITZERLAND	8	32	4	25
FRANCE	9	45	28	1
DENMARK	10	58	10	17
IRELAND	11	5	20	21
GERMANY	12	29	22	9
ITALY	13	63	32	10
MALAYSIA	14	6	42	15
AUSTRALIA	16	108	15	41
RUSSIA	19	35	68	3
JAPAN	21	98	33	23
CHINA	23	25	96	4
INDIA	34	42	113	13
BRAZIL	46	86	77	31

FIND OUT MORE: www2.warwick.ac.uk/fac/soc/csgr/index; www.worldbank.org/globalization; www.globalpolicy.org; www.weforum.org

133

WORLD TRADE ORGANIZATION MEMBERSHIP

MEMBER STATES	
1995	**110 STATES ARE MEMBERS**
1996	**16 MORE STATES JOIN**
1997	**CONGO, CONGO DEM. REP., MONGOLIA, PANAMA**
1998	**KYRGYZSTAN**
1999	**ESTONIA, LATVIA**
2000	**ALBANIA, CROATIA, GEORGIA, JORDAN, OMAN**
2001	**CHINA, LITHUANIA, MOLDOVA**
2002	**TAIWAN**
2003	**ARMENIA, MACEDONIA**
2004	**CAMBODIA, NEPAL**
2005	**SAUDI ARABIA**
2007	**TONGA, VIETNAM**
2008	**CAPE VERDE, UKRAINE**

THE WTO IS THE INTERNATIONAL BODY DEALING WITH THE RULES OF TRADE BETWEEN COUNTRIES. IT CAME INTO BEING IN 1995, A SUCCESSOR TO THE GATT (GENERAL AGREEMENT OF TARIFFS AND TRADE), AND NOW 151 COUNTRIES ARE MEMBERS. ITS MAIN AIM IS SIMPLY TO REMOVE THE BARRIERS TO TRADE, SUCH AS EMBARGOES, IMPORT TAXES, AND OTHER TRADE RESTRICTIONS. MOST NON-MEMBERS ARE LESS-PROSPEROUS COUNTRIES, THOUGH A FEW MAJOR ECONOMIES, MOST NOTABLY RUSSIA, ARE STILL NEGOTIATING TO JOIN.

APPLICATIONS IN PROGRESS INCLUDE:
ALGERIA, IRAN, IRAQ, LIBYA, RUSSIA
NON-MEMBERS INCLUDE: CUBA, NORTH KOREA, SYRIA

TRADE BLOCS

TRADE BLOCS NOW COVER LARGE AREAS OF THE WORLD, WITH NEIGHBOURING COUNTRIES GROUPING TOGETHER TO ALLOW THE FREE MOVEMENT OF GOODS BETWEEN THEM. THE LEVEL OF ECONOMIC INTEGRATION VARIES, FROM SIMPLY BEING A FREE TRADE AREA, THROUGH THE EXISTENCE OF A CUSTOMS UNION OR SINGLE MARKET, TO THE SHARING OF A SINGLE CURRENCY. THEY CAN ALSO HAVE POLITICAL AND MILITARY DIMENSIONS.

NORTH AMERICAN FREE TRADE AGREEMENT	NAFTA	CANADA, USA, MEXICO	1994
EUROPEAN ECONOMIC AREA	EEA	27 EU MEMBERS PLUS ICELAND, NORWAY, LIECHTENSTEIN	1994
ASSOCIATION OF SOUTHEAST ASIAN NATIONS	ASEAN	BRUNEI, BURMA (MYANMAR), CAMBODIA, INDONESIA, LAOS, MALAYSIA, PHILIPPINES, SINGAPORE, THAILAND, VIETNAM	1967
SOUTH ASIAN ASSOCIATION FOR REGIONAL COOPERATION	SAARC	AFGHANISTAN, BANGLADESH, BHUTAN, INDIA, MALDIVES, NEPAL, PAKISTAN, SRI LANKA	1985
UNION OF SOUTH AMERICAN NATIONS	UNASUR/ UNASUL	MERCOSUR MEMBERS (BRAZIL, ARGENTINA, PARAGUAY, URUGUAY, VENEZUELA), ANDEAN COMMUNITY MEMBERS (BOLIVIA, COLOMBIA, ECUADOR, PERU) PLUS CHILE, GUYANA, SURINAME	2004
CARIBBEAN COMMUNITY	CARICOM	ANTIGUA & BARBUDA, BAHAMAS, BARBADOS, BELIZE, DOMINICA, GRENADA, GUYANA, HAITI, JAMAICA, MONTSERRAT, ST. KITTS & NEVIS, ST. LUCIA, ST. VINCENT & THE GRENADINES, SURINAME, TRINIDAD & TOBAGO	1973
SOUTHERN AFRICAN CUSTOMS UNION	SACU	BOTSWANA, LESOTHO, NAMIBIA, SOUTH AFRICA, SWAZILAND	1969

UNFAIR TRADE?

THE BANANA STORY

THE EU USED TO GIVE CARIBBEAN BANANA PRODUCERS PREFERENTIAL ACCESS TO ITS MARKETS. THE USA, BACKED BY MAJOR MULTINATIONALS, PUSHED FOR A WTO RULING DECLARING THIS WAS UNFAIR TRADE. SOMETIMES IT WORKS THE OTHER WAY ROUND; A RECENT WTO RULING IN BRAZIL'S FAVOUR ORDERED THE USA TO STOP SUBSIDIES TO ITS OWN COTTON-GROWERS, BUT IT HAS YET TO COMPLY.

MEXICO'S MAQUILADORAS

FACTORIES JUST OVER THE MEXICAN BORDER FROM THE USA IMPORT MATERIALS AND EQUIPMENT (WITH NO DUTY OR TARIFFS) FOR ASSEMBLY OR MANUFACTURING, EXPLOITING LOCAL CHEAP LABOUR, AND THEN RE-EXPORT BACK TO THE ORIGINATING COUNTRY. MEXICO'S POSITION IS NOW UNDER THREAT FROM CHINA, DESPITE THE HIGHER TRANSPORTATION COSTS.

THE PUBLIC VIEW OF GLOBALIZATION

Unfortunately for politicians, most of their voters think globalization is a bad thing. Of the people questioned in this 2007 Harris Poll, only in Germany did less than half of the respondents say that it was having a negative effect.

"DO YOU THINK GLOBALIZATION IS HAVING A POSITIVE OR NEGATIVE EFFECT IN YOUR COUNTRY?"

A POSITIVE EFFECT

NOT SURE

A NEGATIVE EFFECT

| UK | FRANCE | ITALY | SPAIN | GERMANY | USA |

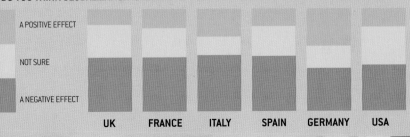

A BIGGER, BETTER WORLD?

Globalization is decried as one of the evils of the modern world. Multinationals can have an unfair sway over the policies of governments, eager for them to base their operations within the country to reap the benefits of employment, investment, and increased tax revenue.

Free trade agreements are negotiated selfishly to maximize benefits to countries' own exporters while losing as little control as possible on imports from the other side. This is frequently done by creating subsidies or grants to price national products below imports. Inevitably the largest economies end up with the best deals, and the poorer nations have to toe the line, though some come out well, such as the hugely beneficial effect of NAFTA on the Mexican economy. Even the WTO itself is manipulated by the likes of the USA and the EU, whose unilateral trade embargoes put pressure on it to take certain actions. The biennial WTO summits, and meetings of the World Economic Forum at Davos in Switzerland, are increasingly disrupted by vehement anti-globalization protestors. Since 2001 social movements opposed to globalization have had a voice through the World Social Forum.

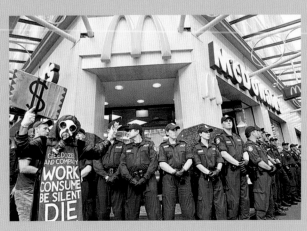

WHO WORKS WHERE?

A mere couple of centuries ago, all but the few were peasants, labourers, serfs, or plantation slaves. Those days are gone for good ir developed countries, where agriculture now accounts for less than 10 the workforce. Worldwide, however, 37.6% of all employment still falls wi this sector (involving everything from subsistence farming upwards), more than 60% of the world's working-age population lives in regions w agriculture dominates.

AGRICULTURE

WORK

Work typically takes up more time than anything else (except perhaps sleeping) in our adult lives. Most people, at least in the developed world, do have some leisure, and holidays too, often as hard won entitlements from past labour reforms and struggles. But work – or the search for it – determines much of how and where we live, our relative prosperity, well-being, and security.

Long-term unemployment, on the other hand, tends to marginalize people from society. Even in rich, developed countries it is so hard to find work in some areas that this social exclusion can become permanent – particularly with youth unemployment typically at least twice as high as the adult rate. Education remains a key factor: someone with only basic schooling is three times more likely to be unemployed than a college graduate.

We have come to define childhood as largely separate from the world of work, although some opportunity to get working experience and earn some money in a safe, healthy environment is generally seen as a good thing if it does not get in the way of schooling. Child labour, however, is another story – and out of the 218 million (one in six children worldwide) who do work, around 60% face hazardous conditions, such as those in mines or in agriculture, using dangerous machinery, chemicals, or pesticides.

BRAZIL	19%
SOUTH AFRICA	7%
CHINA	45%
INDONESIA	40%
GERMANY	2%
MEXICO	15%
JAPAN	4%
RUSSIA	9%
UK	1%
USA	2%

AGRICULTURE 37.6% IN 2005

HOW AGRICULTURE AND INDUSTRY RANK IN THE MAJOR COUNTRIES' LABOUR FORCES

BRAZIL	19%
SOUTH AFRICA	18%
CHINA	22%
INDONESIA	16%
GERMANY	27%
MEXICO	25%
JAPAN	27%
RUSSIA	27%
UK	21%
USA	19%

INDUSTRY 19.7% IN 2005

TRADES UNIONS

Trade union power is in decline in a globalized world labour market, but in most developed countries somewhere between a quarter and one third of all workers are still members of a union. In Scandinavian countries it is nine out of every ten.
Union membership in the USA is much lower – at 12% in 2006, and falling. US public sector workers are more likely to be union members than those who work in the private sector, where just 7.4% are now union members (down from an all-time high of 35% in 1955).

INDUSTRY

The former spearheads of the industrial revolution – above all the UK and the – have now seen the proportion of their workers employed in industry fall bac just above one in five – only marginally more than the global average of 19.7%. It little higher in other established "industrial giants" like Germany, Japan, and Rus – but what is most striking is the growth of the industrial workforce in the ne industrializing countries, and above all in China, the new "workshop of the world"

In every country of what is still often called "the industrialized world", far fewer people actually now work in industry than in the ever-growing service sector – in offices, retail, catering, transport, education, and so on. Worldwide, the service sector accounts for 36.4% of the employed workforce. Some developing countries have switched directly from a mainly agricultural to a mainly service sector workforce. Information and communications technology is making it possible to outsource more such work to developing countries, most obviously in areas like call centres and "back office" computing.

SERVICES

SERVICES 36.4% IN 2005

52%	BRAZIL
47%	SOUTH AFRICA
29%	CHINA
34%	INDONESIA
61%	GERMANY
57%	MEXICO
64%	JAPAN
55%	RUSSIA
73%	UK
74%	USA

HOW SERVICES AND UNEMPLOYMENT RANK IN THE MAJOR COUNTRIES' LABOUR FORCES

UNEMPLOYMENT 6.3% IN 2005

10%	BRAZIL
27%	SOUTH AFRICA
4%	CHINA
10%	INDONESIA
10%	GERMANY
3%	MEXICO
5%	JAPAN
8%	RUSSIA
5%	UK
6%	USA

A figure of 6.3% is currently cited for global unemployment – but this involves counting only those who did not have even a single hour's work in the week. So it excludes all those, particularly in poor countries, who have to survive on whatever irregular and casual labour they can get. A very different figure emerges – calculated at 21% in Italy and France, and certainly substantially more in the developing world – if you add in all the part-timers who would do more hours if the work were available.

UNEMPLOYMENT

THE WORLD'S WORKFORCE

WORKING WOMEN

Women, as the slogan goes, hold up half the sky. Much of their work may be invisible to the employment statistician, but nevertheless the number of women of working age with full or part-time jobs has grown steadily to reach 70% or more in most developed countries, and a global average of well over 50%. Cultural norms in India and the Islamic world, however, dictate that women with jobs are still the exception. Africa shows the sharpest contrast within any continent, with strikingly high rates of female employment in sub-Saharan countries and low rates in North Africa.

WAGE-EARNING WOMEN
AS PERCENTAGE OF FEMALE WORKFORCE

SAUDI ARABIA	18.5
EGYPT	21.6
OMAN	23.6
SUDAN	24.2
TURKEY	27.2
INDIA	36.0
WORLD AVERAGE	57.9
USA	70.1
CHINA	75.8
ICELAND	82.9
MOZAMBIQUE	84.9
MALAWI	86.2
TANZANIA	88.2
BURUNDI	92.8

WHO WORKS HARDEST?

PROPORTIONS OF THE MAJOR COUNTRIES' WORKFORCE WHO WORK MORE THAN 48 HOURS PER WEEK

50.9%	PERU
49.5%	SOUTH KOREA
46.7%	THAILAND
44.1%	PAKISTAN
41.2%	ETHIOPIA
30%	TANZANIA
29.9%	ARMENIA
29.3%	JAPAN
28.4%	ARGENTINA
26.2%	MEXICO
25.7%	UK
22.1%	MAURITIUS
20.4%	AUSTRALIA
19.2%	SWITZERLAND
18.1%	USA
14.7%	FRANCE
9.8%	ESTONIA
7.3%	HUNGARY
7.0%	NETHERLANDS
5.3%	NORWAY

NUMBER OF DAYS' HOLIDAY TAKEN EACH YEAR IN THE MAJOR COUNTRIES

13 DAYS	USA
25 DAYS	JAPAN
25 DAYS	SOUTH KOREA
26 DAYS	CANADA
28 DAYS	UK
34 DAYS	BRAZIL
35 DAYS	GERMANY
37 DAYS	FRANCE
42 DAYS	ITALY

SWEATSHOPS

Slavery is supposed to have been abolished worldwide – but in practice it still exists for many indentured labourers, domestic workers, and the 8.4 million children who are made to do illegal, degrading, or dangerous work that is classified as slave labour by the campaign organization Save the Children. Then there is prison labour: there were nearly 2.2 million "victims of state-imposed forced labour" in the Asia-Pacific region alone in 2005, according to the UN's International Labour Organization.

SOURCES: International Labour Organization (ILO); World Tourism Organization; World Bank: *World Development Indicators*

DAYS LOST TO STRIKES

ertain countries may get a reputation as particularly
trike-prone – as Britain did, before the Thatcher
overnment of the 1980s took on the power of the
nions it saw as "the enemy within". French public
ector strikes frequently get a high profile, whereas
uch action is rare in Japan. In practice, strike levels
uctuate widely year to year in most places; in South
merica, for instance, Brazil had a turbulent year in
004, losing over 150 million person/days, whereas
wo years later it was Argentina which was worst
ffected.

AYS LOST TO STRIKES, PER 100 WORKERS
atest year available)

RI LANKA	595
RINIDAD & TOBAGO	39
RAZIL	28
CELAND	10.5
NDIA	8.4
RGENTINA	6.7
OUTH AFRICA	3.3
ERU	2.2
ANADA	0.58
K	0.28
TALY	0.27
SA	0.2
RANCE	0.17
ERMANY	0.11
USSIA	0
APAN	0

NDING MONEY BACK HOME

TRIES WITH SIGNIFICANT INCOME FROM WORKERS ABROAD

KICO **US$23.1** (2.7% OF TOTAL GDP)

A **US$21.6** (3.6% OF TOTAL GDP)

IPPINES **US$10.7** (10.8% OF TOTAL GDP)

PT **US$5.0** (5.6%)

ROCCO **US$4.6** (8.9%)

NGLADESH **US$4.3** (7.2%)

ISTAN **US$4.3** (3.8%)

ANON **US$4.3** (19.8%)

OMBIA **US$3.9** (2.9%)

AND **US$3.8** (1.1%)

MANIA **US$3.8** (3.8%)

ERIA **US$3.3** (3.4%)

RTUGAL **US$3.0** (1.6%)

ATEMALA **US$3.0** (9.4%)

ALVADOR **US$2.8** (16.7%)

MINICAN REPUBLIC **US$2.4** (8.3%)

DAN **US$2.2** (17.1%)

ADOR **US$2.0** (5.6%)

IT IS BETTER EMPLOYMENT PROSPECTS THAT
ATTRACT WORKERS FROM ABROAD, YET THE "HOST"
COUNTRIES OFTEN USE THEM TO DO UNPOPULAR
LOW-STATUS WORK – OR, CONVERSELY, FAVOUR
APPLICANTS WITH SKILLS IN SHORT SUPPLY.
NEVERTHELESS, RIGHT-WING POPULIST POLITICIANS
TEND TO PRESENT "ECONOMIC MIGRANTS" AS A
THREAT TO LOCAL JOB PROSPECTS AS WELL AS
TO SCARCE RESOURCES (NOTABLY HOUSING AND
SOCIAL SERVICES) AND CULTURAL IDENTITY. ILLEGAL
IMMIGRANTS MAKE AN ESPECIALLY OBVIOUS TARGET.
IN WESTERN EUROPE, HOWEVER, THE DOMINANT
RECENT PHENOMENON IS THE INFLUX OF LITERALLY
MILLIONS OF WORKERS FROM POLAND AND OTHER
COUNTRIES OF THE RECENTLY-ENLARGED EUROPEAN
UNION, FOR WHOM THERE ARE NO IMMIGRATION OR
WORK PERMIT RESTRICTIONS.

WHERE DOES THE TIME GO?

In the 1960s and 1970s, the affluent West thought it faced
a "crisis of leisure", with technology making much tedious
work redundant. Many looked forward to the three-day
working week, even the six-month working year. The
prediction of economist John Maynard Keynes was widely
cited, that the biggest problem for future generations
would be what to do with all their free time.

It hasn't happened. Statistics on working hours show
a modest drop, but tell only part of the story. A recent
US study by the National Sleep Foundation showed that
38 per cent of full-time workers spend 50 or more hours
on the job each week. The contemporary notion of the
always-open "24/7 city" creates more service sector work
(not all captured by official statistics). A sense of constant
"busyness" extends beyond the workplace; people feel
their leisure time is eaten up. Most prevalent in the USA,
it is a problem that crosses demographic categories, from
the single parent to the dual-earner couple. We have
hardly even been "liberated from housework" by labour-
saving devices; instead, aspirational standards have
risen, and 45 hours a week remains the norm in the US
household, as it was in 1975.

Skilled professionals and managerial workers are
increasingly "connected" to work, enabled by (and at the
same time prisoners of) their supposedly time-saving
information and communications technology. The
tyranny of the mobile phone and e-mail come together
symbolically in the BlackBerry, which by mid-2007 had
over 10 million user accounts worldwide. Flexible working
can make its beneficiaries their own hardest taskmasters,
and concern about work/life balance has become the
hallmark of the progressive employer, not least because of
the lack of productivity caused by excessive stress.

ADVERTISING

The advertising industry brings together some of the smartest and most creative minds in design, writing, and film – to sell us soap, cars, and cosmetics. It is all about attracting attention and making a statement, so when Gucci commissioned art-house film-maker David Lynch to create a series of enigmatic video adverts they were creating an "event" in every sense of the word.

Procter & Gamble remain by far the largest global advertiser with an annual budget of US$8.5 billion, while six car companies feature on the list of the top 20 spenders. Shell spent a record US$3.9 million on shooting a single television commercial in 2007, in which historic Ferrari Formula 1 cars tore round the streets of London, New York, and Rio.

Newsprint and television have been the main advertising media and beneficiaries of promotional spend over the last 40 years, but are now under pressure as new media and new forms of advertising are being developed – direct mail and sponsorship are increasingly pervasive and unavoidable, while the Internet offers new forms of specialized and individualized advertising.

The global market for advertising is now worth over US$600 billion. Nearly half of this is spent targeting US consumers, but nowhere with money is immune. Africa, however, with over ten per cent of the world's population, gets less than one per cent of global advertising.

GLOBAL ADVERTISING SPENDING BY MEDIA 2005–2008

- TELEVISION: 37.9% IN 2008, UP FROM 37.7% IN 2005
- NEWSPAPERS: 28% IN 2008, DOWN FROM 29,9% IN 2005
- MAGAZINES: 13% IN 2008, DOWN FROM 29.9% IN 2005
- RADIO: 8% IN 2008, DOWN FROM 8.6% IN 2005
- INTERNET: 7.3% IN 2008, UP FROM 4.7% IN 2005
- OUTDOOR: 5.7% IN 2008, UP FROM 5.5% IN 2005
- CINEMA: 0.4%, UNCHANGED FROM 2005

TOP TEN GLOBAL AD AGENCIES

TOKYO AGENCY DENTSU [...] THE LARGEST OF THE [...] AGENCIES, BUT THE IND[...] REMAINS DOMINATED B[...] YORK'S MADISON AV[...] SEVEN OF THE WORLD[...] TEN AGENCIES ARE BA[...] TH[...]

BBDO Worldwide – New York **US$2099.8 m**

McCann-Erickson Worldwide – New York **US$2127.4 m**

Dentsu – Tokyo **US$2487 m**

Le[...] W[...] US[...]

Young & Rubicam Brands – New Yo[...] **US$1588.3 m**

DDB Worldwide Communications Group – New York **US$2077.8 m**

Publicis Worldwide – Paris **US$1243.8 m**

JWT – New Yo[...] **US$14[...]**

Ogilvy & Mather Worldwide – New York **US$1714.1 m**

TBWA Worldwide – New York **US $1523.1 m**

GLOBAL AD SPEND 1990–2007 (BILLION US$)

		1990	1991	1992	1993	1994	
REST OF THE WORLD		145.9	153.9	165.4	163.2	179	20[...]
USA		130	128.4	133.8	141	153	1[...]

SOURCES: Advertising Age (2007) *Global Marketers*; Universal McCain (2007) *Insider's Report: Presentation on Advertising Expenditures.*

GLOBAL AD SPEND BY COMPANY 2006 [BILLION US$]

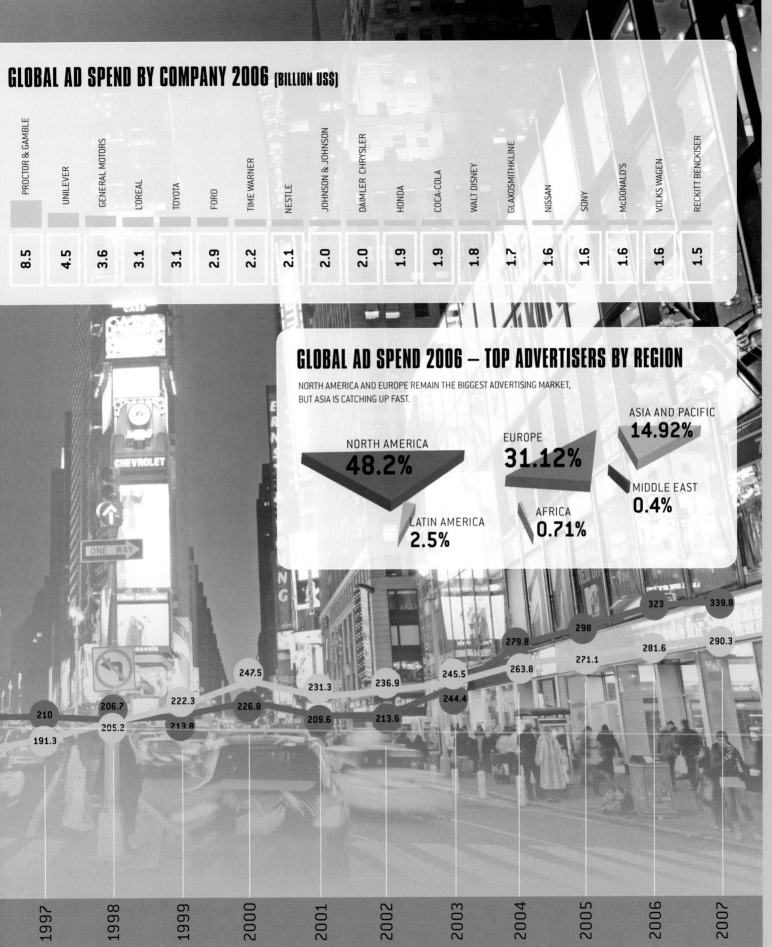

PROCTOR & GAMBLE	UNILEVER	GENERAL MOTORS	L'OREAL	TOYOTA	FORD	TIME WARNER	NESTLE	JOHNSON & JOHNSON	DAIMLER CHRYSLER	HONDA	COCA-COLA	WALT DISNEY	GLAXOSMITHKLINE	NISSAN	SONY	McDONALD'S	VOLKS WAGEN	RECKITT BENCKISER
8.5	4.5	3.6	3.1	3.1	2.9	2.2	2.1	2.0	2.0	1.9	1.9	1.8	1.7	1.6	1.6	1.6	1.6	1.5

GLOBAL AD SPEND 2006 – TOP ADVERTISERS BY REGION

NORTH AMERICA AND EUROPE REMAIN THE BIGGEST ADVERTISING MARKET,
BUT ASIA IS CATCHING UP FAST.

NORTH AMERICA
48.2%

EUROPE
31.12%

ASIA AND PACIFIC
14.92%

MIDDLE EAST
0.4%

LATIN AMERICA
2.5%

AFRICA
0.71%

1997	1998	1999	2000	2001	2002	2003	2004	2005	2006	2007
210	206.7	222.3	247.5	231.3	236.9	245.5	279.8	298	323	339.8
191.3	205.2	213.8	226.8	209.6	213.6	244.4	263.8	271.1	281.6	290.3

ADVERTISING

COMMERCIAL BREAKS

US$12 BILLION IS SPENT IN THE US PER ANNUM ON TV ADVERTISING DIRECTED AT CHILDREN

40,000 TV ADVERTS ARE SEEN BY THE AVERAGE AMERICAN CHILD EVERY YEAR

200 US TV ADVERTS PER YEAR PROMOTE HEALTHY FOOD

1965: UK BANS CIGARETTE ADVERTISING ON TV (AND ALL TOBACCO PRODUCTS IN 1991); SIMILAR RESTRICTIONS IN THE US BY 1971

BETWEEN 1985-96 JAPANESE TOBACCO SALES INCREASE TENFOLD DUE TO PRESSURE EXERTED BY TOBACCO MULTINATIONALS TO DELAY A BAN ON TV ADVERTISING. PHILIP MORRIS CAMPAIGN FEATURES STARS LIKE JAMES COBURN, ROGER MOORE, AND PIERCE BROSNAN

80% OF GLOBAL BRANDS HAVE A "TWEENS" STRATEGY, TARGETING 9-12-YEAR-OLDS

UK 2005: PRESSURE TO BAN ADVERTISING OF "UNHEALTHY" FOODS BEFORE THE 9PM TV WATERSHED

TV ADVERTISING OF ALCOHOL IS OFFICIALLY BANNED IN INDIA, BUT A THIRD OF ALL COMMERCIALS THERE ARE PLACED BY DRINKS MANUFACTURERS, TO BUILD BRAND AWARENESS

TV BAN ON TOBACCO ADVERTISING LEADS TO RESTRICTION OF TOBACCO SPONSORSHIP OF TELEVISED EVENTS, THE MOST PROMINENT BEING THE GRAND PRIX IN THE UK, 2003

SWEDEN HAS BANNED TV ADVERTISING TARGETING CHILDREN

THE COG HONDA ACCORD ADVERT REQUIRED 606 TAKES, MAKING IT THE MOST COMPLICATED ADVERT EVER FILMED

150 TIMES AS MUCH MONEY IS NOW SPENT ON ADVERTISING TO CHILDREN IN THE US AS IN 1983

SOURCES: Zenith Optimedia; www.etcnewmedia.com

OVERTISING AND THE POPULAR MEDIA

V, drug of the nation, breeding ignorance and feeding radiation" rapped the
sposable Heroes of Hiphopcracy and they weren't entirely wrong. In the United
ates in particular, but increasingly all over the world, advertisers pay the
.evision broadcasters for the rent of people's eyeballs and attention.
elevision and advertising have their most potent effect, slowly and
mulatively, as part of the whole complex of beliefs and attitudes that
nstitute advanced Western consumerism; there is an upcoming generation
uich has been trained to associate material acquisition with self-esteem by
eir early teens. In the USA, 62% of 13-year-olds say buying products makes
em feel better, while ten per cent of 12-year-olds ask their parents for a TV-
.vertised product more than fifty times.

Ve may have reached saturation point. There are just not enough hours in the
y to get more TV viewing in, so advertisers and their clients are pioneering new
ys to engage us.

Advertorials: magazines, particularly those devoted to crafting
aspirational lifestyles through consumption – be it cars, clothes, holidays,
or property – continue to provide a platform almost indistinguishable
from the advertising copy that sustains them. Newsprint too has been
suffering from declining ad spend, but increasing amounts of newsprint
real estate is given over to supplements and shrink-wrapped wads of copy
masquerading as content.

Product placement: while spend on cinema advertising is in decline,
the main features now provide a perfect platform for advertising brands.
Product placement is an increasingly important component of Hollywood
budgets. The 2002 James Bond film *Die Another Day* had 20 firms paying
over US$40 million to weave their cars and vodka into the movie.

THE BIG OPPORTUNITY: THE INTERNET

Five years ago, everyone was saying "How do we make
money out of the Internet?" The answer was simple:
advertising. The promotion industry, like so much else, is
being transformed by the Internet. The fastest-growing
sector by far, it has already eclipsed the cinema and
outside billboard as a medium, and will soon pass radio's
share of advertising income. Print is next in line. In the US,
Google, which offers advertisers a link to users who might
actually have some interest in their product, has captured
half of all online advertising income. It will soon surpass
the income of all the biggest TV networks. Other online
sites are busy maximizing their value as advertising
platforms. Tracking consumers' buying and taste patterns
is the key; targeted advertising the holy grail.

Alongside Google, sites that are dependent on user-
generated content – from e-Bay and You Tube to social
networking hubs like My Space, Facebook, and Bebo
– are raking in the advertising dollars, showing increases
of over 1000% in the last two years. Global Internet
advertising spend is chalk-marked to grow by 28.2%,
while other media advertising spend will grow by only
3.9%. In Norway, Sweden, and the UK the Internet already
attracts over ten percent of advertisers' budgets, and
by 2009 Zenith Optimedia expect to achieve similar
results in Australia, Canada, Israel, South Korea, the USA,
and Taiwan. The UK remains the most avid consumer
of Internet ad spend, reaching 13.5% in 2008, with a
projected 21.15% by 2010. The "ad growth hotspots"
are Brazil, Russia, Indonesia, and China. Currently they
account for only six to ten per cent of ad spend, but are
predicted to reach 26% by the end of the decade.

FAIR TRADE

Amid all that is perverse and dysfunctional in the global agricultural system, the growth of the Fairtrade movement stands out as a rare beacon of hope. It is simultaneously a strategy for fighting poverty, an opportunity for Western consumers to take an ethical stand, and a counterweight to the exploitation of small farmers in developing countries. Instead of being totally exposed to the vagaries of world commodity markets and fluctuations in demand, and perhaps driven by desperation into something more lucrative like narcotics, local farmers supplying their coffee, cocoa, tea, bananas, or an expanding range of other produce under a fairtrade agreement can plan their future production with greater security, and enjoy the chance of improvement to their communities, thanks to the guarantee of a stable and worthwhile price plus a "social premium".

The movement is rapidly moving from niche to mainstream, with produce more readily available even in many major retail chains. Consumers committed to buying Fairtrade remain a minority, however – partly because of the price premium, and partly because it takes time and effort to develop the local agreements to support a fairtrade supply chain, thus limiting the range of what is available in the shops. Also important are the competing claims of the organic food movement, and the local food movement, with its emphasis on sourcing close to home.

THE FAIRTRADE MARK GUARANTEES

- A FAIR AND STABLE PRICE FOR FARMERS FOR THEIR PRODUCTS
- EXTRA INCOME FOR FARMERS AND ESTATE WORKERS TO IMPROVE THEIR LIVES
- A GREATER RESPECT FOR THE ENVIRONMENT
- A STRONGER POSITION FOR SMALL FARMERS IN WORLD MARKETS
- A CLOSER LINK BETWEEN CONSUMERS AND PRODUCERS

THE SPREAD OF FAIRTRADE LABELS WORLDWI

THE WORLDWIDE FAIRTRADE MOVEMENT HAS ONLY TAKEN OFF IN THE LAST 20 YEARS. THE LABELLING SIDE OPERATES UNDER THE UMBRELLA OF FLO (FAIRTRADE LABELLING ORGANIZATIONS INTERNATIONAL NATIONAL BODIES ADMINISTER THEIR LABELLING SCHEMES WITHIN THIS FRAMEWORK. A RECOGNIZED LABEL IS AN IMPORTANT GUARANTEE TO THE CONSUMER THAT A PRODUCT IS SOURCED FROM SUPPLIERS UNDER GENUINE FAIRTRADE AGREEMENTS. IN THE USA AND CANADA, THE FAIR TRADE FEDERATION IS AN ASSOCIATION OF BUSINESSES AND ORGANIZATIONS COMMITTED TO FAIR TRADE.

	YEAR JOINED FAIRTRADE LABEL ORGANIZATIONS (AND LABEL)	RETAIL VALUE FAIRTRAD (US$ MILLION 2
NETHERLANDS	1988 (MAX HAVELAAR)	51
BELGIUM	1991 (MAX HAVELAAR)	35
SWITZERLAND	1992 (MAX HAVELAAR)	169
LUXEMBOURG	1993 (TRANSFAIR)	4
GERMANY	1993 (TRANSFAIR)	138
FRANCE	1993 (MAX HAVELAAR)	200
JAPAN	1994 (TRANSFAIR)	5
UK	1994 (FAIRTRADE)	512
AUSTRIA	1994 (TRANSFAIR)	52
ITALY	1995 (TRANSFAIR)	43
DENMARK	1995 (MAX HAVELAAR)	27
SWEDEN	1997 (RÄTTVISEMÄRKT)	20
NORWAY	1998 (MAX HAVELAAR)	11
IRELAND	1998 (FAIRTRADE)	15
CANADA	1998 (TRANSFAIR)	67
FINLAND	1999 (FAIRTRADE)	28
USA	2000 (TRANSFAIR)	624
AUSTRALIA & NEW ZEALAND	2003 (FAIRTRADE)	9
SPAIN	2005 (FAIRTRADE)	2

SALES VOLUMES OF THE MAJOR FAIRTRADE PRODUCTS

	2006
BANANAS*	135,763
COCOA*	10,952
COFFEE*	52,077
COTTON**	1,551,807

* million tonnes   ** items

SOURCES: Fairtrade Foundation; Fairtrade Labelling Organizations (FLO) International: Annual Report (2006/07)

COCOA

FAIR TRADE GUARANTEES ITS COCOA FARMERS A "FLOOR PRICE" OF US$.80 PER POUND (US$0.89 FOR ORGANIC BEANS). WORLD MARKET PRICES WERE LESS THAN HALF THAT AT THEIR 2000 LOW POINT.

FAIRTRADE COCOA SALES 2006 (METRIC TONNES)	
USA	3864
UK	2947
FRANCE	1088
GERMANY	967
REST OF EUROPE	957
OTHER	364
TOTAL	**10,952**

TEA

FAIRTRADE TEA SALES 2006 (METRIC TONNES)	
USA	286
UK	2839
FRANCE	279
GERMANY	163
REST OF EUROPE	265
OTHER	55
TOTAL	**3887**

COFFEE

WORLD MARKET PRICES FOR COFFEE ARE NOTORIOUSLY VOLATILE, SOARING AND PLUMMETING BETWEEN US$2 PER POUND AND UNDER 50 CENTS. FAIRTRADE FARMERS GET A GUARANTEED US$1.26 (OR US$1.31 WHEN WORLD PRICES ARE HIGHER).

" WITHOUT FAIRTRADE WE WOULD PROBABLY HAVE GONE OUT OF BUSINESS DURING THE COFFEE CRISIS. **"**

GERARDO CAMACHO, COFFEE FARMER, LLANO BONITO CO-OPERATIVE, COSTA RICA

FAIRTRADE COFFEE SALES 2006 (METRIC TONNES)	
USA	23,568
UK	6238
FRANCE	6175
GERMANY	3908
REST OF EUROPE	9476
OTHER	2714
TOTAL	**52,077**

BANANAS

BANANA PRICES IN UK IN VARIOUS SUPERMARKETS	LOOSE BANANAS PRICE PER KILO (£)	FAIRTRADE BANANAS PRICE PER KILO (£)
END 2002	1.10	1.50
END 2003	0.74	1.50
2005-2006	0.85	1.14–1.38
APRIL 2007	0.68	1.14–1.38
JUNE 2007	0.59	1.14–1.38
SEPTEMBER 2007	0.85	1.14–1.38

FAIRTRADE TEA SALES 2006 (METRIC TONNES)	
USA	2594
UK	60,276
SWITZERLAND	27,981
FINLAND	7306
FRANCE	4547
REST OF EUROPE	18,904
OTHER	141
TOTAL	135,763

UK FAIR TRADE MARKET SHARES

BANANAS ARE THE STAR OF THE BOOMING UK FAIRTRADE MARKET, WITH SALES INCREASING BY 130% IN 2007 (COMPARED WITH 80% FOR FAIRTRADE PRODUCTS AS A WHOLE). MANY MAJOR STORES NOW STOCK NO OTHER KIND. THE CONVERSION OF SUPERMARKET OWN BRANDS SHOULD BOOST FAIRTRADE TEA'S MARKET SHARE TO TEN PER CENT BY THE END OF 2008, WHILE SUGAR GIANT TATE & LYLE IS SWITCHING ITS ENTIRE RETAIL CANE SUGAR RANGE TO FAIRTRADE.

BANANAS 25% OF ALL BANANAS

COFFEE (ROAST AND GROUND) 20%

COFFEE (INSTANT) 3%

TEA 3%

FAIRTRADE CERTIFIED BANANA PRODUCERS

The Windward Islands Farmers' Association (WINFA) began working with Fairtrade in the 1990s, setting up Fairtrade Groups on each island. There are now 48 of these, with a total of 3347 members, and virtually all the banana growers in the islands are Fairtrade certified. Since the first shipment of Fairtrade bananas to the UK in July 2000, the percentage of Windward Islands bananas sold to the Fairtrade market has grown to over 80% in 2006. In the words of Dominica's Prime Minister Roosevelt Skerrit: "Fairtrade is providing a vital livelihood for small farmers.... It is giving people a legal way of earning a living and maintaining stability."

MEMBERSHIP OF WINFA

ISLAND	NO. OF FARMERS
DOMINICA	856
GRENADA	31
ST. LUCIA	1300
ST. VINCENT	1191

SOURCES: Fairtrade Foundation; Windward Islands Farmers' Association (WINFA); Oromia Coffee Farmers Cooperative Union Ltd

THE FAIRTRADE PREMIUM AT WORK IN ST. LUCIA

NON-FAIRTRADE BANANA SUPPLIERS WERE GETTING EC$16.00 PER 18.14KG BOX IN 2006. THOSE WHO BECAME FAIRTRADE MEMBERS BENEFITED FROM AN IMMEDIATE EC$7.00 INCREASE, TO EC$23.00 PER BOX. OTHER BENEFITS INCLUDED:

- MEDICAL ASSISTANCE FOR FARMERS, AND SUPPORT WITH FERTILIZERS, DIOTHENE, PROPPING TWINE, POST-HARVEST INPUTS, CLUSTER BAGS, BOXES, ETC.

- EDUCATIONAL PROJECTS TO ASSIST LOCAL SCHOOLS.

- ENVIRONMENTAL PROJECTS: COLLECTION OF NON-BIODEGRADABLE FARM WASTE, MOTORIZED WEED CUTTERS FOR USE IN BANANA FIELDS, TREE PLANTING.

- SOCIAL PROJECTS: BUS SHELTERS, SPONSORSHIP OF SPORTING ACTIVITIES, FARM ROAD IMPROVEMENT PROJECTS, AND NEW EQUIPMENT FOR THE "HOME FOR THE AGED" AT SOUFRIERE.

- BUSINESS DEVELOPMENT: DEVELOPMENT OF A LOCAL BANANA RIPENING CENTRE ON THE ISLAND.

❝ TO ME, FAIRTRADE MEANS A BUYING AND SELLING PROCESS IN WHICH HUMANITARIANISM HAS A BIG PART. IT IS CREATING A FAMILY RELATIONSHIP BETWEEN PEOPLES WHO LIVE ON THIS PLANET. ❞

TADESSE MESKELA, OROMIA GENERAL MANAGER, JANUARY 2005

ETHIOPIAN COFFEE PRODUCERS TURN TO FAIRTRADE

CREATED IN MAY 2000, THE OROMIA COFFEE FARMERS' CO-OPERATIVE UNION (OCFCU) GROUPS TOGETHER 11 PRODUCER CO-OPERATIVES WHO GAINED FAIRTRADE CERTIFICATION AT THAT TIME. THEY REPRESENT 8963 FARMERS AND PRODUCE 2830 TONNES OF ORGANIC COFFEE.
FARMERS HAVE USED THEIR EXTRA INCOME TO BUILD OR REPAIR HOUSES AND PURCHASE LIVESTOCK. THE FAIRTRADE PREMIUM FOR SOCIAL DEVELOPMENT HAS BEEN USED TO BUILD FOUR PRIMARY SCHOOLS, TWO CLINICS, AND TWO CLEAN WATER PUMPS.

FAIRTRADE CERTIFIED SPORTS BALLS

TO COUNTERACT THE EXPLOITATION OF CHILD LABOUR AND SWEATSHOP WORKING CONDITIONS, FAIRTRADE SPORTS BALLS ARE GUARANTEED TO HAVE BEEN HAND-STITCHED BY ADULT WORKERS PAID A FAIR WAGE AND ENSURED HEALTHY WORKING CONDITIONS. AFTER-TAX PROFITS ARE DONATED TO CHILREN'S CHARITIES. SALES ROCKETED FROM 56,479 WORLDWIDE IN 2004 TO 152,412 IN 2006, BOOSTED BY 83,617 BOUGHT BY GERMANY FOR SOCCER'S WORLD CUP.

TRANSFORMING TRADE?

There are currently around 600 Fairtrade partner organizations in developing countries certified to international FLO standards, and over a million families reaping the benefits.

It's a drop in the ocean, however, compared with the total numbers tied into supplying the global food economy, or struggling to gain access to markets in Western countries, whose own farming lobbies still manage to defend a level of subsidy and protection that sits oddly with the "free trade" rhetoric of the World Trade Organization. Fairtrade has made only the smallest of inroads, too, outside the area of luxury agricultural produce that has so far been its mainstay; footballs and small amounts of fairtrade cotton are among the few exceptions.

Nevertheless, buoyed up by its success so far, the UK's Fairtrade Foundation has set itself the ambitious objective of "begining to truly transform trade in favour of the poor and disadvantaged" by 2012, and "enabling the voice of the poorest to be heard at the highest level". In practical terms, having built the UK market to almost £500 million already, it now aims to quadruple that by 2012, doubling both the number of producers selling Fairtrade goods in the UK, and the proportion of the crop sold by existing producers via the Fairtrade system.

ARMS

The USA spends almost nine times more than any other single country on arms. It is responsible for almost half of the global arms trade, which has risen every year this century and now tops US$1 trillion. The UK, France, and China each spend over US$50 billion. Fifth and sixth are Japan and Germany, although both have constitutional restraints on the deployment of their armed forces.

All the biggest spenders have substantial domestic defence industries. Many of them make more money out of selling arms to poor countries than they provide in aid, while for the latter the buying of weapons can be ruinously expensive. The spread of nuclear weapons may conjure up the greatest terrors. Arms expenditure, however, goes overwhelmingly on conventional weapons – which have been used for all the killing in all the wars of the last 60 years.

 THE USA HAS THE LARGEST NUMBER OF GUNS IN PRIVATE HANDS OF ANY COUNTRY IN THE WORLD, WITH 60 MILLION PEOPLE OWNING A COMBINED ARSENAL OF OVER 200 MILLION FIREARMS.

 THERE ARE 640 MILLION GUNS IN THE WORLD, ONE FOR EVERY TEN PEOPLE ON EARTH. ANOTHER EIGHT MILLION GUNS ARE MANUFACTURED EVERY YEAR, ALONG WITH 10–14 BILLION UNITS OF AMMUNITION, ENOUGH TO KILL EVERYONE ON EARTH TWICE OVER.

THE TOP MILITARY SPENDERS
WORLD TOTAL SPEND ON ARMS US$1158 BILLION

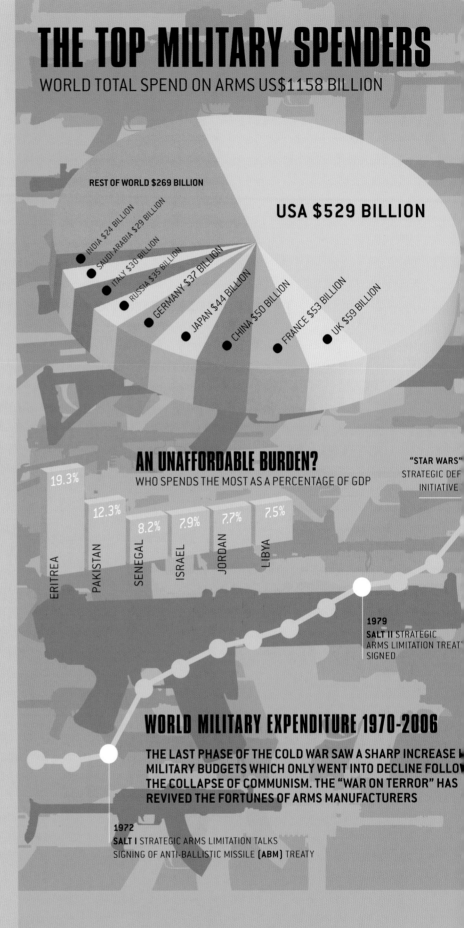

REST OF WORLD $269 BILLION

INDIA $24 BILLION
SAUDI ARABIA $29 BILLION
ITALY $30 BILLION
RUSSIA $35 BILLION
GERMANY $37 BILLION
JAPAN $44 BILLION
CHINA $50 BILLION
FRANCE $53 BILLION
UK $59 BILLION

USA $529 BILLION

AN UNAFFORDABLE BURDEN?
WHO SPENDS THE MOST AS A PERCENTAGE OF GDP

"STAR WARS" STRATEGIC DEF INITIATIVE

ERITREA	PAKISTAN	SENEGAL	ISRAEL	JORDAN	LIBYA
19.3%	12.3%	8.2%	7.9%	7.7%	7.5%

1979
SALT II STRATEGIC ARMS LIMITATION TREAT SIGNED

WORLD MILITARY EXPENDITURE 1970-2006

THE LAST PHASE OF THE COLD WAR SAW A SHARP INCREASE I MILITARY BUDGETS WHICH ONLY WENT INTO DECLINE FOLLOW THE COLLAPSE OF COMMUNISM. THE "WAR ON TERROR" HAS REVIVED THE FORTUNES OF ARMS MANUFACTURERS

1972
SALT I STRATEGIC ARMS LIMITATION TALKS
SIGNING OF ANTI-BALLISTIC MISSILE (ABM) TREATY

NUMBERS OF MILITARY PERSONNEL

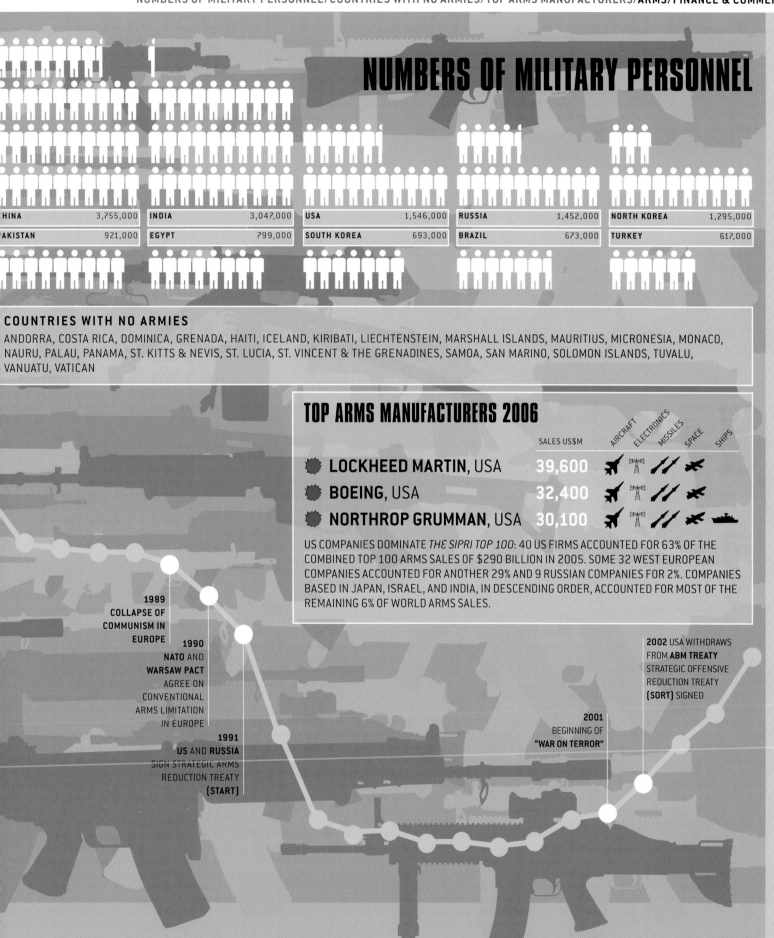

HINA	3,755,000	INDIA	3,047,000	USA	1,546,000	RUSSIA	1,452,000	NORTH KOREA	1,295,000
AKISTAN	921,000	EGYPT	799,000	SOUTH KOREA	693,000	BRAZIL	673,000	TURKEY	617,000

COUNTRIES WITH NO ARMIES

ANDORRA, COSTA RICA, DOMINICA, GRENADA, HAITI, ICELAND, KIRIBATI, LIECHTENSTEIN, MARSHALL ISLANDS, MAURITIUS, MICRONESIA, MONACO, NAURU, PALAU, PANAMA, ST. KITTS & NEVIS, ST. LUCIA, ST. VINCENT & THE GRENADINES, SAMOA, SAN MARINO, SOLOMON ISLANDS, TUVALU, VANUATU, VATICAN

TOP ARMS MANUFACTURERS 2006

	SALES US$M	AIRCRAFT	ELECTRONICS	MISSILES	SPACE	SHIPS
● LOCKHEED MARTIN, USA	39,600	✈	T	//	✈	
● BOEING, USA	32,400	✈	T	//	✈	
● NORTHROP GRUMMAN, USA	30,100	✈	T	//	✈	⛴

US COMPANIES DOMINATE *THE SIPRI TOP 100*: 40 US FIRMS ACCOUNTED FOR 63% OF THE COMBINED TOP 100 ARMS SALES OF $290 BILLION IN 2005. SOME 32 WEST EUROPEAN COMPANIES ACCOUNTED FOR ANOTHER 29% AND 9 RUSSIAN COMPANIES FOR 2%. COMPANIES BASED IN JAPAN, ISRAEL, AND INDIA, IN DESCENDING ORDER, ACCOUNTED FOR MOST OF THE REMAINING 6% OF WORLD ARMS SALES.

1989
COLLAPSE OF COMMUNISM IN EUROPE

1990
NATO AND WARSAW PACT AGREE ON CONVENTIONAL ARMS LIMITATION IN EUROPE

1991
US AND RUSSIA SIGN STRATEGIC ARMS REDUCTION TREATY (START)

2001
BEGINNING OF "WAR ON TERROR"

2002 USA WITHDRAWS FROM ABM TREATY STRATEGIC OFFENSIVE REDUCTION TREATY (SORT) SIGNED

ARMS

GOING NUCLEAR

ARCTIC OCEAN

Novaya Zemlya

RUSSIA

UK
c.160 warheads
45 tests last on November 26 1991

5614 warheads
715 tests including
as Soviet Union, last
on October 25 1990

FRANCE
348 warheads
210 tests last on January 27 1996

UKRAINE

Orenburg

KAZAKHSTAN

Azgir

Semipalatinsk

Alaska
(Amchitka)

SERBIA

NORTH KOREA ▲
unknown number of warheads
1 suspected test, 2006

NORTH
ATLANTIC

UZBEKISTAN

Lop Nor

▲ **ISRAEL**
c.100 warheads

SYRIA

TURKMENISTAN

ALGERIA

IRAN

CHINA

PAKISTAN ▲
c.60 warheads
6 tests last on May 30 1998

c.145 warheads
43 tests last possibly 1996/97

LIBYA

EGYPT

SAUDI
ARABIA

Reggane

Chagai

Pokhran

HIROSHIMA US detonation of uranium
isotope bomb **AUGUST 6 1945**
NAGASAKI US detonation of plutonium
fission bomb **AUGUST 9 1945**
These two bombs were the first and
only uses in war to date

Hoggar Massif

TAIWAN

INDIA ▲
c.50 warheads
5 tests last on May 13 1998

Johnston Atoll

INDIAN OCEAN

INDONESIA

Eniwetok Atoll

Bikini Atoll

Christmas Island

Malden Island

PACIFIC

rocket launched tests

SOUTH
ATLANTIC

Monte Bello Island

AUSTRALIA

SOUTH AFRICA

Emu Fields

Maralinga

SINCE JULY 16 1945 THERE HAVE BEEN 2044 NUCLEAR TESTS WORLDWIDE, THE EQUIVALENT OF ONE EVERY ELEVEN DAYS.

1968 NUCLEAR NON-PROLIFERATION TREATY

DESIGNED TO PREVENT THE SPREAD OF NUCLEAR WEAPONS BEYOND THE FIVE "OFFICIAL" NUCLEAR STATES (THE USA, RUSSIA, THE UK, FRANCE, AND CHINA), AND TO ENCOURAGE EVEN THEM TO DISARM, THE 1968 NUCLEAR NON-PROLIFERATION TREATY (NPT) HAS BEEN SIGNED BY EVERY COUNTRY IN THE WORLD EXCEPT INDIA, PAKISTAN, AND ISRAEL; HOWEVER, NORTH KOREA WITHDREW IN 2003 (TWO YEARS BEFORE OFFICIALLY ANNOUNCING THAT IT HAD NUCLEAR WEAPONS). SOUTH AFRICA ONLY ACCEDED IN 1994, AFTER DISMANTLING ITS APARTHEID-ERA WEAPONS PROGRAM. MEMBERS MUST ALLOW THE INTERNATIONAL ATOMIC ENERGY AGENCY (IAEA) TO VERIFY THAT ANY CIVILIAN NUCLEAR POWER PROGRAMS ARE NOT BEING USED TO DEVELOP A WEAPONS CAPABILITY. LIBYA CONFESSED IN 2003 TO A CLANDESTINE WEAPONS PROGRAM, WHICH IT DECLARED IT WOULD ABANDON IMMEDIATELY AND ACCEPT FULL IAEA INSPECTION. IRAN WAS DECLARED IN 2005 TO BE IN BREACH OF ITS OBLIGATIONS ON IAEA "SAFEGUARDS" INSPECTIONS, AND HAS CLAIMED THE RIGHT TO DEVELOP NUCLEAR WEAPONS SO LONG AS ISRAEL POSSESSES THEM.

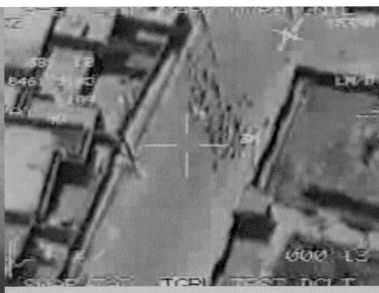

THE NUCLEAR WORLD	
nuclear weapons ownership	
technological potential for developing nuclear weapons	
▲ non-participation in the 1968 Non-proliferation Treaty ▲	
use of atomic weapons in war	
site of US nuclear test	
site of French nuclear test	
site of UK nuclear test	
site of Chinese nuclear test	
site of Soviet/Russian nuclear test	
site of Indian nuclear test	
site of Pakistan nuclear test	
possible North Korean nuclear test	

USA 5045 warheads
1030 tests last on September 23 1993

Nevada
Creek Valley)

New Mexico
(Alamogordo)
(Carlsbad)
(Farmington)

Colorado
(Grand Valley)
(Rifle)

Mississippi
(Hattiesburg)

OCEAN

rua Atoll

Fangataufa Atoll

BRAZIL

OTHER WEAPONS OF MASS DESTRUCTION

The use of chemical and biological weapons is outlawed worldwide, but their illegal manufacture is difficult to control as the technology required can be much simpler than making and firing nuclear warheads. Classed along with nuclear arms as weapons of mass destruction (WMD), they loom large in the public mind. The fear that Saddam Hussein was developing WMD capabilities secretly in Iraq, although later shown to be unfounded, was instrumental in gaining support for a pre-emptive invasion in 2003.

Chemical and biological weapons capable of killing at a distance could also be attractive to those engaged in non-conventional conflict. Letters containing anthrax sent through the US postal system in late 2001 killed five people and infected 17 others; the perpetrators have never been caught.

BROTHERS IN ARMS

The sophistication of military technology, delivery and defence systems, and precise missile guidance equipment creates a huge overlap with other hi-tech areas in the so-called "military-industrial complex". This term is also used as a derogatory reference to the institutionalized complicity between the US armed forces, arms manufacturers, the Department of Defense in the Pentagon, and "pork barrel" politicians, who seek lucrative defence contracts for their local firms regardless of the military necessity of the orders.

Strict rules now govern where certain US equipment and technology can be sold. US allies may face the cancellation of arms supply contracts if they seek to sell restricted items on elsewhere. Thus Spain was forced to withdraw from an agreement to sell weapons to Venezuela in 2006, as it might have involved the transfer of proprietary technology.

The small arms industry worldwide is worth $7.5 billion annually and is responsible for half a million deaths a year. Easy access to guns directly contributes to high crime rates, international narcotics trafficking and associated violence, and the continuation of civil conflict. Lax gun control laws in southern US states, for instance, cause problems in neighbouring Mexico and the Caribbean, while the vast stocks of weapons left over from the conflicts in the Balkans have only in part been destroyed – many finding their way into the hands of terrorist groups and to civil conflicts in Africa and Asia.

TYPES OF ORGANIZED CRIM

Organized crime has traditionally focused on extortion rackets, counterfeiting, the supply of illegal goods (particularly drugs), and the "shady" areas of prostitution and gambling. Human trafficking now includes would-be migrants too. The rise of global brands has created vast opportunities for counterfeit products, clothes, watches, DVDs, cosmetics, and pharmaceuticals. Electronic systems are highly susceptible to manipulation by fraudulent insiders, and identity theft is a major growth area.

ORGANIZED CRIME

Organized crime has always operated beyond and between the boundaries of legitimate states. Medieval vagabond groups crossed borders with ease, while *banditti* lurked in mountains other remote places, kidnapping or robbing travellers. The most notorious were the rovers, *boucaniers*, and pirates who plundered the Spanish Main and other maritime routes. Little has changed. Organized crime was the first truly international industry, exploiting the gaps between nations in a way which many legitimate globalized corporations do today, and it is still proving to be one of the world's most successful enterprises. Global networks of organized crime have become so powerful and sophisticated in recent decades that the so-called "shadow economy" now accounts for between 15 and 20 per cent of world turnover. That, at least, is the estimate of Misha Glenny in his book *McMafia*, tracing how it has shot up "since the liberalization of international financial and commodity markets on the one hand and the fall of Communism on the other".

At the simplest level, a gang with sufficient discipline to run a racket counts as organized crime. It becomes more insidious when parts of mainstream society are co-opted, usually via the corruption of police, state officials, and the legal system. Banning something that people want, as with the prohibition of alcohol in the USA from 1920 to 1933, can be a spectacular "own goal". The opportunities it creates for organized crime were quickly exploited on that occasion by the Mafia (a name now often used generically for organized crime, although the original Sicilian society regarded as its first incarnation referred to itself simply as Cosa Nostra or "our thing"). The powerful Russian "mafiya" got its own great boost by grabbing former state assets in the "gangster capitalism" of the immediate post-Soviet years, whereas many Chinese Triad gangs developed from 19th-century resistance groups, often travelling with emigrants to Western cities. "Snakehead" gangs, usually members of a Triad, now control much of the international human trafficking business.

SMUGGLING

- DRUG TRAFFICKING
- HUMAN TRAFFICKING
- TOBACCO SMUGGLING

INTERNET

- PAEDOPHILIA ON THE INTERNET
- PHISHING
- CYBERCRIME

SUBVERSION

- ARMS TRADE
- TERRORISM
- OUTLAW MOTORCYCLE GANGS

FINANCIAL

- MONEY LAUNDERING
- COUNTERFEITING AND FORGERY
- IDENTITY THEFT
- CAROUSEL (VAT) FRAUD

VEHICLES

- ROAD FREIGHT THEFT
- VEHICLE THEFT

MONEY LAUNDERING

- In 2000–2002 the Financial Action Task Force identified 23 countries or territories that it blacklisted for money laundering: by 2006 all had reformed their financial regimes.
- Tightening of banking regulations has repercussions in everybody's lives: merely opening an account now requires much stricter proofs of identity and address.
- Money is laundered through legitimate businesses that regularly deal in large amounts of cash, such as casinos, bars, restaurants – and even laundries.
- Over US$30 billion is estimated to have passed through Swiss banks from eastern Europe following the collapse of communism. Cypriot banks also processed large sums.

COUNTERFEIT AND FORGERY

- Fakes cost the global economy over US$1 trillion a year; almost a quarter of this is borne by the USA.
- The forgery of banknotes has becoming increasingly difficult, so gangs have turned to counterfeiting designer clothes, shoes and watches, DVDs and CDs.
- China is the largest source of counterfeit products.
- Counterfeit drugs account for 10% of all pharmaceuticals.
- Counterfeit car parts cost the industry US$12 billion, resulting in the loss of 750,000 jobs.
- Counterfeit cosmetics cost the European cosmetic industry US$3 billion.

CIGARETTE SMUGGLING

- Cross-border smuggling cashes in by undercutting highly taxed legitimate sales in the target country. This costs governments heavily in lost tax revenue.
- Smuggled cigarettes account for over half of domestic sales in Albania, Georgia, Iran, and Burma (Myanmar), and at least a quarter in many Balkan countries, Costa Rica and El Salvador, Ecuador and Peru, Estonia and Finland, Laos, Nigeria, Sudan, Syria, Uzbekistan, Yemen, and Zambia.
- Hubs of smuggling networks include Andorra, Cyprus, Dubai, Port Said in Egypt, Hong Kong, Singapore, Vladivostok, Montreal, and Iguazu on the border between Brazil and Argentina.

ID THEFT

- A third of all ID thefts occur or are originated in the USA.
- Almost half of all known "phishing" websites are located there. These attempt to get ordinary computer users to part with personal and banking information.
- Over 8 million US adults suffered identity fraud in 2007.
- Total fraud amount was almost US$50 billion – on average US$6000 per victim.
- 12% of all identity theft victims in the USA end up with a wrongful criminal record.
- 127 million data records were breached in the USA in 2007.
- In Brazil, Valdir Paulo de Almeida was arrested in 2005 for leading a phishing ring which stole up to US$37 million in two years.

FIND OUT MORE: anti-money-laundering.offshore-journals.com; www.thetruecosts.org; www.privacyrights.org/identity.htm; policy-traccc.gmu.edu

153

RUSSIA

- Russian mafia groups deal in drugs, guns, gambling, contract killings, black gold (caviar), and the sex trade. Several thousand contract killings occur each year.
- Five out of six Russian banks are not considered legitimate enterprises.
- Jews, Georgians, and Chechens are disproportionately represented in the Russian underworld.
- Russia's Interior Ministry estimates that more than 2000 industrial entities have fallen under criminal control, and that there are 450 mafia groups with a total membership of 12,000. Non-government estimates put the numbers much higher, at 10,000 groups with a membership of 300,000.

CHINA

- Chinese Triads, or Black Societies, deal in drugs, contract killings, money laundering, gambling, prostitution, car theft, extortion, and counterfeiting of intellectual property such as clothing, computer software, music CDs, and movie DVDs.
- There are an estimated 80 million Triad members worldwide. There are over 50 Triads in Hong Kong alone, with a membership of 80,00

JAPAN

- The Japanese Yakuza, literally "violence groups", claim 85,000 members.
- They are semi-open societies with an official headquarters.
- Yakuza income comes mainly from protection rackets and sex-related industries
- They smuggle pornography and foreign women into Japan, and control large prostitution rings.

WEST AFRICA: THE NEW HUB

Traffickers bringing drugs from South America to Europe increasingly use West Africa as a stopping-off point to divide shipments into smaller quantities that are harder to detect. According to the 2006 United Nations Office on Drugs and Crime World Drug Report, Western and Central Africa saw a sixfold increase in cocaine seizures in 2004 alone. It has also become a transit point for people and vehicle trafficking, and the history of conflict and instability has left a legacy of easy access to firearms, increasing the incidence of armed robbery and gun smuggling.

Legend:
→ TRAFFICKING IN HUMAN BEINGS
→ FIREARMS TRAFFICKING
→ DRUG TRANSIT ROUTES
→ DRUG TRAFFICKING
→ VEHICLE THEFT AND TRAFFICKING
● ARMED ROBBERY
● FRAUD (INC. IT FRAUD)
○ MONEY LAUNDERING

Map labels: MAURITANIA, MALI, NIGER, MIDDLE EAST, SENEGAL, GAMBIA, BURKINA FASO, GUINEA, GUINEA-BISSAU, BENIN, SIERRA LEONE, GHANA, CHINA, COTE D' IVOIRE, NIGERIA, SOUTHERN AFRICA, INDIA, LEBANON, LIBERIA, UK, TOGO, ASIA, LATIN AMERICA, NORTH AMERICA, EUROPE

LATIN AMERICA

- Latin America accounted for up to three-quarters of the world's kidnappings in 2003.
- São Paulo has more heliports than New York because company executives are afraid to travel in cars – just one sign of the gang rule in Brazil's major cities.
- Criminal violence costs Latin America US$30 billion a year – and perhaps 13% of GDP in Colombia.
- The Mexican drug business is worth around US$150 billion a year.
- Up to 100,000 youths in Central America belong to "mara" gangs, which originated in Los Angeles.

CARIBBEAN

- The Netherlands Antilles accounts for 60% o cocaine seized in the Caribbean: up to 100 couriers a day pass through its airports.
- Jamaica is the largest cocaine producer in the region.
- 241 people were kidnapped in Haiti in just one month in December 2005.
- Six Caribbean island states were blacklisted for money laundering in 2000–03.

SOURCES: UN Office on Drugs and Crime; TRAFFIC International; Coalition Against Trafficking in Women

WILDLIFE AND BUSHMEAT TRAFFICKING

- Interpol estimates that illegal trafficking of wildlife and wildlife parts is worth US$20 billion a year.
- 322 tonnes of ivory has been seized worldwide since 1989 – representing the tusks of over 3000 elephants each year.
- 56 African rhinos a year were found dead, poached for their horns, in 2002–05.
- Despite China's 1993 ban on trading in tiger parts, three per cent of its medicine shops still stock tiger bone, and tiger-skin cloaks remain popular in Tibet.

THE SEX TRADE

- There are an estimated eight million women and two million children trapped in the global sex trade.
- 1.4 million more people are ensnared every year – half of whom are children.
- Filipinas and Thais are particularly exploited: they account for 90% of Japan's imported prostitutes. On their arrival in Japan, Thai women have a debt of US$25,000 to pay off to their pimps.
- Thailand has 5.1 million sex tourists a year.

COMBATING CRIME

Collusion between criminal organizations in different parts of the world, now amounting to the effective globalization of crime, has outpaced both the development of international commercial law, and the gradual rise in co-operation between national police networks. Organizations such as Interpol and Europol struggle to keep up. One key objective of the UN Convention against Transnational Organized Crime is to get states to commit to establishing domestic laws that can be used to target organized criminals operating outside their borders. Extradition agreements are an important part of this, as is allowing investigators to have access to suspect bank accounts and business records. It was, after all, a tax evasion charge that famously nailed Al Capone. With business fraud rife, proving that profits have been made illegally is a big part of the anti-crime battle.

It is not all about paperwork and legal argument, of course. Police raids, border checks, and covert surveillance all have their role, together with the dangerous work of informers infiltrated into criminal gangs, and the use of witness protection programmes to break through powerful codes of silence and revenge when cases are eventually brought to trial. The trade in illegal weapons, and the need for untraceable cash, may bring crime gangs into close contact with terrorists and rebel groups fighting against the state. Powerful organized crime groups can even behave much like insurgents themselves – and elicit a similar response. In Mexico, for example, where drug trafficking has become the major threat to security, 30,000 security personnel were deployed in 2007 in a "frontal war" against the drug cartels.

The supercomputer ASC Purple comprises a ring of 196 IBM Power5 SMP servers, containing 12,544 microprocessors with 50 terabytes of memory and 2 petabytes of disk storage. It uses 7.5 megawatts of electricity (enough to power 7500 domestic homes), and requires a purpose-built cooling system. It has a processing speed of 100 teraflops (or 100 million floating-point operations per second). It is designed to continually monitor the US nuclear defense system.

TECHNOLOGY CONTINUES TO OUTSTRIP THE CULTURE WHICH PRODUCES IT, AND IN DOING SO RAISES MANY ETHICAL QUESTIONS WHILST PROVIDING SOME POTENTIAL SOLUTIONS

ENERGY
ELECTRICITY PRODUCTION, NUCLEAR POWER, OIL, RENEWABLE ALTERNATIVES, ENERGY CONSUMPTION

TECHNOLOGY

COMMUNICATIONS
TELECOMS AND MOBILE PHONES, CONNECTIVITY, PUBLISHING TODAY, THE MAIL SYSTEM

THE INTERNET
GROWTH OF THE INTERNET, ACCESS, SEARCH ENGINES, IMPACT ON BUSINESS, SOCIAL NETWORKING SITES

SURVEILLANCE
METHODS, IN THE HIGH STREET/IN THE WORKPLACE, CCTV REVOLUTION, ID/LOYALTY/ CREDIT CARDS

TRANSPORT
MODES OF TRAVEL, CARBON FOOTPRINTS, COMMUTING, GASOLINE PRICES, HOW MUCH ROAD?

NEW TECHNOLOGIES
R&D BUDGETS, PATENTS, NANOTECHNOLOGY, GENETIC ENGINEERING, ROBOTICS, DIGITAL DEVELOPMENTS

ENERGY

Life in the modern era is more energy-dependent than ever, to power our industries, grow our food, heat (and cool) our homes and workplaces, fuel our transport and trade, and drive our communications technology and entertainment media. In the 20th century, oil and gas exploitation grew to rival "King Coal" as major energy sources. But none of these three fossil fuels can last forever – and anyway the carbon dioxide emitted by burning them to the bitter end would warm the world so much as to make human life on this planet intolerable.

This is the fundamental cause of our current energy crisis. It's made more acute by the rising energy demands of China, India, and other developing countries, and the knowledge that we are approaching (or may even have reached) "peak oil" – the point where we have used up more than half of the oil that ever was, and we enter an era of inexorably dwindling oil resources.

Geopolitics comes into the energy security picture too, as energy-hungry Western nations depend heavily on the turbulent Middle East for oil, and on an increasingly assertive Russia for gas supplies to Europe.

Hydroelectricity and (especially) nuclear power, the first great hopes for everlasting clean power, are still widely touted as the best answers to the looming "energy gap". But large-scale hydro can be horribly damaging to the local environment and to vital water courses, while nuclear power has yet to solve its radioactive waste disposal problem, or calm post-Chernobyl safety fears.

THE ELECTRIC WORLD

- TODAY'S WORLD DEPENDS ALMOST ENTIRELY UPON ELECTRICITY
- 200 YEARS AGO THE WORLD WAS ENTIRELY INDEPENDENT OF ELECTRICITY
- THE GENERATION OF ELECTRICITY IS THE SINGLE GREATEST CONSUMER OF ALL FUEL RESOURCES

GLOBAL ENERGY
METHODS OF ELECTRICITY PRODUCTION AROUND THE WORLD

0.9% WIND, SOLAR, TIDE, WAVE, GEOTHERMAL

15.2% NUCLEAR

17.4% HYDRO

66.5% THERMAL— COAL, GAS, OIL, AND BIOMASS

Two-thirds of our electri is derived by burning coa gas, oil, and biomass. Ove 30 countries utilize nucle technology. Many Africa countries are almost enti dependent on hydropowe leaving them vulnerable t droughts. Other renewabl sources are still a very sm wedge in the energy mix, provide no more than a q of any countries' electrici

For more on production and reserves gas, and oil, see Resources pp26-29

RELIANCE ON NUCLEAR POWER

FRANCE 78%
LITHUANIA 64%
SLOVAKIA 58%
BELGIUM 57%
SWEDEN 50%
UKRAINE 45%
SWITZERLAND 42%
BULGARIA 41%
ARMENIA 40%
SOUTH KOREA 38%
SLOVENIA 37%
HUNGARY 32%
CZECH REPUBLIC 31%
GERMANY 28%
FINLAND 27%
SPAIN 24%
JAPAN 23%
UK 22%
TAIWAN 22%
USA 20%
RUSSIA 16%
CANADA 13%
ROMANIA 9%
ARGENTINA 8%
SOUTH AFRICA 5%
MEXICO 5%
NETHERLANDS 4%
BRAZIL 4%
INDIA 3%
PAKISTAN 2%
CHINA 2%

1980
711 TERAWATT/HOURS

1975
365 TERAWATT/HOURS

1970
77 TERAWATT/HOURS

THE RISE AND RISE OF NUCLEAR POW
TOTAL WORLD USE SINCE 1970

SOURCES: *BP Statistical Review of World Energy* June 2007; International Atomic Energy Agency (IAEA); Energy Information Administration

WATTS TO TERAWATTS
Electricity-generating capacity is usually measured in kilowatts (kW), megawatts (1MW=1000kW), or gigawatts (1GW=1000MW). A 1GW power station operating at full capacity for one hour has an output of one gigawatt/hour (GW/h). Global electricity output (and consumption) is measured in terawatt/hours (where 1TW=1000GW).

2005
2771 TERAWATT/HOURS

2000
2582 TERAWATT/HOURS

1995
2324 TERAWATT/HOURS

1990
2002 TERAWATT/HOURS

1985
1481 TERAWATT/HOURS

THE TOP TEN OIL IMPORTERS
METRIC TONS

609,476,000 USA

254,214,000 JAPAN
171,471,000 CHINA
123,840,000 GERMANY
107,232,000 SOUTH KOREA
94,414,000 FRANCE
84,140,000 INDIA
77,706,000 ITALY
77,556,000 SPAIN
46,983,000 TAIWAN

CHINA'S ENERGY CRAVING

- 80% OF CHINA'S ELECTRICITY COMES FROM COAL, TWICE THE GLOBAL AVERAGE
- CHINA ACCOUNTS FOR 37% OF GLOBAL COAL CONSUMPTION AND 14% OF GLOBAL HYDROPOWER CONSUMPTION
- ALMOST 6000 CHINESE COAL MINERS DIE EACH YEAR IN DISASTERS
- CHINA STILL HAS 70 MILLION HOMES WITHOUT ELECTRICITY
- NEW POWER STATIONS ARE BEING COMPLETED AT A RATE OF ONE EVERY FIVE DAYS
- RENEWABLES TARGETS IN BEIJING AIM TO CUT POLLUTION BY THE 2008 OLYMPICS
- THE THREE GORGES DAM ON THE YANGTZE RIVER WILL PROVIDE 22GW OF HYDROPOWER GENERATING CAPACITY BY 2009
- ELECTRICITY GENERATING CAPACITY IS EXPECTED TO DOUBLE TO ALMOST 1000GW BY 2020, WITH A TARGET OF 15% OF PRODUCTION FROM RENEWABLES
- THE PLANNED QUADRUPLING OF NUCLEAR POWER CAPACITY TO 40GW BY 2020 WOULD STILL ONLY PROVIDE 4% OF ELECTRICITY NEEDS

RENEWABLE ENERGY

WIND, SOLAR, TIDE, WAVE, GEOTHERMAL, AND WOOD & WASTE POWER GENERATION (TERAWATT/HOURS)

Year	TWh
2005	370
2004	341
2003	308
2002	284
2001	253
2000	242
1999	221
1998	207
1997	194
1996	178
1995	172
1994	164
1993	156
1992	150
1991	135
1990	127
1989	118
1988	69
1987	66
1986	60
1985	55
1984	52
1983	46
1982	43
1981	33
1980	31

ENERGY CONSUMPTION PER CAPITA

EXPRESSED AS KILOGRAMMES OF OIL EQUIVALENT

CHAD	5
AFGHANISTAN	13
INDIA	316
CHINA	687
BRAZIL	728
ITALY	3077
JAPAN	3725
UK	3767
GERMANY	3888
FRANCE	4108
RUSSIA	4142
USA	7717
CANADA	7876

SOURCES: Energy Information Administration: *International Energy Annual 2005*; World Bank: *World Development Indicators*

A GLIMMER OF HOPE

ICELAND ALREADY PRODUCES ALL OF ITS ELECTRICITY FROM RENEWABLE SOURCES (HYDRO AND GEOTHERMAL). BY CONVERTING ITS TRANSPORT SYSTEMS TO HYDROGEN FUEL, IT AIMS TO BE THE FIRST COUNTRY ENTIRELY RUNNING ON RENEWABLE ENERGY BY 2050.

SAVE YOUR ENERGY

Cutting energy use and increasing efficiency are sure cost-effective ways of reducing demand. Existing renewable energy sources like windpower and burning biomass already do a little to help on the supply side. Windpower is expanding rapidly as the cheapest source of electricity in many developed countries, and in China. New renewable technologies may yet be our best answer, if advances in solar, wave and tidal power can live up to their promise.

ARE BIOFUELS THE ANSWER?

Use biofuel and you can keep on driving? Cereals, soya beans, rapeseed, sugar cane, and palm oil can all be refined or fermented into biofuel. The carbon dioxide released by burning them is no more than they absorbed as they grew, so there is no net contribution to global warming either.

The US wants biodiesel and other alternative fuels to replace 15% of the country's gasoline sales over the next decade. The EU stipulated in 2003 that biofuels should make up at least 5.75% of transport fuels by 2010. Further expansion targets are, however, controversial.

One big problem, though, is that we need agricultural land to grow food. We can ill afford to devote 9% of it worldwide to growing fuel crops – which we'd need, to meet just 10% of global transport fuel needs.

Clearing forests to make way for palm oil plantations is a bad bargain on the climate change front, too. We lose the trees that crucially soak up so much of world carbon dioxide emissions – and burning forests in Indonesia releases 33 metric tons more of this "greenhouse gas" for every ton of palm oil it makes space to grow.

But biofuels can also be made from plants like prairie grasses – and jatropha, which could grow all along the railways in India. Better yet, a new generation of "cellulosic biofuels" is on the horizon, made from inedible cereal stalks and other woody leftovers.

President George W. Bush visited Brazil in March 2007 to confirm US interest in buying as much biofuel as possible from south of the Equator. The opportunity offered to developing countries for new and lucrative cash cropping is rich with ambiguities for the future.

EUROPEAN UNION ENERGY TARGETS FOR 2020

- IMPROVING ENERGY EFFICIENCY BY 20%
- TREBLING THE SHARE OF RENEWABLE ENERGY CUTTING
- GREENHOUSE GAS EMISSIONS BY 20% OR MORE

BAHRAIN 14,501

QATAR 23,679

THE INTERNET

The INTERconnected computer NETworking system, developed by US scientists in the 1960s and 1970s, has now taken over the world. It has revolutionized the way we live, the way we work, and the way we relax. Whatever we want to know or buy, hear or see, it is out there some-where – and the enormous search engines, dominated by Google, will find it for you. The only question is the reliability of the information.

Google has been named as the world's most valuable brand. Its simple, clean search system has mushroomed into a complete Internet service: Google Mail, Google News, Google Chat, Google Maps, Google Earth – you can even tailor-make a Google homepage to integrate your news, email, work, and Web access.

By 2011 it is predicted that there will be 1.5 billion people online – 22% of the world's population. With China reaching 17% penetration and India 7%, Asians will ac-count for 42% of this global online community, and China will have overtaken the USA as the country with most Internet users. Africa's connectivity is increasing from a very small base, with a growing number of users there go-ing online in Internet cafes or at workplaces.

TOP FIVE COUNTRIES WITH LARGEST PERCENTAGE OF POPULATION ONLINE

1	Iceland 86.3%
2	New Zealand 74.9%
3	Sweden 74.7%
4	Portugal 73.8%
5	Australia 70.2%

GOING ONLINE

- 1244 million people use the Internet worldwide
- This total has more than tripled since 2000

Although Internet use is growing everywhere, the most dramatic increases are currently being seen in India (up 33% in 2006), Russia (up 21%), and China (up 20%). Average growth in Internet users worldwide was ten per cent in that year.

% of region's population that is online

Asia	12.4%
Europe	41.7%
North America	70.2%
Latin America/Caribbean	20.8%
Africa	4.7%
Middle East	17.3%
Oceania/Australia	55.2%

% of online population that lives in that region

Asia	36.9%
Europe	27.2%
North America	18.9%
Latin America/Caribbean	9.3%
Africa	3.5%
Middle East	2.7%
Oceania/Australia	1.5%

Total population online in that region

Asia	459,476,825
Europe	337,878,613
North America	234,788,864
Latin America/Caribbean	115,759,709
Africa	43,995,700
Middle East	33,510,500
Oceania/Australia	19,039,390

SOURCES: ETC: New Media Review, World & Regional Overview; Pew Internet Project; comScore, qSearch 2.0

TOP 20 COUNTRIES IN TERMS OF THE NUMBER OF INTERNET USERS 2007

#	Country	Users	Percentage
1	US	210,575,287	69.7%
2	CHINA	162,000,000	12.3%
3	JAPAN	86,300,000	67.1%
4	GERMANY	50,426,117	61.1%
5	INDIA	42,000,000	3.7%
6	UK	37,600,000	62.3%
7	BRAZIL	39,140,000	21.0%
8	SOUTH KOREA	34,120,000	66.5%
9	FRANCE	32,925,953	53.7%
10	ITALY	31,481,928	52.9%
11	RUSSIA	28,000,000	19.5%
12	MEXICO	22,700,000	21.3%
13	CANADA	22,000,000	67.8%
14	INDONESIA	20,000,000	8.9%
15	SPAIN	19,765,033	43.9%

One in three North Americans (USA and Canada) has accessed the Internet wirelessly in the past 30 days. In the USA, one in five Internet users have the necessary wi-fi connections at home, and one in three have logged on using a laptop computer, hand-held device, or mobile phone.

SEARCH ENGINES
TOP SEARCH SITES – AUGUST 2007

More than 61 billion searches were performed by more than 750 million users:

GOOGLE SITES	37 BILLION SEARCHES
YAHOO SITES	8.5 BILLION SEARCHES
BAIDU	3.2 BILLION SEARCHES
MICROSOFT SITES	2.1 BILLION SEARCHES
NHN	2 BILLION SEARCHES
EBAY	1.3 BILLION SEARCHES
TIME WARNER	1.2 BILLION SEARCHES
ASK	743 MILLION SEARCHES
FOX	683 MILLION SEARCHES
LYCOS	441 MILLION SEARCHES
TOTAL WORLDWIDE SEARCHES	61 BILLION SEARCHES

At the end of 2007 there were

1.4 billion

email accounts in active use worldwide. This includes 542.9 million Web email users, plus non-Web-based email such as the accounts provided by businesses for their staff at work. Use of online social networks had grown to 483.7 million users worldwide.

THE INTERNET

LIVING ONLINE

INTERNET IMPACT ON BUSINESS

The Internet allows even the smallest specialist businesses a global shop window. Their online presence may just be a listing in online directories, or a simple static website about their operations. More sophisticated are the interactive online shops, linked to instant dispatch or access to downloadable products. Email has also changed business communications dramatically, while Internet conferencing facilities and remote access to business networks help with staff working outside the office and international collaboration.

NETWORKED READINESS INDEX

From the World Economic Forum.
The index looks at various factors such as how much countries are using the Web to increase competitiveness.

The top ten list in the Index is as follows:

1	US	6	CANADA
2	SINGAPORE	7	TAIWAN
3	DENMARK	8	SWEDEN
4	ICELAND	9	SWITZERLAND
5	FINLAND	10	UK

THERE ARE OVER

75 MILLION

DOMAIN NAMES WORLDWIDE

Percentage of businesses that have their own website

Sweden 82%
Japan 78%
Germany 72%
UK 66%
Canada 64%
South Korea 53%
Australia 48.4%
Italy 44%

...AND ON GOVERNMENT

The Center for Public Policy at Brown University studied 1782 government websites in 198 different countries in 2006 to determine the level of e-government services across the globe. Features assessed included the availability of online information and electronic services, privacy and security, and public access.

TOP TEN E-GOVERNMENT COUNTRIES WORLDWIDE 2006 (SCALE OF 1–100)

1	South Korea 60.3	6	UK 42.6
2	Taiwan 49.8	7	Ireland 41.9
3	Singapore 47.5	8	Germany 41.5
4	USA 47.4	9	Japan 41.5
5	Canada 43.5	10	Spain 40.6

WHAT YOU CAN DO ONLINE IN THE UK
• file tax returns
• buy car tax
• buy TV licence
• pay parking fines
• university applications and admission

SELLING ON THE INTERNET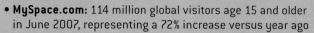

Marketing methods on the Internet are evolving rapidly, the biggest current area of expansion being the utilization of tailored advertising opportunities.

MARKETING TACTICS USED BY ONLINE COMPANIES WORLDWIDE:

Email **83%**
Display ads **73%**
Paid keyword search **63%**
Branded sponsorship **48%**
Blogs, online games, social networks, virtual worlds, widgets, and wikis **44%**
Referrals **39%**
Video ads **33%**
Podcasts **25%**

SOCIAL NETWORKING

• **MySpace.com:** 114 million global visitors age 15 and older in June 2007, representing a 72% increase versus year ago
• **Facebook.com:** 52.2 million visitors, jumping 270%
• **Bebo.com:** 18.2 million visitors (up 172%)
• **Tagged.com:** 13.2 million visitors (up 774%)

HOW MANY ONLINE CUSTOMERS VISIT SOCIAL NETWORKING SITES?:

South Korea **66%**		Canada **25%**
Brazil **47%**		India **24%**
China **42%**		Germany **19%**
Mexico **36%**		France **18%**
USA **32%**		Japan **22%**
UK **28%**		Russia **3%**

SOURCES: ETC: New Media Review; Harris Interactive Inc: *The Harris Poll*® #8 (January 29 2007); GBGC: *Global Gambling Report*

ENTERTAINMENT ONLINE

video-sharing phenomenon YouTube was created in February 2005, and is now
ed by Google. In January 2008 alone, nearly 79 million users watched over three
on video clips posted on YouTube.

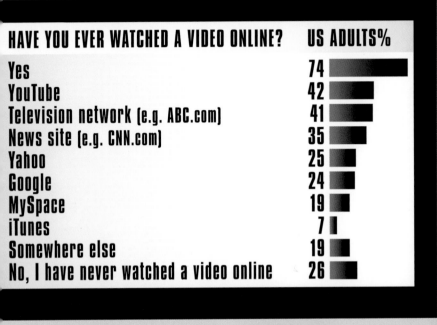

HAVE YOU EVER WATCHED A VIDEO ONLINE?   US ADULTS%

Yes	74
YouTube	42
Television network (e.g. ABC.com)	41
News site (e.g. CNN.com)	35
Yahoo	25
Google	24
MySpace	19
iTunes	7
Somewhere else	19
No, I have never watched a video online	26

04:12 / 06:30

X AND THE WEB

NEWS POLL: AMERICAN SEX SURVEY	MEN	WOMEN
ve visited sex Web site	34	10
ve participated in sex chat room	5	2
nk visiting sex Web site is cheating	25	42
nk participating in sex chat room is cheating	54	72

NLINE GAMBLING

007 there were over 2400 online gaming sites, and as many as 23 million people may have
ed bets online. Revenues from these sites currently account for only 5.4% of the global
ing revenue, but it is the fastest-growing sector. The international nature of websites has
ed many governments to review gambling legislation.

2006 revenues
US$15.2 billion (up 22% in a year)
of which
- **40%** is sports betting
- **22%** is poker
- **31%** other casino games

- **47%** generated in North America
- **28%** in Europe
- **14%** in Asia

2012 projected revenues
US$26.1 billion of which
- **36%** will be generated
  in North America
- **39%** in Europe
- **15%** in Asia

WEB DEVELOPING

Increasing demand for Internet services could see it
running out of capacity by 2010, says a US study by
Nemertes Research — unless US$130 billion is spent
worldwide (a third of it in the USA) on increasing
bandwidth on broadband networks. Users could otherwise
rediscover the frustrations that characterized the earlier
era of dial-up access.

By that time, the number of Web users creating
content is expected to double to 238 million, creating
three times more Internet content than the combined
total put up by publishers or brands. Sites like YouTube,
MySpace, Facebook, and Photobucket are leading this
key development area of user-generated content (UGC).
Blogging will spread within companies for information-
sharing, and lifelogs (24/7 streaming of an individual's
life) will digitally record biodata, memories, habits,
and preferences.

BLOGGING
- Over 75,000 new weblogs are created every day
- In 2006 there were over 35 million blogs
- More than half of all bloggers are still updating
  their sites
- Around four million update their sites weekly
- Chinese actress-turned-director Xu Jinglei's blog
  has had over 100 million page views

COMMUNICATIONS

Telecommunications have been shrinking space and reshaping the world for over 160 years since the introduction of the telegraph in the 1840s. By 1900 there was a worldwide network of land and sea cables linking and traversing the inhabited continents. In the 20th century the telegraph was complemented and then eclipsed by the telephone. Despite the spread of global networks, the landline telephone remained expensive and limited to sound alone, until the invention of facsimile image transfers down the line in the 1970s.

Over the last 30 years digital, satellite, and mobile technologies, combined with the Internet (page 162), have again transformed communication, making information exchange of all kinds easier, cheaper, and more widespread than ever. These technologies are now merging as increasing processing power allows mobile phones to use the Internet.

Texting has made critical data available to all: a farmer in Africa can finally cut out the middle-man by receiving the prices for his products direct from the market. The addition of cameras to cell phones has democratized news-gathering. The tracking data from mobile phones is increasingly important to police and security investigations, while children's access to mobile phones is changing the nature of parental supervision.

TELECOMS

THE INTERNET STEALS THE HEADLINES AS THE DEFINING TECHNOLOGY OF THE EARLY 21ST CENTURY, BUT THE EXPLOSIVE GROWTH AND ENORMOUS USE OF MOBILE TELEPHONY IS ALMOST AS ASTONISHING.

In 1981 NMT (Nordic Mobile Telephony) was launched in Saudi Arabia, Norway, and Sweden, and the first mobile telephone networks were established. Growth was slow over the first decade, but the following 15 years have been explosive – adding 400 million Chinese users alone. In 2007 the world's 3.3 billion mobile phone subscribers were equal to half the global population.

FOCUS ON AFRICA

The International Telecommunications Union Digital Opportunity Index ranks Africa as the least connected continent. However, everywhere on the continent the mobile phone is spreading. The picture above shows cell phones recharging at a Sudanese refugee centre in Uganda.

THE CELL PHONE IN AFRICA

Africa's demand for the mobile phone is insatiable. In a continent where landlines are rare, expensive and unreliable, the cell phone flourishes. The pervasiveness of the mobile phone is transforming agricultural markets, economic prospects, and even banking.

CELL PHONES IN AFRICA (MILLIONS)

1996 1M
2006 100M
2007 215M

M-BANKING IN KENYA

Number of Kenyans with bank account: 19%
Number of Kenyans with access to mobile phone: 58%
Cost of remitting £50 from UK to Kenya: £9
Cost using m-banking: £3
Cost of sending £260 by text in Kenya: 22p

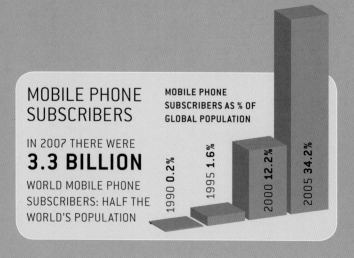

MOBILE PHONE SUBSCRIBERS

IN 2007 THERE WERE
3.3 BILLION
WORLD MOBILE PHONE SUBSCRIBERS: HALF THE WORLD'S POPULATION

MOBILE PHONE SUBSCRIBERS AS % OF GLOBAL POPULATION

1990 0.2%
1995 1.6%
2000 12.2%
2005 34.2%

SOURCES: International Telecommunications Union (2007); World Information Society 2007, Geneva; World Bank, World Development Indicator

CONNECTIVITY AND WEALTH

THE RICHEST 20% OF THE WORLD HAVE 80% OF THE BROADBAND CONNECTIONS. THE POOREST 50% HAVE VIRTUALLY NONE.

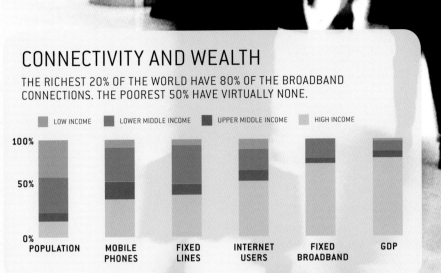

LOW INCOME | LOWER MIDDLE INCOME | UPPER MIDDLE INCOME | HIGH INCOME

POPULATION | MOBILE PHONES | FIXED LINES | INTERNET USERS | FIXED BROADBAND | GDP

LANDLINES VERSUS MOBILES

MOBILE PHONE SUBSCRIBERS PER 1000 PEOPLE

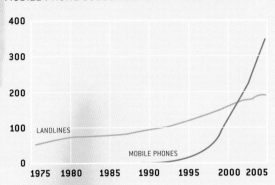

LANDLINES

MOBILE PHONES

1975 1980 1985 1990 1995 2000 2005

20 LARGEST MOBILE PHONE COMPANIES (SUBSCRIBERS IN MILLIONS)

THE MOBILE PHONE HAS CREATED SOME OF THE 21ST CENTURY'S NEW CORPORATE GIANTS.

CHINA MOBILE	CHINA	349.66
VODAFONE	UK	206
CHINA UNICOM	CHINA	156.03
TELEFONICA/MOVISTAR/O2	SPAIN	154.8
AMERICA MOVIL	MEXICO	143.394
T-MOBILE	GERMANY	113.7
MTS	RUSSIA	74.67
ORANGE/FRANCE TELECOM	FRANCE	73.2
TELENOR	NORWAY	68
AT&T MOBILITY	USA	65.7
VERIZON WIRELESS	USA	63.7
TELECOM ITALIA/TIM	ITALY	61.1
SINGTEL	SINGAPORE	56.87
ORASCOM TELECOM	EGYPT	56
SPRINT NEXTEL	USA	54
VIMPELCOM	RUSSIA	53.3
NTT DOCOMO	JAPAN	52.94
BHARTI AIRTEL	INDIA	46.81
TELKOMSEL	INDONESIA	42.81
TELIASONERA	SWEDEN AND FINLAND	41.7

COMMUNICATIONS

HARD COPY : WORLD PUBLISHING TODAY

GLOBAL PUBLISHING IS DOMINATED BY A CLUSTER OF MULTI-IMPRINT, MULTI-MARKET, AND MULTI-NATIONAL CORPORATIONS COVERING A RANGE OF PRINT AND EMERGING DIGITAL MEDIA. THE BIGGEST, ALTHOUGH THEY HAVE AMERICAN OPERATIONS BASED IN CANADA OR EUROPE, HAVE GLOBAL REACH. A FEW SPECIALISTS SURVIVE, LIKE READERS DIGEST IN THE POPULAR AND DIRECT-MAIL MARKET, AND SCHOLASTIC IN THE EDUCATIONAL/CHILDREN'S MARKET. PEARSON, WITH BROADLY-SPREAD INTERESTS IN EDUCATIONAL, PROFESSIONAL, AND FICTION PUBLISHING, ALONGSIDE NEWSPAPERS, ONLINE, AND MAGAZINES, IS MORE REPRESENTATIVE OF THE MODERN PUBLISHING CONCERN.

TOP PUBLISHING HOUSES WORLDWIDE

CONVENTIONAL PRINT PUBLISHING REMAINS BIG BUSINESS, BUT THE SHIFT TOWARDS DIGITAL EDUCATIONAL PRODUCTS, MAGAZINES, SPECIALIST JOURNALS, AND THE AVAILABILITY OF THESE (FOR A PRICE) ONLINE IS SHAPING THE FUTURE MARKET.

PUBLISHER	COUNTRY	TURNOVER 2006 IN BILLIONS OF EUROS
REED ELSEVIER	UK/NETH/USA	5.85
PEARSON	UK/NETH/USA	5.61
THOMSON	CANADA	5.10
BERTELSMANN	GEMANY	4.60
WOLTERS KLUWER	NETHERLANDS	3.70
HACHETTTE LIVRE	FRANCE	1.97
MCGRAW-HILL EDUCATION	USA	1.94
READER'S DIGEST	USA	1.84
SCHOLASTIC	USA	1.76
DE AGOSTINI EDITORE	ITALY	1.61
HOLTZBRINCK	GERMANY	1.23
GRUPO PLANETA	SPAIN	1.02
HARPER COLLINS	USA	1.00
HOUGHTON MIFFLIN	USA	0.99
INFORMA	UK	0.98
SPRINGER SCIENCE AND MEDIA	GERMANY	0.92
KODANSHA	JAPAN	0.91
SHOGAKUKAN	JAPAN	0.90
SHUEISHA	JAPAN	0.84
WILEY	USA	0.80

BOOKS PUBLISHED PER ANNUM

10,000 BOOKS

BRITAIN REMAINS THE BIGGEST PUBLISHER OF CONVENTIONAL BOOK TITLES PER ANNUM. NEVERTHELESS, THE ANNUAL FRANKFURT BOOK FAIR BOASTS SOME 8000 EXHIBITORS AND OVER 280,000 ATTENDEES, MANY OF WHOM ARE SPECIALIST SUBJECT OR LANGUAGE PUBLISHERS. IN SPAIN, PUBLISHING IN REGIONAL CATALAN ACCOUNTS FOR OVER 30% OF THE NATIONAL PUBLISHING OUTPUT IN TERMS OF TITLES IF NOT TURNOVER.

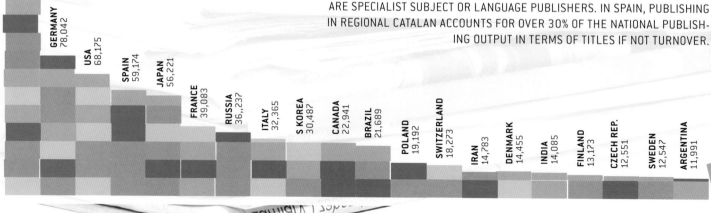

UK 110,965
GERMANY 78,042
USA 68,175
SPAIN 59,174
JAPAN 56,221
FRANCE 39,083
RUSSIA 36,,237
ITALY 32,365
S KOREA 30,487
CANADA 22,941
BRAZIL 21,689
POLAND 19,192
SWITZERLAND 18,273
IRAN 14,783
DENMARK 14,455
INDIA 14,085
FINLAND 13,173
CZECH REP. 12,551
SWEDEN 12,547
ARGENTINA 11,991

SOURCES: Livres Hebdo (2007): The World's Biggest Publishing Groups; Universal Postal Union (2007): Development of Postal Services in 2006

SIGNED, SEALED, DELIVERED...

BUT NOT NECESSARILY TO YOUR DOOR. SIGNIFICANT PARTS OF AFRICA AND POCKETS OF LATIN AMERICA STILL HAVE NO ACCESS TO MAIL NETWORKS. MANY OF THOSE THAT DO ENJOY DAILY MAIL DELIVERY MUST TRAVEL TO A SUB-POST OFFICE TO RECEIVE IT.

	MAIL DELIVERED AT HOME	MAIL DELIVERED AT POST OFFICE	NO ACCESS TO MAIL	PERSONS PER POSTAL WORKER	PARCELS PER 1000 PEOPLE
AFRICA	22%	66%	12%	11,780	6
LATIN AMERICA AND CARIBBEAN	81%	13%	6%	3056	283
ASIA AND PACIFIC	95%	5%	0%	2240	80
EASTERN EUROPE AND FORMER SOVIET UNION	98%	2%	0%	509	140
MIDDLE EAST	64%	32%	4%	2624	5
INDUSTRIALIZED COUNTIRES	95%	5%	0%	343	6375

DIGITAL IMPACTS

Book publishing and the mail are pre-modern inventions. Both can be traced back to 16th century Europe and, despite the emergence of the new digital communications technologies, they remain in business. Book publishing continues, in the absence of an effective digital reader, to have a product – bound books – that has a tactile and practical edge over all the competition. But increasingly book publishers are product manufacturers, part of a supply chain dominated by corporate retailers rather than by creative instinct. The emergence of print-on-demand technologies, publishing on the Internet, and online bookselling are all changing the business, threatening to cut traditional bookshops and publishers out of the circuit between writers and readers.

The usual corporate response to global markets and technological uncertainty is "merger", and over the last two decades there has been a marked concentration of publishing power within a few large corporations. In addition to books, some have immense stakes in newspapers, magazines, and scientific and journal publication.

The impact of digital technologies on the world's mail services is more complex. On the one hand, email has contributed to the demise of the letter and the postcard; on the other hand, Internet shopping has boosted domestic parcel services. More worryingly, computer records and data analysis have created the avalanche of junk mail that the developed world is choking itself on, while the traditional postal service is in economic meltdown.

BILLIONS OF LETTERS AND PARCELS DELIVERED 2006

DOMESTIC PARCELS **6.2**	INTERNATIONAL PARCELS **0.04**

433.6
DOMESTIC LETTERS

INTERNATIONAL LETTERS **5.5**

CHANGE OF ADDRESS

THE TOTAL VOLUME OF GLOBAL MAIL IS IMMENSE – NEARLY HALF A TRILLION ITEMS A YEAR. ALMOST EVERYWHERE THIS IS CARRIED BY STATE MONOPOLIES OF SOME KIND OR ANOTHER.

Over the last 20 years a range of private alternative courier services have emerged, and many markets have been deregulated to allow more competition. The small but lucrative international parcel trade has been an area of particularly fierce competition, high investment, and high profit.

SURVEILLANCE

You are being watched. Huge numbers of secret police, vast networks of informers and painstaking record-keeping were once necessary for totalitarian regimes to keep their subjects in check. Technology has changed that. Surveillance is no longer a matter of targeting and tracking suspects, but of tapping into a vast reservoir of data collected automatically and indiscriminately, whether by video cameras in public places or via the electronic footprints left by a wide range of our everyday activities. Use a mobile phone, and triangulation from several different masts can pin down pretty exactly where you are. Drive past a speed camera or buy anything with a credit card, and your precise location and time are logged. If the state has the power of access to all this information, its capacity for surveillance is immense.

The UK has more than 4 million CCTV cameras – the most watched place in the world. Automatic face recognition software helps identify individuals from their constant recordings, and work is being done on picking people out from the crowd by their gait too. Vehicle number plate recognition technology is now in widespread use, not only for speed cameras but increasingly for billing for toll roads too. Big cities with mass public transit systems regularly install not only CCTV systems but travel cards – in London for example the Oyster card – which track all the journeys that a user makes.

BITS OF PLASTIC

EACH YEAR FIVE BILLION PLASTIC CARDS CONTAINING PHOTO ID ARE PRODUCED WORLDWIDE. MORE THAN 90% OF THESE ARE NON-FINANCIAL CARDS SUCH AS DRIVING LICENCES OR NATIONAL ID CARDS. ON TOP OF THESE COME ANOTHER 12 BILLION NON-PHOTO CARDS, MOSTLY CREDIT CARDS, ATM CARDS, AND PHONE CARDS. SMART CARDS WITH MICROCHIPS TO STORE ELECTRONIC DATA ARE THE FASTEST-GROWING SECTOR.

SURVEILLANCE METHODS IN THE EVERYDAY WORLD

WHEN PHOTOGRAPHY WENT DIGITAL, IT OPENED UP THE NEW ERA OF THE COMPUTER SEARCHABLE IMAGE. ELECTRONIC TRANSACTION LOGGING IS THE OTHER GREAT LEAP FORWARD FOR SURVEILLANCE.

STORE LOYALTY CARDS
A MINE OF DATA TO PROFILE YOU AS CONSUMER

CCTV
WATCHING IN STREETS, SHOPS, AND PUBLIC BUILDINGS

REGISTRATION PLATE RECOGNITION CAMERAS
TRACKING DRIVERS IN THEIR PASSING CARS

LONDON OYSTER CARDS
CONVENIENT – AND CONVENIENTLY TRACEABLE – TRAVEL PAYMENT

SATELLITES
NOW CAPABLE OF DETAILED PINPOINT PHOTOGRAPHY

PERSONAL VIDEO RECORDERS
PUT IT IN YOUTUBE FOR THE WORLD TO SEE

MOBILE PHONE CAMERAS
MOST PEOPLE CAN NOW GATHER PICTURE EVIDENCE

NHS PATIENT RECORDS
WHERE PATIENT CONFIDENTIALITY BECOMES FULLY SEARCHABLE

WORKER CALL MONITORING
ACCOUNTABILITY IN THE OFFICE

MOBILE PHONE TRIANGULATION
ZEROING IN ON WHERE THE CALL WAS MADE

SHOP RFID TAGS
WHAT YOU BUY HAS A TRACKABLE ID TOO

HIDDEN CAMERAS/BUGGING DEVICES
THE TRADITIONAL TOOLS OF ESPIONAGE GET EVER SMALLER

CREDIT CARD TRANSACTIONS
WHAT YOU SPENT IT ON – AND WHERE AND WHEN

WORKER CLOCKING-IN
WERE YOU WHERE YOU SHOULD HAVE BEEN?

KEYSTROKE PROGRAMMES
NOT JUST YOUR WORK RATE, BUT WHAT YOU WROTE

INTERNET COOKIES
TELLTALE EVIDENCE OF WHERE YOU'VE BEEN ONLINE

ELECTORAL ROLL
CENTURIES OLD – BUT NOW ON COMPUTER FILE

PHONE-TAPPING
RESTRICTED BY LAW BUT WIDELY USED

 SOURCES: IT Strategies: *Digital Printing of Plastic Cards*; American Management Association: 2007 Electronic Monitoring & Surveillance Survey

STORE LOYALTY CARDS

COLLECTING DATA ON CUSTOMERS FOR COMMERCIAL PURPOSES IS NOTHING NEW – BUT THE SCALE ON WHICH IT IS NOW DONE ELECTRONICALLY MAKES THE STORE LOYALTY CARD A TRULY WORLD-CHANGING PHENOMENON.

Supermarket loyalty cards tell the store a great deal more than just how much you spend. An industry has grown up around analysing individual shoppers' purchases, their preferences, and their in-store behaviour. Detailed profiles can be built up, and used for targeted advertising of relevant products. This can not only unleash a torrent of junk mail, but represent what many see as a breach of privacy. Data could be exploited in many ways if it fell into the wrong hands, and would greatly add to the state's power of surveillance over suspected criminals or dissidents.

85% OF UK HOUSEHOLDS BELONG TO AT LEAST ONE LOYALTY PROGRAMME

150 TERABYTES OF DATA OBTAINED ANNUALLY BY US SUPERMARKET CHAIN KRUGER

WORKPLACE MONITORING

65% of US companies use software to block connections to inappropriate websites

45% track computer content, keystrokes, and time spent at the keyboard

45% monitor time spent on the phone and numbers called

43% monitor email, of which **40%** assign an individual to manually review email

7% use video surveillance to track employees' on-the-job performance

8% use GPS to track company vehicles; **3%** use GPS to monitor cell phones; and less than **1%** use GPS to monitor employee ID/Smartcards

INTERNET COOKIES

COOKIES ARE SMALL PARCELS OF TEXT SENT FROM A SERVER TO A WEB BROWSER AND BACK IN ORDER TO AUTHENTICATE INFORMATION ABOUT USERS.

It is possible using cookies to work out what websites a user has been viewing. DoubleClick has agreements with over 11,000 websites and maintains cookies on 100 million users.

PHONE-TAPPING

PHONE-TAPPING HAS MOVED ON CONSIDERABLY. IT IS NOW IMPOSSIBLE TO TRACK WHETHER A CONVERSATION IS BEING TAPED.

Unofficial phone taps can be set up with minimal equipment, but most Western countries severely limit the legality of phone-tapping, and the use of such evidence in court.

SATELLITES

THE FIRST LANDSAT SATELLITE IN 1972 HAD A RESOLUTION OF APPROXIMATELY 80 METRES PER PIXEL. THE BEST SPY SATELLITES NOW HAVE A RESOLUTION OF 10CM PER PIXEL – CAPABLE OF SEEING A SMALL BALL FROM SPACE. GOOGLE EARTH'S IMAGERY VARIES BETWEEN 15M PER PIXEL AND 15CM PER PIXEL.

Satellite imagery is now available not just to the military and intelligence communities, but to most ordinary computer users through Google Earth. For the most part this high resolution, publicly available imagery is confined to the developed world. Google Earth images are also often considerably out of date. Those with access to current satellite data, however, can direct which areas of the world are kept under surveillance in real time.

HIDDEN CAMERAS

PLACING A HIDDEN CAMERA OR SOUND TRANSMISSION DEVICE (OR BOTH) IN A SPECIFIC LOCATION IS A LONG-ESTABLISHED METHOD OF ESPIONAGE OR SURVEILLANCE OF A SPECIFIC SUSPECT.

Far from being a Cold War anachronism, this remains a growing industry, backed by ever more sophisticated and miniaturized technology. Bugging devices have become much harder to detect. Bugs can now be so small that they are indistinguishable from everyday items such as pens – indeed, the use of one everyday item, the mobile phone, was recently ruled admissible in the US. Some models of phone can now be remotely reprogrammed without the knowledge of their owners to transmit conversations even when the phone itself is switched off.

SURVEILLANCE

IN THE NATIONAL INTEREST

THERE HAS ALWAYS BEEN TENSION BETWEEN THE USE OF SURVEILLANCE FOR THE PUBLIC GOOD — AGAINST EXTERNAL THREATS AND CRIME — AND THE PRIVACY AND CIVIL LIBERTIES OF THE INDIVIDUAL. IN A PRE-ELECTRONIC AGE, THE SHEER DIFFICULTY (AND MASSIVE MANPOWER REQUIREMENTS) OF MAINTAINING WIDESPREAD SURVEILLANCE ACTED AS A LIMIT ON WHAT COULD BE JUSTIFIED IN THE NATIONAL INTEREST. NOW THE MAIN LIMITING FACTOR IS PUBLIC ACCEPTABILITY — TOGETHER WITH CONCERNS ABOUT MISIDENTIFICATION AND THE SECURITY OF DATA AGAINST THEFT, LOSS, AND FRAUD.

West hall 43 : 18:34:32

SURVEILLANCE IN THE UK

THERE ARE AN ESTIMATED 20 MILLION CCTV CAMERAS IN OPERATION WORLDWIDE, OF WHICH 4.2 MILLION ARE IN THE UK — ONE FOR EVERY 14 PEOPLE. THE UK HAS MORE THAN THE REST OF WESTERN EUROPE COMBINED (2.3 MILLION). LONDON'S RESIDENTS CAN EACH EXPECT TO BE CAPTURED ON CCTV CAMERAS UP TO 300 TIMES A DAY.

The UK is in some ways one of the most watched societies on earth. Its seemingly ubiquitous CCTV cameras were developed in part as security during a period of heightened vigilance against IRA bombings. Increasingly, however, they were used by local authorities to target crime and anti-social behaviour, initially in city centres. Most railway stations now have them, as do shopping centres, and indeed individual shops, with even small shopkeepers using them to deter shoplifting. Their use in public places is more controversial in terms of the intrusion into personal privacy they represent, but they have become so commonplace that some councils are now to start using CCTV to enforce parking regulations.

MALAYSIA

IN 2001 MALAYSIA INTRODUCED THE MYKAD, A MULTI-PURPOSE COMPULSORY IDENTITY CARD WHICH CONTAINS BIOMETRIC DATA.

All Malaysian citizens must carry them at all times. The MyKad operates as not only an identity card, but as a driving licence and, with some neighbouring countries, a passport, as well as electronic money and as a pass card for toll roads. It contains personal information and health data as well as religious status and education information. Malaysia has also installed cameras and recording instruments in mosques to watch for radical or anti-government sentiment from Imams.

US$43 billion:

estimate of what the Chinese surveillance market will be worth in 2010 — compared with just US$0.5 billion in 2003.

CHINA

SURVEILLANCE OF CHINESE SOCIETY INTENSIFIED WITH THE APPROACH OF THE 2008 OLYMPICS. CCTV CAMERAS HAVE BEEN MOUNTED THROUGHOUT BEIJING.

The US state department has warned that all hotel rooms and offices are subject to "monitoring at all times". China denies that its security measures go beyond international norms, but around 660 cities are installing high-tech surveillance systems.

RUSSIA

THE FEDERAL SECURITY SERVICE (FSB), SUCCESSOR TO THE KGB OF THE SOVIET ERA, HAS GREATLY EXPANDED ITS REMIT TO COVER COUNTER-INTELLIGENCE, ELECTRONIC ESPIONAGE, BORDER CONTROL, AND SOCIAL MONITORING.

The FSB is also responsible for pursuing suspected traitors, including scientists and researchers accused of leaking state secrets. More than one in two employees in Russia is watched by video cameras while they are at work.

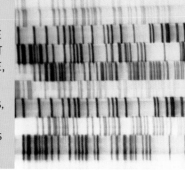

SOURCES: UK Home Office: Harris Interactive Inc: The Harris Poll® #19 (February 24 2006) and #63 (August 17 2006)

"TWO YEARS AGO I WARNED THAT WE WERE IN DANGER OF SLEEPWALKING INTO A SURVEILLANCE SOCIETY. TODAY I FEAR THAT WE ARE IN FACT WAKING UP TO A SURVEILLANCE SOCIETY THAT IS ALREADY ALL AROUND US."

UK INFORMATION COMMISSIONER RICHARD THOMAS

RFIDs

NOT ONLY PEOPLE, BUT OBJECTS TOO, CAN NOW BE GIVEN UNIQUE AND TRACKABLE IDENTITIES BY THE SIMPLE ATTACHMENT OF SMALL AND INEXPENSIVE RADIO FREQUENCY IDENTIFICATION (RFID) TAGS.

- The world's smallest and thinnest RFID tags measure just 0.05 x 0.05 millimetres.
- Over 30 million library items worldwide now contain RFID tags.
- The RFID industry is expected to grow at over 19% a year between now and 2016.
- The first RFID passports ("E-passport") were issued by Malaysia in 1998.
- Heathrow Airport uses RFID-based tags for tracking passenger luggage.
- RFID-activated billboards can communicate directly with passers-by, "personalizing" the advertising or messages they display according to the RFIDs they detect within range.

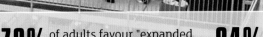

70% of adults favour "expanded camera surveillance on streets and in public places".

84% of adults favour stronger document and physical security checks for travellers.

61% favour "closer monitoring of banking and credit card transactions".

82% adults favour expanded undercover activity to penetrate groups under suspicion.

62% favour "law enforcement monitoring of Internet chat rooms and other forums".

64% favour adoption of a national ID system for all US citizens, up from 61 per cent in June 2008.

52% favour expanding the "monitoring of cell phones and email".

DO AMERICANS APPROVE?

THESE ARE THE FINDINGS OF A 2006 POLL. THEY REVEAL THE OVERWHELMING IMPORTANCE WHICH ORDINARY AMERICANS ATTACH TO GIVING THE NATIONAL SECURITY SERVICES THE TOOLS THEY WANT TO GUARD AGAINST THE THREAT OF TERRORISM.

Fear of crime, and of predatory use of the Internet to ensnare children, also shows up strongly in this survey – whereas it is notable that monitoring person-to-person phone calls and emails gets less support.

ON CAMERA – AND ON TAG

Governments that impose widespread surveillance measures routinely insist that they are doing so for the safety and welfare of their citizens. In the USA, the strong attachment of most Americans to privacy has been outweighed by the anxiety fostered by "9/11" and the ensuing "war on terror". The US public is not alone in this response. In the UK, despite considerable controversy, a poll in 2004 recorded 61 per cent in favour of compulsory identity cards. The proliferation of CCTV cameras in the UK has also enjoyed substantial public support, boosted whenever the perpetrators of major crimes are caught on film. The abduction and murder of toddler James Bulger in 1993 (opposite), and the 2005 London Underground terrorist bombings, can be regarded as horrible milestones along this road.

Data compression and nanotechnology hold out almost limitless possibilities for the use of RFID tags. It is conceivable that most ordinary objects could each have a unique identity and in effect their own mini "website", traceable by anyone searching online. Already RFIDs are increasingly being incorporated into products, and used to tag people and animals. There are worries that the information on RFIDs can be intercepted, and the US government demands that its employees with RFID cards house them in shielded holders.

Major current growth areas include supply chain management, where they provide an easy way of measuring inventory and confirming provenance, and mass transit, whether in cars for toll road payments or, as with the Oyster card in London, for public transport. RFID chips have even been implanted in people so that VIP customers in nightclubs can use them to pay for drinks.

WHERE THE CARS ARE
GLOBAL SHARE OF MOTOR VEHICLES

REST OF THE WORLD 22.9%

USA 27.6%

JAPAN 8.7%

CHINA & INDIA 4.7%

RUSSIA & EASTERN EUROPE 8.7%

WESTERN EUROPE 27.4%

TRANSPORT

Three-quarters of the world's motor vehicles are to be found in countries where just one-sixth of its population lives. However, even in China the car has overtaken the once-ubiquitous bicycle as the main mode of travel, as a car-hungry population seeks the benefits and status afforded by economic growth. Over half of all bicycles are still made in China; worldwide production has remained fairly static for the last 20 years at 100 million a year. World car production, meanwhile, is still steadily rising – now reaching almost 70 million a year.

For passenger travel, mass transit land-based systems including buses and trains are far more energy-efficient than cars and planes. Ever faster high speed trains can also compete time-wise with air travel for inter-city journeys of up to three or four hours. Cars use slightly less fuel per passenger mile than planes – but rack up so many more passenger miles that they stand invidiously at the top of the global gas-guzzling league table. The picture is rather different when you look at the movement of freight. Waterborne freight transport has a significant energy advantage, and hence a lower carbon footprint, compared with overland freight. But if ships score better than trains, the latter in turn outperform trucks in energy terms.

THE USA ALONE OWNS 28% OF THE WORLD'S MOTOR VEHICLES, which devour almost half of the world's annual car gasoline consumption. Developing countries average one vehicle per 24 people. The massive populations of India and China are still well below this.

OTHER ASIA & OCEANIA 5%

CHINA & INDIA 5%

JAPAN 5%

AFRICA 3%

EASTERN EUROPE 6%

OTHER WESTERN HEMISPHERE 11%

WESTERN EUROPE 14%

USA 44%

GASOLINE CONSUMPTION
WHO'S USING THE FUEL?

WAY TO GO?

THE NETHERLANDS WAS THE FIRST COUNTRY TO ESTABLISH AN OFFICIAL NATIONAL BICYCLE POLICY: IT CURRENTLY HAS ALMOST 19,000 KILOMETRES (11,875 MILES) OF PATHS AND LANES EXCLUSIVELY FOR BICYCLES.

MODES OF TRAVEL, PERCENTAGES BY COUNTRY	BY BICYCLE	BY FOOT	BY CAR	BY PUBLIC TRANSPORT	OTHER MEANS OF TRAVEL
NETHERLANDS	30%	18%	45%	5%	2%
DENMARK	20%	21%	42%	14%	3%
GERMANY	12%	22%	49%	16%	1%
SWITZERLAND	11%	29%	38%	20%	2%
SWEDEN	10%	39%	36%	11%	4%
AUSTRIA	9%	31%	39%	13%	8%
ENGLAND+WALES	8%	12%	62%	14%	4%
FRANCE	5%	30%	47%	12%	6%
ITALY	5%	28%	42%	16%	9%
CANADA	1%	10%	74%	14%	1%
USA	1%	9%	84%	3%	3%

THE FASTEST TRAINS : TOP SPEEDS

JAPAN: MAGLEV 580.9kph

FRANCE: TGV Est 574.8kph

SOURCES: Transportation Quarterly 98-1 (J. Pucher); EIA; EUROSTAT (2003); Ecoinvent (2007); UBA (2006)

RAIL FREIGHT 23

AIR FREIGHT 607

ROAD HAULAGE 84

15 LARGE CARGO VESSEL
over 8000 dwt

CARGO VESSEL 21

CARBON FOOTPRINTS

CARBON DIOXIDE GRAMS PER METRIC TON, PER KILOMETRE

Seen in this form, air freight looks like the villain of the piece. Nevertheless, air freight is comparatively extremely expensive and tends to be avoided except for emergency, luxury or highly perishable goods. In terms of sheer detriment to the environment the internal combustion engine still far outweighs the airplane, partly due to the sheer numbers of cars, vans and trucks constantly moving across the planet's surface, and partly due to the inefficient planning and use of most journeys.

TRAVELLING LITE

THE FUEL EFFICIENCY OF CARS IS NOW A MAINSTREAM DESIGN ISSUE FOR MANUFACTURERS AND A KEY PURCHASING POINT FOR DRIVERS.

Hybrid cars and buses have come on the market in recent years that achieve fuel savings by combining a fuel system with electric batteries that are recharged in the course of the driving process. Cars powered by ethanol/biofuel, natural gas, compressed air, hydrogen combustion, and hydrogen fuel cells have also been developed – and fully electric vehicles are shedding their old "milk float" image. But manufacturers have a tough target to beat: a combustion engine record was set in the 2004 European Shell Eco-marathon by a car that managed to travel 3410 km (2131 miles) on the equivalent of a single litre of fuel – while a prototype vehicle using hydrogen fuel cells has covered 3836 km (2397 miles) – the distance from Paris to Moscow – with equally miserly fuel needs.

WE TRAVEL FURTHER BECAUSE WE CAN TRAVEL FASTER

YORK 200 miles/320km

LINCOLN 130 miles/208km

CAMBRIDGE
60 miles/96km

ANNUAL TRAIN TICKETS
YORK	£3800
LINCOLN	£3400
BRISTOL	£3200
SOUTHAMPTON	£2900
IPSWICH	£2700
CAMBRIDGE	£2500
BRIGHTON	£2400

BRISTOL
120 miles/192km

IPSWICH
70 miles/112km

LONDON

SOUTHAMPTON
75 miles/120km

BRIGHTON
55 miles/ 88km

Despite attempts to limit car use by commuters, the lack of investment in the rail infrastructure in the UK, spiralling fare costs, and chronic overcrowding make taking the train an unattractive option for many. Two significant developments are the advent of cheap air travel and the Eurotunnel rail link, which have made it possible for some to commute to London from homes abroad.

EXTREME COMMUTING

In the UK people travel for an average of 45 minutes per day and spend some 8% of their income simply getting to work. The magnetic effect of London now sees some commuters travelling for one quarter of their waking hours from locations as distant as Bristol or York. The work/life balance has been sold as a justification for living further and further from the workplace. However, many long-distance commuters do not see their gardens on weekdays in daylight for six months of the year.

THE COST OF COMMUTING I

NOBODY LIKES COMMUTING – BUT WE DO IT MORE AND MORE. 3.4 million Americans endure a daily commute of 90 minutes or more each way to work. Advertisements on London commuter trains warn UK commuters that they will spend three years of their lives doing precisely that. And the travel doesn't end once you get to work. A quarter of European business executives make more than 100 rail journeys a year to meetings outside the office, and one in eight take more than 50 flights.

AVERAGE COMMUTES
UK: **45** MINUTES	FRANCE: **36** MINUTES
GERMANY: **44** MINUTES	SPAIN: **33** MINUTES
NETHERLANDS: **43** MINUTES	USA: **26** MINUTES
EU AVERAGE: **38** MINUTES	ITALY: **23** MINUTES

SWITZERLAND: 989 METRES TO THE DOCTOR

554	834	869	989	1084

HOME KINDERGARTEN = 554M POST OFFICE = 834M GAS STATION = 869M DOCTOR = 989M BAKERY = 1084M CITY HALL = 1099M

A recent study by the Swiss Federal Statistical Office (SFSO) calculated the distance from the average Swiss home to local shops and services. The accessibility of these basic amenities is a useful measure of quality of life – and the Swiss are clearly streets ahead.

 1 km (0.625 miles) is considered the "psychological threshold" for walking distance.

SOURCES: Swiss Federal Statistical Office (SFSO); World Bank: *World Development Indicators*

HE COST OF COMMUTING II

GASOLINE PRICES AROUND THE WORLD

AVERAGE PRICE PER LITRE

USA 6,407,637km/4,004,773 miles

TURKEY **US$2.67**
ERITREA **US$2.40**
NORWAY **US$2.22**
NETHERLANDS **US$2.21**
ICELAND **US$2.17**

UK **US$2.05**
INDIA **US$1.10**
USA **US$0.81**
RUSSIA **US$0.77**
CHINA **US$0.72**

LIBYA **US$0.13**
SAUDI ARABIA **US$0.12**
IRAN **US$0.11**
VENEZUELA **US$0.03**
TURKMENISTAN **US$0.02**

HOW MUCH ROAD?
THE TOP TEN COUNTRIES

INDIA 2,411,001km/1,506,875 miles

CHINA 1,438,633km/899,145 miles

JAPAN 914,745km/571,715 miles

FRANCE 891,290km/557,056 miles

SPAIN 659,629km/412,268 miles

UK 619,398km/387,123 miles

ITALY 479,688km/299,805 miles

CANADA 415,600km/259,750 miles

RUSSIA 362,133km/226,333 miles

TRAVEL DAMAGE LIMITATION

The motor car is still unrivalled as the most convenient means of personal transport outside towns and cities. In congested urban areas, however, its advantages are less apparent, notably on the speed front. The average speed of journeys in London has not risen appreciably in the last 100 years and bicycles regularly outstrip all other options when contests are held across the city. A congestion charge was introduced on cars in London's central zone in 2003, and widened in 2007. Similar schemes operate in Stockholm, Rome, Singapore, and Valletta (Malta), while Bergen in Norway has had a small-scale congestion charge scheme running since 1986. A proposal to apply this principle in Manhattan in 2007 was soon shelved amid an outcry from car-addicted New Yorkers, but London's success has got other cities around the world watching closely. Many city/motorway toll systems give incentives for sharing cars, and membership of car-share clubs has increased fivefold over the last five years.

£8 per day
Mon - Fri
7 am - 6.30 pm

½ mile

Central London's congestion charge has been deemed a success in turning the rising tide of vehicles on the metropolitan roads, and is being extended to cover a larger area of the city. It also generates useful revenues, which are earmarked for improving the infrastructure.

Along with car manufacturers, civil aircraft suppliers are developing increasingly efficient modes of transport, lighter, with greater passenger capacity and – significantly – lower fuel consumption. Boeing unveiled their "eco-friendly" answer to this challenge in 2007 (the Dreamliner, below), replacing their enormously successful long-haul gas-guzzler, the Jumbo Jet.

NEW TECHNOLOGIES

Communications technology and computing have revolutionized not just our gadgets but our daily lives – and continue to do so at accelerating pace. Technological advances feed off one another, and can open up new possibilities in what once seemed unrelated fields. Where this takes us, seems limited only by the scope of human imagination – and the drive for power and profit

Modern genetics and the understanding of DNA, for instance, are allowing us to manipulate the fundamental building blocks of nature, creating new foods, enabling new medical diagnostics and disease prevention, and giving us daunting moral choices on selective breeding. In quantum physics, delving into the sub-particles of matter could help develop new materials, and new solutions on key issues such as energy – while artificial intelligence is being used to facilitate our interaction with machinery and create highly realistic virtual worlds.

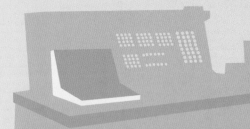

- IN 1954, WHEN IBM PRODUCED ITS FIRST COMMERCIALLY AVAILABLE COMPUTER (THE IBM 704), ITS MARKETING DEPARTMENT PREDICTED A MARKET OF ONLY SIX MACHINES

- TO DATE ALMOST TWO BILLION COMPUTERS HAVE BEEN SOLD, AND THERE ARE CURRENTLY OVER A BILLION IN USE WORLDWIDE

INVESTMENT AND SUCCESS

MONEY SPENT ON R&D

COUNTRY	GROSS EXPENDITURE ON RESEARCH & DEVELOPMENT (US$ BILLIONS)	% OF WORLD GROSS EXPENDITURE ON RESEARCH & DEVELOPMENT	% OF NATIONAL GDP	GROSS EXPENDITURE ON RESEARCH & DEVELOPMENT PER INHABITANT (US$)
USA	290	35.0	2.8	1006
JAPAN	106	12.8	3.1	837
CHINA	72	8.7	1.2	56
GERMANY	56	6.7	2.5	678
FRANCE	35	4.2	2.2	592
UK	29	3.5	1.8	490
INDIA	21	2.5	0.7	20
RUSSIA	15	1.8	1.3	102
BRAZIL	13	1.6	1.0	75
ISRAEL	6.1	0.7	4.9	922
MEXICO	3.5	0.4	0.4	35
SOUTH AFRICA	3.1	0.4	0.7	69

THE PATENTS SCRAMBLE

MAJOR PATENT OFFICES AROUND THE WORLD MUST ASSESS EVER MORE APPLICATIONS EACH YEAR, REFLECTING THE INCREASING VALUE PLACED ON INTELLECTUAL PROPERTY AND THE PRESSURE ON SCIENTISTS TO SHOW RESULTS. THE JAPANESE IN PARTICULAR FILE HUGE NUMBERS OF APPLICATIONS DOMESTICALLY. WHETHER THEY THEN PROCEED WITH THE EXPENSE AND EFFORT OF SECURING INTERNATIONAL PATENTS IS OFTEN A BETTER INDICATOR OF THE LIKELIHOOD OF ACTUALLY PROCEEDING TO MARKET.

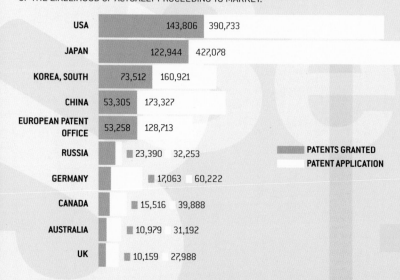

Country	Patents Granted	Patent Application
USA	143,806	390,733
JAPAN	122,944	427,078
KOREA, SOUTH	73,512	160,921
CHINA	53,305	173,327
EUROPEAN PATENT OFFICE	53,258	128,713
RUSSIA	23,390	32,253
GERMANY	17,063	60,222
CANADA	15,516	39,888
AUSTRALIA	10,979	31,192
UK	10,159	27,988

SOURCES: UNESCO Institute for Statistics; UK Dept for Innovation, Universities & Skills: 2006 R&D Scoreboard; WIPO: *Patent Report* (2007)

COMPANIES SPENDING OVER US$5BN ON R&D EXPENDITURE WITHIN EACH SECTOR

COMPANY	SECTOR	COUNTRY	R&D $ BN
INTEL	TECHNOLOGY HARDWARE	USA	6.0
NOKIA	TECHNOLOGY HARDWARE	FINLAND	5.4
PFIZER	PHARMACEUTICALS	USA	8.6
JOHNSON & JOHNSON	PHARMACEUTICALS	USA	7.3
GLAXOSMITHKLINE	PHARMACEUTICALS	UK	6.3
NOVARTIS	PHARMACEUTICALS	SWITZERLAND	5.6
SANOFI-AVENTIS	PHARMACEUTICALS	FRANCE	5.5
FORD MOTOR	AUTOMOTIVE	USA	9.3
GENERAL MOTORS	AUTOMOTIVE	USA	7.8
DAIMLERCHRYSLER	AUTOMOTIVE	GERMANY	7.7
VOLKSWAGEN	AUTOMOTIVE	GERMANY	5.6
TOYOTA MOTOR	AUTOMOTIVE	JAPAN	7.4
MICROSOFT	ELECTRONICS	USA	7.7
SIEMENS	ELECTRONICS	GERMANY	7.1
SAMSUNG ELECTRONICS	ELECTRONICS	S.KOREA	6.3
IBM	ELECTRONICS	USA	6.2
MATSUSHITA ELECTRIC	OTHER	JAPAN	5.6
SONY	OTHER	JAPAN	5.2

THE USA REMAINS THE GIANT OF THE RESEARCH AND DEVELOPMENT WORLD, NOT ONLY SPENDING MOST IN ABSOLUTE TERMS BUT ALSO SPENDING MORE PER CAPITA THAN ANY OTHER COUNTRY. R&D BUDGETS ARE OVERWHELMINGLY CONCENTRATED IN THE TOP 100 COUNTRIES, WHICH ACCOUNT FOR OVER 60% OF THE TOTAL SPEND. IN EVERY ONE OF THE FOUR MAJOR SECTORS, A US CORPORATION TOPS THE LIST FOR TOTAL R&D SPENDING.

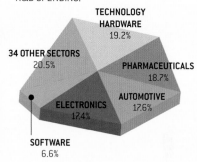

TECHNOLOGY HARDWARE 19.2%
34 OTHER SECTORS 20.5%
PHARMACEUTICALS 18.7%
AUTOMOTIVE 17.6%
ELECTRONICS 17.4%
SOFTWARE 6.6%

US PATENTS GRANTED PER US$20M R&D INVESTMENT

RESEARCH AND DEVELOPMENT IN ESTABLISHED INDUSTRIES LIKE TELECOMS OR AUTOMOTIVE ENGINEERING CAN BE HUGELY EXPENSIVE. OFTEN IT INVOLVES LARGE PROJECT TEAMS COMPETING TO MAKE TECHNOLOGICAL ADVANCES WHICH WILL DELIVER A MARGINAL IMPROVEMENT IN PERFORMANCE – BUT A SIGNIFICANT COMMERCIAL ADVANTAGE FOR ONE OF RELATIVELY FEW MULTINATIONAL COMPANIES CAPABLE OF BRINGING IT TO MARKET. NEW PATENTS IN SUCH AREAS ARE FEW AND FAR BETWEEN. IN NUMERICAL TERMS, INVESTING IN R&D IN ELECTRONICS IS SIX TO TEN TIMES MORE LIKELY TO YIELD PATENTABLE RESULTS, BUT THE FAST-CHANGING NATURE OF THE MARKET MEANS THAT A SMALLER PROPORTION OF THOSE PATENTS WILL MAKE IT PAST THE PROTOTYPE STAGE. FEWER STILL WILL TURN INNOVATION INTO SUFFICIENT SALES TO MAKE A WORTHWHILE PROFIT.

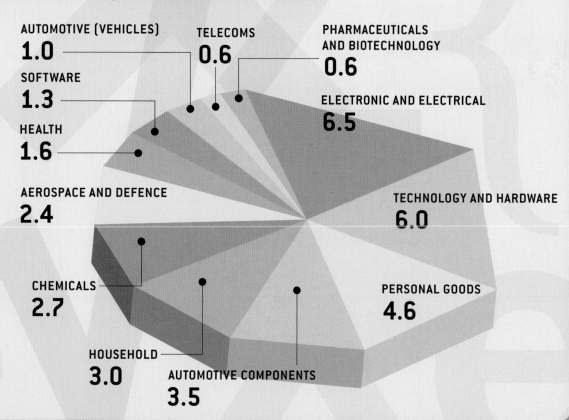

AUTOMOTIVE (VEHICLES) 1.0
TELECOMS 0.6
PHARMACEUTICALS AND BIOTECHNOLOGY 0.6
SOFTWARE 1.3
ELECTRONIC AND ELECTRICAL 6.5
HEALTH 1.6
AEROSPACE AND DEFENCE 2.4
TECHNOLOGY AND HARDWARE 6.0
PERSONAL GOODS 4.6
CHEMICALS 2.7
HOUSEHOLD 3.0
AUTOMOTIVE COMPONENTS 3.5

NEW TECHNOLOGIES

WHAT THE WORLD'S WORKING ON

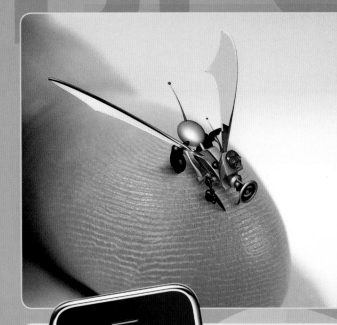

NANOTECHNOLOGY

This so-called "science of the very small" is technology at a molecular scale, where everyday materials exhibit different properties – such as becoming transparent, liquid, conductive, or combustible. Among the first commercial applications are cosmetics and sunscreen creams; the next wave could include spray-on solar photovoltaic film. Nano-sized gadgetry – which we can't even design and build without improved technology – might usher in an era of nanoflies performing discreet surveillance, or nanocars doing highly targeted drug delivery within the human body. Inventor Ray Kurzweil predicts that we will have intelligent nanobots whizzing around our capillaries on health protection missions and interacting with the neurons in the brain to improve memory and intelligence.

ENTERTAINMENT IN THE PALM OF YOUR HAND

Integrating multiple functions into ever-smaller devices reached a new high with Apple's iPhone. Within one slim pocketbook case, it combines Internet access, phone, email, music system, camera, and TV and video playback, and weighs in at just 135g. Third-party services can be linked in: location information through Google maps, music downloads from iTunes, or AOL's Mobile Search engine. Touchscreen interfaces maximize the viewing area for Internet, photos, and video. Other handhelds make different choices – the BlackBerry, for example, has a tiny keyboard for use with PC-style applications such as Microsoft Office. 14 million BlackBerrys have been sold worldwide – and over 140 million iPods. These portable media players from Apple can weigh as little as 15g, and have memory options up to 4GB (as of early 2008), enough to hold most people's entire music collection.

CLONING SPECIES

1952: Tadpole, 1963: Carp, 1986: Mouse, 1996: Sheep, 2000: Rhesus Monkey, 2001: Cow and Cat, 2003: Mule and Horse. A hybrid human embryo was created in 1998 but not allowed to develop.

ROBOTICS

Robots can perform precise actions – but can they think and feel? Designers of Toyota's robots aim to make them fuller partners in our lives by building in agility, kindness, warmth, and intelligence.

SOURCES: Intel®; World Bank: *World Development Indicators*; www.mkaku.org

DATA STORAGE – SIZE HAS SHRUNK WHILE CAPACITY HAS GROWN

YEAR FIRST COMMERCIALLY AVAILABLE	PERSONAL DATA STORAGE DEVICE	ACRONYM	CAPACITY (ORIGINAL/LATEST)	STORAGE METHOD
1846	PUNCHED PAPER TAPE			PAPER
1885	PUNCH CARD			PAPER
1950S	MAGNETIC TAPE		(= 10,000 PUNCH CARDS)	MAGNETIC
1956	HARD DISK DRIVE	HDD	4.4MB/1000GB	MAGNETIC
1963	COMPACT CASSETTE TAPE		20KB PLUS	MAGNETIC
1969	FLOPPY DISK 8"		80KB	MAGNETIC
1976	FLOPPY DISK 5.25"		256KB	MAGNETIC
1979	COMPACT DISC	CD-ROM	700MB	OPTICAL
1983	FLOPPY DISK 3.5"		1.44MB	MAGNETIC
1994	ZIP DRIVE		100MB/750MB	MAGNETIC
1994	MEMORY CARDS: COMPACT FLASH, MEMORY STICK (1998), SECURE DIGITAL (2000), XD PICTURE CARD (2002)	CF, SD, XD	2MB/64GB	SOLID STATE
1995	DIGITAL VERSATILE DISC	DVD-ROM	8.5GB	OPTICAL
2000	FLASH DRIVES		128MB/64GB	SOLID STATE
2004	ULTRA DENSITY OPTICAL DISC	UDO	30GB	OPTICAL
2006	HIGH DEFINITION DVD	HD DVD	30GB	OPTICAL
2006	BLU-RAY DISC	BD	50GB	OPTICAL
2007	SOLID STATE DRIVE		32GB/832GB	SOLID STATE

MOORE'S LAW

THE NUMBER OF TRANSISTORS ON A CHIP (WHICH DETERMINES PROCESSING POWER) DOUBLES EVERY TWO YEARS. THIS WAS FIRST OUTLINED IN 1965 BY GORDON MOORE, CO-FOUNDER OF INTEL.

		NUMBER OF TRANSISTORS	MAX PROCESSING SPEED
1971	FIRST INTEL CHIP	2300	0.74MHZ
1993	FIRST PENTIUM	3,100,000	300MHZ
2006	FIRST CORE 2 DUO	291,000,000	3200MHZ

PCs PER 1000 POPULATION TOP FIVE COUNTRIES

SWITZERLAND	865
SAN MARINO	857
SWEDEN	763
USA	762
ISRAEL	740
OTHER COUNTRIES	
CANADA	700
UK	600
FRANCE	575
GERMANY	545
JAPAN	542
ITALY	367
RUSSIA	122
BRAZIL	105
CHINA	41
INDIA	15.5
BOTTOM FIVE COUNTRIES	
BURKINA FASO	2.4
MALAWI	2.0
ANGOLA	1.9
CHAD	1.6
NIGER	0.7

A STEP TOO FAR?

How far will technology take us? American innovator Chip Walter predicts our evolution into "Cyber sapiens – a creature part digital and part biological that will have placed more distance between its DNA and the destinies they force upon us than any other animal".

Yet Mary Shelley's fictional Frankenstein, the over-ambitious scientist who unleashed a terrible power he could not control, casts a long shadow. For every technology of supposedly limitless promise, from nuclear power "too cheap to meter", to genetically modified crops claiming to revolutionize low-input farming, there is a nightmare scenario of how it could all go wrong. The disaster at Chernobyl in 1986 set the nuclear industry back by decades. Responses to the threat of climate change again show us veering erratically from fear to faith in technology – looking to ward off global warming not just by low carbon energy solutions, but to geo-engineering "technofixes" like giant sunshields in space.

AMERICAN THEORETICAL PHYSICIST MICHIO KAKU CHALLENGES TODAY'S SCIENTISTS TO BREAK THROUGH THE BARRIERS OF "REALITY". IN *PHYSICS OF THE IMPOSSIBLE* HE EXPLAINS THAT TIME TRAVEL AND INVISIBILITY ARE NOT WILD IMAGININGS BUT JUST ENGINEERING PROBLEMS. HIS 2058 VISION IS OF A WIRED WORLD FULL OF AMBIENT TECHNOLOGY.

TV family, China/Mark Wallinger's *State Britain* installation, Tate Britain, 2007. Opium for the masses or brain-food? Either way, global culture permeates our way of life.

THE EMERGENCE OF A GLOBAL CULTURE IS BOTH A SOURCE OF WONDER AND FOR MANY A VERY REAL THREAT

LANGUAGE
WORLD LANGUAGES AND ALPHABETS, MOTHER TONGUES, SECOND LANGUAGES, OFFICIAL LANGUAGES

TELEVISION
TV SET OWNERSHIP, CORPORATE CONTROL, SATELLITE AND CABLE, HOW MUCH DO WE WATCH?

NEWS
NEWSPAPERS AND MARKETS, NEWS ON TV AND ONLINE, AGENCIES, CHEQUEBOOK JOURNALISM

TOURISM
GROWTH, ATTRACTIONS, DESTINATIONS, SPEND, AIRLINES, EXTREME TOURISM

CULTURE

SPORT
LEADING SPORTS, HIGHEST PAID ATHLETES, THE BIG LEAGUES, THE PREMIERSHIP, GLOBALIZATION

ART
MARKETS, COLLECTORS AND MUSEUMS, ART PRICES, ART PRIZES, FORGERIES, THE NEW ART MARKETS

FASHION
SIZE ZERO, THE GARMENT VALUE CHAIN, FAST FASHION, SUPPLYING THE WEST, DESIGNER LABELS

MUSIC
THE BIZ, MARKET SHARES, DIGITAL MUSIC AND DOWNLOADING, MONEY, CLASSICAL AND WORLD MUSIC

FILM
HITS AND MISSES, GLOBAL MOVIE PRODUCTION, BOX OFFICE, PIRACY, PRODUCTION COSTS

LANGUAGES AND ALPHABETS

English is the language with the most words (approx. 250,000)

Taki Taki or Sranan (Suriname) is the language with the fewest words (340)

Khmer is the language with the largest alphabet (74 letters)

Rotokas (Papua New Guinea) is the language with the shortest alphabet (12 letters). It is also the language with the fewest sounds (11 phonemes)

The language with the most sounds is !Xóõ (Botswana). It has 112 phonemes and is also the living language with the most consonants

The most common consonant sounds in the world's languages are **P, T, K, M, N**

The language with the fewest irregular verbs is Esperanto (none)

Symbol-based writing can be used to transliterate varying tongues – as in the adaptation of Chinese script by the Japanese

LANGUAGE

Today's world has 6912 languages – but interconnected communication is killing them off. By 2020 there could be only 700 left. Languages with only a handful of speakers can be isolating, discouraging integration into a wider community, yet each lost language deprives us of access to its distinct cultural heritage.

Spoken languages change over time, and borrow words from others. Contact between languages also creates new forms. Pidgins simply take terms at will from either original source, mixed with no recognizable grammar. Once passed on to a "native" generation of speakers, a pidgin can quickly develop into a fully-fledged mixed-origin creole.

In the classical period, Greek became the *lingua franca* or common language among scholars, succeeded by Latin – whose use was perpetuated through the Catholic Church – and by Arabic. French later claimed the status of "language of diplomacy"; now displaced by the hegemony of English, its international use is still actively promoted and subsidized by Paris.

WORLD LANGUAGES

347 OF THE WORLD'S LANGUAGES (THE TOP 5%) HAVE AT LEAST ONE MILLION SPEAKERS AND ACCOUNT FOR 94% OF THE WORLD'S POPULATION. BY CONTRAST, THE REMAINING 95% OF LANGUAGES ARE SPOKEN BY ONLY 6% OF THE WORLD'S PEOPLE. ENGLISH IS THE MAIN LANGUAGE OF THE INTERNET, BOOKS, NEWSPAPERS, AIRPORTS AND AIR TRAFFIC CONTROL, INTERNATIONAL BUSINESS AND ACADEMIC CONFERENCES, SCIENCE, TECHNOLOGY, DIPLOMACY, SPORT, INTERNATIONAL COMPETITIONS, POP MUSIC, AND ADVERTISING. OVER TWO-THIRDS OF THE WORLD'S SCIENTISTS READ IN ENGLISH.

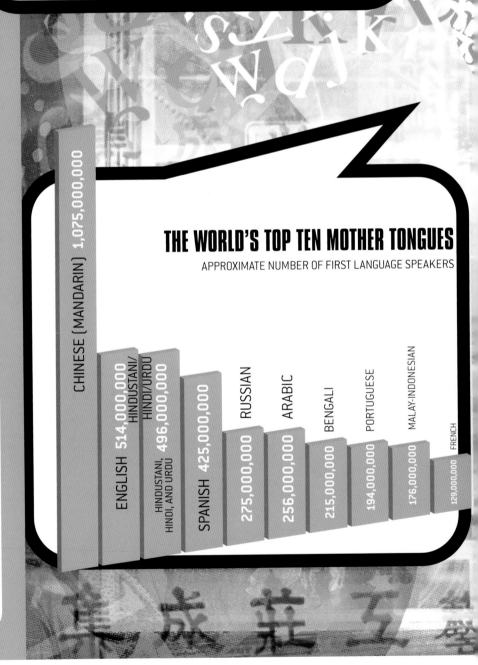

THE WORLD'S TOP TEN MOTHER TONGUES
APPROXIMATE NUMBER OF FIRST LANGUAGE SPEAKERS

- CHINESE (MANDARIN) 1,075,000,000
- ENGLISH 514,000,000
- HINDUSTANI, HINDI, AND URDU (HINDUSTANI/HINDI/URDU) 496,000,000
- SPANISH 425,000,000
- RUSSIAN 275,000,000
- ARABIC 256,000,000
- BENGALI 215,000,000
- PORTUGUESE 194,000,000
- MALAY-INDONESIAN 176,000,000
- FRENCH 129,000,000

SOURCES: Raymond G. Gordon Jr (ed.): *Ethnologue: Languages of the World*; US Census Bureau: American Community Survey

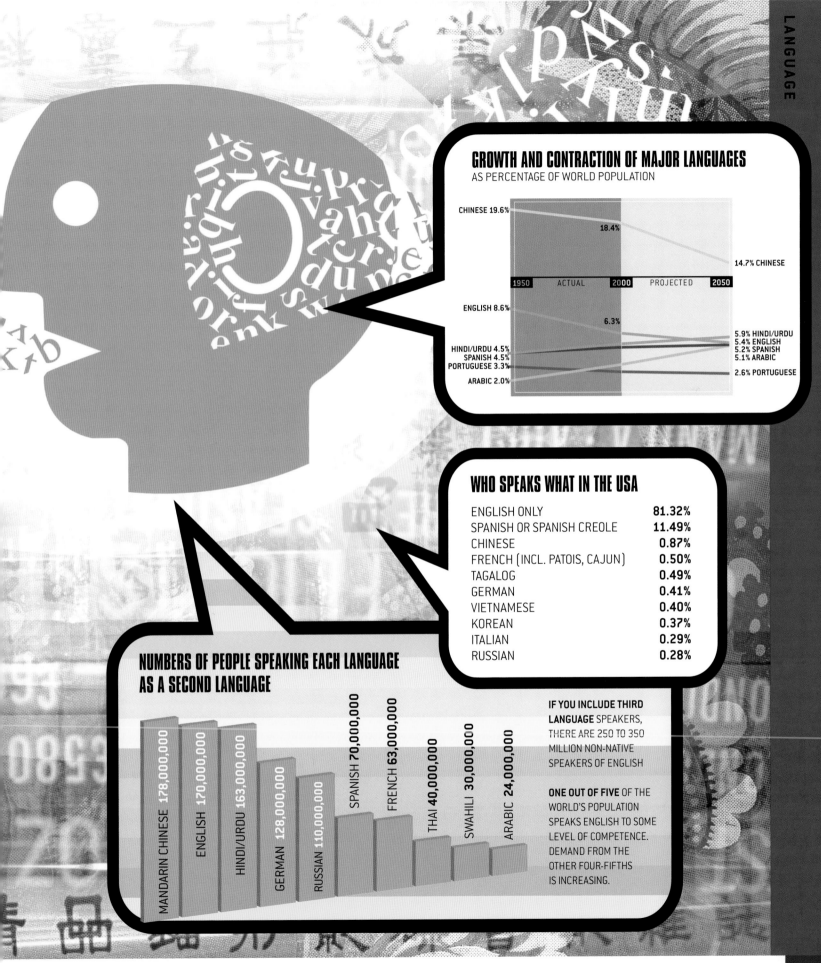

GROWTH AND CONTRACTION OF MAJOR LANGUAGES
AS PERCENTAGE OF WORLD POPULATION

CHINESE 19.6% — 18.4% — 14.7% CHINESE
ENGLISH 8.6% — 6.3%
HINDI/URDU 4.5%
SPANISH 4.5%
PORTUGUESE 3.3%
ARABIC 2.0%

5.9% HINDI/URDU
5.4% ENGLISH
5.2% SPANISH
5.1% ARABIC
2.6% PORTUGUESE

1950 ACTUAL 2000 PROJECTED 2050

WHO SPEAKS WHAT IN THE USA

ENGLISH ONLY	81.32%
SPANISH OR SPANISH CREOLE	11.49%
CHINESE	0.87%
FRENCH (INCL. PATOIS, CAJUN)	0.50%
TAGALOG	0.49%
GERMAN	0.41%
VIETNAMESE	0.40%
KOREAN	0.37%
ITALIAN	0.29%
RUSSIAN	0.28%

NUMBERS OF PEOPLE SPEAKING EACH LANGUAGE AS A SECOND LANGUAGE

MANDARIN CHINESE 178,000,000
ENGLISH 170,000,000
HINDI/URDU 163,000,000
GERMAN 128,000,000
RUSSIAN 110,000,000
SPANISH 70,000,000
FRENCH 63,000,000
THAI 40,000,000
SWAHILI 30,000,000
ARABIC 24,000,000

IF YOU INCLUDE THIRD LANGUAGE SPEAKERS, THERE ARE 250 TO 350 MILLION NON-NATIVE SPEAKERS OF ENGLISH

ONE OUT OF FIVE OF THE WORLD'S POPULATION SPEAKS ENGLISH TO SOME LEVEL OF COMPETENCE. DEMAND FROM THE OTHER FOUR-FIFTHS IS INCREASING.

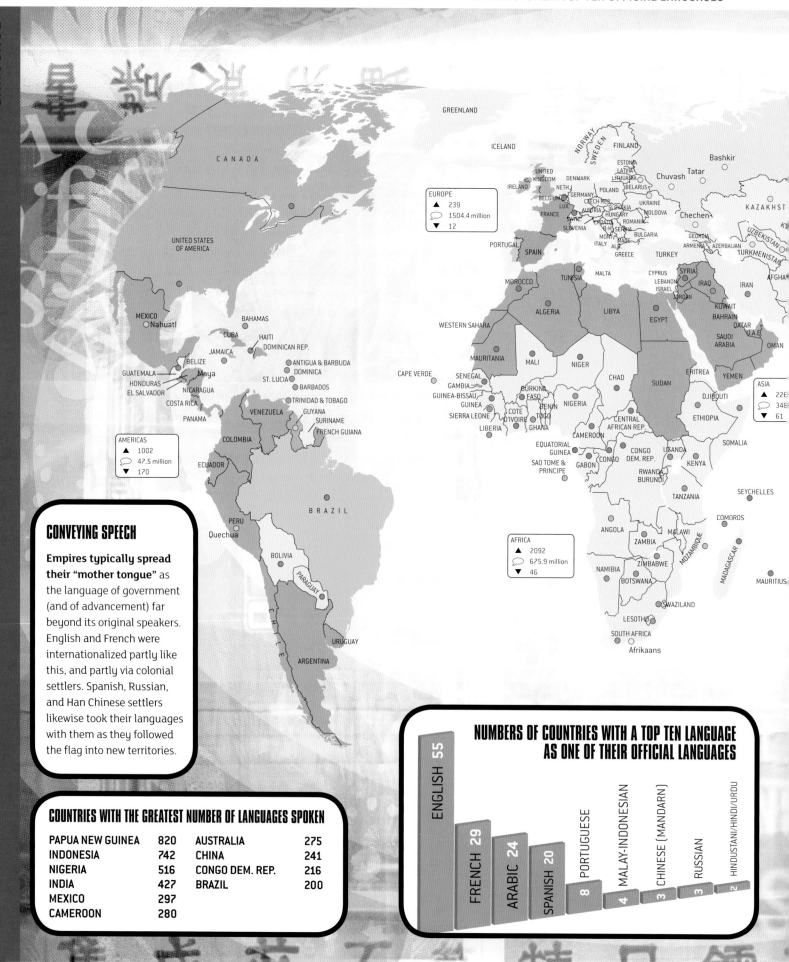

EUROPE
▲ 239
💬 1504.4 million
▼ 12

ASIA
▲ 228
💬 348...
▼ 61

AMERICAS
▲ 1002
💬 47.5 million
▼ 170

AFRICA
▲ 2092
💬 675.9 million
▼ 46

CONVEYING SPEECH

Empires typically spread their "mother tongue" as the language of government (and of advancement) far beyond its original speakers. English and French were internationalized partly like this, and partly via colonial settlers. Spanish, Russian, and Han Chinese settlers likewise took their languages with them as they followed the flag into new territories.

NUMBERS OF COUNTRIES WITH A TOP TEN LANGUAGE AS ONE OF THEIR OFFICIAL LANGUAGES

ENGLISH 55
FRENCH 29
ARABIC 24
SPANISH 20
PORTUGUESE 8
MALAY-INDONESIAN 4
CHINESE (MANDARN) 3
RUSSIAN 3
HINDUSTANI/HINDI/URDU 2

COUNTRIES WITH THE GREATEST NUMBER OF LANGUAGES SPOKEN

PAPUA NEW GUINEA	820	AUSTRALIA	275
INDONESIA	742	CHINA	241
NIGERIA	516	CONGO DEM. REP.	216
INDIA	427	BRAZIL	200
MEXICO	297		
CAMEROON	280		

SOURCES: National Government information, constitutions, and censuses

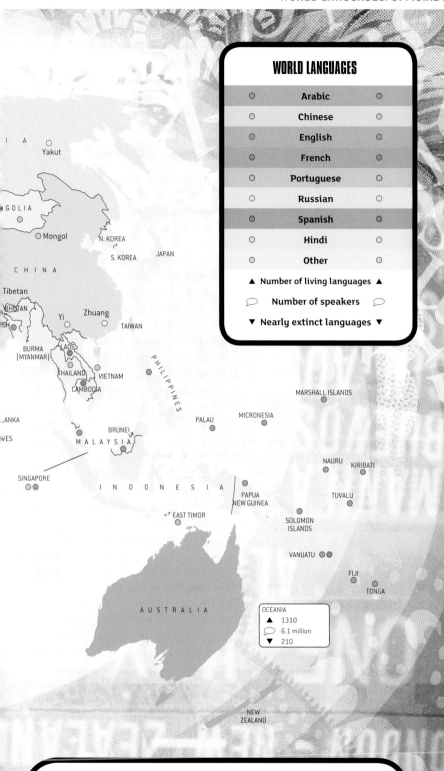

WORLD LANGUAGES

○	Arabic	○
○	Chinese	○
○	English	○
○	French	○
○	Portuguese	○
○	Russian	○
○	Spanish	○
○	Hindi	○
○	Other	○

▲ Number of living languages ▲

💬 Number of speakers 💬

▼ Nearly extinct languages ▼

OCEANIA
▲ 1310
💬 6.1 million
▼ 210

COUNTRIES WITH THE MOST OFFICIAL LANGUAGES

SOUTH AFRICA AFRIKAANS/ENGLISH/ISINDEBELE/ISIXHOSA/
ISIZULU/NORTHERN SOTHO/SESOTHO/
SETSWANA/SISWATI/TSHIVENDA/XITSONGA

SINGAPORE MALAY/ENGLISH/MANDARIN/TAMIL

SPAIN SPANISH/GALICIAN/BASQUE/CATALAN

TOWARDS A GLOBAL LANGUAGE

Is English the obvious choice as a global language? It is already an official language in over a quarter of the world's countries, spoken widely in a further quarter and in global business, and ever more familiar from popular music, film, and the ubiquitous Internet.

Yet the trend is not all in that direction, even in the "English-speaking world". Around 12% of the US population, for instance, is more at home in Spanish. Then there is the enormous weight of numbers behind languages such as Chinese and Hindi/Urdu.

Some countries make proficiency in their official language an essential part of qualifying for citizenship. On the other hand, invented languages such as Esperanto and Interlingua aim to provide a "neutral" auxiliary language, without idiosyncracies, for international discourse.

The richness of mother tongues, however, can be seen as a vital safeguard against imposed conformity. UNESCO's Babel Project encourages the use of community languages to guarantee engagement in the world. Conversely, George Orwell's *1984*, written in 1948, foresaw how a totalitarian state could control language to control thought. By gradually reducing the number of words in existence, "Newspeak" would ultimately "make thoughtcrime literally impossible, because there will be no words in which to express it".

Advances in translation software could in theory make the learning of other languages unnecessary, allowing anyone to use their own personal language to communicate via computer — just as Douglas Adams's fictional Babelfish, placed in the ear, made any language intelligible to the hearer.

THE GLOBAL OPIATE

Until the 1970s mass television ownership was confined to the richer parts of the West. No technology or media has spread so widely since. The last 30 years has seen a five-fold increase in the global number of TV sets, the vast majority of the new sets appearing in the developing world – and one third of them in China alone.

Television has become the prime manipulator of public opinion, whether that be political mind control, achieved by confining public access to state-controlled channels, or the subtle allure of the advertising industry which, for the most part, funds television programming.

TELEVISION

The transmission of sound and vision through electromagnetic waves from a central point to many dispersed television sets trumped radio and cinema, its early competitors. First trialled in the 1930s in Britain, Germany, and the US, television only emerged as a regular media service in the 1940s and early 1950s.

By the mid 1960s television had embedded itself in the life of the West, and acquired its own aesthetic codes and conventions. The 1960 US presidential campaign marked the moment when the medium began to transform the conduct of politics. Now political life, particularly elections, in most of the world is conducted through the television. By 2000, in the West, just under a quarter of adult waking hours were devoted to watching it.

In its classical analogue form, the number of channels available was sharply restricted, giving rise to many public and private monopolies and duopolies. The arrival of multichannel satellite and cable broadcasting has swept this restriction aside and made international boundaries increasingly permeable. So far, new media conglomerates have managed to hold on to a significant share of output and power, but as TV merges with the Internet the fragmentation of the audience threatens even these titans.

BROADCASTING FACTS

- 46 countries have only one TV broadcast channel, all of which are government-controlled
- 122 countries have ten or fewer channels, including one or more government-controlled stations
- Two countries, Andorra and Tuvalu, have no national broadcasting system

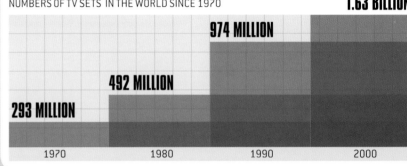

WORLD TV SETS

NUMBERS OF TV SETS IN THE WORLD SINCE 1970

1.63 BILLION

974 MILLION

492 MILLION

293 MILLION

| 1970 | 1980 | 1990 | 2000 |

CORPORATE CONTROL

- The two giants of world broadcasting are Ted Turner and Rupert Murdoch (right), both moguls who grasped the opportunity of satellite broadcasting early in the game.
- Turner (background: American, outdoor advertising) turned WTBS into a US national station through satellites, invented CNN, acquired MGM/UA, created TNT, merged to form Time Warner and now also owns AOL.
- Murdoch (background: Australian, newspapers) used News International (now News Corporation) to launched Sky TV (now Sky BSB) in the UK, acquired 20th Century Fox in the US and Star TV in Asia. His holdings include 157 newspapers, MySpace, IGN, and Dow Jones.

Behind every television set is a television company, but the technological and economic upheavals of the last few years have transformed the old corporate giants. In the 1970s the big three US networks, CBS, NBC, and ABC could claim over 95% of prime-time audiences; now they command less than a quarter, and have all either bought into cable channels or been bought up themselves. The arrival of Spanish language network Univision has cut into the share even further.

THE RISE OF SATELLITE AND CABLE

NUMBERS OF BROADCAST TV STATIONS: THE TOP 20 COUNTRIES

he new technologies of broadcasts created the bandwidth for TVs to eceive innumerable channels. While richer countries now suffer from n overload of output, over 50 countries have only two channels or less. Vhat fills this extraordinary amount of airtime? Not much new programming, but a lot of live chat and confrontation airtime, pecialist interest broadcasting, shopping and auctions, fashion,

round-the-clock news and sport and, of course, local and regional stations serving the immediate community. In addition there are innumerable repeat channels.

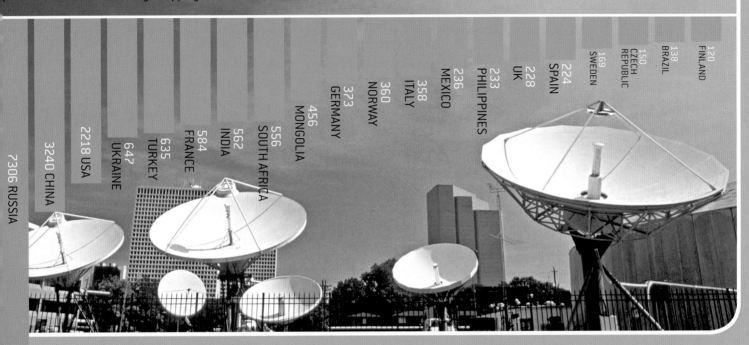

- 120 FINLAND
- 138 BRAZIL
- 150 CZECH REPUBLIC
- 169 SWEDEN
- 224 SPAIN
- 228 UK
- 233 PHILIPPINES
- 236 MEXICO
- 358 ITALY
- 360 NORWAY
- 373 GERMANY
- 456 MONGOLIA
- 556 SOUTH AFRICA
- 562 INDIA
- 584 FRANCE
- 635 TURKEY
- 647 UKRAINE
- 2218 USA
- 3240 CHINA
- 7306 RUSSIA

SETS PER 1000 PEOPLE TODAY, BY REGION

GLOBAL AVERAGE NUMBER OF TV SETS PER 1000 PEOPLE TODAY: 270

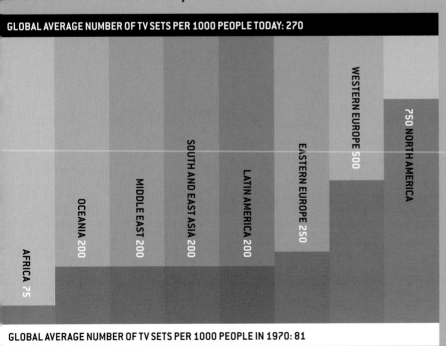

- 750 NORTH AMERICA
- WESTERN EUROPE 500
- EASTERN EUROPE 250
- LATIN AMERICA 200
- SOUTH AND EAST ASIA 200
- MIDDLE EAST 200
- OCEANIA 200
- AFRICA 75

GLOBAL AVERAGE NUMBER OF TV SETS PER 1000 PEOPLE IN 1970: 81

GROWTH OF TV SETS IN CHINA

TV SETS PER 1000 PEOPLE TODAY: 306

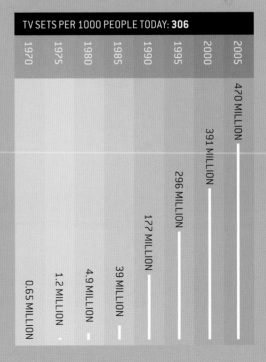

- 1970 — 0.65 MILLION
- 1975 — 1.2 MILLION
- 1980 — 4.9 MILLION
- 1985 — 39 MILLION
- 1990 — 177 MILLION
- 1995 — 296 MILLION
- 2000 — 391 MILLION
- 2005 — 470 MILLION

TELEVISION

ONE-WAY TRAFFIC: TRANSATLANTIC TV
US TV IN EUROPE, AND EUROPEAN TV IN THE USA

IT SOMETIMES SEEMS THAT EUROPEANS CANNOT GET ENOUGH OF AMERICAN TELEVISION. US SITCOMS, DRAMAS, COMEDIES, AND MOVIES FLOW IN HUGE NUMBERS ACROSS THE ATLANTIC, SUCH AS *THE SOPRANOS* (BELOW), PROVIDING A CORE PART OF MANY EUROPEAN CHANNELS' OUTPUT. THE FLOW IN THE OPPOSITE DIRECTION IS MINUSCULE, AND OVERWHELMINGLY BRITISH. US BROADCASTERS HAVE HOWEVER IMPORTED FORMATS AND IDEAS FROM EUROPE, INCLUDING PUBLIC VOTING SHOWS SUCH AS *POP IDOL*, REALITY SHOWS SUCH AS *BIG BROTHER*, AND ADAPTATIONS OF UK SUCCESSES SUCH AS *THE OFFICE*.

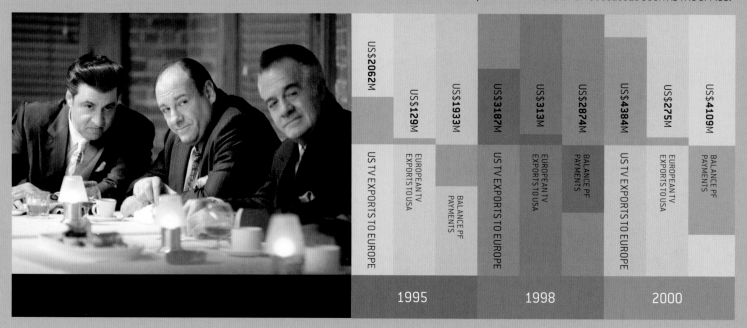

1995			1998			2000		
US$2062M	US$129M	US$1933M	US$3187M	US$313M	US$2874M	US$4384M	US$275M	US$4109M
US TV EXPORTS TO EUROPE	EUROPEAN TV EXPORTS TO USA	BALANCE PF PAYMENTS	US TV EXPORTS TO EUROPE	EUROPEAN TV EXPORTS TO USA	BALANCE PF PAYMENTS	US TV EXPORTS TO EUROPE	EUROPEAN TV EXPORTS TO USA	BALANCE PF PAYMENTS

HOW MUCH DO WE WATCH? AVERAGE TV HOURS PER WEEK

USA:	**4 HOURS** DAILY	**28 HOURS**
UK:	**4 HOURS** DAILY	**28 HOURS**
ITALY:	**3.85 HOURS** DAILY	**27 HOURS**
IRELAND:	**3.28 HOURS** DAILY	**23 HOURS**
GERMANY:	**3.28 HOURS** DAILY	**23 HOURS**
FRANCE:	**3.28 HOURS** DAILY	**23 HOURS**
AUSTRALIA:	**3.14 HOURS** DAILY	**22 HOURS**
DENMARK:	**2.85 HOURS** DAILY	**20 HOURS**
NETHERLANDS:	**2.85 HOURS** DAILY	**20 HOURS**
BELGIUM:	**2.71 HOURS** DAILY	**19 HOURS**
SWEDEN:	**2.57 HOURS** DAILY	**18 HOURS**
NORWAY:	**2.57 HOURS** DAILY	**18 HOURS**

LIKE A GLOBAL PANDEMIC OF NARCOLEPSY, THE NUMBER OF HOURS SPENT IN FRONT OF THE TELEVISION RISES. IN THE UNITED STATES AND BRITAIN THE AVERAGE IS AROUND ONE QUARTER OF PEOPLE'S WAKING HOURS. THE ARRIVAL OF TV SCREENS IN SHOPPING MALLS, GARAGES, AND ON PUBLIC TRANSPORT ENSURES ANY DOMESTIC DEFICIT IS TOPPED UP. SCANDINAVIANS FIND THAT BY GETTING OFF THE SOFA THEY GAIN ANOTHER TEN HOURS A WEEK IN THEIR LIVES. THE SHEER MULTIPLICITY OF CHANNELS IN MANY COUNTRIES HAS ENCOURAGED "CHANNEL-HOPPING," CONTRIBUTING TO A DIMINISHED ATTENTION SPAN AND AN INCREASING DEMAND FOR SHEER VARIETY AMONG VIEWERS. FEW PROGRAMMES ARE WATCHED IN THEIR ENTIRETY.

 SOURCES: UNESCO (2004) *International Flows of Selected Cultural Goods and Services*

TV AND VIOLENCE

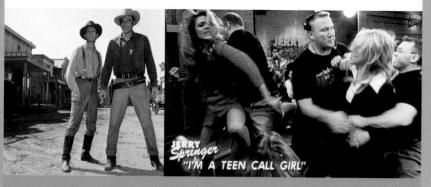

Violence is a staple of contemporary television. The Western may be a minority genre these days but dramas and thrillers continue to centre on police work, the underworld, and crime. News output provides a more sanitized version of the real thing, while chat shows and daytime TV have discovered the ratings potency of staged conflict and public loss of control by their guests.

| 200,000 | THE NUMBER OF VIOLENT ACTS THE AVERAGE AMERICAN CHILD SEES ON TV BY AGE 18 |
| 16,000 | THE NUMBER OF MURDERS VIEWED BY THE AVERAGE AMERICAN CHILD BY AGE 18 |

TV AND FAMILY LIFE

Since the arrival of television both conservatives and radicals have been critical of its impact on family life and the socialization of children. These critiques have often relied on an invented golden age of domestic harmony, collective meals, and self-generated entertainment. However, given that families are spending on average up to a quarter of their waking hours in front of it, it is no surprise that the older patterns of domestic life have been disrupted. Families eat together less often, and are more sedentary.

The content of television's output has proved equally contentious. Radicals have argued that the relentless and unabashed consumerist ethic of television and its aggressive advertising have eaten into the fabric of family life by creating unfulfillable needs and material desires. Conservatives have tended to argue that the crudity of the language used and the immodest and casual eroticism of TV's attitude to sex are distasteful at best and harmful at worst. Literary critic, Kenneth Tynan (above), shocked the British nation when he uttered the first four-letter word on UK television in the 1960s, but in the end issues of language are a sideshow: even the unstoppable wave of aestheticized violence pale into insignificance against the medium's capacity to disable rather than enrich consciousness.

TELEVISION AND REALITY

Television has been exploring, blurring, and generally messing with the line between reality and artifice since its invention – an endless pursuit of the fantasy that one can make unconstructed television, in which the vast technological and cultural apparatus of its creation is made invisible. The earliest takes on this were the low-brow *Candid Camera* shows which showed unscripted reactions of the public to comic set-ups and the high-brow fly-on-the-wall methods of highly personalized and intimate documentary-making. The docu-soaps that follow the daily life of institutions, police officers, etc. are their late 20th-century populist descendants.

Reality TV in its current incarnation can be traced to the Dutch show *Number 28* which threw together members of the public who were strangers to each other and filmed their interactions – adding confessionals from participants, post-encounter reflections and highly-edited summaries. MTV popularized the genre with its version in 1992's *Real World*. The arrival of digital editing technologies made these shows possible, allowing much faster editing of an unlimited supply of imagery. However, these programmes proved too tame and too unreliable in their narrative rhythms and ratings. Reality TV was transformed by turning the encounters into game shows or employment agencies.

Big Brother (above) was the key game show variant of this development, and added public voting and 24-hour coverage to the mix. Combined with the ever-rising demand for celebrity news from the press, it achieved blanket coverage to the point where the real prize was not the paltry cash from the TV producers but the endorsements, photo shoots, and kiss-and-tell stories available after the show.

NEWS

Our appetite for "news" – from simple gossip to international politics – reflects every community's need and desire to gather and spread information among its members. Satisfying this appetite has spawned a huge industry. For many people, events close to home are the most fascinating, so any country's foreign news coverage focuses heavily on stories involving its own nationals abroad.

Television and radio have long overtaken the press as most people's main source of news. Yet paid daily newspapers have held up surprisingly well in the face of a spread of "freesheets" and free online access to newspaper websites. Total printed newspaper sales have actually risen in the last five years in the majority of countries – but not in the UK or the USA, where there has been a drop of ten million since the early 1990s. More Americans now visit newspaper websites online – if only a few times a month – than buy daily papers.

THE TOP TEN DAILY NEWSPAPERS

YOMIURI SHIMBUN IS THE WORLD'S LARGEST NEWSPAPER, WITH A DAILY CIRCULATION GREATER THAN THE COMBINED TOTAL CIRCULATION OF THE TOP NINE US NEWSPAPERS.

PUBLICATION	CIRCULATION	COUNTRY
YOMIURI SHIMBUN	14,246,000	JAPAN
THE ASAHI SHIMBUN	12,326,000	JAPAN
MAINICHI SHIMBUN	5,635,000	JAPAN
NIHON KEIZAI SHIMBUN	4,737,000	JAPAN
CHUNICHI SHIMBUN	4,571,000	JAPAN
BILD	4,220,000	GERMANY
THE SUN	3,461,000	UK
SANKEI SHIMBUN	2,665,000	JAPAN
USA TODAY	2,603,000	USA
CANAKO XIAOXI (BEIJING)	2,530,000	CHINA

READ ALL ABOUT IT

- MORE THAN 515 MILLION PEOPLE BUY A NEWSPAPER EVERY DAY, UP FROM 488 MILLION IN 2002. AVERAGE READERSHIP IS ESTIMATED TO BE MORE THAN 1.4 BILLION PEOPLE EACH DAY.
- SEVEN OUT OF TEN OF THE WORLD'S 100 BEST-SELLING DAILIES ARE NOW PUBLISHED IN ASIA. CHINA, JAPAN, AND INDIA ACCOUNT FOR 60 OF THEM.
- NEWSPAPER ONLINE CONSUMPTION MORE THAN TREBLED BETWEEN 2000 AND 2005. THE NUMBER OF NEWSPAPER WEBSITES INCREASED BY 20% IN 2005.
- INTERNET ADVERTISING REVENUES BEGAN TO TAKE OFF IN 2005, AND BY 2007 WERE SHOWING DRAMATIC GROWTH.

THE FIVE LARGEST MARKETS FOR NEWSPAPERS

	2006	2005
CHINA	98.7 MILLION COPIES DAILY	96.6 MILLION COPIES DAILY
INDIA	88.9 MILLION COPIES DAILY	78.7 MILLION COPIES DAILY
JAPAN	69.1 MILLION COPIES DAILY	69.7 MILLION COPIES DAILY
USA	52.3 MILLION COPIES DAILY	53.3 MILLION COPIES DAILY
GERMANY	21.1 MILLION COPIES DAILY	21.5 MILLION COPIES DAILY

 SOURCES: World Association of Newspapers: *World Press Trends 2007*; Harris Interactive Inc: The Harris Poll® #52 (June 11 2007)

CABLE V NETWORK NEWS IN THE USA

CNN, THE FIRST 24-HOURS-A-DAY CABLE TELEVISION NEWS CHANNEL, WAS LAUNCHED IN 1980. INTENSE MEDIA COVERAGE IN THE IRANIAN HOSTAGE CRISIS SPARKED "REAL-TIME" INTEREST IN AMERICAN POLITICAL, DIPLOMATIC, AND SECURITY MATTERS. FOX NEWS AND MSNBC WERE LAUNCHED IN 1996. CABLE NEWS VIEWERS HAVE RISEN OVER THE LAST DECADE, NOW AT 2.6 MILLION FOR PRIME TIME AND 1.5 MILLION FOR DAYTIME VIEWING, THOUGH ARE STILL ONLY A FRACTION OF THE NETWORK VIEWING FIGURES: 26.1 MILLION FOR EVENING NEWS (THOUGH THIS HAS DROPPED BY A QUARTER OVER THE LAST DECADE) AND 13.6 MILLION FOR MORNING NEWS.

HEARD THE NEWS?

NEWS AND INFORMATION SOURCES NOW

(PERCENTAGES)	USA	UK	FRANCE	ITALY	SPAIN	GERMANY	AUSTRALIA
TV NETWORK NEWS	25	36	29	30	22	28	35
ONLINE SITES	18	14	17	22	18	16	18
MAJOR DAILY NEWSPAPERS	15	17	13	14	25	18	17
CABLE NETWORK NEWS	14	2	9	5	7	7	3
RADIO	12	16	20	11	16	18	17
LOCAL NEWSPAPERS & NEWSLETTERS	9	7	4	8	4	5	7
MAGAZINES	4	3	5	5	4	5	3

NEWS AND INFORMATION SOURCES IN FIVE YEARS

(PERCENTAGES)	USA	UK	FRANCE	ITALY	SPAIN	GERMANY	AUSTRALIA
ONLINE SITES	26	26	26	39	28	23	30
TV NETWORK NEWS	22	33	24	22	17	26	30
CABLE NETWORK NEWS	15	4	11	8	10	6	5
MAJOR DAILY NEWSPAPERS	13	15	11	12	22	17	14
RADIO	11	14	16	9	15	17	13
LOCAL NEWSPAPERS & NEWSLETTERS	7	4	3	5	3	4	5
MAGAZINES	3	2	4	4	3	4	2

HARRIS INTERACTIVE: 8749 ADULTS WERE SURVEYED ACROSS SEVEN COUNTRIES

A WORLDWIDE SURVEY OF 287 FREE DAILY NEWSPAPERS IN 2006 RECORDED A 55% INCREASE IN THEIR COMBINED CIRCULATION IN THE PREVIOUS YEAR, TO A TOTAL OF 40.7 MILLION, OF WHICH 27 MILLION, INCLUDING ALL THE TOP FIVE TITLES, WERE DISTRIBUTED IN EUROPE. FIVE YEARS EARLIER THE WORLDWIDE TOTAL FIGURE HAD BEEN JUST 17 MILLION.

TOP FREE DAILY NEWSPAPERS 2006

RANK	TITLE	COUNTRY	CIRCULATION
1	**METRO**	UK	1,130,000
2	**LEGGO**	ITALY	1,050,000
3	**20 MINUTOS**	SPAIN	997,000
4	**QUE!**	SPAIN	970,000
5	**ADN**	SPAIN	914,000

ONLINE NEWSPAPERS

MORE THAN 66 MILLION PEOPLE A MONTH (OVER 40% OF ALL ACTIVE INTERNET USERS IN THE USA) WERE VISITING US NEWSPAPER WEBSITES BY EARLY 2008. MOST VISITED, NOT SURPRISINGLY, WERE THE SITES OF THE COUNTRY'S FOUR BEST-KNOWN PAPERS — *THE NEW YORK TIMES*, *WASHINGTON POST*, *USA TODAY* AND THE *WALL STREET JOURNAL*. IN THE UK, THE RELATIVELY SMALL-CIRCULATION *GUARDIAN* RANKS AS THE TOP NEWSPAPER WEBSITE, WITH ALMOST 20 MILLION VISITORS IN FEBRUARY 2008, FOLLOWED BY THE *DAILY MAIL*, *THE TIMES* AND THE LEADING MASS-MARKET TABLOID *THE SUN*.

NEWS

FOCUS ON US MEDIA

USA SURVEYS, 2008

In recent years Harris Interactive have surveyed various groups of US adults on their views about news sources in the media. Here are some of their findings:

IS THERE A BIAS IN NEWS REPORTING?

BASE: 1179 US ADULTS (PERCENTAGES ROUNDED)

THERE IS A LIBERAL BIAS IN THE MEDIA	38%
THERE IS NO BIAS IN THE MEDIA	5%
THERE IS A CONSERVATIVE BIAS IN THE MEDIA	25%
NOT AT ALL SURE	31%

WHICH MEDIA HAS THE GREATEST BIAS IN NEWS REPORTING?

BASE: 743 US ADULTS SAYING THERE IS A BIAS IN THE MEDIA (PERCENTAGES ROUNDED)

TELEVISION	41%
PRINT	17%
RADIO	7%
ALL ARE EQUALLY BIASED	31%
NONE IS MORE BIASED THAN ANOTHER	4%
NOT SURE	1%

TIME SPENT ONLINE FOR NEWS IN THE LAST WEEK

BASE: 1932 US ADULTS WHO HAD GONE ONLINE FOR NEWS (PERCENTAGES ROUNDED)

29 MINUTES OR LESS	23%
30–59 MINUTES	25%
1–2 HOURS	25%
MORE THAN 2 HOURS TO 4 HOURS	14%
MORE THAN 4 HOURS TO 5 HOURS	6%
MORE THAN 5 HOURS	8%
MEDIAN	**1 HOUR**

WHAT SITE OR SITES DO YOU RELY ON MOST?

BASE: 1303 US ADULTS SAYING THEY RELY ON INTERNET SITES "A LOT" OR "SOME" FOR INFORMATION ABOUT POLITICAL ISSUES (MULTIPLE RESPONSES ALLOWED)

CNN	26
YAHOO	12
FOX NEWS	12
MSNBC	10
MSN	8
NEW YORK TIMES	6
AOL	4
GOOGLE	3
WASHINGTON POST	3
ABC NEWS	3
DRUDGE REPORT	3
BBC	3

BBC V CNN

BBC NEWS	CNN
3500 STAFF, 2000 OF WHOM ARE JOURNALISTS	**3300 NEWS PROFESSIONALS**
48 NEWSGATHERING BUREAUX, 41 OF WHICH ARE OVERSEAS	**36 NEWSGATHERING BUREAUX**, 26 OF WHICH ARE OVERSEAS
MORE THAN **260 MILLION VIEWERS WORLDWIDE** IN 40 LANGUAGES	**150 MILLION INTERNATIONAL VIEWERS** IN SIX LANGUAGES

SOURCES: Harris Interactive Inc: The Harris Poll® #35 (May 19, 2004), #52 (June 30 2006), and #75 (October 7 2004); BBC; CNN; Reuters; AFP; AP

NEWS AGENCIES

REUTERS	AP	AFP
196 BUREAUX IN 94 COUNTRIES SERVING APPROXIMATELY 131 COUNTRIES	243 BUREAUX IN 97 COUNTRIES SERVING 121 COUNTRIES	BUREAUX IN 110 COUNTRIES; WORLDWIDE NETWORK SPANS 165 COUNTRIES
APPROXIMATELY 16,900 STAFF; 2400 EDITORIAL STAFF, JOURNALISTS, PHOTOGRAPHERS, AND CAMERA OPERATORS	4100 EMPLOYEES WORLDWIDE, 3000 JOURNALISTS	4000 EMPLOYEES WORLDWIDE
IN 2006 REUTERS FILED 2.5 MILLION NEWS ITEMS, INCLUDING 656,500 ALERTS, FROM 209 COUNTRIES AROUND THE WORLD, PUBLISHED IN 18 LANGUAGES. FINANCIAL DATA UPDATED OVER 8000 TIMES PER SECOND, AND AT PEAK TIME MORE THAN 23,000 TIMES PER SECOND	AP SENDS NEWS IN FOUR LANGUAGES. THE REPORT IS TRANSLATED INTO MANY MORE LANGUAGES BY INTERNATIONAL SUBSCRIBERS	400,000–600,000 WORDS IN OVER TEXT, 2000–3000 PHOTOS, 80 NEWS GRAPHICS, AND 30 VIDEO CLIPS PER DAY

CHEQUEBOOK JOURNALISM

- THE *NEW YORK TIMES* SCOOPED AN EXCLUSIVE INTERVIEW WITH THE *TITANIC* WIRELESS OPERATOR FOR JUST OVER US$1000 IN 1912.
- TWO DECADES LATER, THE HEARST NEWSPAPER CHAIN PAID THE LEGAL BILLS OF THE DEFENDANT IN THE LINDBERGH BABY KIDNAPPING CASE TO ENSURE SCOOPS DURING THE TRIAL.
- THE UK'S CHANNEL FOUR PAID £400,000 FOR AN INTERVIEW WITH FORMER WHITE HOUSE INTERN MONICA LEWINSKY IN 1999 OVER THE BILL CLINTON SEX SCANDAL.
- *HELLO!* MAGAZINE WAS ORDERED TO PAY £1,047,756 IN DAMAGES TO *OK!* MAGAZINE, MICHAEL DOUGLAS, AND CATHERINE ZETA-JONES FOR INFRINGING THE DEAL THEY HAD MADE FOR *OK!* TO HAVE EXCLUSIVE RIGHTS TO THEIR WEDDING PHOTOS IN 2000.
- REBECCA LOOS MADE £800,000 FROM VARIOUS MEDIA FOR HER STORY OF SEX WITH FOOTBALLER DAVID BECKHAM IN 2004.
- TENNIS PLAYER LLEYTON HEWITT AND ACTRESS BEC CARTWRIGHT GAVE THEIR A$200,000 PAYMENT FOR THE EXCLUSIVE STORY OF THEIR 2005 ENGAGEMENT TO AN AIDS CHILDREN'S CHARITY.

MISINFORMED, ALIENATED, OR BEWILDERED?

The news is indispensable to keep people aware of events that may impact directly on their lives. That is one reason why a free press is an essential feature of democratic society – and why authoritarian states such as China, Iran, and Zimbabwe control the news media, allowing them to report only what the government wants people to know. Yet the seemingly constant presence of "the media" in the lives of most people in the developed world leaves many feeling that we are excessively bombarded with news, and increasingly suspicious of the big news organizations' agenda.

Television news broadcasting in the West is largely controlled by just a few companies and individuals. News Corporation, built up by Australian-born tycoon Rupert Murdoch, is the archetype. It owns both a vast press empire – including *The Australian*, the UK *Times* and *Sun*, the *New York Post* and *Wall Street Journal* – and television news stations such as Fox in the USA, a stake in ITV in the UK, channels across mainland Europe, ANTV in Indonesia, and the international satellite channel Sky. Interestingly, its Starry Sky channel in China has moved away from airing news at all, instead flooding the Chinese market with imitations of popular US shows.

A news counter-culture has emerged with the growth of blogging, whereby any individual can make their "take" on the news accessible across the Internet. Cameras on mobile phones have also made it possible to disseminate "first-hand" images, even in mainstream news footage of major events. Vanished are the days when the only way to bring ordinary people's views to the global news feed was via the editor's filter and the newspaper "letters" page. If this is truly democratized journalism, it does raise other issues over bias. With no professional training, no industry regulation, and no pretence of objectivity, blogging brings the validity of news increasingly into question.

TOURISM

Tourism is thriving, in spite of threats from terrorism, bird flu and other health scares, rising oil prices, and much publicity about the impact of flights on the environment. 842 million international journeys were made in 2006, up 4.5% over 2005, driven by the world's increasingly wealthy and better educated population. Further growth is projected between now and 2020, at 4.1% a year.

Tourism now provides the main source of foreign earnings for at least 74 countries. Even the Middle East achieved a 4% rise in 2006 in spite of the Israel-Lebanon crisis. However, these floods of visitors can cause damage at tourist sites and drain countries' resources. Emerging countries are also particularly vulnerable to the kind of fluctuations in the global tourism industry that can rapidly be triggered by changes in the world economy and also by international terrorism: after the Luxor massacre in 1995, Egypt's tourist arrivals more than halved; and far fewer Americans ventured abroad in the years after 9/11.

THE GLOBAL EXPANSION OF TOURISM
INTERNATIONAL ARRIVALS IN MILLIONS

1990 — 439 MILLION
1995 — 541 MILLION
2000 — 687 MILLION
2005 — 806 MILLION

5% BY RAIL
7% BY WATER
43% BY ROAD
45% BY AIR

THE TOP TEN GALLERIES AND MUSEUMS

MILLIONS OF VISITORS

7.5 **LOUVRE MUSEUM** PARIS
5.1 **POMPIDOU CENTRE** PARIS
4.9 **TATE MODERN** LONDON
4.8 **BRITISH MUSEUM** LONDON
4.6 **NATIONAL GALLERY** LONDON
4.5 **METROPOLITAN MUSEUM** NEW YORK
4.2 **THE VATICAN AND ITS MUSEUMS** ROME
4.0 **AMERICAN MUSEUM OF NATURAL HISTORY** NEW YORK
3.7 **NATURAL HISTORY MUSEUM** LONDON
2.5 **HERMITAGE MUSEUM** ST. PETERSBURG

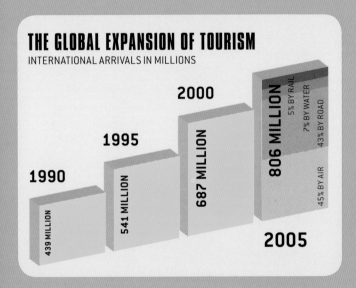

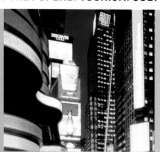

THE TOP TEN MOST VISITED ATTRACTIONS

MILLIONS OF VISITORS

COMPILED BY FORBES TRAVELER

35	**TIMES SQUARE** NEW YORK CITY	
25	**NATIONAL MALL & MEMORIAL PARKS** WASHINGTON D.C.	
6.6	**DISNEYWORLD** FLORIDA	
15	**TRAFALGAR SQUARE** LONDON	
4.7	**DISNEYLAND** CALIFORNIA	
14	**NIAGARA FALLS** ONTARIO AND NEW YORK STATE	
13	**FISHERMAN'S WHARF/GOLDEN GATE** SAN FRANCISCO	
2.9	**DISNEYLAND/DISNEYSEA** TOKYO	
12	**NOTRE DAME** PARIS	
0.6	**DISNEYLAND** PARIS	

WHERE TOURISTS GO, AND WHAT THEY SPEND

TOP SIX DESTINATIONS

FRANCE 76 million visitors

SPAIN 55.6 million visitors

USA 49.4 million visitors

CHINA 46.8 million visitors

ITALY 36.5 million visitors

UK 30 million visitors

EARNINGS FROM TOURISM

USA US$81.7 billion

SPAIN US$47.9 billion

FRANCE US$42.3 billion

ITALY US$35.4 billion

UK US$30.7 billion

CHINA US$29.3 billion

987	882	560	514	385	295	234	124	1?
BRITISH	GERMANS	CANADIANS	FRENCH	ITALIANS	JAPANESE	AMERICANS	RUSSIANS	CHINESE

ANNUAL PER CAPITA SPEND ON FOREIGN VACATIONS (IN US$)

France still tops the list of most visited places, with its good climate and wide range of attractions located in the heart of affluent western Europe. As many visits to France are short (because of the ease of getting there), people actually spend considerably more money during a trip to the USA or Spain, the two top earners in terms of annual tourist revenue.

So which nations are the big spenders? The British, closely followed by the Germans, spend nearly US$1000 per person annually on international tourism, more than four times the equivalent spend by the average American. Part of this difference is due to many Americans holidaying "at home" within their own diverse country.

THE WORLD'S FAVOURITE AIRLINES

Budget airlines have both fuelled and benefited from the rapid growth of tourism, especially in the USA, China, and Europe. The UK's Ryanair, set up only 20 years ago, now ranks 12th worldwide in terms of number of passengers carried:

1	AMERICAN AIRLINES INC.	99,835,000
2	SOUTHWEST AIRLINES	96,277,000
3	DELTA AIR LINES	73,584,000
4	UNITED AIRLINES	69,265,000
5	NORTHWEST AIRLINES	55,925,000
6	LUFTHANSA	51,213,000
7	AIR FRANCE	49,411,000
8	ALL NIPPON AIRWAYS	49,226,000
9	JAPAN AIRLINES INTERNATIONAL	48,911,000
10	CHINA SOUTHERN AIRLINES	48,512,000
11	US AIRWAYS	40 MILLION +
12	RYANAIR	40,532,000

A VIRTUAL PARADISE

Japanese beachgoers can rel₂ in ideal surroundings at th₂ world's first indoor beach. ₂ blue "sky", clean salt-free wate₂ ideal waves for surfing, ar₂ an hourly show from a mi₂ flame-spitting volcano provide ₂ perfectly specified day out, wi₂ no bugs and no risks – not eve₂ melanoma!

THE NEW SEVEN WONDERS OF THE WORLD

An Internet website vote named the New Seven Wonders of the World on 07/07/07. Egypt's Pyramids were withdrawn from the vote and granted honorary status, as the only remaining member of the original Seven Wonders.

COLOSSEUM, ITALY

TAJ MAHAL, INDIA

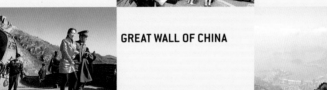

GREAT WALL OF CHINA

CHRIST THE REDEEMER, BRAZIL

PETRA, JORDAN

CHICHEN ITZA, MEXICO

MACHU PICCHU, PERU

SOURCES: IATA: World Air Transport Statistics: 51st Edition; International Association of Antarctica Tour Operators (IAATO)

XTREME TOURISM

ver 2500 people have climbed Mount Everest (current cost: $65,000). Trips to Antarctica have tripled the last decade, and you can take ice-breaker cruises to the North Pole, or be helicoptered in and en ski the last 100km (62 miles). But the latest fix is a trip into space. Individual space tourists have ade headlines, but more regular space travel will soon be launched, such as Virgin Galactic's 2.5-our suborbital flight, costing over US$20 per second. For that you should get three to six minutes of eightlessness, a view of a twinkle-free starfield, and a vista of the curved Earth below.

PACE "TOURISTS"

S$20m	**DENNIS TITO** (AMERICAN) 2001
S$20m	**MARK SHUTTLEWORTH** (SOUTH AFRICAN) 2002
S$20m	**GREGORY OLSEN** (AMERICAN) 2005
NDISCLOSED	**ANOUSHEH ANSARI** (IRANIAN/AMERICAN) 2006
S$25m	**CHARLES SIMONYI** (HUNGARIAN/AMERICAN) 2007
S$200,000	**VIRGIN GALACTIC'S** INITIAL PRICE FOR THE PASSENGER SERVICE IT PLANS TO LAUNCH IN 2008

OLAR TOURISM

OURISTS FIRST PAID TO GO TO ANTARCTICA IN 1967. SINCE THE EARLY 1990S SITOR NUMBERS HAVE GROWN DRAMATICALLY.

| 6704 | 8016 | 8120 | 9367 | 7413 | 9604 | 10,013 | 13,826 | 12,248 | 11,588 | 13,571 | 19,886 | 22,712 | 26,245 |

992/3 1993/4 1994/5 1995/6 1996/7 1997/8 1998/9 1999/0 2000/1 2001/2 2002/3 2003/4 2004/5 2005/6

VIRTUAL TOURISM

The facilities expected by some tourists can cause serious environmental damage: a golf course in Thailand needs 1500kg (3307lbs) of chemical fertilizers, pesticides, and herbicides every year and uses as much water as 60,000 rural villagers. 77% of all ship waste comes from cruise-ships, and over 80% of the world's coral sites have suffered from cruise-ship pollution. A growing trend for "responsible travel" or sustainable tourism focuses on being sensitive to the local environment and cultures.

The travelling, too, has a serious impact on climate change. But amid the expansion in destinations, flights, and money being spent on travel, there is also another increase – the rise in the virtual traveller. Travel books, TV programmes, and the Internet are bringing the world to you, with virtual tours allowing you to explore inside fabulous sites or view the highlights of museums – no need for injections, advanced planning, and those interminable queues at the airport!

Modern trends for Top Ten lists and popular votes have provided the virtual traveller with fascinating (and inevitably controversial) reads. *The Forbes Traveler's Most Visited Attractions* makes a valiant attempt at defining an "attraction", but discerning readers may wonder how visitor numbers to Times Square or Trafalgar Square are actually counted. *1000 Places to See Before You Die* and similar titles are great reference guides but often suffer from a strong US-UK bias in their listed attractions.

The 2007 website vote for "The New Seven Wonders of the World" began with a long list of nominations recommended by the countries themselves, whittled down to 21 (limited to at most one per country) by the competition's architects and then voted on by the public – requiring Internet access, but no necessity of actually having seen any of these wonders in the flesh.

THIS SPORTING PLANET

THE LEADING SPORTS AROUND THE WORLD

THE WORLD'S LEADING COMMERCIAL SPORTS ARE THE TEAM GAMES OF THE 19TH CENTURY, BUT THERE IS PLENTY OF MONEY ELSEWHERE. THE CHART OF THE WORLD'S HIGHEST-PAID ATHLETES SHOWS THAT GOLF, MOTOR SPORTS, BOXING, AND TENNIS ARE THE CURRENT TOP EARNERS.

 FOOTBALL

 BASEBALL

 CRICKET

 RUGBY

 BASKETBALL

 AMERICAN FOOTBALL

CYCLING

ICE HOCKEY

 AUSSIE RULES FOOTBALL

NORDIC AND ALPINE SPORTS

SPORT

"Sport is global culture," said Phil Knight, CEO of giant sportswear company Nike. He may be right. In the early 21st century sport, as a spectacle and as a business, has never been more successful or more global. TV viewing figures for the mega-events – like the Olympics and football's World Cup – are huge; sponsorship and merchandising money rolls in.

The sports that proved most successful in the 20th century were inventions of the 19th century. British sports were codified at home but spread through the tentacles of empire; football to almost everywhere and cricket to South Asia, Southern Africa, the Caribbean, and Australasia.

In North America, baseball, American football, and basketball triumphed – but have proven less powerful as exports. American football has barely travelled; baseball has staked a claim in Central America, the Caribbean, and East Asia but little beyond; and basketball, while now global, is still rarely professional.

Climate has also been a factor, giving ice hockey and winter sports an edge in Scandinavia, Northern and Alpine Europe, and Canada, while cycling occupies a place in the culture of Western Europe that is just as strong.

GOLF GOES GLOBAL

GOLF IS ONE OF THE FASTEST-GROWING GLOBAL GAMES. FROM ITS PREDOMINANTLY ANGLO-SAXON/SCOTTISH ROOTS, IT HAS IN THE LAST 30 YEARS BECOME THE GAME OF THE ELITES OF EAST ASIA, EUROPE, AND LATIN AMERICA.
IN THE USA ONE IN TEN ADULTS ARE REGISTERED GOLFERS.
THE GOLF COURSES OF THE WORLD NOW OCCUPY AN AREA LARGER THAN BELGIUM.

THE WORLD'S HIGHEST-PAID ATHLETES
THE TOP TEN MEN AND TOP FIVE WOMEN

ATHLETE	SPORT	AGE	EARNINGS 2006-07	ATHLETE	SPORT	AGE	EARNINGS 2006
TIGER WOODS	GOLF	31	US$100 million				
OSCAR DE LA HOYA	BOXING	34	US$43 million				
PHIL MICKELSON	GOLF	37	US$42.2 million				
KIMI RAIKKONEN	F1	27	US$40 million				
MICHAEL SCHUMACHER	F1	38	US$36 million	MARIA SHARAPOVA	TENNIS	19	US$19 million
DAVID BECKHAM	FOOTBALL	32	US$33 million	MICHELLE WIE	GOLF	17	US$17 million
KOBE BRYANT	BASKETBALL	28	US$32.9 million	SERENA WILLIAMS	TENNIS	25	US$10 million
SHAQUILLE O'NEAL	BASKETBALL	35	US$31.9 million	ANNIKA SORENSTAM	GOLF	36	US$8 million
MICHAEL JORDAN	BASKETBALL	44	US$31 million	VENUS WILLIAMS	TENNIS	26	US$7 million
RONALDINHO	FOOTBALL	27	US$31 million				

SOURCES: Forbes.com: World's Top-earning Athletes (2007) and Celebrity 100 (2006); M. Van Bottenburg: *Global Games*

SPORTING HIGHLIGHTS ON TV
VERIFIABLE LIVE TV AUDIENCES
IN MILLIONS 2006

- US OPEN GOLF, FINAL DAY **10M**
- TOUR DE FRANCE, FINAL STAGE **15M**
- NBA FINALS, GAME 6 **15M**
- WIMBLEDON MEN'S SINGLES FINAL **17M**
- US MASTERS GOLF, FINAL DAY **17M**
- WORLD SERIES GAME 5 **19M**
- NASCAR DAYTONA 500 **20M**
- F1 BRAZILIAN GRAND PRIX **83M**
- CHAMPIONS' LEAGUE FINAL **86M**
- WINTER OLYMPICS OPENING CEREMONY **87M**
- SUPER BOWL **98M**
- WORLD CUP FINAL **260M**

THE WORLD CUP ON TV
Cumulative global audiences
and broadcast hours

Year	Audience	Countries	Broadcast hours
1986	13.5 BILLION	166 COUNTRIES	9900 hours
1990	26.7 BILLION	167 COUNTRIES	14,700 hours
1994	32.1 BILLION	188 COUNTRIES	16,400 hours
1998	24.7 BILLION	196 COUNTRIES	29,100 hours
2002	28.8 BILLION	213 COUNTRIES	41,300 hours
2006	26.2 BILLION	214 COUNTRIES	73,100 hours

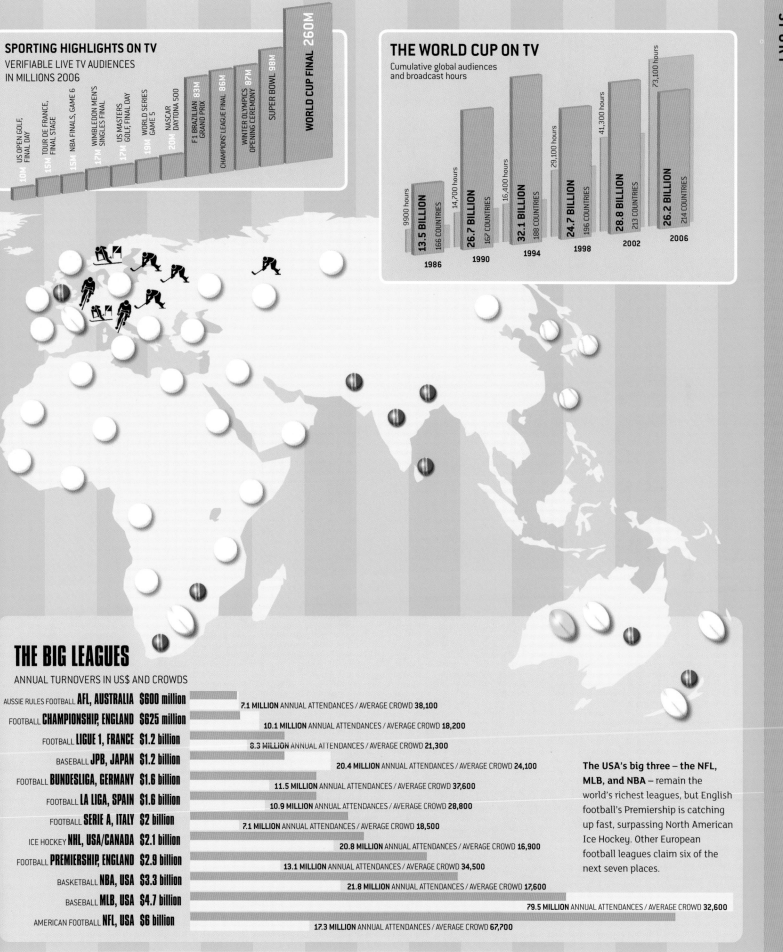

THE BIG LEAGUES
ANNUAL TURNOVERS IN US$ AND CROWDS

AUSSIE RULES FOOTBALL **AFL, AUSTRALIA** **$600 million** — 7.1 MILLION ANNUAL ATTENDANCES / AVERAGE CROWD **38,100**

FOOTBALL **CHAMPIONSHIP, ENGLAND** **$625 million** — 10.1 MILLION ANNUAL ATTENDANCES / AVERAGE CROWD **18,200**

FOOTBALL **LIGUE 1, FRANCE** **$1.2 billion** — 8.3 MILLION ANNUAL ATTENDANCES / AVERAGE CROWD **21,300**

BASEBALL **JPB, JAPAN** **$1.2 billion** — 20.4 MILLION ANNUAL ATTENDANCES / AVERAGE CROWD **24,100**

FOOTBALL **BUNDESLIGA, GERMANY** **$1.6 billion** — 11.5 MILLION ANNUAL ATTENDANCES / AVERAGE CROWD **37,600**

FOOTBALL **LA LIGA, SPAIN** **$1.6 billion** — 10.9 MILLION ANNUAL ATTENDANCES / AVERAGE CROWD **28,800**

FOOTBALL **SERIE A, ITALY** **$2 billion** — 7.1 MILLION ANNUAL ATTENDANCES / AVERAGE CROWD **18,500**

ICE HOCKEY **NHL, USA/CANADA** **$2.1 billion** — 20.8 MILLION ANNUAL ATTENDANCES / AVERAGE CROWD **16,900**

FOOTBALL **PREMIERSHIP, ENGLAND** **$2.9 billion** — 13.1 MILLION ANNUAL ATTENDANCES / AVERAGE CROWD **34,500**

BASKETBALL **NBA, USA** **$3.3 billion** — 21.8 MILLION ANNUAL ATTENDANCES / AVERAGE CROWD **17,600**

BASEBALL **MLB, USA** **$4.7 billion** — 79.5 MILLION ANNUAL ATTENDANCES / AVERAGE CROWD **32,600**

AMERICAN FOOTBALL **NFL, USA** **$6 billion** — 17.3 MILLION ANNUAL ATTENDANCES / AVERAGE CROWD **67,700**

The USA's big three – the NFL, MLB, and NBA – remain the world's richest leagues, but English football's Premiership is catching up fast, surpassing North American Ice Hockey. Other European football leagues claim six of the next seven places.

FIND OUT MORE: A. Guttman: *Sport: The First Five Millennia*; www.forbes.com; www.thesportseconomist.com

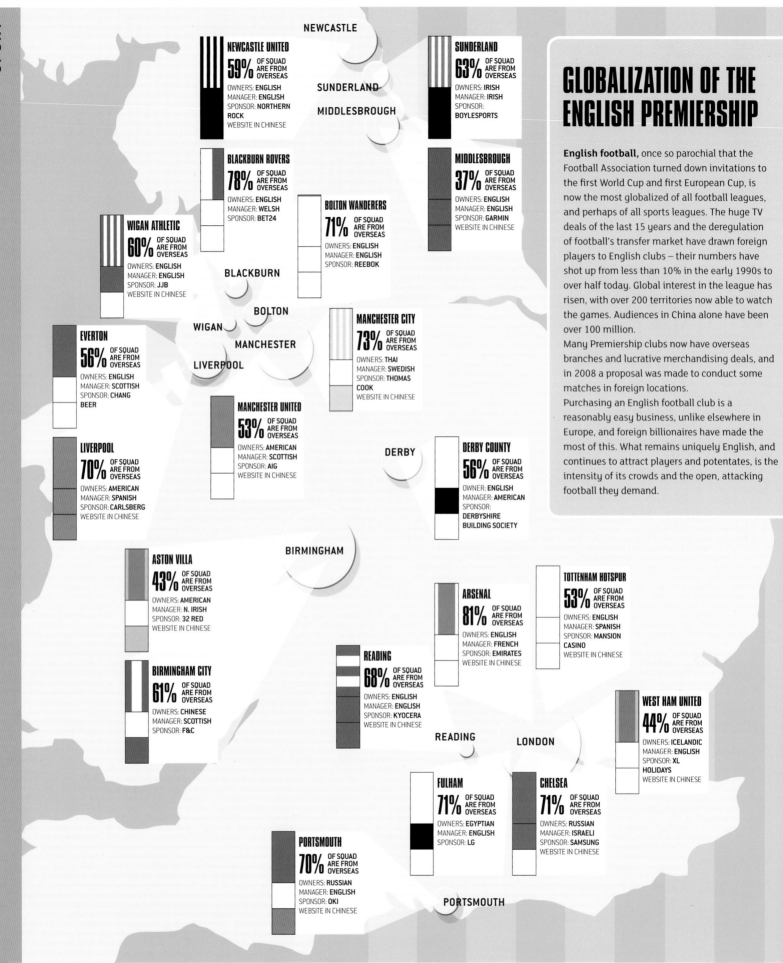

NEWCASTLE

NEWCASTLE UNITED
59% OF SQUAD ARE FROM OVERSEAS
OWNERS: ENGLISH
MANAGER: ENGLISH
SPONSOR: NORTHERN ROCK
WEBSITE IN CHINESE

SUNDERLAND

SUNDERLAND
63% OF SQUAD ARE FROM OVERSEAS
OWNERS: IRISH
MANAGER: IRISH
SPONSOR: BOYLESPORTS

MIDDLESBROUGH

MIDDLESBROUGH
37% OF SQUAD ARE FROM OVERSEAS
OWNERS: ENGLISH
MANAGER: ENGLISH
SPONSOR: GARMIN
WEBSITE IN CHINESE

BLACKBURN ROVERS
78% OF SQUAD ARE FROM OVERSEAS
OWNERS: ENGLISH
MANAGER: WELSH
SPONSOR: BET24

BOLTON WANDERERS
71% OF SQUAD ARE FROM OVERSEAS
OWNERS: ENGLISH
MANAGER: ENGLISH
SPONSOR: REEBOK

WIGAN ATHLETIC
60% OF SQUAD ARE FROM OVERSEAS
OWNERS: ENGLISH
MANAGER: ENGLISH
SPONSOR: JJB
WEBSITE IN CHINESE

BLACKBURN

MANCHESTER CITY
73% OF SQUAD ARE FROM OVERSEAS
OWNERS: THAI
MANAGER: SWEDISH
SPONSOR: THOMAS COOK
WEBSITE IN CHINESE

BOLTON

WIGAN

MANCHESTER

LIVERPOOL

EVERTON
56% OF SQUAD ARE FROM OVERSEAS
OWNERS: ENGLISH
MANAGER: SCOTTISH
SPONSOR: CHANG BEER

LIVERPOOL
70% OF SQUAD ARE FROM OVERSEAS
OWNERS: AMERICAN
MANAGER: SPANISH
SPONSOR: CARLSBERG
WEBSITE IN CHINESE

MANCHESTER UNITED
53% OF SQUAD ARE FROM OVERSEAS
OWNERS: AMERICAN
MANAGER: SCOTTISH
SPONSOR: AIG
WEBSITE IN CHINESE

DERBY

DERBY COUNTY
56% OF SQUAD ARE FROM OVERSEAS
OWNER: ENGLISH
MANAGER: AMERICAN
SPONSOR: DERBYSHIRE BUILDING SOCIETY

BIRMINGHAM

ASTON VILLA
43% OF SQUAD ARE FROM OVERSEAS
OWNERS: AMERICAN
MANAGER: N. IRISH
SPONSOR: 32 RED
WEBSITE IN CHINESE

BIRMINGHAM CITY
61% OF SQUAD ARE FROM OVERSEAS
OWNERS: CHINESE
MANAGER: SCOTTISH
SPONSOR: F&C

READING
68% OF SQUAD ARE FROM OVERSEAS
OWNERS: ENGLISH
MANAGER: ENGLISH
SPONSOR: KYOCERA
WEBSITE IN CHINESE

ARSENAL
81% OF SQUAD ARE FROM OVERSEAS
OWNERS: ENGLISH
MANAGER: FRENCH
SPONSOR: EMIRATES
WEBSITE IN CHINESE

TOTTENHAM HOTSPUR
53% OF SQUAD ARE FROM OVERSEAS
OWNERS: ENGLISH
MANAGER: SPANISH
SPONSOR: MANSION CASINO
WEBSITE IN CHINESE

WEST HAM UNITED
44% OF SQUAD ARE FROM OVERSEAS
OWNERS: ICELANDIC
MANAGER: ENGLISH
SPONSOR: XL HOLIDAYS
WEBSITE IN CHINESE

READING

LONDON

FULHAM
71% OF SQUAD ARE FROM OVERSEAS
OWNERS: EGYPTIAN
MANAGER: ENGLISH
SPONSOR: LG

CHELSEA
71% OF SQUAD ARE FROM OVERSEAS
OWNERS: RUSSIAN
MANAGER: ISRAELI
SPONSOR: SAMSUNG
WEBSITE IN CHINESE

PORTSMOUTH
70% OF SQUAD ARE FROM OVERSEAS
OWNERS: RUSSIAN
MANAGER: ENGLISH
SPONSOR: OKI
WEBSITE IN CHINESE

PORTSMOUTH

GLOBALIZATION OF THE ENGLISH PREMIERSHIP

English football, once so parochial that the Football Association turned down invitations to the first World Cup and first European Cup, is now the most globalized of all football leagues, and perhaps of all sports leagues. The huge TV deals of the last 15 years and the deregulation of football's transfer market have drawn foreign players to English clubs – their numbers have shot up from less than 10% in the early 1990s to over half today. Global interest in the league has risen, with over 200 territories now able to watch the games. Audiences in China alone have been over 100 million.

Many Premiership clubs now have overseas branches and lucrative merchandising deals, and in 2008 a proposal was made to conduct some matches in foreign locations.

Purchasing an English football club is a reasonably easy business, unlike elsewhere in Europe, and foreign billionaires have made the most of this. What remains uniquely English, and continues to attract players and potentates, is the intensity of its crowds and the open, attacking football they demand.

SOURCES: The Barclay's Premier League, www.premierleague.com; Major League Baseball, www.mlb.com

Baseball, once the most insular of American sports, has been making major efforts over the last 20 years to reach a global audience and to recruit talent from abroad. As the supply of home-grown, top-class baseball players has declined, so Major League Baseball (MLB) has increasingly recruited Venezuelans, Japanese, Puerto Ricans, and above all Dominicans who alone make up 15% of all MLB rosters. Every MLB franchise now operates an academy and scouting network in the Dominican Republic.

GLOBALIZATION OF THE AMERICAN MLB

1982	1987	1992	1997	2002	2007
12%	14%	19%	25%	27%	29%

PERCENTAGE OF FOREIGN-BORN PLAYERS IN MLB 1982–2007

SPORT IN CHINA

For much of the 20th century Chinese sport stood aside from the global stage. In the first half of the century, Western sports like basketball and football began to make headway among the tiny urban middle classes, while the vast rural hinterland remained oblivious.

Organized sports were destroyed by the long civil war and Japanese occupation. Only after the Communists came to power in 1949 did sport begin to revive; however, the excesses of the Cultural Revolution destroyed much of the sporting infrastructure, and the Party's deep suspicion of international organizations and the endless wrangles over Taiwan's status kept China out of FIFA, the Olympics, and other international sporting bodies.

Over the last 30 years, China's opening to the world and then its breakneck development have been accompanied by a massive and commercialized renaissance of sport, culminating in "Beijing 2008", which at a cost of over US$30 billion – much of this spent on construction (above) – is the most expensive Olympic Games ever. Alongside this China has been joining all manner of international sports organizations, creating professional leagues, and consuming the rest of the world's sports. As well as the Premiership and European football, NBA basketball has been the most successful entrant into the Chinese market. Since signing a number of Chinese stars, notably Yao Ming by the Houston Rockets and Yi Jianlian by the Milwaukee Bucks, NBA TV audiences in China can reach as high as 200 million.

THE PRICE OF VICTORY?

The giddy commercial circus of global sports has personally enriched small elites of predominantly male athletes, but the bigger winners are the corporate television networks and the global sports goods industry. For every Michael Essien or Yao Ming, there are thousands of casualties of the global sport labour market: among them the young Africans abandoned without money or passports on the streets of Europe by unscrupulous football agents.

The global governance of sport remains in the hands of the early 20th-century institutions, like FIFA, the IOC, and the athletics federation (IAAF) – whose design and culture were closer to the elite athletic male sports clubs from which their founders sprung, than to globally responsible non-governmental organizations. Given that these organizations hold precious global cultural resources in trust for the rest of us we should expect the highest levels of transparency, accountability, and probity from them, but the global sporting public is regularly disappointed. Several IOC delegates (including Vice-President Kim Un-yong, above) resigned over "gifts" accepted during Salt Lake City's successful bid for the 2002 Winter Olympics; FIFA expressed disapproval of its Vice-President over links to a 2006 World Cup soccer ticket scam.

The global reach of sport has increased the opportunities for gambling fixes of various kinds. Police investigations into thrown games in football, tennis, and horse racing are currently under way in over 30 countries. Many of these cases have lines of influence stretching to the voracious gambling industries of Vietnam, Thailand, and China.

The enormous rewards for winning and the gigantic interlocking pressures of money, status, and sport have seen an increasing number of sports and athletes take to performance-enhancing drugs, from baseball to football, athletics, cycling, and swimming.

FOR THE LOVE OF MONEY

THIS ARTWORK, *FOR THE LOVE OF GOD*, IS A LIFE-SIZE PLATINUM CAST OF A HUMAN SKULL WITH ITS ORIGINAL TEETH. COVERED ENTIRELY BY 8601 FLAWLESS PAVE-SET DIAMONDS, IT COST AN ESTIMATED US$20 MILLION TO CREATE. DESIGNED BY DAMIEN HIRST, IT WAS MADE BY A LONDON JEWELLER, AND WAS BOUGH BY AN ART INVESTMENT GROUP, WHICH INCLUDED HIRST HIMSELF. IT IS AN INTERESTING EXAMPLE OF BOTH THE RENAISSANCE WORKSHOP SYSTEM OF ART PRODUCTION AND OF THE PRE-ROMANTIC EVALUATION OF ART AS A COMMODITY. AT TIME OF PRESS A WORLD TOUR OF THE SKULL WAS UNDER NEGOTIATION.

ART

Art can be found everywhere, but what happens in New York, London, Paris, Berlin, Geneva, Milan, Tokyo, and Hong Kong defines the global art market. The circuits of power, money, and objects pulsate between these cities, where the key actors are clustered together: artists, dealers, galleries, auction houses, museums, advisers and consultants, art investment services, and funds, and, of course, collectors such as François Pinault (above).

The creation of a work of art is just the beginning of the process. Artists who are unknown must then strive to get their work inserted into the process of recognition, validation, and eventually sales, through grants, prizes, and media coverage, attracting the attention of dealers and curators. Indeed the capacity to mobilize this kind of PR is an essential skill for any contemporary artist to be successful in their own lifetime.

Galleries, with their established networks of buyers and collectors, act as crucial gatekeepers to the market. A prestigious gallery's decision to show an artist instantly confers kudos and market value on their work.

Auction houses are perhaps the key actors in the whole network of institutions, providing the glamorous context in which the most expensive works are bought and sold, and in so doing setting a guide price for the rest of the market.

GLOBAL ART PRICES 1987—2007

THE GLOBAL ART PRICE INDEX IN THE LAST 20 YEARS IS A TALE OF TWO BOOMS. IN THE LATE 1980s A TREMENDOUS SURGE OF MONEY ENTERED THE TOP END OF THE MARKET: JAPANESE INVESTMENT WAS A KEY FACTOR, PARTICULARLY IN EUROPEAN IMPRESSIONISTS. HOWEVER, IN THE EARLY 1990s ALLEGATIONS IN JAPAN ABOUT TAX EVASION ON TOP OF GLOBAL RECESSION PULLED THE MARKET DOWN. IN THE LAST DECADE RISING INVESTMENT WORLDWIDE HAS DRIVEN PRICES TO NEW HIGHS. HOWEVER, THE MARKET IS NOTORIOUSLY UNTRANSPARENT AND IS RIFE WITH UNDISCLOSED AND RUMOURED PRICES, UNCOMPLETED AND HIDDEN SIDE DEALS.

1990 The market peaks as Japanese investors send Impressionist values sky-high: Renoir's *Bal au Moulin de la Galette* is sold for US$78.1 million and Van Gogh's *Portrait of Dr. Gachet* for US$82.5 million

1987 Global stock market crash: Japanese money abandons stocks for art. Van Gogh's *Irises* sells for US$53.9 million and *Sunflowers* for US$39.7 million

1991 Many Japanese art purchases are exposed as elements of corporate fraud and tax evasion. With the onset of the First Gulf War, the global art market collapses

THE ART MARKET AND MUSEUMS

MOST OF THE WORLD'S MOST FAMOUS PICTURES ARE NOW OWNED BY MUSEUMS AND ARE UNLIKELY EVER TO COME ONTO THE MARKET. DA VINCI'S *MONA LISA* WAS VALUED IN 1962 FOR INSURANCE PURPOSES AT US$100 MILLION — NEARLY US$700 MILLION TODAY. THE LOUVRE DECIDED TO FORGO INSURANCE AND SPEND THE MONEY ON A MASSIVELY IMPROVED SECURITY SET-UP.

SOURCES: www.artprice.com; www.theartwolf.com

THE TURNER PRIZE

ORGANIZED BY THE TATE GALLERY, THE TURNER PRIZE IS THE LEADING AWARD FOR CONTEMPORARY ART IN THE UK. SINCE 1984 MANY OF BRITAIN'S LEADING ARTISTS HAVE FEATURED ON ITS LISTS. THE PRIZE ATTRACTS CONSIDERABLE CONTROVERSY, PARTICULARLY WHEN AWARDED TO ARTISTS WORKING IN NON-TRADITIONAL MEDIA, SUCH AS MARK WALLINGER FOR HIS INSTALLATION *STATE BRITAIN* (2007).

2006 David Geffen sells Pollock's *No.5*, 1948, and de Kooning's *Woman III* for a total of US$277.5 million – the two most expensive paintings ever. **Klimt's** *Portrait of Adele Bloch-Bauer* sells for US$135million

2004 Breaking through the US$100 million barrier: Picasso's *Garçon à la Pipe* sells for **US$104.2 million**

1998 Creeping back: Van Gogh's *Portrait de l'Artiste sans Barbe*, sells for **US$71.5 million**

2000 Price-fixing case against the auction houses finally ends with Christie's and Sotheby's sharing a US$500 million fine

FINE ART SALES AT AUCTION TURNOVER IN US$

- 4.7 BILLION
- 4.1 BILLION
- 4.9 BILLION
- 4.1 BILLION
- 3.8 BILLION
- 4.3 BILLION
- 3.1 BILLION
- 3.2 BILLION

1998 1999 2000 2001 2002 2003 2004 2005

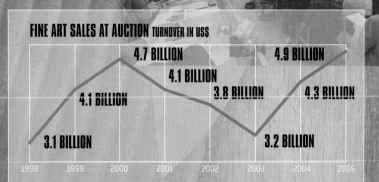

THE GLOBAL ART MARKET — TOTAL TURNOVER 1998–2005

MOST ART SALES USED TO BE PRIVATE, NOW ALMOST HALF OF THE GLOBAL ART MARKET GOES THROUGH THE MAIN AUCTION HOUSES. IN 2007 THE TOTAL VALUE OF THEIR TURNOVER WAS APPROACHING US$12 BILLION.

1992 Bottom of the market: Warhol's *210 Coca Cola Bottles* fails to make its reserve price at a New York auction. Price-fixing investigation into Sotheby's and Christie's begins

ART

THE GLOBAL ART MARKET

WHILE THE ART MARKET CONTINUES TO HAVE A SECRETIVE, PRIVATE NETWORK OF BUYING AND SELLING, MORE AND MORE OF THE MAJOR WORKS PASS THROUGH THE MAIN AUCTION HOUSES. SOTHEBY'S AND CHRISTIE'S DOMINATE THE GLOBAL ART MARKET. COLLUSION BETWEEN THEM IN THE 1980s AND 1990s WAS SUBSEQUENTLY EXPOSED THROUGH COURT PROCEEDINGS. CONTROVERSY PERSISTS OVER THE OPERATIONS OF THIS DUOPOLY, ESPECIALLY THE INCREASING ROLE OF GUARANTEED PRICES FROM THE AUCTION HOUSES, WHICH KEEP OUT COMPETITORS AND ARTIFICIALLY INFLATE THE MARKET.

THE AUCTION HOUSES RETAIN OUTPOSTS IN THE RICHER PARTS OF EUROPE AND ASIA FOR AUTHENTICATION AND REGIONAL SALES, BUT THREE-QUARTERS OF THE GLOBAL AUCTION HOUSE MARKET FLOWS THROUGH JUST TWO CITIES — LONDON AND NEW YORK.

THE REALITIES OF ART

It has been estimated that 40% of the upper end of the art market is made up of forgeries. There are only some 320 paintings accurately attributed to Rembrandt; however, recently there were over 600 "Rembrandts" in public collections around the world, and a further 300 in private hands.

Transience of art: of the 1000 contemporary artists who had gallery shows in New York and London in the 1980s, only 20 were still being exhibited in comparable venues by 2007.

LOS ANGELES

NEW YORK

AMSTERDAM
LONDON
PARIS
ZURICH
GENEVA
MILAN
TEL AVIV

DUBAI

HONG KONG

SINGAPORE

SYDNEY

○ SOTHEBY'S   ○ CHRISTIE'S   ○ BONHAMS

THE TOP TEN COLLECTORS

ONLY THE VERY RICHEST CAN NOW SERIOUSLY COLLECT ART AT THE TOP END OF THE MARKET. IN 2007 NINE OF THE TOP TEN COLLECTORS WERE US DOLLAR BILLIONAIRES, SUCH AS ELI BROAD (LEFT). OLD MONEY IS BEING JOINED BY FINANCIERS WITH FORTUNES FROM THE HEDGE FUND AND DERIVATIVE BUSINESSES. EVEN THE RICHEST MUSEUMS ONLY HAVE ANNUAL BUDGETS IN THE TENS OF MILLIONS.

Name	Estimated Wealth	Source of Wealth	Citizenship
FRANCOIS PINAULT	US$14.5 billion	Retail	French
ELI BROAD	US$6 billion	Real Estate Finance	American
CHARLES SCHWAB	US$5.2 billion	Finance	American
SAMMY OFER	US$3.9 billion	Shipping	Israeli
STEVEN COHEN	US$3 billion	Hedge Funds	American
RONALD LAUDER	US$3 billion	Cosmetics	American
MITCHELL RALES	US$2.8 billion	Manufacturing	American
HENRY KRAVIS	US$2.6 billion	Private Equity	American
KENNETH GRIFFIN	US$1.7 billion	Hedge Funds	American
CHARLES SAATCHI	> US$500 million	Advertising	British

SOURCES: Sotheby's, Christie's, and Bonhams auction houses; ARTnews (www.artnews.com)

THE EMERGING MARKETS

RUSSIA

NEW MONEY IN RUSSIA IS DRIVING UP DEMAND FOR RUSSIAN ANTIQUES, WITH THE MARKET NOW WORTH OVER US$1 BILLION A YEAR. SPECIALIZED RUSSIAN SALES OF MAINLY PRE-REVOLUTION PAINTINGS HELD IN THE WEST BROUGHT IN US$126 MILLION IN 2006 AND DOUBLE THAT IN 2007, AND SUPPORT A BURGEONING TRADE IN MODERN FACSIMILE PAINTINGS (AND OUTRIGHT FORGERIES). PASTORAL IDYLLS OF IMPERIAL RUSSIA SEEM TO APPEAL MORE TO THE AVERAGE OLIGARCH THAN THE RADICAL ABSTRACTIONISM OF THE 20TH CENTURY.

CHINA

WITH THE NEW CHINESE INDUSTRIAL REVOLUTION HAS COME A FRESH CLASS OF ENTREPRENEURS SEEKING CULTURAL ROOTS AND SOCIAL STATUS THROUGH THE PURCHASE OF CHINESE ART. WESTERN COLLECTORS LOOKING FOR AN INVESTMENT ARE JOINING THEM. PAINTINGS FROM THE LATE 1980s AND 1990s IN THE STYLES CALLED "POLITICAL POP" AND "CYNICAL REALISM" ARE FETCHING THE HIGHEST PRICES. YUE MINJUN'S *ENCHANTED SPRING* SOLD IN NEW YORK FOR ALMOST US$5 MILLION IN 2005

INDIA

INDIA'S ART MARKET IS THE LATEST BOOM ZONE WITH WORKS BY LIVING INDIAN PAINTERS NOW GOING FOR RECORD PRICES. IN 2005 TYEB MEHTA'S *MAHAISASURA* WAS THE FIRST INDIAN WORK TO FETCH OVER US$1 MILLION. THE GLOBAL MARKET FOR INDIAN ART IS NOW WORTH US$350 MILLION A YEAR, DRIVEN BY THE NEW RICH AT HOME AND THE HUGE NUMBER OF WEALTHY INDIANS ABROAD.

AUSTRALIA

FROM ALMOST NOTHING IN THE 1970s, THE MARKET FOR AUSTRALIA'S ABORIGINAL ART IS NOW ESTIMATED TO BE WORTH US$150 MILLION A YEAR. WHAT WERE ONCE DESPISED AS THE SCRIBBLINGS OF A MARGINAL RACE ARE NOW THE GRAPHIC SIGNATURE OF THE AUSTRALIAN TOURIST INDUSTRY. CONTROVERSY PERSISTS OVER THE AUTHENTICITY OF MANY WORKS AND WHETHER THE ARTISTS ARE RECEIVING ANY MORE THAN A SMALL FRACTION OF THEIR WORK'S REAL VALUE.

NOT ALL THAT MEETS THE EYE

The total value of the art market is impossible to quantify precisely, with many transactions going unreported and prices on reported sales often more rumour than fact. The market is among the least transparent in the world. Forgeries and fakes are the least of its problems. The leading auction houses have been fined for market carve-ups, and their current practice of offering high, guaranteed prices to sellers is thought by many to be a major market distortion. Valuations are shamelessly manipulated by coteries of artists, collectors, curators, and publicists who constitute an interlocking set of elites. The sceptical stance of "anonymous" graffiti artists such as Banksy (above) was soon undercut when his outlaw works were preserved and became high-value collectible items.

The tastes of a very narrow band of rich collectors can temporarily transform the value of a particular artist or style. The arrival of the new and nationalist rich in Russia and China has certainly boosted the value of their national art. Charles Saatchi's control of much of British contemporary art has enriched both him and the most recent generation of British artists.

Museums and public institutions are part of the process too. The purchase of contemporary art by museums is important in validating an artist's status. Similarly, when a museum hosts an exhibition drawn from a private collection (often receiving follow-on donations), this enhances the prestige, perceived market value, and ultimate cash value of the collection.

In 2008, however, as the USA passes into what appears to be a deep recession, auction houses are reporting low prices and falling levels of turnover. They must be hoping that the insatiable hunger for cultural capital among the new rich of China, Russia, and India can come to their rescue.

WHO GETS WHAT IN THE GARMENT VALUE CHAIN?

The global garment industry relies on the extraordinary hard work of factory hands in the developing world, but they are at best getting six per cent of the final sale value of a garment. Retailers take half themselves, textile another quarter, and the rest goes to the factory owners and shippers.

FASHION

Clothing is amongst the most basic of human needs. In the early 21st century the fashion industry has come to express some of the key features of our turbo-charged capitalism.

Domestic production of garments has been quashed by industrial production. In the West clothes have become commodities *par excellence*, valued for what they say over what they are. The relentless cycle of the fashion industry's *haute couture* shows and collections is designed to render past purchases redundant and to force the consumer to look for something new. When the vast fashion media are insufficient to the task of educating the consumer, companies are increasingly turning to celebrities to endorse their garments.

Few industries have exploited the new global division of labour with the creativity and cruelty of the fashion industry. Using the most advanced systems of global outsourcing and stock management, the giant retailers and brands have found the world's cheapest labour markets and created sensational profits from making cheaply and selling expensively.

GARMENT RETAIL PRICE $100

SIZE ZERO

The fashion industry has always exerted a kind of tyranny over permissible body shapes and sizes. In recent years the obsession has taken on an anorexic pallor. The notion of size zero is its nihilistic limit. Now a number of governments have insisted that the industry regulate itself and take better care of the models it celebrates but often condemns to ill health.

EL SALVADOR

- A living monthly wage in El Salvador is **US$650**
- The actual monthly wage in the Salvadoria garment industry is **US$162**
- Tommy Hilfiger (left) earned **US$10,679** per hour in 2003, equivalent to the hourly earnings of over 10,000 Salvadorian garment workers

SOURCES: American Apparel and Footwear Association (AAFA): *Trends*

BANGLADESH

- Number of Bangladeshis employed in the garment industry: **two million**
- Garments as percentage of the nation's exports: **67%**

Nazmul, 24, garment worker in Dhaka, Bangladesh:
- Working week: 80 hours; two days off per month; monthly pay **US$34**
- A living monthly wage in Bangladesh is **US$40**

INDONESIA

- A living monthly wage in Indonesia is **US$244**
- The actual monthly wage in the garment industry is **US$102**
- David Beckham's sponsorship income from Adidas is **US$24** million, equivalent to the living wages of 100,000 Indonesians

RETAILER
$50

MANUFACTURER
$50

CONTRACTOR
$15

EXPENSES & PROFIT
$12.50

TEXTILES
$22.50

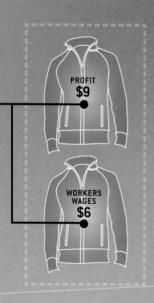

PROFIT
$9

WORKERS WAGES
$6

MEN'S COTTON T-SHIRTS IMPORTED INTO THE USA 2005

AMOUNT	UNIT PRICE	
US$163 MILLION	US$1.50	HONDURAS
US$95 MILLION	US$1.97	MEXICO
US$62 MILLION	US$1.45	EL SALVADOR
US$32 MILLION	US$1.49	CHINA
US$22 MILLION	US$1.32	HAITI
US$17 MILLION	US$1.95	PAKISTAN
US$15 MILLION	US$2.17	DOMINICAN REPUBLIC
US$14 MILLION	US$2.58	INDIA
US$11 MILLION	US$1.22	BANGLADESH
US$10 MILLION	US$4.11	PERU

FASHION

FAST FASHION

Today, in the developed world, we buy 40% of our clothes from "value" retailers with 17% of our budget. Retailers are constantly forcing down prices from their suppliers, who in turn look out the lowest wages and insist upon price cuts from contractors who are completely dependent on their business.

Suppliers respond by:

- **Increasing work rates and length of work days**
- **Cutting costs and health and safety**
- **Cutting wages: the real value of the minimum wage in the Bangladeshi garment industry has fallen by 50% over the last five years**

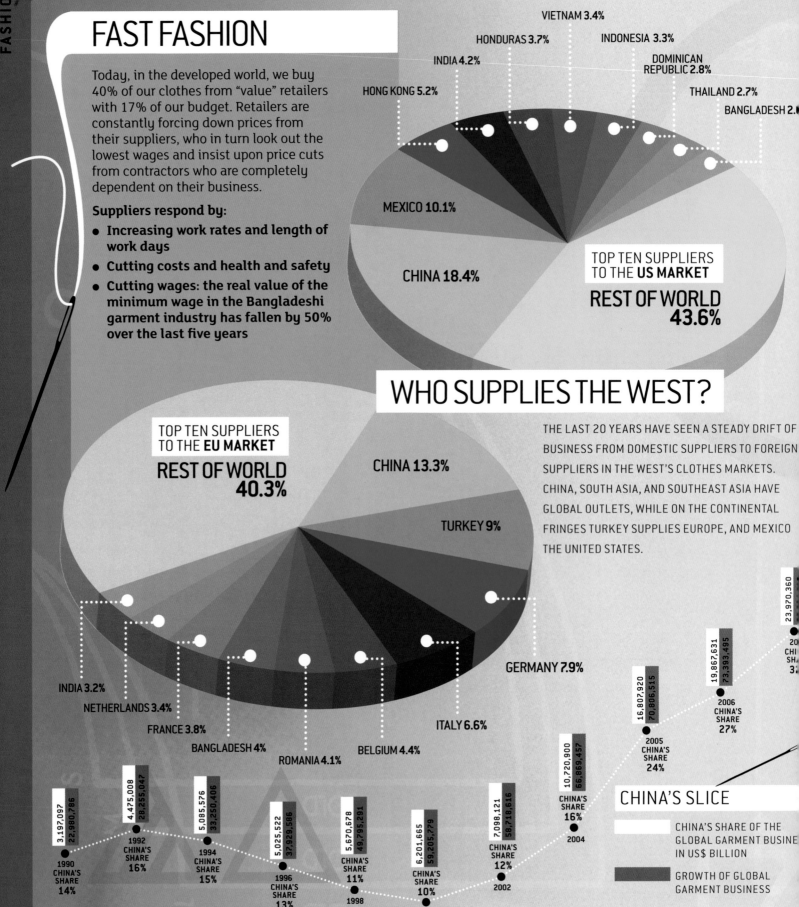

VIETNAM 3.4%

HONDURAS 3.7%   INDONESIA 3.3%

INDIA 4.2%   DOMINICAN REPUBLIC 2.8%

HONG KONG 5.2%   THAILAND 2.7%

BANGLADESH 2.

MEXICO 10.1%

CHINA 18.4%

TOP TEN SUPPLIERS TO THE **US MARKET**
REST OF WORLD
43.6%

WHO SUPPLIES THE WEST?

TOP TEN SUPPLIERS TO THE **EU MARKET**
REST OF WORLD
40.3%

CHINA 13.3%

TURKEY 9%

THE LAST 20 YEARS HAVE SEEN A STEADY DRIFT OF BUSINESS FROM DOMESTIC SUPPLIERS TO FOREIGN SUPPLIERS IN THE WEST'S CLOTHES MARKETS. CHINA, SOUTH ASIA, AND SOUTHEAST ASIA HAVE GLOBAL OUTLETS, WHILE ON THE CONTINENTAL FRINGES TURKEY SUPPLIES EUROPE, AND MEXICO THE UNITED STATES.

GERMANY 7.9%

INDIA 3.2%

NETHERLANDS 3.4%

FRANCE 3.8%

BANGLADESH 4%

ROMANIA 4.1%   BELGIUM 4.4%

ITALY 6.6%

23,970,360

20
CHI
SH
3

19,867,631
73,393,495

**2006
CHINA'S
SHARE
27%**

16,807,920
70,806,515

**2005
CHINA'S
SHARE
24%**

10,720,900
66,869,457

**CHINA'S
SHARE
16%
2004**

CHINA'S SLICE

CHINA'S SHARE OF THE GLOBAL GARMENT BUSINE IN US$ BILLION

GROWTH OF GLOBAL GARMENT BUSINESS

7,098,121
58,718,616

**CHINA'S
SHARE
12%
2002**

4,475,008
28,255,047

**1992
CHINA'S
SHARE
16%**

5,085,576
33,250,406

**1994
CHINA'S
SHARE
15%**

3,197,097
22,980,786

**1990
CHINA'S
SHARE
14%**

5,025,522
37,929,586

**1996
CHINA'S
SHARE
13%**

5,670,678
49,795,291

**CHINA'S
SHARE
11%
1998**

6,201,665
59,205,779

**CHINA'S
SHARE
10%
2000**

SOURCES: Labour Behind the Label (2006): *Who Pays for Cheap Clothes*; Interbrand (2007) The World's Top 100 Brands 2006

THE TOP FASHION BRANDS – ESTIMATED VALUE OF BRAND 2006

LOUIS VUITTON (LVMH)•	FRANCE	US$17.6 BILLION
NIKE	USA	US$10.8 BILLION
GUCCI	ITALY	US$7.1 BILLION
GAP	USA	US$6.4 BILLION
CHANEL	FRANCE	US$5.1 BILLION
ADIDAS	GERMANY	US$4.3 BILLION
ZARA	SPAIN	US$4.2 BILLION
HERMES	FRANCE	US$3.8 BILLION
BULGARI	ITALY	US$2.8 BILLION
PRADA	ITALY	US$2.8 BILLION
ARMANI	ITALY	US$2.7 BILLION
BURBERRY	UK	US$2.7 BILLION
LEVI'S	USA	US$2.6 BILLION

LVMH comprises 60 or so "world leader in luxury" brands, including Dior and Givenchy (perfume), and Moët Hennessy (rinks); the group has expressed interest in the automobile brand Aston Martin

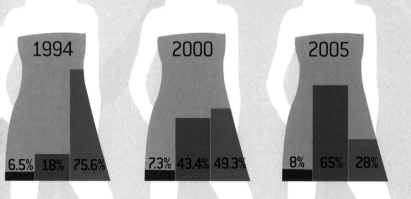

1994 6.5% 18% 75.6%　**2000** 7.3% 43.4% 49.3%　**2005** 8% 65% 28%

CHANGING EMPLOYMENT IN THE NORTH AMERICAN GARMENT INDUSTRY

CANADA

MEXICO

USA

THREE-QUARTERS OF THE US GARMENT WORKFORCE WAS AMERICAN IN THE EARLY 1990s. IT IS NOW BARELY A QUARTER; THE JOBS HAVE SWITCHED TO MEXICO AND OTHER, EVER-CHEAPER, OUTSOURCED SUPPLIERS.

WORLD GARMENT IMPORTS

THE GROWTH OF THE FASHION INDUSTRY IN THE LAST TWO DECADES HAS BEEN PHENOMENAL, THE DEMAND FOR STYLISH LABELS AND CHEAPER PRICES ECHOING FROM EVERY HIGH STREET AND SHOPPING MALL IN THE DEVELOPED WORLD. IN 2006 THE MULTI-FIBRE AGREEMENT (WHICH HAD HEAVILY REGULATED DEVELOPING WORLD EXPORTS TO THE DEVELOPED WORLD) CAME TO AN END. SINCE THEN, THE SHARE OF CHINESE EXPORTS TO THE US – THE MOST IMPORTANT TRADING RELATIONSHIP IN THE SECTOR – HAS SOARED, PUTTING IMMENSE PRESSURE ON BOTH US FIRMS BUT ALSO MUCH OF THE DEVELOPING WORLD THAT IS TRYING TO TAKE A SHARE OF THE US MARKET.

BRANDS, LABELS, FAKES, AND FANTASY

The great panoply of couture houses, driven by seasonal catwalk shows in Milan, Paris, London, and New York, drives an ever-churning turnover of goods and money on the high street. Four times a year, mass-produced variants and changes of style and look are loaded into the shops well in advance of the changing weather patterns, and remaining overstocks cleared out at end-of-season sales with ruthless efficiency.

Fast fashion and global networks of production are key components of the fashion industry, but almost as much time, energy, and money goes into branding; the stardust of glamour or borrowed chic is one route, with names like David Beckham (Adidas), Kate Moss (Topshop), Keith Richards (Louis Vuitton), amongst others, selling their names at enormous cost to the brands. There is also the cultural alchemy that turns a $20 shirt into a $200 must-have, or tatty bags and sunglasses into objects of desire by the mere addition of a logo or label. At the other end of the market is the high street, where a mainstream label can combine street smarts with driven-down prices. Companies like Gap and Zara have combined elements of these strategies and have joined the world's most valuable brands. Leading sportswear companies, like Nike and Adidas, are equally active in the creation of meaning around their clothes.

All the fashion houses are remarkably litigious when it comes to searching out fakes and copies – in itself a burgeoning industry, with counterfeit accessory pedlars a regular feature (often brazenly sited outside the brand shops) in most tourist cities.

MUSIC

Until the end of the 19th century music had to be listened to at concerts, or you made your own. The 20th century saw music become available as a recorded or broadcast product, one of the signal commercial success stories of the era. The notion of "popular" music was to develop by mid-century into a global, often youth-oriented, phenomenon, creating stars and fortunes, while also bringing a wide range of musical styles into the home. But the increasingly monolithic music business of the late 20th century, after 50 years of lavish profits and immense cultural power, is now at a point of crisis. Recordings on vinyl, cassette tape, and then CD, had been the industry's core for half a century. Since the mid-1990s, revenue has been in steady decline and profits have fallen even further. The arrival of recordable CDs, and ripping and copying software, destroyed much of the CD retail market.

Making your own music has revived with digital technology, while artists such as Radiohead (above) are now releasing their own material on the Internet, and relying on viral marketing, social networking sites, and live performance to build an audience.

THE MUSIC BIZ

Through a steady process of a consolidation the global music industry is now dominate by four huge corporations who control over 70% of the world market. However, all of the companies look vulnerable in the new technological and economic climate.

The arrival of file-sharing technologies on the Internet saw illegal downloading taking another great slice out of the industry's profits. The creation of corporate downloadable music sites has sliced the business a different way, allowing customers to buy a much r select body of music – no-one has to buy a whole album for one or two songs any more. EMI, for example, was bought up by a venture capital firm Terra Nova in 2007 at just a th of the value mooted when Universal contemplated a takeover ten years earlier. EMI's on truly profitable arm was its publishing and copyright.

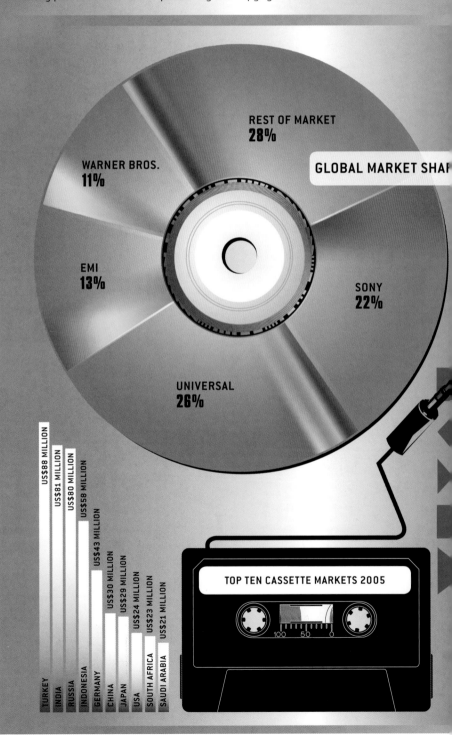

GLOBAL MARKET SHAR

REST OF MARKET
28%

WARNER BROS.
11%

EMI
13%

SONY
22%

UNIVERSAL
26%

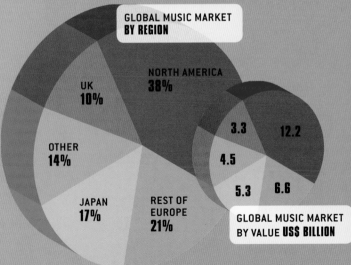

GLOBAL MUSIC MARKET BY REGION

NORTH AMERICA
38%

UK
10%

OTHER
14%

JAPAN
17%

REST OF EUROPE
21%

3.3
4.5
5.3
12.2
6.6

GLOBAL MUSIC MARKET BY VALUE US$ BILLION

TOP TEN CASSETTE MARKETS 2005

TURKEY	US$88 MILLION
INDIA	US$81 MILLION
RUSSIA	US$80 MILLION
INDONESIA	US$58 MILLION
GERMANY	US$43 MILLION
CHINA	US$30 MILLION
JAPAN	US$29 MILLION
USA	US$24 MILLION
SOUTH AFRICA	US$23 MILLION
SAUDI ARABIA	US$21 MILLION

SOURCES: IFPI: *The Recording Industry World Sales; Rolling Stone*

DECLINE IN GLOBAL MUSIC INDUSTRY REVENUES 1998 – 2006

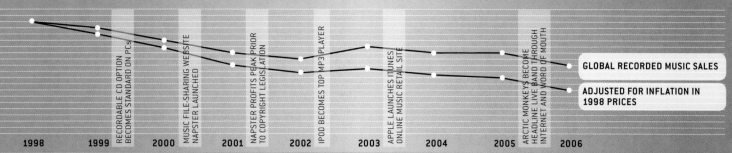

Timeline annotations:
- RECORDABLE CD OPTION BECOMES STANDARD ON PCs
- MUSIC FILE-SHARING WEBSITE NAPSTER LAUNCHED
- NAPSTER PROFITS PEAK PRIOR TO COPYRIGHT LEGISLATION
- IPOD BECOMES TOP MP3 PLAYER
- APPLE LAUNCHES ITUNES ONLINE MUSIC RETAIL SITE
- ARCTIC MONKEYS BECOME HEADLINE LIVE BAND THROUGH INTERNET AND WORD OF MOUTH

Years: 1998 1999 2000 2001 2002 2003 2004 2005 2006

- GLOBAL RECORDED MUSIC SALES
- ADJUSTED FOR INFLATION IN 1998 PRICES

DIGITAL V PHYSICAL SALES

Legal digital downloads are the great hope of the music industry. Sales through the Internet and mobiles are growing, and in the US have touched over a billion dollars in 2006, but the value of CD and other format sales is falling even more quickly.

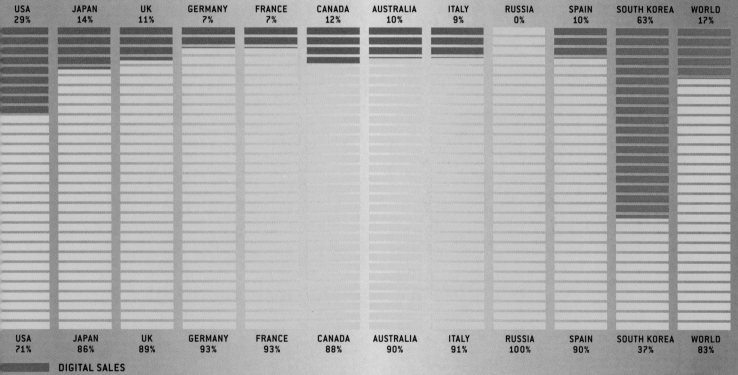

	USA	JAPAN	UK	GERMANY	FRANCE	CANADA	AUSTRALIA	ITALY	RUSSIA	SPAIN	SOUTH KOREA	WORLD
Digital (top)	29%	14%	11%	7%	7%	12%	10%	9%	0%	10%	63%	17%
Physical (bottom)	71%	86%	89%	93%	93%	88%	90%	91%	100%	90%	37%	83%

- DIGITAL SALES
- PHYSICAL SALES

GLOBAL MARKET 2005 NON-DIGITAL FORMATS

- VINYL US$77 MILLION
- CASSETTE US$633 MILLION

GROWTH OF DOWNLOADING

2005

UK	ONLINE: **US$41 MILLION**	MOBILE: **US$30 MILLION**
NORTH AMERICA	ONLINE: **US$212 MILLION**	MOBILE: **US$424 MILLION**
JAPAN	ONLINE: **US$23 MILLION**	MOBILE: **US$240 MILLION**

2006

UK	ONLINE: **US$81 MILLION**	MOBILE: **US$42 MILLION**
NORTH AMERICA	ONLINE: **US$710 MILLION**	MOBILE: **US$384 MILLION**
JAPAN	ONLINE: **US$36 MILLION**	MOBILE: **US$354 MILLION**

MUSIC

MONEY, MONEY, MONEY

Abba, the Swedish pop queens, made it, but it is becoming harder and harder to do so by just selling music. Nearly all of the highest earning artists today make their money from tours, ticket sales, and merchandising. The model was pioneered by West Coast rock band Grateful Dead, who set up their own label in the early 1970s, toured prodigiously, and by 1990 were regularly featured in the *Forbes* list of highest earners.

Even U2, who receive around US$20 million advance on each new album, make their main money from performance – their North American tour alone grossed US$135 million. By contrast, Mariah Carey who played live rarely but had the top-selling CD of the year does not make it onto the rich list at all.

As the pop/rock audience ages, ticket prices have soared. Elton John and Celine Dion make the rich list on the basis of their lucrative Vegas shows.

A-LIST TICKET PRICES

ROLLING STONES
1990 BEST SEAT, WEMBLEY £25
2006 BEST SEAT, TWICKENHAM £350

MADONNA
1988 WEMBLEY £15
2006 WEMBLEY £160

COLDPLAY
CHARGED $160 A SHOT TO SEE THEM AT
ESPACIO RIESCO, SANTIAGO, CHILE
AVERAGE MONTHLY WAGE IN SANTIAGO $500

HIGHEST-SELLING ARTISTS OF ALL TIME	EST. GLOBAL RECORD SALES (MILLION)
ELVIS PRESLEY	1000
THE BEATLES	1000
MICHAEL JACKSON	750
FRANK SINATRA	600
BING CROSBY	500
ABBA	350
MADONNA	350
NANA MOUSKOURI	350
LED ZEPPELIN	300
PINK FLOYD	300
QUEEN	300
CLIFF RICHARD	250
ELTON JOHN	250
JULIO IGLESIAS	250
THE ROLLING STONES	250

HIGHEST-EARNING ARTISTS OF 2006	US$ MILL
U2	154
THE ROLLING STONES	92
EAGLES	63
PAUL McCARTNEY	56
ELTON JOHN	49
NEIL DIAMOND	44
JIMMY BUFFETT	41
ROD STEWART	40
DAVE MATTHEWS BAND	39
CELINE DION	38

SOURCES: Robert Sandall: "Off the Record", *Prospect* 137, Aug. 2007; *Rolling Stone*; *Forbes*

CLASSICAL MUSIC

The orchestra pit is, today, an expensive money pit, and the price of opera tickets in turn excludes much of the audience. And, while live performance of classical music simply doesn't earn on the scale of pop stars, the sector has shrunk to less than three per cent of the recorded global market. "Silver surfers" lately adopting downloading is giving a temporary boost to sales, but the desperate attempts of the big companies to create cross-over acts, such as Vanessa Mae, to appeal to a younger market, have failed to halt a relative decline.

WORLD MUSIC

World Music is the catch-all title invented by Western journalists and companies in order to get the extraordinary treasure trove of the rest of the planet's music into the industry's pigeon-holes. The category covers everything from Latino sambas to the poppy rai of the Maghreb. Although its market share in the West is rising, and its musical impact belies the numbers, sales remain no bigger than those of classical music – although here again, live exposure on the festival scene is earning bucks for many artists from the developing world.

MUSIC FOR A JADED PALATE

While the global music industry continues to face a tidal wave of technological and economic change, there is no shortage of making and listening to music. And no shortage of personal wealth-making: Paul McCartney, Jagger and Richards, Elton John, and many others regularly feature in *The Sunday Times* Rich List.

In an era in which we now have more access to the music and artists of increasingly distant cultures, we seem to prefer the well-known and familiar. No contemporary artists appear likely to approach the enduring universality and popularity of the key mainstream acts of the pop industry's first four decades: while performances by Frank Sinatra, Elvis, and The Beatles might now only live in memory (or virtually-real concert formats), Bob Dylan, Van Morrison, the Rolling Stones, and Madonna continue what seem like never-ending tours.

We also seem to enjoy being present at a unique event: sales of tickets for arena concerts – whether it be Live Aid, the Three Tenors, or the latest chartbusters – have been steadily climbing, enhanced by bands such as Cream, The Who and Led Zeppelin reuniting for money-spinning jamborees. Meanwhile, the number of music festivals (and cost of entry) has been rising across Europe and elsewhere. These have become increasingly specific (reggae, ram-jam bands, dance raves, or world music), and multi-staged, while the desire for novelty has seen the likes of Shirley Bassey and the English National Opera (above) gracing the main stage at Glastonbury. As platforms for launching new bands, festivals have replaced in large part the old clubs and dives of the mid-20th century, in much the same way as the PC has replaced the gramophone.

GLOBAL MOVIE PRODUCTION

OVER 7000 MOVIES WERE MADE IN 2006, BUT THE VAST MAJORITY WERE PRODUCED IN THE SIX KEY MOVIE GLOBAL INDUSTRIES — THE USA, EUROPE, CHINA, JAPAN, INDIA, AND NIGERIA.

FILM

After the Second World War, national cinemas in Europe and Japan prospered on state subsidies and domestic audiences, but the US film industry continued to set global standards of genre, production methods, and profitability. Now, new technologies and new forms of globalization are changing the world's film industry.

Although US movies are by far the most successful internationally, they face increasing competition in the huge Indian and Chinese markets, while national cinema continues to take a large chunk of the Japanese and Korean box office. Few, however, have proved able to export films beyond their ethnic and linguistic diasporas.

The Indian film industry is emblematic of the new shape of global cinema. It has learnt some of Hollywood's tricks but created its own distinctive genres and conventions for its booming audience: brash and brassy, all-dancing, all-singing, Bollywood's hold is strong enough to ensure that no American movie can make it into the top ten at the sub-continent's box office. Only Iran, where film importing is subjected to strict controls, has a lower share for importing foreign films. South Korea, Turkey, and Japan have strong domestic industries, but most national box offices remain dominated by Hollywood. Even France, where cultural pride and government money are lavished upon native film-making, can only capture 37% of the national box office.

USA – 699

HOLLYWOOD MAY NOT MAKE THE MOST MOVIES BUT IT CONTINUES TO MAKE THE MOST MONEY.

Movie-going in the West continues to be an ever — although one now enjoyed in a shopping mall, offering a panoply of merchandising opportunit

MOVIES PRODUCED IN 2006

DOMESTIC SHARE OF BOX OFFICE			FOREIGN SHARE OF BOX OFFICE
37%	FRANCE	203	73%
17%	GERMANY	174	83%
17%	SPAIN	150	83%
19%	ITALY	117	81%
59%	SOUTH KOREA	108	41%
99%	IRAN	83	1%
5%	CANADA	80	95%
34%	UK	78	66%
11%	ARGENTINA	74	89%
12%	BRAZIL	70	88%
35%	HONG KONG	51	65%
14%	MALAYSIA	0	86%
5%	MEXICO	0	95%

THE TOP FIVE BIGGEST EARNERS

1	US$1,835,400,000	TITANIC	1997
2	US$1,133,027,325	THE LORD OF THE RINGS: THE RETURN OF THE KING	2003
3	US$1,065,659,812	PIRATES OF THE CARIBBEAN: DEAD MAN'S CHEST	2006
4	US$976,457,891	HARRY POTTER AND THE SORCERER'S STONE	2001
5	US$952,404,152	PIRATES OF THE CARIBBEAN: AT WORLD'S END	2007

BOX OFFICE

	DOMESTIC	IMPORTED
USA	95%	5%
INDIA	95%	5%
CHINA	68%	32%
JAPAN	41%	59%

EUROPE – 862

FRANCE, GERMANY, SPAIN, ITALY, AND THE UK ACCOUNT FOR OVER THREE QUARTERS OF THE EUROPEAN UNION'S FILM-MAKING.

CHINA – 330

STRICT IMPORT QUOTAS AND A MASSIVE DOMESTIC MARKET HAVE KEPT THE CHINESE FILM INDUSTRY BUOYANT.

JAPAN – 417

IN JAPAN THE DESIRE FOR NATIONAL STORIES IN THE NATIONAL LANGUAGE REMAINS STRONG, BUT HOME-GROWN FILMS STILL ONLY ACCOUNT FOR LESS THEN 50% OF THE BOX OFFICE.

NIGERIA – 2000

NOLLYWOOD HAS PERFECTED THE LOW-BUDGET MOVIE IN THE DIGITAL AGE – ADDING A WHOLE NEW DIMENSION TO THE NOTION OF MASS PRODUCTION.

INDIA – 1041

BOLLYWOOD HAS TAKEN THE NUMBER TWO SPOT, DRIVEN BY ITS MUSICALS, EPICS, AND EXTRAVAGANZAS.

One area in which Asian cinema successfully penetrated global markets was with martial arts movies, a trend followed up in recent years with violent thrillers and horror movies.

MOVIES PRODUCED IN 2006

PHILIPPINES	56
EGYPT	39
AUSTRALIA	32
PAKISTAN	17
ISRAEL	17

FILM

CINEMA ADMISSIONS AND BOX OFFICE

AS CINEMA SCREENS AND RELATIVE PROSPERITY SPREAD, THE GLOBAL BOX OFFICE IS DOING RECORD LEVELS OF BUSINESS. THE DEVELOPED COUNTRIES CONTINUE TO PAY OUT THE MOST PER TICKET, BUT AUDIENCES IN ASIA AND THE PACIFIC FAR OUTSTRIP THE OTHER REGIONS IN TERMS OF ADMISSIONS.

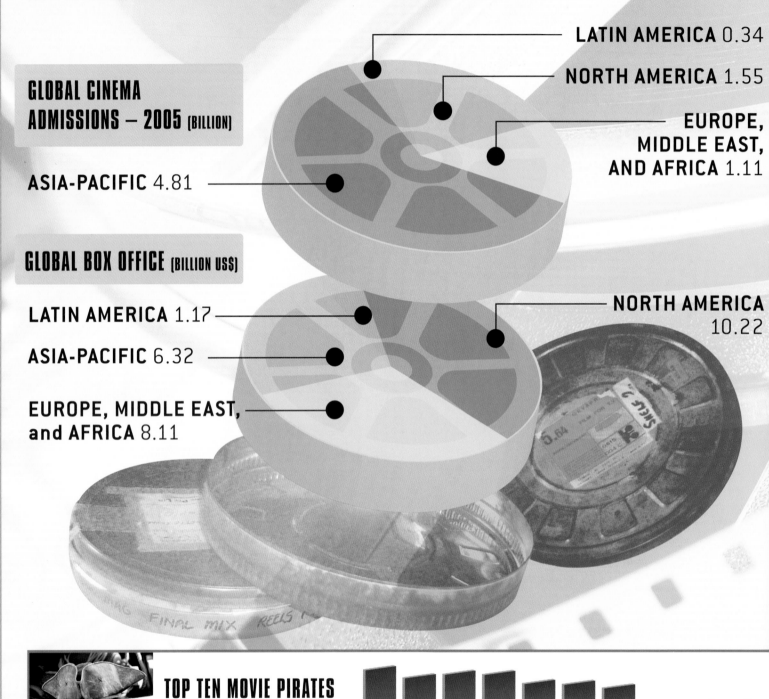

GLOBAL CINEMA ADMISSIONS – 2005 (BILLION)

LATIN AMERICA 0.34

NORTH AMERICA 1.55

EUROPE, MIDDLE EAST, AND AFRICA 1.11

ASIA-PACIFIC 4.81

GLOBAL BOX OFFICE (BILLION US$)

LATIN AMERICA 1.17

ASIA-PACIFIC 6.32

EUROPE, MIDDLE EAST, and AFRICA 8.11

NORTH AMERICA 10.22

TOP TEN MOVIE PIRATES

THE ADVENT OF VIDEO AND DVD TECHNOLOGIES HAS CREATED A HUGE MARKET FOR PIRATED COPIES OF FILMS. IN SOME PARTS OF THE WORLD THE BLACK MARKET DWARFS THE LEGAL MARKET, WITH CHINA THE WORST OFFENDER.

CHINA	RUSSIA	THAILAND	HUNGARY	POLAND	MEXICO	TAIWAN	SPAIN	INDIA	ITALY
90	79	79	76	65	61	54	32	29	25

percentage of potential film market lost to piracy

 SOURCES: MPA (2006) *The Cost of Movie Piracy*; European Audiovisual Observatory (2007) *World Film Market Trends*; www.itssamsview.blogspot.com

INDIAN FILMS BY LANGUAGE

INDIA'S FILM INDUSTRY REFLECTS SOMETHING OF ITS LINGUISTIC DIVERSITY WITH HINDI MOVIES SERVING A NATIONAL PUBLIC ALONGSIDE FOUR OTHER INDIAN LANGUAGE FILM INDUSTRIES.

26%	24%	15%	13%	12%	8%	2%
TELUGU	HINDI	MALAYALAM	TAMIL	OTHER	KANNAD	ENGLISH

CHINA GOES TO THE MOVIES

● BOX OFFICE (US$ MILLION)
● ADMISSIONS (MILLIONS)

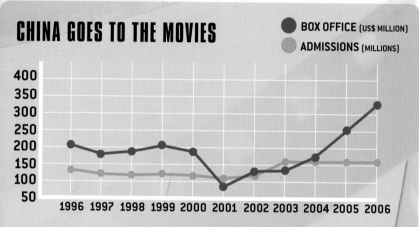

(Chart y-axis: 400, 350, 300, 250, 200, 150, 100, 50)
(Chart x-axis: 1996 1997 1998 1999 2000 2001 2002 2003 2004 2005 2006)

AVERAGE COST OF FILM PRODUCTION

WITH AVERAGE COSTS AROUND EIGHT TIMES ITS COMPETITORS, THE US MOVIE IS A HIGH RISK/HIGH RETURN INVESTMENT – AND ONLY HOLLYWOOD SEEMS ABLE TO PUT THIS KIND OF FINANCE TOGETHER. A LARGE SLICE OF HOLLYWOOD MOVIES ARE TODAY MADE IN THE UK DUE TO LOWER OVERHEADS.

● FRANCE
● US
● UK
(US$ MILLION)

(Chart y-axis: 70, 60, 50, 40, 30, 20, 10, 0)
(Chart x-axis: 1996 1997 1998 1999 2000 2001 2002 2003 2004 2005 2006)

CHANGING LOCATIONS

The cinema continues to be the first outlet for films – with continuing growth in admissions in Asian markets – although the exotic dream palaces of old have been mostly rationalized into multiplexes. But movies are increasingly viewed via DVD rental and purchase, on-line and on television, providing new revenue streams. Re-releases of classics on DVD (pioneered by Disney's recycling of its old movies) also provide new turnover for backlist owners.

The arrival of digital technologies has, at one end, transformed the economics of film-making – as Nigeria in particular has demonstrated; cheaply-made movies distributed on DVD can reap considerable profits. Ironically, at the upper end of film budgets, the extravagances of computer-generated imagery (CGI) and animation can make movies even more expensive to create. Hollywood blockbusters can have astronomical budgets, but can make spectacular returns as well.

Film-making is an expensive and risky process. When it goes wrong, it really goes wrong. Heaven's Gate didn't just lose money – it shattered Universal Studios. Predicting whether a film can make a return on its investment and controlling production budgets are fiendishly difficult – the film industry today has yet to resolve this problem.

THE TOP FIVE BIGGEST MOVIE LOSSES

1	US$99,109,016	HEAVEN'S GATE	1980
2	US$95,600,000	THE ADVENTURES OF PLUTO NASH	2002
3	US$94,382,589	CUTTHROAT ISLAND	1995
4	US$90,089,425	INCHON	1981
5	US$81,500,000	TOWN & COUNTRY	2001

INDEX

This Index is not intended to be comprehensive. Many subjects are adequately referenced in the Contents list at the beginning of the book, and this Index is intended to give the reader an idea of where further information on specific topics may be found. References to individual countries and places which appear on the many maps and graphs in the book are also not included, with the exception of those instances in which a country or location has been analysed as part of a particular topic.

9/11 attacks 114–117
abortion 55
Afghanistan 103
Africa
    debt 131
    disease 45
    famine 18
    health care 47
    trafficking/smuggling 154
    urbanization 40
    war 18
ageing 60–63
agriculture 15, 136
AIDS 18, 44, 45
air transport 174–177
    accidents 20
    hijackings 114–115
alcohol 79
al-Qaeda 115–117
Andrew, Hurricane 19
Anti-Corruption Resources Centre 83
Aral Sea 24
arms, trade, manufacturers 148–151
art, market 204–207
ASEAN (Association of Southeast Asian States) 134
Australia 25, 63, 123
automobiles 174–175
    fuel efficiency 175

Baha'i Faith 56–59
Bangladesh 31
Barcelona 37, 41
baseball 200–203
    MLB 203
basketball 200–201
Beijing (Peking) 39
Berlin 39
Bhopal 20
bicycles 174
biodiversity 14–17
biomes 14
    protection 16
biometrics 96–97
birth rates 31–32, 54
    teenage birth rates 54
blasphemy 59, 98
Boeing 149
Bofors arms deal scandal 83
Bolivia, ethnicity 64
    coups 90
boxing 200
Brazil
    ethnicity 64
    population 30
bribery 80–81
Buddhism 56–59

cable TV broadcasting 189
Canada, ethnicity 64
Cao Dai 56–59
capital punishment 74–75
carbon dioxide (CO$_2$) 10–11
CARICOM (Caribbean Community) 134
"cash-for-honours" scandal 82
CFA Franc zone 120
children 54
China, People's Republic of
    2008 Olympics 203
    disasters 18–21
    organized crime 154
    politics 90

pollution 11, 13
population 31–33, 62, 67
religion 56–59
TV ownership 189
urbanization 34–36
water needs 25
cinema 140
climate change 10–13, 17
cloning (see also genetic engineering) 55
coal 27, 28
Colombia 112–113
commodities 26–27
communications industries 162–165
communism 90
commuting 174–177
Comoros, politics 90
Congo, Democratic Republic 31
contraception 54
coral reefs 12–13, 14
corruption 80–83
counterfeit, money 152–155
    goods 211, 212–215, 219
Christianity 52, 56–59
crime 72–75
    organized 152–155
CSGR (Centre for the Study of Globalization and Regionalization) 133
Curitiba 37

dams 15, 25
death rates 32, 60–61
    penalty 75
debt 128–131
deforestation 11
democracy 86–89, 90–91
diet 48–51
disasters, man-made, natural 18–21
disease 12–13, 18, 44
divorce rates 52
drought 18
drugs 76–79
    illicit, abuse 76–77

prescription 78
production, seizures 112–113
trafficking 112–113

earthquakes 18–19
ecology, impact of climate change 12
ecological footprint 14, 29
ecosystems 12–13
education 68–71
electoral systems 89
employment 136–139
energy, sources, renewable 158–161
epidemics 18
Ethiopia, population 31
European Economic Area (EEA) 134
European Union (EU) 13
  membership 91
  Euro zone 120
  trade 135
Evangelism 59
execution *see* capital punishment
exchange rates 122
extinctions 12–13, 15
extraordinary rendition 116
extreme weather *see* weather

fair trade 144–147
families
  average size 54
  family planning 54
famine 18, 51
fashion industry 208–211
fast food 51
FIFA 203
Fiji, ethnicity 65
film industry 216–219
fingerprinting 96
fires 12–13, 15
fish 17, 28
FLO (Fair Trade Labelling Organization) 144–147
flooding 12–13, 18–19
food 48–51

changing production patterns 12
football 200–201
  American (NFL) 201
  UK Association 202
  Australian Rules 201
  UK Association 202
  UK Premiership 201–202
  World Cup 201
forests 16
Forest Stewardship Council 29
Formula One 200
fossil fuels 10–11
France 120
Fujimori, Alberto 83

gambling 153, 169
gas, natural 27, 28
gender balance 30, 52–53, 69, 72
genetic engineering/modification 51, 52
genocide 67
globalization 132–135
GNA (Gross National Happiness) 124
gold, reserves 122
golf 200
Gore, Al 10
greenhouse gases (GHG) 10–11
Guantánamo Bay 117
guns 72–73, 148–149
Guyana, ethnicity 64

health 44–47
  health care 46, 63
heat waves 18–19
higher education *see* universities
Hinduism 56–58
homosexuality 52
human trafficking 110–111
hurricanes 18–19
hyperinflation 120–121

IAAF 203
ice cover 10

ice hockey 201
identity cards 95, 96–97
identity theft 153
IDPs (Internally Displaced Persons) 106–109
immunization 47
India
  pollution 13
  population 31
  water needs 25
Indonesia, population 31
industry, industrialization 136–139
  accidents 20
infanticide 30
inflation 120–121
Internet, the 166–169
  advertising 140–14
  news broadcasting 194–195
  suppression of 97, 101
IPCC (International Panel on Climate Change) 10
Iraq 98–99
Islam/Islamic world 52, 56–59, 138
Israel 65
Italy 90
Ivan, Hurricane 19
IVF 54

Jainism 56–59
Japan, population 31
  organized crime 154–155
  religion 56–59
journalists 100–101
Judaism 52, 56–59

Katrina, hurricane 18, 19
Keynes, John Maynard 139
Kierval, Jacques 83
Kobe, earthquake 18, 19
Korea, ethnicity 65
Kyoto Protocol 10, 13

labour force 136–139
Lagos 34

languages 184–187
Latin America
  drugs 112–113
  organized crime 154
  population 30–33
  Leeson, Nick 83
LETS (Local Exchange Trading Scheme) 120
literacy 68–69
Live 8 concert 128
Living Planet Index 14
Lockheed Martin 149
London, UK
  disasters 21
  sanitation 25
  urbanization 38

McDonald's 51, 133
malnutrition 12–13
Marine Stewardship Council 29
Marcos, Ferdinand 129
marriage 52–53
  same-sex unions 53
MBAs 71
megacities see urbanization
Mexico 135
Mexico City 25, 34
Microsoft 133
migrant workers 139
mining 15
  accidents 20
mobile phone technology 139
Monaco 32
money 120–123
  laundering 152–155
Mongolia 32
monoculture 14
Monsanto 14
Montesinos, Vladimiro 83
Mumbai (Bombay) 21
murder 72–73
Murdoch, Rupert 188
music industry 212–215

Muslims see Islam

NAFTA (North American Free Trade Association) 134
news 192–195
newspapers 192–193, 140–141
New York 37, 38
NFL 201
Nigeria, population 31
Nike 200
Northrop Grumman 149
nuclear energy 159–159
  accidents 21
  weaponry, tests 150–151

obesity 50
oil 26–27, 28
  spills 20
  for food scandal 82
Olympics, the 203
  IOC scandal 203
organic foods 50

Pakistan 31, 90
Palestinians 65
Paris, France 38
peacekeeping 104–105
pensions 62
Pearl, Daniel 98
petroleum costs 177
pharmaceuticals 78
  herbal/organic 17
Philippines, The 47
police 72–74, 94–97
politics 86–93
Politkovskaya, Anna 98
population 30–33
press, the 98–101, 192–195
prison, populations 74–75
Privacy International 94–95
Procter & Gamble 140
protected areas 16

punishment 72–75

Qatar, ethnicity 65

race/racial issues 64–67
radio/wireless 140
rail transportation 174–175
  accidents 20
rainforests 15
recycling 29
refugees 106–109
religion 56–59
Reporters Without Frontiers 98–99
resources, depletion 26–29
roads 15
  accidents 20, 44, 45
Russia, population 31, 66
  organized crime 154

SAARC (South Asian Association For Regional Cooperation) 134
SACU (Southern African Customs Union) 134
St. Petersburg 39
satellite, surveillance 171
  TV broadcasting 189
service industries 137
sex trade 110–113, 155
sexual consent, age of 53
Sharia law 75
shipping 175
  accidents 20
Shinto 56–59
Sikhism 56–59
SIPRI Top 100 149
smuggling 110–113, 152–155
Somalia 103
South Africa, ethnicity 65
  crime rates 72–73
  health 47
species, endangered 12–13, 15
  reintroductions 17
sport 200–203

strike action 139
student debt 130
Sudan, ethnicity 65
  war 103
surveillance 170–173
sweatshops 138

technology, new 178–181
  accidents 18
  transportation 174–175
  digital 166–169, 180, 188–191
television 188–191
  advertising 140–143
  news broadcasting 194–195
  sport on TV 201
  World Cup 201
temperature, global average 10
tennis 200
terrorism 114–117
tobacco 76
trade blocs 134
trades unions 136
trafficking 110–113
trains see rail
Transparency International 82–83
transportation 174–177
  accidents 18
Trinidad, ethnicity 6
Turner, Ted 188
Tuvalu 21

UAE (United Arab Emirates) 65
UNASUR/UNASOL (Union of South American
  Nations) 134
unemployment 137
Union Carbide 20
United Kingdom
  crime rates 72–73
  prison population 74–75
United Nations (UN)
  Millennium Development Goals 124
  Millennium Target Goals 131

peacekeeping 104–105
United States of America (USA)
  crime rates 72–73
  debt, national 128–129
  education 71
  Kyoto protocols 13
  languages 185
  money 120–123
  population 30, 66
  presidential elections 86–87
  religion 59
  TV broadcasting 190
universities 70–71
urbanization 15, 32, 34–37, 38–41

vegetarians/vegans 51
volcanoes 18–19
voting 86–89
  ages 86

Wal-Mart 133
war 18–19, 102–105
water 22–25
  shortage/stres 12–13
wealth, disparities 124–127
weapons of mass destruction 151
weather, extreme events 13, 17, 18
wetlands 16
Wilma, Hurricane 19
women, in workplace 138
  suffrage 89
World Trade Organization (WTO) 134, 135
work 136–139
Worldcom 82
World War I 18, 102
World War II 102

Yellowstone, supervolcano 21

Zimbabwe 90

ACKNOWLEDGEMENTS

The publisher would like to thank the following for their kind permission to reproduce their photographs:

(Key: a-above; b-below/bottom; bg-background; c-centre; f-far; l-left; r-right; t-top)

1 NASA: Johnson Space Center / STS096-705-066. **2-3 iStockphoto.com:** (2, 10); Frank van den Bergh (4); Mark Evans (12); Robert Kohlhuber (17); Jan Kranendonk (15); Yong Hiam Lim (3); Ivan Mateev (5); Andrew Penner (18); Malcom Romain (8); Fanelie Rosier (7); Przemyslaw Rzeszutko (11); Roberto A. Sanchez (13); Robert Simon (16); Len Tillim (9); Josh Webb (1); **NASA:** STS-49 (14). **Wikipedia, The Free Encyclopedia:** (14). **5 iStockphoto. com:** (bl); Wolfgang Amri (tl); René Mansi (cl). **6 iStockphoto.com:** (tl); Darko Novakovic (bl); Anatoly Vartanov (cl). **8 Corbis:** EPA / Chris Hocking (bc); EPA / Vincent Laforet (t); Frans Lanting (br); Reuters / Kimimasa Mayama (fbr). **9 Alamy:** Michael Howard (fbl); **Corbis:** Yann Arthus-Betrand (br); Reuters / Keith Bedford (bc); **Getty Images:** David Einsel (t); **iStockphoto.com:** Phil Augustavo (bl); Malcom Romain (fbr). **10 Corbis:** EPA / Chris Hocking (tl). **10-11 NASA:** Johnson Space Center / STS096-705-066 (bg). **12-13 NASA:** Johnson Space Center / STS096-705-066 (bg). **13 Corbis:** Layne Kennedy (c); David Madison (tr). **14 Corbis:** Frans Lanting (tl); **iStockphoto.com:** Wolfgang Amri (br). **15 Getty Images:** Altrendo (bl). **17 iStockphoto.com:** Len Tillim (ca). **Still Pictures:** Mark Edwards (c). **18 Corbis:** Reuters / Kimimasa Mayama (tl). **18-19 Jim Reed** (bg). **19 Alamy:** Pacific Press Service (c). **20 Alamy:** Peter Bowater (cr); **Getty Images:** Liaison / Sandro Tucci (tr); **Rex Features:** Sipa Press (t). **21 Corbis:** Reuters / David J. Phillip (tr); **Still Pictures:** UNEP / H. Windeck (tr). **22 Alamy:** Michael Howard (tl). **23 iStockphoto.com:** Kevin Tavares (tl). **24 Corbis:** David Turnley (cr). **25 Getty Images:** National Geographic (l); **PlayPumps International:** (br). **26 iStockphoto.com:** Phil Augustavo (tl); Mark Evans (bc); Steve Foerster (br); **Wikipedia, The Free Encyclopedia:** (cr). **27 iStockphoto.com:** (c); Melissa Carroll (bl); Klaus Meindl (cr); Donall O'Cleirigh (bc); Andrew Penner (t); **Wikipedia, The Free Encyclopedia:** (cl, br). **28 Photolibrary:** Animals Animals / Shane Moore (bl). **29 Rex Features:** Image Source (bl); Zuma / KPA (tr). **30 Corbis:** Reuters / Keith Bedford (tl). **32 Corbis:** Dean Conger (tr); **iStockphoto.com:** René Mansi (tl). **33 Getty Images:** AFP / Deshakalyan Chowdhury (tr). **34 Corbis:** Yann Arthus-Betrand (tr); **Panos Pictures:** Qilai Shen (tr). **36 Catherine Jagger:** (br); **Panos Pictures:** Ian Teh (br). **37 Corbis:** Lucille Reyboz (bl); **Getty Images:** AFP / Lands Department (tr). **38 iStockphoto. com:** (cra, cb, br); Sebastian Bayram (cr); Arseniy Federoff (cfra); Marek Pawluczuk (bc); Malcom Romain (tl). **39 iStockphoto.com:** Frank van den Bergh (cra); Stéphane Bidouze (tr); Matjaz Boncina (cr); Jan Kranendonk (bl); Elena Korenbaum (cla); Russell McBride (br); Nigel Merrick (tc). **40 iStockphoto.com:** Nigel Merrick (bl); Marek Pawluczuk (bl). **41 iStockphoto.com:** Stéphane Bidouze (t); Joselito Briones (tl); Arseniy Federoff (tl); Russell McBride (c); **Still Pictures:** Zachary L. Powers. **42 Corbis:** Reuters (fbl); Reuters / Ajay Verma (tl); Zefa / Fridmar Damm (bc); **Getty Images:** AFP / Robyn Beck (tr); Paula Bronstein (tr); **Panos Pictures:** Justin Jin (fbr). **42 Corbis:** Dallas Morning News / Michael Ainsworth (bc); EPA / Diego Azubel (t); **Getty Images:** AFP / Prakash Singh (fbr); Stone+ / Ryan McVay (fbl); **iStockphoto.com:** Paul Kline (bl); **Panos Pictures:** Heldur Netocny (br). **44 Corbis:** EPA / Photomig (cr); Reuters (tl). **45 Alamy:** Steve Hotson (cl). **46 Alamy:** John Angerson (bl); Les Gibson (tl). **47 Alamy:** John Angerson (tr); **Panos Pictures:** Dieter Telemans (tl). **46-47 Alamy:** John Angerson (bg). **48 Getty Images:** AFP / Robyn Beck. **49 Alamy:** Mark Baynes (tr/Oil Crops); **iStockphotos.com:** (tr/Eggs, tr/Sugar, tr/Vegetables); Christine Balderas (tr/Milk); Kelly Cline (tr/Starchy Roots); Sharon Day (tr/Pulses); Jon Helgason (tr/Plate); Ivan Mateev (tr/Cereals); Fanelie Rosier (tr/Fish); Robert Simon (tr/Meat); Klaudia Steiner (tr/Fruit); Josh Webb (tr/Nuts). **51 Getty Images:** Graeme Robertson (bc); Michael Smith (tr). **52 Corbis:** Zefa / Fridmar Damm (tl). **54 Alamy:** David Gregs (bl). **55 Alamy:** ClassicStock (tr). **56 Corbis:** Reuters / Ajay Verma (tl). **58 Getty Images:** AFP / Marai Shah (bl). **59 Corbis:** Reuters / George Esiri (tr). **60 Panos Pictures:** Justin Jin (tl). **61 Getty Images:** John Rowley (cra); **Panos Pictures:** Tim Dirven (tr). **62 Getty Images:** Adam Crowley (bl). **63 Alamy:** Angela Hampton Picture Library (tl); David Hoffman Photo Library (tr); **Corbis:** Jose Luis Pelaez, Inc. (bc). **64 Getty Images:** Stone+ / Ryan McVay (tl). **67 Panos Pictures:** Sven Torfinn (tr). **68 iStockphoto.com:** Nicholas Belton (cr); Winston Davidian (br); Paul Kline (tl); Chen Ping-Hung (c). **68-69 Nicola Plumb:** (bg). **69 iStockphoto.com:** (car, br); Elman Alexander (tr); Winston Davidian (cl); Christopher Hudson (tr). **70-71 Alamy:** Colin Underhill (bg). **71 iStockphoto.com:** Elman Alexander (tr). **72 Corbis:** Dallas Morning News / Michael Ainsworth (tl); **Getty Images:** AFP / Photo STR (bc). **72-73 Corbis:** William Whitehurst (bg). **74 Corbis:** Bettmann (bl). **74-75 Corbis:** Bettmann (bg). **75 Corbis:** John Zich (tr); **Getty Images:** AFP / Samad Jewel. **76 Panos Pictures:** Heldur Netocny (tl). **77 Still Pictures:** Argus / Hartmut Schwarzbach (bl). **80 Corbis:** Bettmann (cra); **Getty Images:** AFP / Mark Phillips (ca); AFP / Prakash Singh (tl). **81 Corbis:** Reuters (ca); Reuters / Fred Ernst (cra); Sygma / Jacques Pavlovsky (cla). **83 Corbis:** Reuters / Paul McErlane (tr). **84 Corbis:** Kevin P. Casey (fbr); Reuters / Jim Bourg (br); David Turnley (bc); **Getty Images:** Brian Sokol (t). **85 Corbis:** Reuters (fbl); Reuters / Dimitar Dilkoff (br); **Panos Pictures:** Espen Rasmussen (bc); **Rex Features:** Sipa Press (t); **Still Pictures:** Das Fotoarchiv / Sebastian Bolesch (bl); **Duncan Youel:** (fbr). **86 Corbis:** Reuters / Jason Reed (br); David Turnley (tl). **88 Getty Images:** Marco Garcia (cr); **89 Corbis:** EPA / Altaf Qadri (tl); **Getty Images:** Mario Tama (br). **90 Corbis:** Reuters / Jim Bourg (tl); Reuters / Howard Burditt (bc). **94 Corbis:** Kevin P. Casey (tl). **95 Corbis:** Reuters / Jim Bourg (tl). **96 Corbis:** David Brabyn (tl). **96 iStockphoto.com:** Andrew Brown (t). **97 Corbis:** Kevin P. Casey (br); **Getty Images:** Brian Sokol (tc, c); **Rex Features:** Steve Bent (t). **98 Corbis:** Reuters (tl). **99 Duncan Youel:** (c). **100-101 Corbis:** Horacio Villalobos (tl). **102 Still Pictures:** Das Fotoarchiv / Sebastian Bolesch (tl). **104 Corbis:** Bettmann. **105 Getty Images:** Time Life Pictures / Department of Defense (tr); **Panos Pictures:** Sven Torfinn (tr). **106 Panos Pictures:** Espen Rasmussen (tl). **106-107 Corbis:** Lynsey Addario. **108 Panos Pictures:** Jenny Matthews (tl); **Still Pictures:** UNEP / Art Chen Soon Ling (bl). **109 Getty Images:** Scott Nelson (tr); **Still Pictures:** Sean Sprague (bl). **110 Corbis:** EPA (cr); Reuters / Dimitar Dilkoff (tl). **110-111 Rex Features:** Sipa Press (bg). **112 Panos Pictures:** Jeroen Oerlemans (clb); **112-113 Corbis:** Reuters / Dimitar Dilkoff (bg). **113 Getty Images:** AFP / STR (tl); Peter Macdiarmid (tr). **114 Magnum Photos:** Steve McCurry (r); **Duncan Youel:** (tl). **116 Getty Images:** AFP / Asif Hassan (cl); AFP / Gerdende Rambourg (br). **117 Corbis:** Reuters (tr); **Getty Images:** Time Life Pictures / Shane McCoy (l). **118 Alamy:** Todd Muskopf (br); **Corbis:** Robert Essel NYC (t); Lester Lefkowitz (fbr); **Getty Images:** Liaison / Netphoto / Pablo Bartholomew (br); **Panos Pictures:** Mark Henley (bl); **Photolibrary:** Diaphor La Phototheque (l); **Still Pictures:** (fbl). **119 Corbis:** EPA / Adrian Bradshaw (bc); In Visu / Olivier Coret (fbr); **Getty Images:** Photographer's Choice / Alvis Upitis (bc); **iStockphoto.com:** (bl). **119 Corbis:** EPA / Adrian Bradshaw (bc); In Visu / Olivier Coret (fbr); **Getty Images:** Photographer's Choice / Alvis Upitis (bc); **iStockphoto.com:** (bl). **120 iStockphoto.com:** (tl). **121 Corbis:** Reuters / Howard Burditt (tr). **123 Corbis:** Alan Schein Photography (l/bg); **iStockphoto.com:** David Franklin (tr). **124 Getty Images:** Photographer's Choice / Alvis Upitis (t); **iStockphoto.com:** Tomislav Forgo (tr). **124-125 iStockphoto.com:** Tomislav Forgo (bg). **126 iStockphoto.com:** Tomislav Forgo (bg). **127 Panos Pictures:** Dieter Telemans (tr); **Rex Features:** Tim Rooke (tl); Solent News (cl); John Wrights (c). **128 Alamy:** eStock Photo (tr); Todd Muskopf (tl). **129 Corbis:** Anna Clopet (br). **130 www.crescentlodge.co.uk:** (cl). **131 Corbis:** Images.com (tr); **Getty Images:** Cate Gillon (br); **Panos Pictures:** Sven Torfinn (bc). **132 Corbis:** Lester Lefkowitz (tl); **iStockphoto:** (tr); **Photolibrary:** Nordic Photos / Chad Ehlers (bc). **132-133 Corbis:** Steve Raymer (bg). **133 Corbis:** Alan Schein Photography (clb). **134-135 Photolibrary:** Photononstop / Marc Vérin (bg). **135 Corbis:** EPA / Dennis M. Sabangan (tr); Reuters / David Gray (br); **iStockphoto.com:** Roberto A. Sanchez (tl); **Panos Pictures:** Fernando Moleres (cl). **136 Still Pictures:** (tl); CNS / Sinopictures (br); Mark Edwards (tr). **137 Getty Images:** AFP / Mauricio Lima (tr); Travel Pix (tr). **138 Corbis:** Yves Gellie (b). **139 Corbis:** Ted Soqui (tl); **iStockphoto.com:** (tr). **140 Panos Pictures:** Mark Henley (tl). **140-141 Corbis:** Alan Schein Photography (bg). **143 Getty Images:** Photonica / Tony Cordoza (tl); **www.yahoo.com:** (tr). **144 Corbis:** EPA / Adrian Bradshaw (tl). **145 iStockphoto.com:** Josh Webb (b); **Getty Images:** Karen Robinson (t); **Photolibrary:** Jon Arnold Travel / Peter Adams (t). **146 iStockphoto.com:** (bl/Bananas, bl/Tea); Roberto A. Sanchez (bg); Josh Webb (bl/Roasted Coffee); Asher Welstead (bl/Ground Coffee); **Still Pictures:** Ron Gilling (t). **147 Alamy:** Aliki Sapountzi (tr); **iStockphoto.com:** Dan Thornberg (bc); **Panos Pictures:** Sven Torfinn (cl). **148 Corbis:** Zuma / Robin Nelson (bl); **Getty Images:** Liaison / Netphoto / Pablo Bartholomew (tr). **150-151 Corbis:** (bg). **151 Wikipedia, The Free Encyclopedia:** (tr). **152 Corbis:** In Visu / Olivier Coret (tl). **153 Corbis:** Saba / Sherbell Shepard (crb); **iStockphoto.com:** (cra, br); Przemyslaw Rzeszutko (tr). **154 Corbis:** Reuters / Michel Filho-Ag O Globo (bl); **Getty Images:** AFP / Alexey Kondrashkin (tl). **155 Alamy:** Iain Masterton (bl); **Getty Images:** AFP / Hashem Nawfal (tr); **Photolibrary:** OSF / Roger de la Harpe (tl). **156 Corbis:** Zefa / Benelux (br). **156-157 Corbis:** Kim Kulish (t). **157 Corbis:** Bettmann (fbr); Reuters / B. Mathur (br); **iStockphoto.com:** Alexander Hafemann (bl); **Panos Pictures:** Penny Tweedie (fbl); **Still Pictures:** Philippe Hays (bc). **158 Corbis:** Zefa / Benelux (tl). **158-159 Corbis:** Tibor Bognr (bg). **160-161 Corbis:** Bob Sacha (bg). **161 Still Pictures:** images.de / Kessler (br). **162 Panos Pictures:** Abbie Trayler-Smith (cr); Penny Tweedie (bl). **162-163 Photolibrary:** It Stock (bg, br). **164 iStockphoto.com:** Michal Koziarski (bg). **165 iStockphoto.com:** (cb); **Panos Pictures:** Mark Henley (tr). **166 iStockphoto.com:** Alexander Hafemann (tl); **Photolibrary:** Index Stock Imagery / Ed Lallo (br/bg). **167 iStockphoto.com:** Yong Hiam Lim (br/bg); Anatoly Vartanov (c/bg). **168 www.ebay.co.uk:** (bl); **www.facebook.com:** (tr); **iStockphoto.com:** Robert Kohlhuber (tr). **169 www.myspace.com:** (tr); **www.partypoker.com:** (bl). **170 Still Pictures:** Philippe Hays (tl). **170-171 Photolibrary:** View Pictures / Hufton + Crow (bg). **171 Wikipedia, The Free Encyclopedia:** (ca, tl). **172 Corbis:** Zefa / Josh Westrich (br); **Getty Images:** First Light / John Hasyn (tl). **172-173 Getty Images:** First Light / John Hasyn (bg). **173 Photolibrary:** PicturePress / Maximillian Stock (tr). **174 Alamy:** qaphotos.com (bl); Liu Xiaoyang (fbl); **Corbis:** Reuters / B. Mathur (tl). **174-175 Duncan Youel:** (bg). **175 Corbis:** Car Culture (bl). **176 Corbis:** EPA / Chamussy (tr); **Getty Images:** Stone / Sandra Baker (cl); Mario Tama (c); **Photolibrary:** Macia Rafael (fcl). **177 Wikipedia, The Free Encyclopedia:** (br). **178 Corbis:** Bettmann (tl, cr). **180 Courtesy of Apple Computer, Inc.:** Doug Rosa (cl); **Corbis:** Digital Art (tl); Reuters / Eriko Sugita (tr); **Getty Images:** Erik S. Lesser (bl). **181 Getty Images:** Time Life Pictures / Ted Thai (bc); **iStockphoto.com:** Steve Declemente (tr). **182 Corbis:** Liu Liqun (t); **Getty Images:** Time Life Pictures / Ralph Crane (bc); **Magnum Photos:** Martin Parr (fbr); **Rex Features:** Qilai Shen (bl); Sipa Press (br). **183 Alamy:** Sergio Pitamitz (fbr); **Corbis:** Micheline Pelletier (bl); **Getty Images:** AFP / Adrian Dennis (t); Jo Hale (br); Chris Jackson (bc); **iStockphoto.com:** Geoffrey Black (fbl). **184 Rex Features:** Qilai Shen (tl). **187 Pictures:** Tack / Freelens Pool (tr). **188 Corbis:** David Brabyn (br); **Getty Images:** Time Life Pictures / Ralph Crane (tl). **189 Corbis:** Progressive Image / Bob Rowan (cl). **190 Corbis:** Liu Liqun (clb); **Rex Features:** Everett / © HBO (cla). **191 Getty Images:** CBS Photo Archive (tl); Evening Standard / Roy Jones (cl); Keystone (tc); **Kobal Collection:** (tc); **Rex Features:** (tl). **192 Still Pictures:** Visum / Carsten Koall (br); Visum / Tomasz Tomaszewski (crb). **192-193 Rex Features:** Sipa Press. **193 Rex Features:** Patrick Frilet (tr); Alisdair Macdonald (cr); **www.thesun.co.uk:** (bl). **194 Corbis:** Wally McNamee (tl). **194-195 Rex Features:** Sipa Press. **195 Rex Features:** Sipa Press (tr). **196 Corbis:** Morton Beebe (tr); EPA / Lindsey Parnaby (bc); **Getty Images:** Image Bank / Eric Van Den Brulle (c); **Magnum Photos:** Martin Parr (tl); **Panos Pictures:** Martin Roemers (cb). **197 Getty Images:** Joe Cornish (cr); Riser / Cosmo Condina (cra); **Panos Pictures:** Teun Voeten (tr). **198 Corbis:** Owen Franken (b/Italy); Thom Lang (b/Mexico); Gregg Newton (b/Brazil); Reuters / Colin Braley (tl); **Magum Photos:** Martin Parr (tr); **Panos Pictures:** Paul Lowe (b/China); Paul Smith (b/Peru); **Still Pictures:** Martin Harvey (b/India); images.de / Jespersen (b/Jordan). **199 NASA:** Johnson Space Center / AS17-148-22727 (tl/Earth); STS-49 (tl/Shuttle). **200 iStockphoto.com:** Geoffrey Black (tl); Dan Thornberg (bl). **203 Alamy:** Danita Delimont (tc); **Getty Images:** Sung-Jun Chung (tr); **Still Pictures:** sinopictures / Ma Wenxiao (c). **204 Alamy:** Ian Shaw (cr); **Corbis:** Christie's Images (c); Micheline Pelletier (tl); **Damien Hirst** For the Love of God, 2007. Platinum, diamonds and human teeth. 6 3/4 x 5 x 7 1/2 in. (17.1 x 12.7 x 19.1 cm) © the artist. Photo: Prudence Cuming Associates Ltd / Courtesy Jay Jopling / White Cube (London) (tl). **205 akg-images:** Erich Lessing (cra); **Alamy:** Patrick Ward (crb); **Corbis:** EPA / Peter Foley (cla); Sygma / Jason Szenes (clb); **Getty Images:** AFP / Adrian Dennis (tr). **206 Corbis:** Tim Rue (tl). **207 Alamy:** Dinodia Images (clb); Thomas Lehne (tr); Iain Masterton (cla); **Corbis:** The Gallery Collection (tl); **Getty Images:** AFP / William West (bl). **208 Corbis:** Reuters / Charles Platiau (bl); Sygma / Eric Robert (bc); **Getty Images:** Chris Jackson (tl). **209 Getty Images:** Adidas / Gary M. Prior (ca); **Panos Pictures:** Dieter Telemans (tc). **211 Alamy:** WM (tr). **212 Getty Images:** Jo Hale (tl). **214-215 Alamy:** Everynight Images (bg). **215 Corbis:** BelOmbra / Jean Pierre Amet (c); EPA / Angel G. Medina (tc); **Getty Images:** Matt Cardy (tr). **216 Alamy:** Sergio Pitamitz (tl); **Getty Images:** Newsmakers / Chris Hondros (cra). **216-217 iStockphoto.com:** Darko Novakovic (bg). **217 Rex Features:** Frank Monaco (br). **218 Rex Features:** Everett / © Walt Disney (bl). **218-219 iStockphoto.com:** Darko Novakovic (bg). **219 Corbis:** Robert Holmes (tr).